DISSIDENT ACTS

A series edited by Macarena Gómez-Barris and Diana Taylor

Duke University Press   *Durham and London*   2024

PAUL AMAR,
EDITOR

Rio as Method

Collective Resistance for a New Generation

Printed in the United States of America on acid-free paper ∞
Project Editor: Liz Smith
Designed by Courtney Leigh Richardson
Typeset in Portrait and Retail by Westchester Publishing Services

Library of Congress Cataloging-in-Publication Data
Names: Amar, Paul (Paul Edouard), [date] editor.
Title: Rio as method : collective resistance for a new generation / Paul Amar, editor.
Other titles: Dissident acts.
Description: Durham : Duke University Press, 2024. | Series: Dissident acts | Includes bibliographical references and index.
Identifiers: LCCN 2024011039 (print)
LCCN 2024011040 (ebook)
ISBN 9781478031130 (paperback)
ISBN 9781478026891 (hardcover)
ISBN 9781478060123 (ebook)
Subjects: LCSH: Politics, Practical—Brazil—Rio de Janeiro. | Politics and culture—Brazil—Rio de Janeiro. | Political participation—Brazil—Rio de Janeiro. | Rio de Janeiro (Brazil)—Ethnic relations—Political aspects. | Rio de Janeiro (Brazil)—Politics and government. | Rio de Janeiro (Brazil)—Civilization. | BISAC: SOCIAL SCIENCE / Ethnic Studies / Caribbean & Latin American Studies | POLITICAL SCIENCE / Globalization
Classification: LCC JL2481 .R57 2024 (print) | LCC JL2481 (ebook) | DDC 306.20981/53—dc23/eng/20240807
LC record available at https://lccn.loc.gov/2024011039
LC ebook record available at https://lccn.loc.gov/2024011040

Cover art: Photo by Pedro Garcia, 2021.

Contents

Acknowledgments

With the collective creation of *Rio as Method*, we have incubated a process of reconceptualizing the global from a location in the Global South fraught with struggle, crisis, and creativity. We generated this collection and maintained these dynamic, difficult, and inspiring conversations during an arc of unbearable difficulties and occasional exhilarating triumphs. Much of this volume was completed during the darkest times of the COVID-19 pandemic, which struck Rio de Janeiro and Brazil with particularly grim ferocity. Our colleagues, authors, translators, and editors were forced to be isolated, distanced, and debilitated, with many of our contributors under relentless political attack, their jobs threatened, medical care denied by an inept government, and several losing family members during the seasons of tragedy. Yet there were also moments of hope and triumph as the author-activists gathered here also led the resistance and forged the future out of the ruins. Two of our authors ran for public office, one for federal congress, and another for Rio city council. Several assumed new prominence as leaders in universities and religious institutions even as they suffered withering attacks. Almost all our contributors participated in the massive national front in Brazil that emerged and worked tirelessly to ensure President Bolsonaro and his genocidal presidential administration did not win a second term. And this volume was completed after the inauguration of the new administration of President Luiz Inácio Lula da Silva in January 2023, which opened space for many of this volume's contributors to generate new policies, plans, and visions stemming from the methods and concepts we convey in these chapters.

This intensely moving and challenging set of moments and contexts resulted in a more beautiful, agonizing, and vividly inventive conversation than any of us could have imagined. *Rio as Method* is not just a collection of studies and think pieces. It is a manifesto and an archive of agony and of the future.

Although painstakingly and lovingly compiled in the virtual underground, it shines bright with the hopes, visions, and contributions by a group of scholar-activist-researchers who bonded and evolved during the process of generating ideas, models, methods, and texts. I am grateful to take the opportunity here to thank the many individuals who inspired, labored over, and shepherded this book from start to finish.

Rio as Method, as a book project, was born from a long-term working group formed in Rio to highlight the work of scholar-activists who have been striving to reconceptualize or rehistoricize the global twenty-first-century surge of authoritarian belief systems and governance regimes. We convened the meetings of those who came to constitute this set of contributors via working group while I (this volume's editor) was serving at regular intervals as visiting professor, center codirector, and grant principal investigator in Rio de Janeiro's federal university system since 2003, even as I established my academic base at the University of California, Santa Barbara (UCSB). During the past twenty years, it has been my privilege to serve on committees with institutes of the Rio municipal and state governments, and also as an ally, rapporteur, and interlocutor with NGOs and social movements around racism, sexuality justice, and police violence. I was honored to have published in Portuguese with university presses in Rio and to have collaborated in the submission of successful Brazilian National Science Foundation (CNPq) grant applications. During my time there, I served on Brazilian MA and PhD committees, and recently secured funding to create a long-term research partnership hub in Rio that supports several professors' and students' research projects, including one Fulbright fellowship (2003–4) in which I cofounded with Prof. Paulo Pinto the Center for Middle East Studies. I was also among the launching team for a new, critical, and interdisciplinary international relations graduate program at the Fluminense Federal University and pursued a second Fulbright fellowship (2023) where I worked with the faculty and students at the State University of Rio de Janeiro to create a new kind of activist, social justice–modeled global studies program there.

This specific *Rio as Method* collaborative group, which was hosted at the Fluminense Federal University in Niterói in the state of Rio de Janeiro and at the Institute of Philosophy and Social Sciences at the Federal University of Rio de Janeiro, came together in a series of four workshops and conferences between 2016 and 2020. At these events, a group of about twenty-five academics, researchers, and graduate students united to formulate global strategies, committing themselves to reimagine the epochal moments that dismantled a fractured liberal-left consensus of the Lula-Dilma era. These moments of violent dismantlement included the impeachment of President Dilma Rousseff;

the assassination of Black/queer/favela resident, scholar, and galvanizingly successful municipal political leader Marielle Franco; the catastrophic presidency of Jair Bolsonaro; and the horror of the 2020–22 COVID-19 pandemic. But we also experienced uplift and transformation through innovation at a global scale. Our contributors were particularly equipped to bring new tools and concepts to bear throughout the struggles to shape a new intersectional antiracist and antipatriarchal left, which culminated in a broad coalition that flowered after the inauguration of President Lula in January 2023.

I would like to first and foremost acknowledge the tremendous work, guidance, insights, and brilliance of Prof. Ana Paula Miranda, Department of Anthropology, Fluminense Federal University (UFF), and Prof. Fernando Brancoli, Department of International Security and Geopolitics at the Federal University of Rio de Janeiro (UFRJ). Fernando and Ana Paula were my primary partners in managing this book. They are based in Rio de Janeiro and endured my daily WhatsApp messages and audios, and relentless Zoom meetings. These two are among my dearest of friends, brilliant intellectual guides, and research collaborators. They both worked tirelessly over a period of two years with me identifying participants and managing financial streams. And, most important, they worked to mediate and cultivate conversations about ideas, translations, reconceptualizations, publishing norms, and revision practices. I am more than grateful for their fellowship, solidarity, hard work, and brilliance. I would also like to thank Prof. Roberto Kant de Lima, coordinator of the Institute for Comparative Studies in Conflict Resolution (InEAC), who, alongside my dear colleagues on his team, hosted and guided research related to this project over the years. And I would like to convey my gratitude to Profs. Michel Misse, Beatriz Bissio, and Maria Celi Scalon, who hosted me for crucial research and writing trips at UFRJ's Institute of Philosophy and Social Sciences during this period.

I am so happy to acknowledge the incredibly heroic efforts and genius of our other translators and editors who were central to this dialogue around reconceptualizing processes of reconceptualization for each chapter. And we thank Rodrigo Bezerra for his Portuguese-English translation work.

And I underline my profound recognition, acknowledgment, and thanks to my associate editor Dr. Hatem Hassan, my friend and comrade. Hatem drew upon his lifetime of experience as an antiracism, anticarceral, and police violence activist and researcher in several international contexts. This experience positioned him perfectly to mediate the editing and thorough revision, round after round, of each text. Hatem and I worked with each author to pinpoint the essence of their intervention, contextualize its significance within vernacular and activist publics, and enable each concept to jump scale in order to best inform global public and transnational debates. For example, Hatem worked with loving care and surgical precision to edit and polish the translation of Marielle Franco's thesis.

Also, I feel such gratitude and limitless appreciation for the efforts of my associate editor Dr. Thaddeus Blanchette, who was once a student of mine when I taught ethnographic methods at the Afro-Brazilian Studies Center at Candido Mendes University in Rio de Janeiro during my postdoc stay in 2003. By the time this book project began, Thaddeus had become a leading anthropologist in both Brazil and the United States, living in Rio and professionally based at UFRJ-Macaé and at the prestigious Anthropology doctoral program of the National Museum of Brazil, the oldest scientific research institution in the country, located in Rio. He constitutes the heart of one of the bravest, boldest communities of social justice race/sexuality researcher anthropologists in the world. He provided crucial translations, polishing several chapters where the nuances of translation, revision, and debates—around how to scale up and scale out newly invented concepts from Rio—had become paralyzed by heated (always productive) debates.

I would also like to thank Profs. Laura Murray, Leonardo Vieira, and João Gabriel Rabello Sodré for serving as ambassadors to other contributors, helping to revise and serve as essential mediators and facilitators. And I am deeply grateful to Prof. Flávia Medeiros for giving me a master class, via Zoom conferences, to update me on the essential terminology and philosophy of police investigation practices as they intersect with inquisitorial juridical norms in Brazil. Understanding this cluster of epistemes and practices is so important since these formations manifest in so many chapters in this volume. These practices and notions are relevant to many global forms of criminalization, racialization, and punishment including those in the United States and Europe. This represents an entire regime of global coloniality and race/sex history that I believe only this book captures fully.

I would also like to thank the team at my home campus of the University of California, Santa Barbara. Global studies PhD student Vitória Moreira did a wonderful job as our research assistant, tracking contributions and organizing submissions during the first year of our project. I am deeply grateful to global studies PhD student Amanda Pinheiro for working so hard and so brilliantly to organize the international conference in 2016 at UFF titled "Transregional Summit: The Arab Spring Meets Black Lives Matter in Rio de Janeiro: Activism, Civic Spaces, Human Rights." That summit-conference was an unforgettable historical convergence and alerted us to the emergence in Rio de Janeiro of a revolutionary set of mobilizing concepts and activist social research methods that merited global attention. At UCSB, I would like to thank the Orfalea Center for Global and International Studies, which provided core funding for this book project, research travel, and publication support, through graduate fellowship employment and consultancies. And I'd like to thank Dean Charles Hale, Associate Dean Bishnupriya Ghosh, the Institute for Social, Behavioral and Economic Research (ISBER), and the Office of Research at UCSB. Dr. Melissa Bator, who served until 2022 as academic coordinator, has been a brilliant, friendly, efficient, and encouraging leader, guiding this research and publication process through every stage and ensuring participants are supported, recognized, and paid.

I would also like to express gratitude to the Carnegie Corporation for its generous grant support for parts of this collaboration in the frame of the Security in Context project, spearheaded by the always supportive and ingenious guidance of Prof. Omar Dahi at Hampshire College. And we cannot thank enough Hillary Wiesner, program director at Carnegie, and Nehal Amer, program analyst, for their leadership, guidance, and insights.

I would like to acknowledge the generosity, hard work, and intelligence of the team at Duke University Press and to highlight the positive influence, helpful guidance, acute insights, and visionary encouragement extended by editorial director Ken Wissoker. I am also profoundly grateful to my dear friend and model scholar Prof. Macarena Gómez-Barris and the esteemed Prof. Diana Taylor and their team in the Dissident Acts book series for welcoming this publication project. I'd like to thank the anonymous peer reviewers for their invaluable insights, which significantly improved this volume in so many ways. And I would like to thank Duke's editors, copyeditors, and design and marketing team, including Ryan Kendall, Liz Smith, and Chad Royal, for working so hard to transform this manuscript into a beautiful, accessible set of contributions.

Finally, I would like to recognize and thank the contributors for challenging one another and themselves as they crafted these landmark works, which will excite many readers. And I would like to thank the communities, schools, social movements, and brave political innovators in Rio de Janeiro themselves for bringing this laboratory of new ideas to life.

Introduction

Methods and Concepts for a New Generation

PAUL AMAR

On every continent, new formations of fascism and coloniality—articulated by financial, charismatic, military, and nationalist actors—are being transmitted and shared globally and are animating regimes of polarization and logics of violence. These forces of polarization are spreading virally through disinformation, dogma, (para)militarization, and intimidation. Yet this era also simultaneously features the emergence of fresh leadership, bold concepts, revived histories, and alternative embodiments of the social and of nature. Novel, progressive methods of engaging the political world and decolonizing structures of power are rising to challenge political establishments and forging new tools for dismantling endemic structural injustices. A revolution in the consciousness and strategy of progressives is occurring and mobilizing ideas, perspectives, and populations that have been long excluded, targeted, or rendered incomprehensible by those in power.

Rio as Method, in this context, provides a new set of lenses for apprehending and transforming this world at a critical moment. *Method* here refers less to techniques for gathering data and evidence, and instead represents a politics of knowledge production, articulated through new ways of being, and of being political. This knowledge-politics of this method hinges on linguistic inventiveness, sometimes refusing translation and always pursuing nonextractive relations. We work to generate modes of collaborative praxis that refuse disciplinary boundaries. Through these lenses, the city of Rio de Janeiro—a global megametropolis with a population of 14 million—becomes legible to the reader as a hub of experiences, learning, experimentation, and contestations among activists, scholars, and publicly minded voices. As such, Rio offers frameworks for progress and a set of new methods for identifying sociopolitical problems and for solving them through action. Here, we (*we* refers to the editor, who is the convener of the volume and author of this introductory chapter, along with our thirty-two contributing and conversing authors) conceive of this volume as a manifesto—a toolbox for thinking, teaching, and acting in the world. This manifesto-volume operates as one kind of handbook for energizing public engagement, examining well-informed direct action, and providing resources for building "pedagogies of hope" (Freire 2021) in classrooms and communities. It might also serve as what Argentine writer Jorge Luis Borges might call a "celestial emporium or encyclopedia" (Topinka 2010)—a heterotopia of creative, fanciful, sometimes almost surrealistically unconventional experiments. In this case, we offer a compendium of activist-scholar research and methodological innovations alongside and through no-less-important ethical-political reflections.

This toolbox brings together the creativity and inventiveness of Rio-based activists and scholars striving to escape the regionalizing confines of parochial area-studies frames imposed by the Global North, that would lock our contributors into the periphery as research objects for the field of Latin American studies, rather than at the center of world concern. In doing so, this collection recognizes activists and scholars as engineers of globally relevant and influential methods and models. For example, in the face of global anti-Blackness (Alves 2018), police and paramilitary brutality, displacement, and state violence, late city councilwoman and galvanizing leader Marielle Franco offers a contribution in this volume which provides a road map that moves us away from policing and militarization solutions—branded by government actors as a type of warfare, a pacification of residents. Instead, she moves us toward models of citizen empowerment and self-governance. Franco's participatory models offer Rio-based lessons from intersecting religious, feminist, queer, and Black movements and put forth a method that is globally applicable, for gradual abolition of or alternatives to governance monopolized by militarized policing.

Rio as Method reverses trends that position the Global South as a zone of local informants and footnotes by centering the region as a source of possibilities for new world-making practices. Among our thirty contributions here, for instance, young Rio-based Indigenous scholar-activists Cristiane Gomes Julião and Luiz Enrique Eloy Amado introduce Indigenous epistemologies in the face of environmental disaster. They map out a vision for inspiring a new generation of action—in the wake of a genocidal rollback of environmental policy and the tragic fire that consumed the historical memory of Indigenous Brazil in the National Museum in September 2018. Indianare Siqueira, another of our contributors, spells out the utopian plan of action that their trans and travesti squatter movements and cultural-political mobilizations implement in real space and time across the urban landscape of Rio.[1] Their "travestirevolutionism" is a methodology for occupying and transforming real urban spaces and economies in order to explode the boxes of gender normativity as well as the relations of property ownership and houselessness. These are neither analogous nor residual developments of Global North movements for gender liberation and housing rights.

Our Rio-based network rearticulates global debates that may be familiar to some readers, but on our own terms, introduced schematically in the paragraphs that follow. This collaboration has generated a set of radical, transformative terminologies. For example, Ana Paula Miranda and Maria Pita offer a new approach to reading and responding to "stateness," one that penetrates the myths of state-generated statistics of violent death in Rio and teaches us to countermap the very specific race and class contours of bullets. Fernando Brancoli takes the reader to the "hybrid governance zones" of Rio where the binary of state versus nonstate forces of governance is blurred, revealing and confronting government complicity with narco-traffickers or paramilitary militias. And Roberto Kant de Lima illuminates the urgent contemporary, global relevance of very specific "inquisitorial" methods within Rio's justice system, whose aim is not so much to preserve the equality of each individual under the law but to morally and punitively fix each body in its proper place—mapped onto a carceral-colonial matrix of hierarchies of class, race, gender, and propriety. Kant shows us how this process is dictated by the still-hegemonic norms and judge cultures of Catholic canon law, the relevance of which extends, for example, to the regressive decisions about racial justice and reproductive rights of the 2021 US Supreme Court, whose deciding voices explicitly reference inquisitorial conservative Catholic jurisprudence in their decisions.

With this deparochializing aim in mind, we hope our voices—inscribed in this book—articulate useful insights and models for members of the global public, including activists, interdisciplinary scholars, and bold policymakers concerned with issues of ecological, social, racial, and gender justice, as well as those passionate about urban class inequities, geographies of violence, and grassroots democratization. We provide a united front for rethinking and remobilizing around these intersecting challenges. Our volume aims to generate non-Eurocentric concepts and traveling methodological models, not just to explain Brazil. We carefully translate these new concepts to make them useful for students, scholars, activists, and members of the public in other world contexts—for those who want to see their own worlds differently.

Debates in Brazil and around the world have centered on how researchers draw knowledge from their human sources through systems informed by coloniality and inequality, thus building authority through the knowledge of others that is reductively cited or hardly referenced at all (Cruz and Luke 2020). *Rio as Method* rejects this academic extractivism and presents an alternative model.

Since the 2010s, scholar-activists, community organizers, and writers in Brazil—particularly authors and public figures identified with Black feminism—have initiated transformative conversations around appropriation, recognition, and citation. There has been an explicit attempt to criticize the lack of reflexive scholarship on the region by those in more powerful positions. São Paulo–based philosopher and political theorist Djamila Ribeiro (2017), for example, explores positionality in the now hugely influential *O que é lugar de fala?* (What is the place of speech?).[2] Ribeiro challenges us to rethink who can (or cannot) speak in the context of a patriarchal, colonial, racist, and classist ruling order. She insists that centering authoritative voices of racialized, gendered bodies would establish not an "identity politics" that splits or fragments but one that unites. She insists, "whoever had social privilege has epistemic privilege, since the valued and universal model of knowledge is white" (Ribeiro 2017, 16). In making the link between language, power, gender, race, and knowledge production, Ribeiro offered a generation a framework to practice reflexive scholarship and practice. According to Gilney Costa Santos (2019), Ribeiro's work "recognizes that 'place of speech' is the object of antagonistic disputes. There are those who consider 'place of speech' as the expression of individualized voices, without any reference to the collective experiences shared by groups." Speech has larger implications of erasure, cultural appropriation, and consumerism. In examining the "whitening" of Black Samba music, Ribeiro (2016) delineates between observing and consuming Black women's culture without questioning the position of the consumer relative to those who produced and continue to practice the musical tradition: "To make money, the capitalist [places] white[ness] as the new face of samba. . . . It empties a culture of meaning with the purpose of commodification at the same time that it excludes and makes invisible those who produce it. This cynical cultural appropriation does not translate into respect and rights in everyday practice. Black women were not treated with dignity, for example, because samba gained the status of a national symbol." For Ribeiro and Santos alike, there are structural economic and social implications to unreflexively consuming and producing a cultural practice divorced from those who originally practiced it. And if we look at our contributors in this volume, we see, for example, that Denise da Silva (2017)—a Black philosopher from Rio de Janeiro—elevates the question of positionality and extraction to the global and juridical arena, introducing diasporic analysis of appropriation, the ethics of data gathering, and indebtedness.

In this book, we work to ensure that our concepts and methods remain visibly attached to and owned by their collective and individual originators, not detached or floating in ways that would make them easy to be seized and misused by dominant institutions, media, or universities. Resources from grants and fellowships that enabled the production of this collective dialogue and publication were directed outward toward contributors in Brazil and in many cases those funds were channeled, in turn, by contributors to support community collective action and mutual aid. Participants in this project were self-identified or brought into the conversation by Rio-based colleagues and community organizers. Intellectual production and ideas are presented in this book by their author-originators, many with work appearing for the first time in English (e.g., Marielle Franco's contribution), with the intention that their concepts travel outward under their name and bear their context and social origins.

Nevertheless, even as we have struggled to reverse structures of intellectual appropriation and extractivism, we acknowledge the relations of power and privilege that undergird the production of this work. Grant funding, project management, and book editing were coordinated from the Orfalea Center for Global and International Studies at the University of California, Santa Barbara, in the United States, administered by a Global North–based scholar who serves as this book's editor and this introduction's author, Paul Amar. I have spent twenty-five years shuttling back and forth to Rio, helping to build partnerships, programs, and research centers, as well as identifying and disseminating resources for activist scholarship. These collaborative efforts have unfolded as a continuous partnership with a gradually expanding set of scholar-activists at the Fluminense Federal University, the Federal University of Rio de Janeiro, and the State University of Rio de Janeiro, and with progressive community organizers, political campaigns, and public media leaders in Greater Rio. The production of this set of texts unfolded as a creative, deliberative, and productively contentious process of writing, rewriting, debate, framing, reconceptualizing, translating, retranslating—or detranslating, in those cases where we decided to return and preserve the original Carioca term and import it into English without translation. We worked together to frame and pitch every concept, case study, and approach for our intended broad and engaged readership, working collaboratively and painstakingly through triangulation between authors, editor, coauthors, peer readers on-site, translators, editing assistants, peer reader-revisers, and undergraduate student test readers. Although ultimate convening power did remain with the editor, this capacity was embedded and limited within a process of constant consultation through which contributors and collaborators retained veto power over editorial decisions. Any revenue earned by the editor of this collection will be distributed immediately to these contributors and partners to fund the writing and research of a new generation of thinkers.

Against Carioca Exceptionalism, against New Authoritarianism

This book's collective intervention emerged from Rio de Janeiro, but not because Rio is an exceptional hub of transformational thought or action. We do not see the city of Rio as an extraordinary space that is more progressive, generative, or idealistic than anywhere else. Rio is not an isolated space; its activists and researchers are interconnected with global struggles. As our contributors describe in these chapters, tools for organizing and concepts for alternative governance have been shaped by five centuries of transnational exchanges and comobilizations, not just with the North and across the Americas but with southern Africa, particularly the regions referred to now as Angola and Congo. Also, Rio has been a hub for populations, religious, and cultural articulations with the Arab Levant and Muslim West Africa for centuries (Amar 2014). In turn, today's uprisings and new generations of struggle in southwest Africa— around evangelical churches, paramilitarism, and gender/sexuality—draw upon and rewrite deep transcontinental histories; and they share resources and trade strategies with Rio and Brazil. And Brazil has long been a generative center for global conversations around public health justice and epidemic/pandemic response (whether around cholera, HIV/AIDS, Zika, or COVID-19). In this context, Rio has been a transfer hub for learning and swapping techniques with activist researchers, international organizations, and direct-action movements on all continents. Scholar-activists in Rio have learned much by tracing how new authoritarian trends and white supremacies have been checked and reversed in other contexts, how Indigenous struggles over land demarcation, sovereignty, and recognition have been articulated through transnational and epistemological resistance, and how Black and feminist mobilizations have redirected or taken over branches of the state. *Rio as Method* does not reveal exceptional origins of methods and concepts in one city but highlights reciprocal relationships and a set of relational solutions to emblematic challenges faced in other countries.

As we distance ourselves from exceptionalism or any notion of Rio as inherently more cutting-edge, productive, or progressive than other megacity contexts, it is also important to acknowledge the intensified right-wing profile of the city. The political, social, and religious terrains of Rio de Janeiro in the twenty-first century have been fertile ground for the rise of far-right evangelical dogmatism that relentlessly targets the rights and bodies of cis and trans women, practitioners of religions of African origin, Indigenous people, LGBTQI+ individuals, human rights defenders, social justice advocates, and the Left in general. In Rio, paramilitary and militia governance squads rule a majority of the greater city's neighborhoods by force of arms as unaccountable racketeering and vigilante organizations. And Rio has served as a cradle for a new wave of hard-right "populism" that explicitly celebrates historical fascism, military dictatorship, and anti-Black, anti-Indigenous, anti-queer genocide (Toscano 2022; Melo 2020).[3] This new "authoritarian populism" has been embraced by majorities of the white middle and lower-middle classes of Rio and across the country (Pinho 2021), as well as a significant swath of nonwhite and nonelite populations in the greater urban conglomeration.

The most influential and wealthy televangelists and dogmatic right-wing pastors, not just of Brazil but, arguably, among the world's most powerful, launched their global missionary franchises in Rio de Janeiro. In the 1920s, the Brazilian branch of the neo-Pentecostal Assembly of God (Assembleia de Deus) was founded in Rio's working-class districts of Madureira and Bangu (Palma 2022). This began the pattern of Assembleia churches and evangelical missions planting themselves in neglected communities. There they explicitly provided an alternative to leftist-progressive Catholic liberation theology activism that offered more sympathetic, collective-minded, structurally grounded, and historically informed perspectives on injustice and poverty for residents in those peripheral areas (Cartledge 2021). From the periphery of urban Rio, Pastor Paulo Leivas Macalão launched the first evangelical radio and media networks and a publishing house in the 1940s and '50s. It is no coincidence that these evangelical churches grew quickly in the 1970s and '80s, during the era of military dictatorship in Brazil and the papacy of John Paul II in the Vatican. The junta and that pope together ruthlessly targeted—with arrest or excommunication— progressive and left-leaning Catholic clergy and community organizers (Peritore 1989) as well as Afro-Brazilian faith communities of Candomblé and Umbanda. Such Afro-religious communities had long served as safe and vibrant spaces for embodied spirituality, deep historical continuities, and transcontinental leadership for the African diaspora as well as adherents welcomed from all racial backgrounds, and for nonheteronormative forms of sociability and alternative family (Moutinho 2013). Paradoxically, right-leaning evangelicals restitched Rio's civil and religious fabric by disseminating radically individualist and pro-capitalist dogmas. They reintroduced collective worship and collective action (dogmatically and patriarchally) to the spaces and intersections that their ideological forebears had purged when they targeted left-leaning liberation theology and Afro-Brazilian religious leaders a generation earlier.

One such case was the Universal Church of the Kingdom of God (UCKG), or in Portuguese, the Igreja Universal do Reino de Deus (IURD), that pastor and billionaire media mogul Edir Macedo (Nascimento 2019) established in Rio in 1977. The Universal Church propagates the theology of prosperity, promoting a deeply capitalist worldview that ignores historical, structural patterns and constraints. It spotlights heroic entrepreneurship, shames the poor as responsible for their own misery, offers a theology of a mythically self-oriented entrepreneurialism and privatizing individualism, and nourishes the worship of the wealthy as God's chosen people (Garrard-Burnett 2013). This church now boasts upward of 12 million members across the Americas, Asia, and Africa (Jacob et al. 2003).

The Assembly of God now numbers 67 million believers worldwide (North Central University 2022), within which the Brazil-originating Assembleia denominations remain autonomous and are some of the most archconservative and politically active segments of the larger movement. A significant degree of doctrinal and social diversity does persist among Assembleia congregations and pastors. In fact, several prominent progressive, left-leaning Brazilian politicians and social leaders are Assembleia members, including Benedita da Silva (from Lula's Workers Party, PT), who served as Rio de Janeiro's first governor to identify as Black, a woman, and favela born (M. Santos and de Souza 2022). Another extraordinary progressive leader coming from the Assembleia evangelical fold is Black-Indigenous environmentalist, senator, labor leader alongside Chico Mendes, and former three-time presidential candidate Marina Silva. Marina was born on a rubber-tapping plantation in the Amazon region and rose to become a PT member serving in the presidential cabinet and as founder and spokesperson of the Sustainability Network Party, REDE (Telles and Mundim 2010). On the other end of the evangelical political spectrum is political leader Silas Malafaia, a Pentecostal televangelist, born in 1955 in Rio de Janeiro, who has made an estimated US$150 million as a pastor of the Assembleia de Deus Vitória em Cristo (Assembly of God Victory in Christ) branch. He became infamous for his viciously homophobic and misogynist attacks (Solano 2018), which earned him the moniker "the hate preacher" (Sponholz and Christofoletti 2019). Malafaia was a highly visible and effective vote mobilizer for Bolsonaro and his allies in the 2018–21 period (Fachin and Vitor Santos 2020).

Aside from far-right evangelical social and political formations, many of the country's most ominous paramilitary and death squad commanders hail from the city and have been linked directly to elected municipal leaders (Zaluar and Conceição 2007; Lusquiños and de Rezende Francisco 2022; Arias 2009; Campbell and Brenner 2002). Jair Bolsonaro, president of Brazil from January 2019 through December 2022, is also a product of Rio. Although born in the state of São Paulo in 1955, he settled in Rio in the mid-1970s when he attended the military academy there. He was elected to the city council in 1988 and has based his movement in the state and city of Rio de Janeiro since then. He built his base of power among the military, religious, and real estate oligarchies, which represent very specific class, race, and gender hierarchies of the megacity. His model of rule and his reign of intimidation altered every neighborhood of the metropolis. It transformed Copacabana Beach, a zone in Rio de Janeiro that in the twentieth century was adored by LGBTQI+ communities, samba and bossa nova artists, and bohemians and tourists from around the world. It became instead the primary staging ground for Third Reich–style mass rallies during the Bolsonaro administration; and the neighborhood became a mecca for resentful white reactionaries. This reactionary trend among white middle-class groupings has been thoroughly researched and revealed in the accounts of Sean T. Junge, Alvaro Jarrín Mitchell, and Lucia Cantero (2021) mapping the rise of authoritarian populism in Rio and other Brazilian cities. During both the October 2018 presidential election, which Bolsonaro won handily, and in the October 2022 race, when he lost narrowly to former president Luiz Inácio Lula da Silva, Rio de Janeiro's evangelical church leaders, police and military elites, and voters heavily tilted toward the far-right candidate. But this reality—of Rio as an incubator for Bolsonarismo and other previous and subsequent far-right sociopolitical trends—has not severed it from the global imagination nor purged the city of its spaces and histories of progressive struggle.

In the same period that propelled the emergence of the hard-right political regime, an inspiring alternative progressive model fought its way onto the stage of history. Rio's social movements, media influencers, community organizers, cultural figures, student organizations, Afro-Brazilian religious groupings, and a broad front of new feminist, ecology, Black, queer, and labor mobilizations— with plenty of white allies among progressive student, community, social media, and church activists—did not just provide resistance. These forces engineered a series of triumphs and articulated new methods of being political. They launched a series of alternativas Cariocas that are shaping prospects for transformation. The word Carioca (which some have mistranslated as "home of the white men") is derived from the Tupi-Guarani Indigenous term kariió oka, meaning "house of the Carijó." The Carijó were the original inhabitants of what is now the urban center of Rio, perched on the shores of Guanabara Bay (de Almeida Navarro,

Trevisan, and da Silva Fonseca 2012, 367). *Carioca* now signifies the people, dialect, concepts, and cultures of Rio de Janeiro, regardless of race.

These alternatives have begun to generate success. Black, trans, feminist, Indigenous, and community-organizer candidates (several of whom are authors in this volume) ran for local and federal office, some winning. They recaptured reactionary church and religious spaces and generated new progressive spiritual communities. They fought back against disinformation and troll media, and exposed the brutality and corruption of militia, police, and military forces. They defended schools and universities as spaces of critical thought, upward mobility, and safety for those targeted racially, sexually, or by political purges. And, crucially, they pushed a new vision of government or logic of state beyond the obsession with policing, hyperincarceration, sexual demonization, culture wars, and military securitization.

Eras of Struggle and Inspiration

These emergent or alternative methods and models were born not just of the struggles against new fascism and authoritarian political culture in the Bolsonaro era of 2018–22. Our methods and conceptual innovations are equally shaped by struggles and strategies tested in the context of two previous periods and paradigms.

The first era of struggle that shaped us and our mentors was that against liberal and neoliberal hegemony in the 1980s and '90s under presidents José Sarney (1985–90), Fernando Collor de Mello (1990–92), Itamar Franco (1992–94), and Fernando Henrique Cardoso (1995–2002) (Amann and Baer 2002). During this period, Brazil emerged from more than two decades of military dictatorship, inheriting a dramatically narrowed space of politics dominated by doctrines of so-called color-blind policies of "racial blindness" (Carrillo 2021) that had fostered an elitist educational system. This system fixated on US and French thinkers and academies, a policy environment defined by individualistic privatism (Moreira 2013) and a public sphere that had no place for collective and structuralist expressions or orientations. A second era of struggles played out during the center-left administrations of presidents Lula (2003–10) and Dilma Rousseff (2011–16), both from the PT. During this period, progressives, community organizers, and leaders concerned with reinvigorating public autonomies, participation, and mechanisms of redistribution clashed with the PT's proclivity for top-down statism, repressive securitization of public spaces, and lack of accountability, which was riddled with police and state violence, clientelistic NGO-dispensed paternalism, and sometimes superficial "photo opportunity multiculturalism" that defined many moments of the Lula and Dilma era (Amar 2013, 139–70). And only then came the third era that shaped our authors' concepts and tactics of resistance: the period dominated by the hard-right wing and inquisitorial evangelical pastor and mayor of Rio, Marcelo Crivella (2017–20), and of former president Bolsonaro himself (2019–22).

In the wake of these three periods, our authors fashioned methods and concepts for understanding a new politics of knowledge production, reconceptualizing the meanings and means of political participation and cultural recognition. As a result, we offer an outward-looking, future-oriented program for world making during a globally challenging moment.

New, Strange, and Useful Concepts

We hope the readers will enjoy experimenting with the new terms and ideas we offer as we collectively attempt to refashion how we think, act, and interact. Our contributors are energized by the linguistic resources of Carioca vernacular, activist argots, and African and Indigenous lexicons. Certain authors embrace terminological hybridization in order to give names to previously inconceivable phenomena, and some contributors refuse translation in certain moments if that erases history or epistemological autonomy. In this book, we define new terms or neologisms—consistently in both English and Brazilian Portuguese— and offer them as techniques for challenging binaries or structures of meaning that we might take for granted but which obscure how power or resistance operates. We invite you to experiment with translating them into other languages that you use in your daily life.

For example, our new contributors' concepts of *militiarchy* and *parastatal sexarchy* challenge how the legitimate state or municipal government is conventionally seen as the opposite of nonstate militias or paramilitary groups, or as a civilizing institution that polices public sexuality and sexualized populations. Intentionally provocative—and maybe a bit awkward at first—these newly fashioned terms serve as tools or methods for identifying the operation of a kind of real-world governance that centers, privileges, and codepends on vigilante militias and sexual criminalization as the heart of its functional, economic, and social power. This kind of governance, of course, is not unique to Rio or Brazil. But these concepts and this boldness for conceptualizing this mode of patriarchal, militia-centric rule is a passion for Rio's activist scholars.

Other novel terms that our contributors introduce, such as *genderphobic binarism, puta politics,* and *travestirevolutionary occupy movements,* channel the vital energy in Rio de Janeiro of new feminist and queer movements that simultaneously challenge heteropatriarchal respectability politics, respectability-oriented feminist frameworks, and mainstream liberal or normative gay rights agendas. In addition, our authors' ideas and strategies push back militantly against attempts to purge school curricula of feminist, Black diasporic, and LGBTQI+ ideas or to violently cleanse public spaces of sex workers, crush antihouseless movements, morally discipline popular religiosity, repress Black and Indigenous sovereignties and autonomies, or purge the cityscape of the vibrant trans anarchist leadership and squatter movements.

Methods of challenging the horrors of racialized state violence in Rio produced concepts that we transmit here, such as *de-killing*, the *social life of corpses*, and new *analytics of raciality*. These terms channel Black mobilizations and political methodologies in Rio de Janeiro that recognize and reverse, on the one hand, the necropolitical, genocidal logic of killings committed by police and militias across the city and, on the other, the spectacularization of this violence by media and political discourse.

Our activist authors also reimagine the spaces of the world city and the urbanisms or city logics of transformative resistance. Our term *quilombo portness* illustrates the long tradition of neighborhoods and urban and rural zones that were liberated and self-governed by former slaves and their descendants. These societies are called maroon communities in English, or quilombos in Brazilian Portuguese. The word *quilombo* comes from the African Kikongo and Kimbundu languages and originally meant "camp" but came to mean self-made refuge community for self-emancipated enslaved peoples. *Quilombos* can be a useful way to describe how contemporary downtown communities are reoccupying the ruins of the slave market wharves in the port of Rio de Janeiro. As this term *portness* indicates, these are not mere sites for historical heritage but autonomously occupied ports and portals to Africa and its diaspora, the past, and the future. *Fractalscopic quotidian*, *heartbreaking lyrical ontology*, and *de-hygienization clusivities* are other examples of fabulously Rio de Janeiro–style conceptualizations of how nonrationalized, nonmonolithic modes of living in the city generate alternative epistemologies. But as mentioned previously, our hope is that these epistemologies, concepts, and terms can be experimented with beyond Rio, in accordance with our method, our mode of knowledge production and idea transfer that aims to conjure new world-making practices.

Method Diversity and Epistemology Debates

The term *epistemology* signifies a way of knowing the world or a mode of experiencing and seeing the social, natural, and built spaces of the city—human and nonhuman. Conversations around epistemology are relevant to activists as well as academics since they reflect shifts in generational languages and terminologies, recognize previously erased sources of knowledge, and open up new pathways for rethinking the possibilities of justice and action.

Scholars arguing for the decolonization of politics have claimed that we are currently experiencing an "epistemological turn" (Grosfoguel 2013). This means that Eurocentric and white privilege, not just in representation but in ways of seeing and knowing, are being challenged and replaced by the revitalization and recognition of deep histories of thinking differently. Those frameworks, for example, include Indigenous worldviews or the long inquisitorial legacies of Portuguese and Spanish empires and the counterpublics of race, religion, and sexuality that persisted within and around them. This epistemological turn also implies unleashing creativity in terms of the metaphors and signifiers of knowledge, as some of our contributors have done when they, for example, bring together biomedical and musical metaphors and concepts to describe modes of being and mobilizing in Rio. Mingling medical science and music history to generate new concepts reflects the city's history, marked by periods of plague and pandemic followed by epochs of renowned musical and popular-cultural innovation.

Our book contributes to a broader set of efforts to shape concepts and to re-engineer methods. Through the contributions of this volume, methods refer to research methodologies but also to knowledge politics and political tactics. *Rio as Method*, thus, is in line with kindred movements that reimagine how we all come to understand ourselves, our histories, social and political worlds, pasts, and futures. Inspiring recent books have been crafting alternative models for the coproduction of global knowledges in light of the epistemological turn. These include, of course, a primary inspiration, the volume *Asia as Method: Toward Deimperialization* by Kuan-Hsing Chen (2010), which launched a call to authors and researchers to refuse neocolonial concepts and imperialist imaginaries. *The Brazil Reader* (Green, Langland, and Schwarcz 2018) offered an unparalleled inclusive perspective on the country's history, diversity, and social stratifications. And we have been enriched by the models provided by the manifestos and future-forming works of *Decolonizing Methodologies* (Smith 2021), *The End of the Cognitive Empire* (B. Santos 2018), *Border as Method* (Mezzadra and Neilson 2013), *Beyond the Pink Tide* (Gómez-Barris 2018), and *¡Presente! The Politics of Presence* (Taylor 2020). These works have remapped the horizons of decolonial thinking and relearning. We have also been enriched by the spectacular "Method as Method" issue (Rojas 2019) of the journal *Prism* and its self-satirizing essays: "Translation as Method" (Rojas), "Hoax as Method" (Christopher Rea), "Cannibalism as Method" (Lorraine Wong), "Cold War as Method" (Petrus Liu), and so many others.

This collaborative effort also reflects the inspiration of a new generation of transnational Américas studies scholars, artists, media makers, and public intellectuals who have built upon the critical purchase of activist scholarship within the field of (previously US-centric) American studies and picked up on transglobal and decolonial trends in ethnic studies and Latin American studies fields. Often these Américas studies conversations were catalyzed by the performances and conversations that took place at the Hemispheric Institute of Performance and Politics during workshops in Chile, Brazil, Mexico, New York, and elsewhere, as well as at the dynamic congresses of the American Studies Association, Ethnic Studies Association, Brazilian Studies Association, Brazilian Anthropological Association, and Latin American Studies Association.

Américas studies has been articulated by scholars such as Ricardo Ortiz through work on migration, displacement, and sexuality, and by Macarena Gómez-Barris, who not just decenters the United States but also rejects state-centric politics and displaces Cold War–era area studies approaches (Gómez-Barris 2018, 104) to emphasize hemispheric and South-South solidarities and exchanges. Or the academic-community ethical framework model of critical, transformative, activist research partnerships developed between the Universidad de los Andes and the Asociación Ébano in Colombia (Bello-Urrego 2019). Américas studies advocate Raúl Coronado reflects upon the work of Susan Gillman and states, "It may be that we have a lot to learn from our fellow Americans, those inhabiting the rest of the hemisphere. The task at hand is much more radical than supplementing our reading with a handful of Latin American texts. As Gillman sums up, it 'means a decisive departure from the homogenizing of global English and toward the multicultural babel of the many languages of world literature'" (Coronado 2008, 214).

In dialogue with these brilliant interlocutors, *Rio as Method* elaborates these epistemological interventions and hones the methods captured by our new terms. We cluster these interventions into four thematic sections, which do not interrupt dialogue between all chapters across those sections. But these four sections do establish a particular rhythm and a more comprehensible map of actions and conceptions. Our four sections are designated (I) "State," where we offer new methods for seeing and testing the limits of governance and inserting new activist logics for remaking apparatuses of representation and control; (II) "Space," where we offer new methods for mapping the city, its racial, economic, criminalizing, and emancipatory dynamics and histories; (III) "Subject," where our author-activists identify and give visibility to the vast social locations, voices, identities, and group formations of newly mobilized subjects—ranging from narco-trafficking evangelicals to the city's increasingly conscious Arab community, incarcerated populations that refuse to be silent, and even the haunting presence of unjustly killed Black youth. In the final section, (IV) "Futurity," our authors strive toward path making. Through their contributions, these final chapters have a particularly insistent claim on worlds yet to come, either to redeem catastrophic loss—a loss, say, at the scale of the fire that ravaged the National Museum in Rio de Janeiro, which turned to ash the archives of the country's Indigenous population and halted the academic progress of many Indigenous students and scholars. And we highlight the Bandungian futurities that in times past and to come may define a new global solidarity among Global South peoples, with Rio being one site of possibility.

Engaging Global Debates

The author-activists gathered here engage global debates in public, political, cultural, and academic spheres, providing action models and concepts that illuminate emerging discussions. This book generates new frameworks for activism around specific forms of police and prison abolition including offering comparative insights on global police racism (Amar 2011). And the volume articulates modes of radical participation within and outside the bodies of governance of the state. It offers a lens on decriminalization of drugs, houselessness, sex work, justice, sovereignty, and reparations for Indigenous and historically targeted Black populations, and imagines, instead, convivial and ecologically sustainable urban spaces beyond the logics of hygiene campaigns, crime wars, and gentrification.

With these policy- and justice-based aims in mind, this book generates a set of tools that open new paths for nonbinary theories of the state and of justice. Our author-activists will teach readers the lessons of Rio's histories of "antiwhite-patriarchal" militancy against the gender binary and how this delivers a powerful agenda for reanimating abolitionist politics. This book's science of sovereignty goes beyond elaborating a decolonial critique of the binaries of civil versus criminal, state versus nonstate, or formal versus informal. Those binaries dominated the language of politics in the supposedly liberal era. But as our contributors point out, those liberal binaries were always haunted by the sexual, racial, and theological duos of pastor versus demon, punisher versus monster, crusader versus corrupted, propertied versus unhoused. Since Rio's militants have seen right through the violent binaries of liberal epistemology, they are well placed to articulate a postliberal model of justice scholarship. Here we replace binary models of the state with nonbinary analytics, collectively generated in modes of uniquely Carioca resistance. These include Black autonomist maroonage, sex work labor struggles, popular Black and Indigenous religions' understandings of informal-criminal markets and capitalism, and community mobilization in the context of narco-cartel governance.

Engaged scholars and resistance actors worldwide are searching for ways to center Global South modes of action, postliberal approaches, and nonwhitepatriarchal techniques in order to redesign ways of acting and being. Our writers convey salient lessons about emergent evangelical-Pentecostal regimes of socialization, as well as antiauthoritarian social histories of Afro-Brazilian terreiros (e.g., Candomblé and other Orixa and Nkisi resistance traditions), progressive-feminist evangelical movements, and Catholic Black Brotherhoods. Our writers convey the lessons of their own efforts to establish transanarchist economies of squatter occupation and to implement campaigns of moral de-hygienization and subversive puta politics that does much more than refuse respectability politics and slut shaming. We engage with rebel port and dockworker histories in Rio that are in dialogue with other direct-action protests and movements to take over or reappropriate shopping malls, museums, social media platforms, and political parties themselves.

Ultimately, we ask: How can we deliver a wealth of voices and a promiscuity of archives in the wake of genocidal death and systematic erasure? One way this volume answers this question is to rhythmically and consistently summon the dead and honor them as speakers. It resuscitates and delivers archives that have been systematically burned, shredded, and degraded. We are conscious of the morbid profiteering that can happen around representations of Black suffering. In this context, our collective intervention offers an empowering and inspiring alternative approach that conveys presence, sociality, and futurity even as it theorizes the necropolitical. This book is a cathexis of approaches to scholarship that refuse the limits of positivist recognition and liberal subjectification because we have seen how those approaches intentionally or inadvertently re-kill and re-erase.

Our collection opens with the voice of Marielle Franco, the brave, captivating, and brilliant embodiment of Rio's revolutionary alternative who identified as queer, Black, socialist, liberation theologist, anthropologist, city council leader, and daughter of a favela (Swift 2018). Marielle Franco's assassination on March 14, 2018, was finally in March 2024 linked to politicians Chiquinho Brazão and Domingos Brazão and former Rio police chief Rivaldo Barbosa (*El Pais* 2024). The three were arrested as suspected masterminds of the crime and are being accused of being part of a paramilitary group. This assassination in 2018 marked an escalation of polarization in Rio and the world (Andrade 2019). And this event was followed soon after on September 2, 2018, by a horrifying fire that raged through and incinerated much of the National Museum in Rio, whose archives included centuries of records of Indigenous sovereignty, language, and culture and Black historical memory, economies, and agencies (Angeleti 2022). The museum is also a university that hosted one of the most influential decolonial anthropology departments in the country. With Marielle's presence and voice—along with the articulation of radical postincendiary archives by young Indigenous activist-scholars still affiliated with Rio's torched museum— we offer *Rio as Method* as a new radical research modality that will start global conversations around the coproduction of knowledge and conceptualization of resistance.

Context and Conceptualization

The Rio collaborative group came together in a series of four workshops and conferences between 2016 and 2020, through endless virtual meetings during the lockdowns of 2020–21, and in a celebratory, forward-looking workshop in person in Rio de Janeiro in January 2023, just after the inauguration of President Lula. In these lively working meetings, we committed to identifying alternative ways to think through the epochal moments that dismantled the fractured liberal-left consensus of the Lula-Dilma era, and the social, political, religious, and para- militarist trends and forces that propelled the rise of Bolsonarismo nationwide and the brutality of the mayorship of paramilitary puppeteer, gospel singer, and fundamentalist evangelical pastor Marcelo Crivella, who was mayor of Rio in 2017 through 2020. These moments of violent dismantlement included the impeachment of President Dilma Roussef, the assassination of political leader Marielle Franco, the presidency of Jair Bolsonaro, the catastrophe of the COVID- 19 pandemic, and the recuperation and resurgence of progressive mobilization that swept Lula back into the presidency and secured the election of dozens of progressive Black, trans, women, and Indigenous leaders and organizers across the country in the elections of October 2022.

Throughout this turbulent process, meetings were hosted in person or vir- tually by the Fluminense Federal University in Niterói in the state of Rio de Janeiro and at the Institute of Philosophy and Social Sciences at the Federal University of Rio de Janeiro. At these events, a group of around thirty academ- ics, researchers, and graduate students united to formulate strategies to drive, on a global scale, extraordinary conceptual and methodological research in Rio de Janeiro. This process was informed by strategic planning meetings of the Orfalea Advisory Council, at the Orfalea Center for Global and International Studies, at the University of California, Santa Barbara. The heart of this process was a sustained conversation on knowledge politics and research ethics, allowing us to reflect on challenging Eurocentrism, coloniality, racism, misogyny, and structural homophobia in the social sciences, including those research traditions that are considered progressive or liberal.

Road Map Ahead

The chapters that follow in this volume are gathered loosely into four thematic groups, although dialogue flows across the boundaries, creating multiple planes of resonance. Our first grouping is under the banner of "State," since each of these pieces provides tools for identifying practices of governance, logics of rule, and formations of authority that conventional concepts render invisible or unrecognizable. This is particularly relevant within the context of the racial state, paramilitarized or militia power, shifts in judicial and moral authority, changes in how forensics and policing target certain bodies and enact dominion, and radical autonomy of communities.

Our second grouping, "Space," provides exciting concepts and mappings of radical spaces of urbanism and emergent leadership, where activist city mobilizations take over municipal legislative spaces, where white supremacy and gentrification in the city are challenged by Black ultramodernity, where militarized police embed their cartographies of masculinism and mastery, and where maroon/quilombo communities reinscribed in the streets rebel histories of religious dissidence and slave port uprisings.

Our third grouping, "Subject," gathers analyses of subjectivities, cultural perspectives, personalities, and identities that Rio's activist scholars render visible and powerful as models for action and reinvention. These include examinations of evangelical religiosity and moral redemption cultivated, paradoxically, by narco-trafficking cartel regimes that rule much of the city or, on the other hand, the feminist subject mobilized in the struggle against attempts to erase discussions of gender, trans existence, or LGBTQI+ populations in school curricula and public policy. This section also includes the subjects and social lives of Black practitioners of Afro-Brazilian religions (Candomblé, Umbanda, etc.) in Rio and their success in creating a new collective subject of rights, to counter the genocidal religious persecution by Pentecostal-identified militias and armed vigilante groups.

Finally, our fourth section, "Futurity," brings together bold programs for change, including the revolutionary agenda of the trans/travesti antigentrification movement, plans for restoring the public sexualities and collectives erased by social cleansing dynamics (more urgent than ever in the postpandemic context), a reigniting of the global solidarities of the Bandung era of Global South solidarities with Rio as a hub, tactics for collectively refusing moral panic governance, and a call for redemption and dignity that "de-kills" Rio's victims and reanimates them as agents of justice to come.

NOTES

1   *Travesti* is a very specific term that is not the English equivalent of either the derogatory term *transvestite* nor the more contemporary and neutral term *trans*. A travesti is someone assigned a male gender at birth but who transitions in appearance (with or without surgery) to a female gender, with or without choosing to alter their pronouns or documented gender identity, although transition to female-identity document markers or nonbinary pronouns is more common in the twenty-first century. Travestis may also strongly identify as a set of lived urban communities that make claims on certain territories, streets, economies, and collectivized spaces.

2   A summary of Ribeiro can be found in G. Santos's (2019) work "Ribeiro D. O que é lugar de fala?," which states that "Djamila Taís Ribeiro dos Santos was born in Baixada Santista, São Paulo on August 1, 1980. She is today one of the main black and feminist intellectuals in Brazil. She earned a BA in philosophy in 2012 and a Masters in Political Philosophy, in 2015, both degrees from the Federal University of São Paulo. From an early age, Djamila Ribeiro reflected on the social issue of black bodies due to the influence of her father, a Black Movement activist and one of the founders of the Communist Party of the Port City of Santos. In 2015, she took over as deputy secretary for the department of Human Rights and Citizenship for the city of São Paulo, an experience that marked her trajectory as it made it possible to reflect on the constraints and loneliness that black women experience in spaces of power."

3   I put *populism* in quotes since across Latin America the term often refers to traditions of progressive, left-leaning politics, although in statist and rather clientelist forms. So to use the term as a synonym exclusively for right-wing authoritarian or neofascist politics can be confusing, given this historical context in Latin America.

REFERENCES

Alves, Jaime Amparo. 2018. *The Anti-Black City: Police Terror and Black Urban Life in Brazil.* Minneapolis: University of Minnesota Press.

Amann, Edmund, and Werner Baer. 2002. "Neoliberalism and Its Consequences in Brazil." *Journal of Latin American Studies* 34, no. 4: 945–59.

Amar, Paul, ed. 2011. *New Racial Missions of Policing: International Perspectives on Evolving Law-Enforcement Politics.* London: Routledge.

Amar, Paul. 2013. *The Security Archipelago: Human-Security States, Sexuality Politics, and the End of Neoliberalism.* Durham, NC: Duke University Press.

Amar, Paul, ed. 2014. *The Middle East and Brazil: Perspectives on the New Global South.* Bloomington: Indiana University Press.

Andrade, Miguel. 2019. "Largest Brazilian Media Group Implicates Bolsonaro in Death Squad Execution of Marielle Franco." *World Socialist Web Site*, November 7. https://www.wsws.org/en/articles/2019/11/07/braz-no7.html.

Angeleti, Gabriella. 2022. "After a Devastating Fire in 2018, the National Museum of Brazil Unveils the First Stage of Its Restoration Project." *Art Newspaper*, September 2. https://www.theartnewspaper.com/2022/09/02/after-devastating-fire-in-2018-the-national-museum-of-brazil-unveils-the-first-stage-of-its-restoration-project.

Arias, Enrique Desmond. 2009. *Drugs and Democracy in Rio de Janeiro: Trafficking, Social Networks, and Public Security*. Chapel Hill: University of North Carolina Press.

Bello-Urrego, Alejandra. 2019. "Dialogues between the Academy and the Community: Establishing an Ethical Framework (Part 2)." December 10. Social Publishers Foundation: Practioner Research. https://www.socialpublishersfoundation.org/knowledge_base/dialogues-between-the-academy-and-the-community-establishing-an-ethical-framework-part-2/.

Campbell, Bruce, and Arthur Brenner. 2002. *Death Squads in Global Perspective: Murder with Deniability*. New York: Palgrave Macmillan.

Carrillo, Ian. 2021. "Racialized Organizations and Color-Blind Racial Ideology in Brazil." *Sociology of Race and Ethnicity* 7, no. 1: 56–70.

Cartledge, Mark J. 2021. "Liberation Theology Opted for the Poor, and the Poor Opted for [Neo-]Pentecostalism." In *(De)Coloniality and Religious Practices: Liberating Hope*, edited by Valburga Schmiedt Streck, Júlio Cézar Adam, and Cláudio Carvalhaes, 82–89. International Academy of Practical Theology Conference Series 2. Tübingen: International Academy of Practical Theology.

Chen, Kuan-Hsing. 2010. *Asia as Method: Toward Deimperialization*. Durham, NC: Duke University Press.

Coronado, Raúl. 2008. "The Aesthetics of Our America: A Response to Susan Gillman." *American Literary History* 20, no. 1/2: 210–16.

Cruz, Melany, and Darcy Luke. 2020. "Methodology and Academic Extractivism: The Neo-colonialism of the British University." *Third World Thematics* 5, no. 1/2: 154–70.

da Silva, Denise Ferreira. 2017. "Unpayable Debt: Reading Scenes of Value against the Arrow of Time." *Documenta* 14: 3–28.

de Almeida Navarro, Eduardo, Rodrigo Godinho Trevisan, and Renato da Silva Fonseca. 2012. "Recensão crítica do livro 'O português e o tupi no Brasil.'" *Língua e literatura* 30: 359–77.

El País. 2024. "Brazilian Police Suspected Masterminds behind the Killing of Councilwoman Turned Icon." March 24. https://english.elpais.com/international/2024-03-24/brazilian-police-arrest-suspected-masterminds-behind-the-killing-of-councilwoman-turned-icon.html.

Fachin, Patricia, and João Vitor Santos. 2020. "Cristofascismo, uma teologia do poder autoritário: A união entre o bolsonarismo e o maquinário político sócio-religioso. Entrevista especial com Fábio Py." *Instituto Humanitas Unisinos*, July 1.

Freire, Paulo. 2021. *Pedagogy of Hope: Reliving Pedagogy of the Oppressed*. London: Bloomsbury.

Garrard-Burnett, Virginia. 2013. "Neopentecostalism and Prosperity Theology in Latin America: A Religion for Late Capitalist Society." *Iberoamericana: Nordic Journal of Latin American and Caribbean Studies* 42, no. 1/2: 21–34.

Gómez-Barris, Macarena. 2018. *Beyond the Pink Tide*. Berkeley: University of California Press.

Green, James N., Victoria Langland, and Lilia Moritz Schwarcz, eds. 2018. *The Brazil Reader: History, Culture, Politics*. Durham, NC: Duke University Press.

Grosfoguel, Ramón. 2013. "The Epistemic Decolonial Turn: Beyond Political-Economy Paradigms." In *Globalization and the Decolonial Option*, edited by Walter D. Mignolo and Arturo Escobar, 65–77. New York: Routledge.

Jacob, Cesar Romero, Dora Rodrigues Hees, Philippe Waniez, and Violette Brustlein. 2003. *Atlas da filiação religiosa e indicadores sociais no Brasil*. Vol. 7. São Paulo: Edições Loyola.

Junge, Sean T., Alvaro Jarrín Mitchell, and Lucia Cantero. 2021. *Precarious Democracy: Ethnographies of Hope, Despair, and Resistance in Brazil*. New Brunswick, NJ: Rutgers University Press.

Lusquiños, Mathias, and Eduardo de Rezende Francisco. 2022. "A influência das milícias nas eleições municipais de 2020 no Rio de Janeiro: Uma análise empírica com base em um processo eleitoral local." *FGV Revista de iniciação científica* 3 (November 7).

Melo, Damien. 2020. "O bolsonarismo como fascismo do XXI." In *(Neo)fascismo e educação: Reflexões críticas sobre o avanço conservador no Brasil*, organized by Rebuá Chabalgoity, Eduardo Diego, Reginaldo Costa, and Rodrigo Lima Ribeiro Gomes, 12–46. Rio de Janeiro: Mórula.

Mezzadra, Sandro, and Brett Neilson. 2013. *Border as Method, or, The Multiplication of Labor*. Durham, NC: Duke University Press.

Moreira, João Flávio de Castro. 2013. "As políticas de expansão e privatização do ensino superior no Brasil e na Argentina (1989–2009)." PhD diss., Universidade de São Paulo.

Moutinho, Laura. 2013. "Homosexuality, Skin Color and Religiosity: Flirting among the 'Povo de Santo' in Rio de Janeiro." In *Sexuality, Culture and Politics: A South American Reader*, edited by Horacio Sívori et al., 573–92. Rio de Janeiro: CLAM, Latin American Center on Sexuality and Human Rights.

Nascimento, Gilberto. 2019. *O Reino: A história de Edir Macedo e uma radiografia da Igreja Universal*. São Paulo: Companhia das Letras.

North Central University. n.d. "About Assemblies of God." Accessed April 1, 2024. https://www.northcentral.edu/student-life/spiritual-life-at-north-central-university/about-assemblies-of-god/#:~:text=Doctrine%20and%20mission&text=From%20the%20Assemblies%20of%20God,second%20coming%20of%20Jesus%20Christ.

Palma, Paul J. 2022. "Pentecostal Polity: Shifting Paradigms in Brazil and the United States." In *Grassroots Pentecostalism in Brazil and the United States*, 145–71. New York: Palgrave Macmillan.

Peritore, N. Patrick. 1989. "Liberation Theology in the Brazilian Catholic Church: A Q-Methodology Study of the Diocese of Rio de Janeiro in 1985." *Luso-Brazilian Review* 26, no. 1: 59–92.

Pinho, Patrícia de Santana. 2021. "Whiteness Has Come Out of the Closet and Intensified Brazil's Reactionary Wave." In *Precarious Democracy*, edited by Benjamin Junge,

Sean T. Mitchell, Alvaro Jarrin, and Lucia Cantero, 62–76. New Brunswick, NJ: Rutgers University Press.

Ribeiro, Djamila. 2016. "Apropriação cultural é um problema do sistema, não de indivíduos." *Azimina*, April 5.

Ribeiro, Djamila. 2017. *O que é lugar de fala?* Bairro Caiçara: Pólen Produção Editora Letramento.

Rojas, Carlos, ed. 2019. "Method as Method." Special issue, *Prism* 16, no. 9.

Santos, Boaventura de Sousa. 2018. *The End of the Cognitive Empire: The Coming of Age of Epistemologies of the South*. Durham, NC: Duke University Press.

Santos, Gilney Costa. 2019. "Ribeiro D. O que é lugar de fala?" *Saúde debate* 43, no. 8. https://doi.org/10.1590/0103-1104201982́6.

Santos, Monalisa Pereira, and Lidyane Maria Ferreira de Souza. 2022. "Direitos e fé nas trajetórias de Benedita da Silva e Mônica Francisco: Mulheres negras faveladas evangélicas e ideologia (anti) gênero." *Revista NUPEM* 14, no. 33: 136–54.

Smith, Linda Tuhiwai. 2021. *Decolonizing Methodologies: Research and Indigenous Peoples*. London: Bloomsbury.

Solano, Esther, ed. 2018. *O ódio como política: A reinvenção das direitas no Brasil*. São Paulo: Boitempo.

Sponholz, Liriam, and Rogério Christofoletti. 2019. "From Preachers to Comedians: Ideal Types of Hate Speakers in Brazil." *Global Media and Communication* 15, no. 1: 67–84.

Swift, Jaimee. 2018. "Marielle Franco, Black Queer Women, and Police Violence in Brazil." *Black Perspectives*, March 19.

Taylor, Diana. 2020. *¡Presente! The Politics of Presence*. Durham, NC: Duke University Press.

Telles, Helcimara de Souza, and Pedro Santos Mundim. 2010. "Movilidad cognitiva y religión: Paradojas del voto a Marina Silva en las elecciones presidenciales brasileñas de 2010." *Revista de ciencia política* (Santiago) 35, no. 3: 509–36.

Topinka, Robert. 2010. "Foucault, Borges, Heterotopia: Producing Knowledge in Other Spaces." *Foucault Studies*, no. 9: 54–70.

Toscano, Gabriel Bayarri. 2022. "The Rhetoric of the Brazilian Far-Right, Built in the Streets: The Case of Rio de Janeiro." *Australian Journal of Anthropology* 33, no. 1: 18–33.

Zaluar, Alba, and Isabel Siqueira Conceição. 2007. "Favelas sob o controle das Milícias no Rio de Janeiro que paz?" *São Paulo em perspectiva* 21, no. 2: 89–101.

Part I
State

1

The Conquering State and Police War-ification? /
O Estado Conquistador e a Guerra-ficaçã
de Policiamento?

Community Collective Alternatives to the Police
and Penal Economies of Pacification

MARIELLE FRANCO

The excerpts here are translated directly from the master's thesis of Marielle Franco (Marielle Francisco da Silva), originally titled "UPP—A redução da favela a três letras: Uma análise da política de segurança pública do estado do Rio de Janeiro (UPP—Reducing the favela to three letters: An analysis of public security policy in Rio de Janeiro state). Committee chair: Prof. Dr. Joana D'Arc Fernandes Ferraz. Committee members: Joel de Lima Pereira Castro Jr., Claudio Roberto Marques Guergel, and Lia de Mattos Rocha. Master's thesis presented to the Master's Program in Administration from the Faculty of Administration Science, Accounting and Tourism at the Fluminense Federal University in Niteroi in 2014, in the state of Rio de Janeiro, as part of the requirements for obtaining the title of master in management. The original thesis, in Portuguese, is available for reference purposes.

This chapter title was generated by the editing and translating team of this volume in order to reflect the focus on war discourse, the nature of the militarized state, and law enforcement practices as they are articulated in these specific excerpted sections from the broader MA thesis. Page numbers in brackets refer to Marielle Franco's (2014) master's thesis, which is a public record of the Fluminense Federal University. These extracts were translated carefully by the team that produced this edited volume. Marielle's daughter Luyara F. dos Santos, as representative of the heirs and family, kindly provided permission to Duke University Press (on November 29, 2023) to publish this selection of excerpts in English translation in this volume in printed and electronic form. As agreed, the heirs of Marielle Franco are not ceding rights to this work; this is only a limited permission to reprint this partial reproduction in English.

Pacification and Proximity

The "war on drugs" discourse and control of territories are initiatives that attempt to win the city's support by alluding to peace. This is accomplished using ideological resources as instruments to shape public opinion and common sense in order to sustain the contradictions such policies depend upon. . . . There is no "war" in this process (Machado da Silva 2010). What exists is a policy of exclusion and punishment of the poor, hidden behind the Unidade de Polícia Pacificadora (UPP, or Police Pacification Unit). This security strategy/project has acted to strengthen a model of urban (re)development centered on private profit and not on the needs of city residents. It is supported by a hegemonic state policy characterized by exclusion and punishment . . . [p. 11].

Below, I explore the theoretical bases for reflections and understandings about the state (liberalism, its changes or transmutations in neoliberalism, and its intertwinement with the penal state). I analyze UPP documents collected during my fieldwork, focusing on the militarization of Rio's "pacified" territories. I also look at state documents: legislative decrees, regulations, and the internal bulletins of the military police. I employed participant observation in meetings of social movements, at the Public Security Summit, and with the ALERJ Human Rights and Citizenship Commission. Finally, I address questions regarding possibilities for resistance and organizing in the favelas. In my final considerations, I reflect upon the results this research has achieved and paths for future security reform . . . [p. 11].

The adoption of control, security, and repression strategies has been the hallmark of state action in Rio de Janeiro's favelas. Here, I examine UPPs from the perspective of public administration since these units are key to the process of elaborating and consolidating policies of public security. I ask whether the neoliberal model in Brazil incorporates elements of a penal state, tracing the emergence of UPPs in the favelas of Rio de Janeiro in the period between 2008 and 2013. In particular, I base some of my conclusions on the UPP in the Favela da Maré, occupied by the army in 2014 in order to install its UPP . . . [p. 12].

The Favela da Maré contains some 130,000 inhabitants. It has a significant network of civil society organizations, with sixteen resident associations, more than fifteen NGOs, ten collectives, and dozens of ongoing projects. On April 5, 2014, the armed forces occupied the Maré to enforce the Guarantee of Law and Order (GLO). The occupation and the subsequent creation of the favela's UPP involved three thousand military and security personnel, deployed to protect the most important expressways in the city, which cut through the Maré (i.e., the Linha Amarela, Linha Vermelha, and Avenida Brasil) [pp. 12–13].

The state operated here under the prerogative of guaranteeing rights, while barely investing in the spaces it supposedly governs. . . . It marked its presence with the use of force and repression through police action, reinforcing the prevailing view that favelas and suburbs are places where "criminality" predominates. These spaces were also considered to be the territory of the "poor" and were assumed to almost entirely lack any security or social organization [p. 14].

. . . Given this, the question is whether or not the emergence of UPPs has altered the central elements of state security policies in Rio. The UPPs seem to respond to the needs of the moment (e.g., mega events and investor security) but do not qualitatively change draconian state policies. In this context, punishment and social assistance must be interconnected in order to maintain strict governance. As the state presents a set of compensatory actions, it must simultaneously create new categories in public policies that combine alternatives for aiding populations and fighting crime. To do this, government policies and technologies were forged and presented to the public as a modern and well-tested new security model . . . [p. 15].

Ideology as a Tool for Understanding UPPs

. . . Proximity policing has been implemented by the state in Rio de Janeiro in recent years. This type of policing presents a utopian image that deviates significantly from its practices. Territorial control, previously carried out through the weapons of criminal groups, was permanently shifted to the police and military. . . . Transforming the established order required building an alternative for regulating violence and state power, reducing the logic of warfare by increasing civil society power (especially in territories controlled by armed criminal groups) [pp. 45–46].

It is no wonder then that, upon arriving in the favelas, the UPPs immediately tried to claim territorial control. This is because the territories in question are not seen as belonging to their residents, but rather as "enemy territory" controlled by criminals. But residents must be able to shape their own spaces together with public institutions focused on culture, education, health, sanitation, legalization of commerce, and so on. . . . It is not enough to confront and overcome a neoliberal regime; one must resist military models based on repressive logic. State transformation requires building an alternative to current modes of regulating violence: a move beyond the logic of warfare in territories controlled by armed groups. Alternatives that do not consider the reality of the city as a whole will only expand inequalities. Police institutions must be open to civil complaints [p. 47].

Public security in the favelas of Rio de Janeiro reveals the contradictions that arise in policy implementation. . . . As a by-product of security policies, UPPs don't present improvements in the quality of public life or safety. It is not possible to achieve peace or security through police actions. The growth of the police presence on the street establishes insecurity and creates fear [p. 50].

There is no law that regulates political and police intervention in Maré besides the Guarantee of Law and Order (GLO). . . . In the state of Rio de Janeiro, UPPs were legitimized through the direct action of the executive branch, promulgated by Decree No. 42.787 of January 6, 2011 (Rio de Janeiro 2011). This decree went into effect almost three years after the first physical installation of a UPP. In 2009, the publication of another decree (No. 41.650 of January 21, 2009) "provide[d] for the creation of a peacekeeping police unit—UPP—and other measures" (Rio de Janeiro 2009) [p. 53].

In 2014, there were still inconsistencies in the practices and terms used by official bodies regarding UPPs. Decree No. 42.787 of 2011 outlines five stages of implementation: tactical intervention, stabilization, implementation, evaluation, and monitoring. During these five stages, favelas are occupied by a number of specialized troops—the Special Operations Battalion of the Military Police of Rio de Janeiro (BOPE/PMERJ), Police Shock Battalion (BPChoque), and the armed forces—as well as local police battalions. Each of these forces has its own command structure. . . . To make action feasible, the government of the state of Rio de Janeiro created the Pacification Police Coordinating Group (CPP), also implemented by Decree No. 42.787 of 2011. This "has the mission of strategically directing the actions and operationalizing the plan of deployment of the UPPs" (Rio de Janeiro 2011). As stated in the decree, the management of "pacification" projects in the favelas is based on measures of efficiency and effectiveness, without "reproducing traditionally military management" (Rio de Janeiro 2011) [pp. 54–55].

The state of Rio de Janeiro thus declared that it did not want to follow the "traditional model of policing, proposing a new model of public security" based on "pacification" (Rio de Janeiro 2011). The General Coordinating Group was created to implement this project, bringing together four sectors: administrative, operational, informational, and education and research. Administrative coordination manages the administrative demands of the Pacification Police, offering technical support to personnel, finance, logistics, and engineering sectors to "advise the General Coordinator in decision-making regarding the implementation, modification, and modernization of the physical structures of the UPP" (Rio de Janeiro 2011). Operational coordination aims to collect, process, and analyze data related to the implementation, evaluation, and monitoring phases of the UPPs, advising the general coordinator of the UPP in decision-making. Information coordination gives support for information flow, the production of intelligence, and assessment of police conduct (Rio de Janeiro 2011). Finally, education and research coordination trains and assigns the police officers who work in the UPPs, developing partnerships with other institutions to standardize the actions of these officers. In this way, it seeks to guarantee the training of professionals, ensuring the quality of the services they provide (Rio de Janeiro 2011). . . . However noble its goals, this on-paper organization does not guarantee the effectiveness of the processes it controls. Currently, there are numerous questions about the UPPs and their ability to change patterns of violence [p. 56].

On the one hand, the "pacification" project is seen as positive. On the other, the UPPs have been questioned regarding their treatment of favela residents. The UPPs position themselves as the manifestation of law and administration in the favelas. However, if we understand public policy using the approach employed by Enrique Saravia, then we need to look at UPPs with regard to how they ensure social harmony or reduce inequality (Saravia 2006, 28).

In the UPP models of "pacification" described above, social policies remain in the background. . . . This combination of policing and the social projects promoted by the UPPs has been questioned by researchers, public policymakers, local leaders, and residents. These note the contradictions inherent in a force that supposedly simultaneously provides security and social services. For some critics, the favelas' social structures and programs are being militarized (Fleury 2012) [pp. 55–60].

The UPPs' programs and projects indicate some willingness for public dialogue, or perhaps just "strong listening" to various local actors.[1] This has taken place mainly through field agents, given that all favelas pacified up to 2012 had local forums. Between 2011 and 2012 (the third year of the UPP program), fifteen local forums were held, called UPP Social Forums. I attended at least

70 percent of these. Suelen Guariento (2013, 8–9), from the Institute of Religion Studies (ISER), discusses these forums in more detail: "Initially linked to the State Secretariat for Human Rights, the UPPs' Social Program was shifted to the municipal level in 2011, after political-party changes. . . . In the press, the change was hailed as the result of an agreement between the Governor and the Mayor. Currently . . . the Instituto Pereira Passos [is] responsible for generating data . . . on the favelas of Rio de Janeiro. The program is financed by an agreement between the City Hall and UN-Habitat, the United Nations Program for Human Settlements. The UPP Social Program was born in the context of rhetoric valuing the favela and strengthening public participation." . . . In addition to improving relationships between the favela and the state, the program also established relationships with the UPPs (Fleury 2012), causing confusion regarding the direct association between the UPP Social Program and the UPPs themselves [p. 58].

That said, I noticed during my fieldwork that residents confused many social issues with security issues. Even though they were an integral part of the UPPs' policies, the UPP Social Program influenced actions in favelas alongside the UPPs, through shared personnel across the two entities. A significant change occurred in the management process of the UPP Social Program, especially after the arrival of economist and former municipal secretary of finance Eduarda La Roque on the scene. La Roque became responsible for the program that "connects" the actions of City Hall in the favelas with the UPPs through public-private partnerships. After approximately three years of execution, the UPP Social Program essentially emphasized entrepreneurship, professional management, fundraising, sustainable development, optimization, and partnership: categories widely employed in management models and financial markets. This strengthened the correlation between security and economic policies, creating "an increasingly private and technical conception of social issues," with social inequalities being reduced to "management problems" (Guariento 2013, 62) [pp. 59–60].

According to Siqueira, Rodrigues, and Lissovsky (2012), "pacification" in Rio de Janeiro understands the community police model as its eventual goal. In practice, however, what occurs in favelas is "proximity policing." . . . According to the public security managers I interviewed, this is characterized by the police's "daytime presence in a certain area and their closer interaction with the local population. In the future, this may become community policing" (Siqueira, Rodrigues, and Lissovsky 2012, 41) [p. 70].

We must reflect upon whether there is, in fact, a new security model being employed here. . . . Three different concepts—pacification, proximity policing, and community policing—are promiscuously confused by the secretary of state for security (SESEG) in defining what UPPs do: "Pacifying Policing . . . [involves] broad police force and includes phases of tactical intervention, stabilization, and the implementation of the Proximity Police Unit (UPP), monitoring, evaluation, and the progressive integration of ordinary policing, carried out by simultaneous or nonsimultaneous actions of other specialized policing units and in proximity . . . to create a favorable environment for the development of citizenship" (PMERJ 2013, 5). Pacification policing is not at all narrow in its scope of activities. Here is what SESEG and PMERJ have to say about the proximity policing project:

> Proximity policing is a philosophy in which police officers and citizens from diverse social segments work in partnership, developing actions in specific territorial regions, promoting the control of issues related to crime, and aiming to improve the quality of life for people in those places. To this end, the police proactively seek community participation to build ties of trust, establishing bridges between possibly repressed demands and offers, and consequently legitimizing police actions. Proximity policing, inspired by the same principles as community policing, acts against crime, approaching the citizen wherever he may be, with an inclusive sociological proposal and powerfully transforming . . . the idea of a special police for a particular community, which would reinforce the logic of segregation. . . . [This is] precisely what we want to avoid. . . . The favela, as a social phenomenon, is a proper part of Rio de Janeiro . . . [but it has a distinct] "community police" separate from the Military Police that operates in the rest of the state. (PMERJ 2013, 5)

And this is how security agencies identify a community policing project: "Community Policing . . . is based on the premise that both the police and the community must work together to identify, prioritize, and solve problems such as serious crime, fear of crime and, in general, the decay of the neighborhood, with the aim of improving the quality of life in the area. Note that both the community police and proximity police are, in essence, the same thing" (5).

According to ISER researchers (Siqueira, Rodrigues, and Lissovsky 2012), however, there is a practical distinction between proximity policing and community policing. This can be seen in the periodic police meetings with the local population, since the central premise of community policing is that the public must play a fundamental, active, and coordinated role in achieving security: "The new meetings, though now routine in various units, are far from empowering the local community. Raising questions and local demands does not mean creating agents or protagonists. That would imply the refinement of proximity and community policing to include local leadership in local security management" (Siqueira, Rodrigues, and Lissovsky 2012, 41). Community organizing, local management, and beneficiary actions are not reflected in an equitable way in the city as a whole. The favelas have been chosen as a stage to highlight measures taken under the pressure imposed by major events such as the 2014 soccer World Cup and the 2016 Olympic Games to ensure some level of local control in these territories [p. 72].

But this is not a security model, nor is it only a model of police action: this is a model for the administration of militarized action. . . . Within this model of police occupation, we see an adaptation of the environment so that it can better respond to the demands of major events. The "militarization of the social" (Fleury 2012, 21) means expanding police action beyond its traditional functions [p. 73].

The UPPs are presented by their defenders as a necessary step in overcoming the fallacious "war on trafficking," since neither illicit drugs nor weaponry are produced in the territories against which this war has been declared. There is no guarantee or indication that confronting drug traffickers represents an effective demobilization of the drug trade. What is experienced in these territories of military permanence can be better conceptualized as a "war on the poor." This is based on Leite's (2004) analysis, where "poverty territories" are treated as "violent territories." Through the "war on drugs," a war on poor spaces is legitimized. This justifies militarist incursions that constantly shed the blood of favela residents and end up imposing extrajudicial death penalties [p. 74].

Actions that should guide and support public policies, especially for favelas, have not been contemplated by the UPPs. . . . The social policies presented by the UPPs have not appeared together with their repressive actions. The statements of State Secretary for Public Security José Mariano Beltrame, in May 2011, question society regarding the efficacy of a policy exercised exclusively through policing:

> It won't be a policeman with a rifle at the entrance of a favela who will hold back the tide if things don't work out inside the communities. It's time for social investments. If there is no massive investment in citizens' dignity, in generating prospects for those people . . . I am not saying that the program will fail, but the police cannot guarantee its success. The UPPs create an environment for society to start paying off the debt we all owe to these hitherto excluded areas. The project's success depends on massive investment, and these are not being made fast enough. (Bottari and Gonçalves 2011)

This public request by the secretary of security can be analyzed as a call for help. The UPP Social Program emerged as an attempt to respond to demands of the type made by Secretary Beltrame [p. 75].

UPPs, Social Investments, and the Market

The UPP Social Program officially began in May 2011, two years after the first UPPs were installed in December 2008. . . . In its second phase in 2013, under the direction of the Instituto Pereira Passos (IPP), the program was to unite social investments under the label "pacification." What actually happened was the growth of criticism and pressure for greater control (from the police) and demands for greater "civility" (from residents) that made the program necessary (Machado da Silva and Leite 2014). . . . There have been two criticisms regarding the inefficiency of the UPP Social Program. One was that the delivery of services did not meet the expected speed and quality. The second was that the UPP Social Program became an unnecessary mediator between the favela and the state [p. 77].

The program "UPP Social" took aim at existing cultural policies, such as the ban on funk music or dance parties in favelas (FGV 2008). Bans, censorship, and the persecution of musical genres asserted themselves as recurrent themes in "pacified territories." Regarding the commodification of life in the favela, it was claimed that the program might enhance tax revenues, but this has yet to be seen. Tax collection for social investments or for strengthening the local economy is still almost nonexistent. The legalization that began as soon as the UPPs were established, imposed through local police actions, may in fact generate financial losses for local ventures established before the arrival of the UPPs. These include moto-taxi services, party houses, funk dances, forró in the public square, or pagode in local bars [p. 82].

The economic consequences of the UPPs became manifest during my monitoring of their activities in the favelas. This would often lead to increases in real estate value and spread to communities in the South Zone. The economic impact of the installation of UPPs seems to be positive for real estate speculators. For favela residents, this means an almost unsustainable change in household budgets [p. 84].

Regarding the economic impacts and rising prices in the favelas brought on by the UPPs, some commercial establishments have been forced to close their doors because they're unable to pay fees resulting from the regularization processes. Real estate prices also went up by 200 percent in UPP-occupied favelas, both for rent and sale. . . . Some surveys, such as ones by the Technical Solidarity Nucleus and the Institute for Labor and Society Studies, make reference to these economic pressures, with an increase of 400 percent in property prices around some of the favelas occupied by the UPPs. What has been called "pacification" has thus enabled the implementation of land regularization projects in a framework of cities-as-commodities. . . . These bring with them a virtual transformation of favelas via gentrification. Favelas located in the richest parts of Rio have been particularly hard hit (Mello 2010) [pp. 84–85].

Not only have the neighborhoods surrounding pacified favelas seen price increases; the communities themselves have been hard hit. This can be seen in an interview that Sebastião Alleluia, president of a favela neighborhood residents' association, granted to *Lé monde diplomatique*. In it, Alleluia vented some of his fears. In short, while the surrounding neighborhoods' residents celebrated the "return to order," the changes in the favela's economic order worried their inhabitants: "Today we are entering a new reality, as our land is now desired by capital. Real estate pressure and speculation is our reality. It's just the beginning: we see Brazilians coming in and even many foreigners disembark, brought in by the European crisis and interested in the potential of our neighborhoods. A duplex apartment located in Baixo Vidigal, estimated at R$50,000 a year ago, is now being sold for R$250,000" (Denis 2013, 6). The UPPs' focus on regularization and "formalization" of property and customs has thus had a great impact on local favela economies. Luiz César Queiroz Ribeiro, director of the Institute for Research and Urban and Regional Planning (IPPUR) of the Observatório das Metrópoles, guides us in understanding this phenomenon in an interview with *Le monde diplomatique*: "Controlling the territory also guarantees capital. It is then necessary to regularize and regulate the occupation of the land, allowing the market to have access to these informal zones and establish legal bases for land ownership—put another way, to modernize the country to allow investors to settle in better? Thus, to favor future transactions, the authorities have put in place a real estate regularization program in these favelas that the city had simply ignored since a 1937 law (repealed in 1984 without the situation of the land being really clarified)" (Denis 2013, 7). One indication of the centrality of the market for the UPPs can be seen in an excerpt from a special series on the G1 news portal, which seeks to "tell the story of entrepreneurs in the communities" (Tabak 2011). The relationship between formalization and the UPPs is presented right at the beginning of the first report: "'The UPP is a very cool novelty that meets the need to formalize business activities,' says Carla Teixeira, coordinator of the Program for the Development of Entrepreneurship in Pacified Communities, of the Brazilian Service for Support to Micro and Small Businesses at Rio de Janeiro" (Sebrae 2013). . . . The "need" for formalization presented by the coordinator of Sebrae is a clue for us to analyze how police occupation—which already is problematic in terms of its social and cultural relationships with the communities—is also an economic activity, changing local dynamics. Formalization takes place without an accurate study of the viability of local merchants and businessmen who, for years—in some cases, decades—ensured the functioning of the economy in the region. . . . In the GI News Success Stories reports, the only stories presented applauded the "legalization of commerce in the pacified favelas" (Tabak 2011) [pp. 85–86].

Sovereignty in favela territories should not be analyzed only from an economic perspective: it must also include a broad analysis of security, violence, commodification, and the militarization of social life. . . . Does the UPP "proximity policing" that follows the military incursions represent the arrival of a set of services and rights? Or does it just mean more frequent police intervention? One of the great risks established in the UPPs regards the political control of the population that lives in the "pacified" areas, where the military police becomes a mediator and where residents' organizations are divorced from political power (Machado da Silva 2008). . . . Put differently, the power officially conferred on police captains can weaken favela residents' claims and preexisting associations [pp. 87–88].

Antisocial UPPs: Violence and Social Services

Look at the increasing number of disappearances as an example of the imbalance in UPP services provided to favela residents. In Rio de Janeiro, thousands of people have disappeared: more than six thousand across the entire state. Blame has been placed on the UPPs. In mass demonstrations during the second half of 2013, one of the most common complaints was with regard to public safety. In Rocinha, one of the largest favelas that had been "pacified" up to then, a man named Amarildo had been taken in for investigation and, after a year, disappeared. Demonstrators chanted, "Hey, police, where is Amarildo?" during organized marches. Out of this came the "We Are All Amarildo" Campaign, taking Amarildo's case as emblematic of the commonly occurring disappearances in UPP-occupied areas. According to data from the Public Security Institute (ISP), public authorities registered 4,633 cases of disappearance in 2007. In 2012, 5,934 disappearances were recorded, representing a 23.7 percent increase in six years. Adding up the totals from this period, 32,073 people went missing in Rio de Janeiro [p. 107].

When one compares the rate of missing persons in the year prior to the installation of a UPP across Rio with the year following its inauguration, a pattern emerges. The total number of disappearances in the year prior to the opening of the UPP was 85. In the year of establishment, it dropped to 77. In the following year, it rose to 133. Thus, between the year of establishment and the next, there was an increase of 72.7 percent in the number of disappearances in this favela.

. . . The demilitarization of the police is the main reform needed to change this scenario, but it is not the only one. We must also change state practices in these territories, focusing on public policy rights and urban equipment and not on police. We need to create spaces for dialogue and decision-making by residents, respecting the regulations created by favela residents themselves. These are actions that can take place at the state level: they're not dependent on federal law reform [pp. 106–8].

Community Organizing, Alternatives, and Resistance

A public policy, even if unfinished like that of the UPPs, does not contemplate local collective organization processes. . . . Machado da Silva and Leite (2004) reflect on the fragmentation and dispersion of the political struggle of the population living in favelas. . . . The strengthening of grassroots collective action, neighborhood organization, and/or popular assemblies can be a qualitative "leap" for these ostensibly "needy" populations. According to Machado da Silva and Leite (2004, 72), this ". . . needs to develop as an autonomous project. . . . However, this does not mean that it needs to or can be independent, isolated: above all, it must be collective." Autonomy is the fundamental basis for discussions about action and participation. To this end, a manual was created as one of the key initiatives in the Santa Marta favela. This booklet presented guidelines on the rights and duties of citizens with regard to the police [p. 112].

The first favela to receive a UPP was also the first to denounce arbitrary acts committed by police officers, back in 2009. The Visão da Favela Brasil Collective, coordinated by the rapper Fiell, organized the production of the manual in the community in partnership with state human rights organizations. The objectives of the publication were to equip residents, expand access to citizenship, and strengthen awareness that the favela must be respected by government and security agents [p. 113].

"Bloco se benze que dá" is the result of political actions carried out by young people in the Maré. These youths raised questions about the unequal relationship between the favela and the city following a public demonstration in April 2004. In this, a student at the Economics College of the State University of Rio de Janeiro (UERJ), Jaqueline, was killed. She was yet another victim of a police operation in the Baixa do Sapateiro favela.

"Bloco se benze que dá" is an instrument of political, cultural, and educational struggle. The bloco was created in 2005, protesting the difficulties favela residents had in moving about, given the visible and invisible barriers between the different communities in the Maré. Another objective of the bloco was to positively interfere in the city's social reality, highlighting how residents' rights had been increasingly violated by the territorial limits imposed by criminal factions and police operations [p. 114].

In the 2005 Carnaval, the bloco's first parade established it as an important movement of cultural resistance to the criminalization of poverty and social movements, bringing together residents from all the communities of the Maré and sympathizers from outside the favela. The parade was marked by a party that grew exponentially, with shouts and calls of "Come out into the street, resident!" This alluded to the phrase used by police as they entered the favela during pacification operations, chanting the "call" of fear: "Get off the street, resident!" The fears created by police operations and by the shootings between the factions were rejected. What prevailed during the parade was confetti and streamers announcing life in the favela.

. . . For Silva and Rocha (2008), the political ostracism found in most favela neighborhood associations is linked to a change in demands placed upon these spaces. In the past these were for water, sanitation, and electricity. Today, residents' associations have much to contribute to the debate on Citizen Public Security and Human Rights [p. 115].

. . . In the Favela da Maré, several collectives have organized to guarantee the rights of favelados:

> In the year marking the 50th anniversary of the 1964 military coup, soldiers and tanks from the armed forces are once again occupying the streets of Rio de Janeiro in a sensationalist media spectacle. This time (again), the slums are the targets, treated as sources of violence; enemies of the city. Favelas are the result of decades of incompetence and neglect of public management. At the same time, they represent the struggle of a people to overcome social inequalities and for the right to have rights. We need to mobilize and demonstrate against new forms of dictatorship in strategic spaces in the city. Peace is not a donation; it is an achievement! Let's go to the street with several blocos. "Se Benze que Dá" joins with the APAFUNK bloco and "Nothing Should seem Impossible to Change." The concentration will be at 3 p.m., with a banner workshop. At 4 p.m., the parade will take to the streets with all residents participating! (Maré Vive 2014)

Morro do Borel, in the North Zone of Rio de Janeiro, was synonymous with organized resistance in yet another favela. But on April 16, 2003, the Borel massacre took place. Four young men were murdered during an operation by the Sixth Military Police Battalion (BPM). . . . In August of that same year, a conference was hosted in Borel, with the theme "Ten years of the Vigário Geral massacre." In that conference, Caio Ferraz stated, "The Vigário massacre [in 1993, when twenty-one innocent residents including children were killed by a military police death squad in the favela community of Vigáio Geral] continues and will continue as long as massacres and summary executions are the norm for police and parapolice squads in poor communities. The slaughter only changes name with each macabre fact. Vigario today is called Borel, Acari, Mineira. . . . What will the name be tomorrow?" (Ferraz 2004). Police violence underlies the growth of the UPPs, becoming a memory of oppression for favela residents who were told lies regarding "proximity" and "community" policing [pp. 117–18].

Restructuring public security and demilitarizing the current police model requires policy decisions at various levels. Since legislation is approved at the federal level, states must organize their police into a single force, defined as a civil institution [p. 118].

Demilitarization of the Military Police and PEC-51

The UPPs are a very clear change in the context of public security policy, of state intervention. But change implies other issues. Change in what? And to what extent? You can say that it has changed, but it is the same police, the same corporation, the same structure. The UPPs have changed within their limits, but this is not an intellectual and moral reform of the police, nor a demilitarization of the police.
—L. ANTONIO MACHADO DA SILVA, "Circulacao e fronteiras no Rio de Janeiro" (2013)

In recent years, Rio has seen many economic transformations.[2] These, in turn, strengthened the policies of violent repression of the population in order to guarantee profits and protect the regions chosen to receive urban investments.

The state does not call for the military occupation of the whole city. Ending militias, especially in those areas with a high concentration of state agents acting illegally, did not require a massive occupation of the city, or a military invasion of territories. . . . There is, above all, distinction in the political treatment of the city. Order blitzes, occupation of slums, criminalization of ways of life and popular culture: these are just some of the hallmarks of public power in the occupied regions of Rio de Janeiro.

The demonstrations that erupted in 2013 were expressions of revolt in response to eroding rights in Rio. The street once again became a stage for change. The June uprisings—followed by strikes by education professionals, postal workers, bank workers, oil workers, and so on—proved that rights are achieved by popular resistance [p. 119].

The struggle for the demilitarization of society and the state in its three spheres—municipal, state, and federal—has become a priority for those who dream of a world where lives come before profit. The demilitarization of the military police—with the removal of police from the armed forces, the introduction of civil and political rights to public security workers, and the construction of a new model of civil police—are all necessary and urgent goals.

However, demilitarization of the police is not enough to advance public security policy. We must demand the end of the use of the military apparatus by the police, including helicopters, drones, machine guns, armored cars, and the use of less lethal weapons to control demonstrations, protests, and major events. . . . The revival of the practice of detaining political prisoners (protestors) in Brazil is not acceptable. Fundamental reforms must guarantee life, establishing programs that invest in youth and that can end the increasing deaths of Black youths across the country. The demilitarization of the police is a fundamental step for moving toward these much-needed changes for Rio de Janeiro and for the whole of Brazil [pp. 120–21].

Final Considerations

In the prevailing approach, the police do not only establish themselves as an entity of the state: they become a force for territorial occupation. . . . The call for peace situates police, not politics, in the first place. This is one more symptom of a security policy based on militarization [p. 123].

The symbolism of war—which presents the favelas with the UPPs as if they were occupying conquered territories—transforms the UPPs into an insular and isolated outpost of a conquering state, increasing the potential for militarization. . . . This highlights several points:

a) In public security, there is a need to change the model supported by policing to one supported by public practices, with a new vision of the city as incorporating rights and peoples.

b) Among police, there is a need for demilitarization, changing behaviors, and unification of separate police forces.

c) With regard to police action, there is a need to overcome the ideology that reinforces the common sense of war, moving toward a common sense that presents the city as a holistic territory demanding protection, not repression.

d) As for the UPPs, the challenge is to create regulations that enhance rights and public policies that dialogue with the population, expanding services and urban equipment to improve the quality of life of favela residents [p. 125].

. . . The public security policy of the state of Rio de Janeiro currently maintains all the characteristics of the penal state (Wacquant 2009). The central elements of this finding are in the militarized actions of the police, in the repression of favela residents, in the practical nonexistence of constitutional rights, and in forced population displacement [p. 126].

NOTES

1 *Strong listening* is an expression used in the UPP social forums, which aimed to strengthen existing spaces for participation and also act as intermediaries between the population, local leaders, and the state.

2 PEC-51 was a proposal in 2013 by progressive Rio de Janeiro state senator Lindbergh Farias to demilitarize the police and fold the military police into a new civilianized security service.

REFERENCES

Bottari, Elenice, and Liane Gonçalves. 2011. "Beltrame quer pressa em investimentos sociais pós-UPPs: 'Nada sobrevive só com segurança.'" *Jornal O Globo*. Accessed March 31, 2024. https://oglobo.globo.com/rio/beltrame-quer-pressa-em-investimentos-sociais-pos-upps-nada-sobrevive-so-com-seguranca-2764060.

Denis, Jacques. 2013. "Favelas pacificadas para a nova burguesia brasileira." *Le monde diplomatique Brasil*, January 7. https://diplomatique.org.br/favelas-pacificadas-para-a-nova-burguesia-brasileira/.

Ferraz, Joana. 2004. "A Chacina de Vigário Geral: A violência como princípio." PhD diss., PPCIS/UERJ, Rio de Janeiro.

FGV. 2013. "Indicadores socioeconômicos nas UPPs do Estado do Rio de Janeiro." FGV Projetos, no. 17. Fundação Getúlio Vargas.

Fleury, Sonia. 2012. "Militarização do social como estratégia de integração." *Sociologias* 14, no. 30.

Franco, Marielle. 2014. "UPP—A redução da favela a três letras: Uma análise da política de segurança pública do estado do Rio de Janeiro." MA thesis, Fluminense Federal University.

Guariento, Suelen. 2013. "Participação no contexto das UPP's: Apontamentos a partir do programa UPP Social." MA thesis, Universidade Estadual do Rio de Janeiro.

Leite, Marcia. 2004. "Entrelaçamento entre religião e política: A mediação de conflitos urbanos no movimento de mães de vítimas de violência." Paper presented at "A Questão Social no novo Milénio," University of Coimbra, Portugal, February 7.

Machado da Silva, L. Antonio. 2008. *Vida sob cerco: Violência e rotina nas favelas do Rio de Janeiro*. Rio de Janeiro: FAPERJ/Nova Fronteira.

Machado da Silva, L. Antonio. 2010. "Da metáfora de guerra ao projeto de pacificação, favelas e políticas de segurança pública no Rio de Janeiro." *Revista Brasileira de segurança pública* 6, no. 2: 374–88.

Machado da Silva, L. Antonio. 2013. "Circulacao e fronteiras no Rio de Janeiro: A experiencia urbana de jovens moradores de favelas em context de pacificação." In *Sobre periferias: Novos conflitos no Brasil contemporaneo*, edited by Neiva Vieira da Cunha and Gabriel de Santis Feltran, 146–58. Rio de Janeiro: Lamparina.

Machado da Silva, L. Antonio, and Marcia Leite. 2004. "Favelas e democracia: Temas e problemas da ação coletiva nas favelas cariocas." In *Rio: A democracia vista de baixo*, edited by L. Antonio Machado da Silva et al., 61–78. Rio de Janeiro: Ibase.

Machado da Silva, Luiz Antonio, and Marcia Pereira Leite. 2014. "Continuidades e mudanças em favelas 'pacificadas': Apresentação ao dossiê Unidades de Polícia Pacificadora-Cevis." *Revista Dilemas* 7, no. 4. https://revistas.ufrj.br/index.php/dilemas/article/view/7263.

Maré Vive. 2014. "É tempo de mobilizar: Maré resiste!" Facebook, April 5. https://www.facebook.com/events/223034181236819/?source=3&source_newsfeed_story_type=regular&action_history=[%7B%22surface%22%3A%22newsfeed%22%2C%22mechanism%22%3A%22feed_story%22%2C%22extra_data%22%3A[]%7D]&has_source=1.

Mello, Marco Antonio da Silva. 2010. "Cidades: Commodities para consumo?" *Jornal da UFRJ* 6, no. 53: 13–16.

PMERJ. 2013. "Public Statement." Polícia Militar do Estado do Rio de Janeiro. https://web.archive.org/web/20140617063821/http://www.upprj.com.

Rio de Janeiro. 2009. "Dispõe sobre a criação da Unidade de Polícia Pacificadora—UPP e dá outras providências." Executive Acts, Decree No. 41,650. *Diário oficial do Estado do Rio de Janeiro*, January 22.

Rio de Janeiro State Government. 2011. "Dispõe sobre a implantação, estrutura, atuação e funcionamento das Unidades de Polícia Pacificadora (IUPP) no Estado do Rio de Janeiro e dá outras providências." Executive Acts, Decree No. 42,787. *Diário oficial do Estado do Rio de Janeiro*, January 6. http://arquivos.proderj.rj.gov.br/isp_imagens/Uploads/DecretoSeseg42.787Upp.pdf.

Saravia, Enrique. 2006. "Introdução à teoria da política pública." In *Coletânea de políticas públicas*, edited by Enrique Saravia and Elisabete Ferrarezi, 21–42. Brasília: ENAP.

Sebrae. 2013. "Serviço Brasileiro de apoio às micro e pequenas empresas." http://www.sebrae.com.br.

Silva, Itamar, and Lia de Mattos Rocha. 2008. "Associações de moradores de favelas e seus dirigentes: O discurso e a ação como reversos do medo." In *Justiça global: Segurança, tráfico e milícias no Rio de Janeiro*, 37–47. Rio de Janeiro: Fundação Heinrich Böll.

Siqueira, Raíza, André Rodrigues, and Maurício Lissovsky. 2012. "As Unidades de Polícia Pacificadora: Debates e reflexões." *Comunicações do ISER* 67, no. 31.

Tabak, Bernardo. 2011. "Pacificação abre caminho para formalização nas favelas do Rio." *O Globo*, July 12. https://g1.globo.com/economia/pme/noticia/2011/07/pacificacao-abre -caminho-para-formalizacao-nas-favelas-do-rio.html.

Wacquant, Loïc. 2009. "The Body, the Ghetto and the Penal State." *Qualitative Sociology* 32, no. 1: 101–29.

2

Inquisitorial Model of Juridical Inequality /
Modelo Inquisitorial de Desigualdade Jurídica

*Recognizing the Persistence of the Colonial Inquisition
Regime in Justice Procedure and Police Practice*

ROBERTO KANT DE LIMA

International coverage of the anticorruption task forces launched in Brazil in 2005 and 2014 exposed the world to some of Brazil's ordinary and unique procedures for crime prosecution and the peculiar forms of collaboration between judges, public prosecutors, and civil/judicial police. The anticorruption indictments focused on the launch of investigations in 2005 into the so-called Mensalão scandal, consisting of monthly payoffs made to lawmakers, supposedly engineered by President Lula's government to keep right-wing lawmakers from blocking his legislative agenda (Romero 2012). The second set of scandals, with inquiries launched in 2014, was named Lava-Jato after it was discovered that a car wash was a systematic graft operation and money laundering scheme. This operation involved government officials who received kickbacks from mega contractors and petroleum companies (Fishman, Viana, and Saleh 2020; Estrada 2021).

In the case of the Lava-Jato prosecutions, highly coercive plea bargains and testimony deals pushed by activist right-wing judges enabled the criminal prosecution of certain powerful and rich notables. These campaigns overwhelmingly and unfairly targeted political figures and contractors associated with the left while often ignoring the vast landscape of corruption, graft, racketeering, and money laundering that props up right-wing political parties and the oligarchical Centrão.[1] Nevertheless, this anticorruption wave did, for a moment, decenter the most common targets of ordinary criminal prosecution in Brazil—namely, the poor.

Some journalists and legal experts in the West called this persecution of Lula and his associates an inquisition, and the lead right-wing judge/prosecutor, Sergio Moro, was labeled the grand inquisitor. For example, human rights lawyer Geoffrey Robertson reminded the *Guardian*, as he took the case to the United Nations, that this "legal system in Brazil goes back to the Spanish Inquisition. . . . Justice is not done or seen to be done" (Phillips 2017; also see Wilpert and Meier 2019). Actually, these terms are not mere hyperbole. It is the purpose of this chapter to demonstrate that dominant judicial procedures and policing practices in contemporary Brazil represent the persistence, in form, substance, and reality, of the Inquisition as a judicial and policing regime. The Inquisition is not just a long-gone period of history identified with imperial Spain and Portugal's Catholic canon law regime and the investigative torture and confession-extraction system that it deployed to torment, surveil, ethnically cleanse, and commit genocide against Moors, Muslims, Jews, Indigenous peoples, sexual dissidents, practitioners of African spiritual traditions, and disobedient women, from 1492 well into the 1800s. In reality, the Inquisition is an entire system of legal and judicial interpretation and philosophy, or jurisprudence, that remains dominant in Latin America and the postcolonies of Iberia today.

This lesson is particularly important to learn and to transmit globally, in the third decade of the twenty-first century, since the justice procedures and policing practices of the Inquisition, or inquisitorial models of rule, are rising up to overthrow liberal legal-juridical traditions in places like the United States. For example, US Supreme Court judges Antonin Scalia and his ideological heirs on the Supreme Court, Brett Kavanaugh and Amy Coney Barrett, do not come from Anglo-liberal jurisprudential traditions nor from Protestant-conservative branches of legal-juridical interpretation. These three emerged from highly conservative Catholic canon law traditions, the same juridical models that we technically identify as inquisitorial. They are the same as those models advocated by Francisco Franco's fascist government in Spain, by the Opus Dei and its ultraconservative support for military dictatorships in Latin America, and by Pope Benedict XVI (the German jurist Joseph Ratzinger), who before becoming pontiff had been in charge, as prefect in the Vatican, of the Supreme Sacred Congregation of the Roman and Universal Inquisition.

This chapter explains the inquisitorial model in practice and as a legal doctrine and ordinary practice. And it explains why global activists, scholars, and members of the public need to recognize its contemporary relevance and persistence, in order to better critique and resist its power to reinforce racial, class, gender, and religious hierarchies and violence. Police practices are inquisitorial, and judicial systems represent a secret or veiled surveillance in Brazil. Judges claim that theoretically they have no discretion beyond the rigid interpretations of the law, but police—classified in a lower level of the judicial system—assist the judiciary in identifying criminals and, subsequently, investigating crimes. Judges' tasks necessarily imply a widely unconstrained field of discretion in the application of the law, since they are intended both to prevent future behaviors based on the assumptions of police officers and to carry out investigations (Noronha 2002).[2]

Judicial superiority is justified by alleged distance, objectivity, and exemption in the strict application of the law—a superiority that is related to the accusatory standards of the Brazilian legal tradition. Brazilian police and judicial practices are a reflection of a legal culture that views the Brazilian social structure as hierarchical—with the role of the judicial system to attribute and fix different degrees of citizenship and civilization to different segments of the population. Although the Brazilian Constitution attributes equal rights to all citizens, indiscriminately, the judicial system and the civil (judicial) police implement a mission that aims to provide distinct treatment to distinct segments of the population and to identify criminals before it even identifies crimes. Inquisitoriality is a model of institutional management of conflicts between individuals who are seen naturally and legally as ontologically unequal parties. The arbiter of the process—particularly the civil (judicial) police and its case-shaping judges[3]—is above society and its conflicts.

This chapter also highlights the clash between Brazil's two legal models for society[4]—one, an egalitarian jurisprudence model based on Brazil's 1988 postdictatorship Constitution and its talk of rights, which derive from liberal doctrines championing the equal rights of all individuals, and another conflicting legal doctrine that understands the world as fundamentally hierarchical. In this latter legal/juridical tradition, the aim of the law is to keep groups (not individuals) in their place within the hierarchy and to keep races, classes, and genders in their "naturally" subordinate or privileged positions in the divine order of things. This second doctrine is that of the Inquisition and its epistemologies and norms. Justice system cultures are alive and well in Brazil and around the world, but they clash with explicit intensity in Brazil. The two radically clashing distinct legal-juridical regimes are used alternately to justify judicial decisions. In focusing on Brazilian legal traditions and their relationship to the establishment and constant undermining of civil rights, this chapter shows how an aristocratic/hierarchically focused legal model of equality remains a site of inquisitoriality.[5] In this section, I map out the key characteristics of contemporary Brazilian criminal processes and briefly describe legal models in criminal procedural law. This is followed by a discussion of the effects that legal ambiguity has on citizenship. Our laws, in fact, favor a type of coexistence between explicit representations—which are presented in the form of legal and doctrinal texts, referring to aspirational practices by lawmakers, guided by implicit and traditional principles, which actually guide the majority of their practices (Baptista 2008; Figueira 2008).[6]

Brazilian legal tradition contrasts with more familiar liberal forms of Western legal traditions. After national independence in 1822, the study of law was transformed in Brazil in the bill that authorized the opening of the first two law schools, whose purpose was to form the cadres for administering the Brazilian Empire (Falcão Neto 1988, 400–442), newly independent at that time from the Portuguese crown. Whereas some Western legal traditions teach through precedent, Brazilian traditions privilege the state's prerogative over either precedent or any notion of citizens' equal rights. The imperial regime continued, after independence, to explicitly support legal inequality between Brazilians, a dynastic continuation of the Portuguese absolute monarchy established in Brazil from 1808 to 1821, when the Portuguese King D. João VI came to Rio de Janeiro fleeing from Napoleon's army, ideologically committed to slavery. With this exile, the king brought with him the Portuguese absolute monarchical institutions (police, judiciary, administration, etc.) from Lisbon to Rio de Janeiro. Slavery was only abolished in 1888, with the first Civil Code published only in 1916, despite the fact that a penal code and penal procedure codes were published in the 1830s (the last one receiving significant reformulations in the 1840s and 1870s).

The monarchical tradition of legal inequality and unequal policing and judicial treatment was established in Rio de Janeiro in 1763 when Rio became the capital of the Portuguese colony of Brazil. Later, it also became the capital of the Empire of Brazil in 1822, when the son of King Dom João VI, King Pedro IV of Portugal, moved to Rio to rule over the independent Empire of Brazil as Pedro I. The Portuguese court came to Rio de Janeiro in 1808, fleeing Napoleon's invasion and occupation of the Portuguese mainland. Between 1808 and 1821, the Lisbon court brought political and legal institutions of repression and absolute monarchy to Rio, including the Royal Guard, a protomodern police authority. This entity was nothing like the bourgeois police established in France and England during the nineteenth century. Rio remained the capital of Brazil after the monarchy was overthrown in 1889 and until the 1960s, when the capital was transferred to the newly created Federal District of Brasília in the central zone of the country. To this day, however, Rio has more federal civil servants than Brasília. Due to this historical legacy, this tradition of unequal security coverage, which permeates the whole of Brazil, was concentrated in Rio, where Brazil's first uniformed police forces were created and deployed. The royal and imperial courts continued to operate in Rio de Janeiro throughout the nineteenth century and into the first decades of the twentieth century, even though the monarchy had been abolished in 1889. The traditions, practices, and institutional relationships within the justice tribunals of Rio de Janeiro reflect the momentum of this history even today.

For almost eighty years of its formative history, Brazil had no civil code and was governed by a highly hierarchical penal code that deployed structural and state violence to keep races and classes in their places through punishment and penal sanction. This legal posture persisted in the concept of legal equality so emphatically described by Rui Barbosa (1995, 26) in his Prayer to the Young in the twentieth century, still current in the twenty-first: "The rule of equality is to treat (give) unequally (to) the unequal to the extent that they are unequal. It is in this social inequality, proportioned to natural inequality, that the true law of equality is found." Rui Barbosa, a liberal jurist, is committed to the formation of a republic that transforms "natural differences" of race, class, and gender into "proportional" or right-sized social inequality, thus reaffirming, in Aristotelian and legal terms, the inequality of legal treatment as the essence of the founding order of Brazil (Mendes 2005). According to this inquisitorial notion of justice, through the application of unequal treatment, a fair hierarchical and material legal order would be reproduced—an absurd claim in the capitalist model, which starts from the permanent creation of material and symbolic inequalities across the market, not by the law (Marshall 1967).

Attributing rights based on natural differences reveals a mismatch in the construction of citizenship—"regulated" (dos Santos 1987), "relational" (DaMatta 2000), or through a logic of state-imposed, top-down "patrimonialism" (estadania, in Portuguese; de Carvalho 2002)—and constitutes what reform-minded scholars of the law consider to be a "badly conformed civic world" (Cardoso de Oliveira 2018, 2020). Estadania in Portuguese captures the state's logic within this inquisitorial epistemology, describing the state's patrimonialist relationship to its citizens, protecting, punishing, rendering them dependent, at best as clients, at worst as servants. But the people are not truly sovereign in this model, and certainly, individual citizens are not hegemonic subjects. In a society of legally unequal individuals (in the context of the inquisitorial model), obedience to the rules takes on a negative value of servility and subordination (R. Lima 2008). Their disobedience may even be illegal, but it appears as an affirmation of freedom. Conceptions of liberal law—represented as a protection for citizens against abuse from the government or other citizens—are reproduced as abstract rhetorical forms in the Brazilian judicial system, with no correspondence in daily institutional practices. Unequal treatment detaches the law and/or rule from those being accused, who are deemed distinct in nature, rendering their legal circumstances external to the control of those who are subjected to it.

On the contrary, in an inquisitorial legal model, the application of the same law in the context of similar facts or events is unequal. This is because the law, to be just, must be applied unequally to people of unequal status. In this context, everyone's obedience to the law is discouraged since their disobedience may be illegal. But it is not immoral, as it is perceived as an expression of hierarchical privilege (which is good, in this context), not of rights, which are seen as far less important than privilege. This is the case, for example, for special prisons, which continue to exist in Brazil for all those who have completed higher education. "Special prison" is provided for in article 295 of the Brazilian Criminal Procedure Code. It is a procedural privilege that guarantees unequal treatment for Brazilian citizens, depending on their position, function, employment, activity, or degree of university education. It authorizes them to be confined in a special cell, different from the common prison system, which is a massively violent warehousing system for the racialized criminal class. By contrast, privileged individuals stay in special prison until transit in res judicata for criminal sentencing. The privileged jurisdiction—or jurisdiction by prerogative of function—is provided for in articles 53 and 102 of the Constitution of the Republic and is a mechanism that gives relative immunity to at least forty thousand public servants in Brazil, who are removed from a single judge's jurisdiction to the jurisdiction of appeal and superior courts (Cavalcante Filho, Trindade, and Lima 2017).

Inquisitorial Tradition in the Brazilian Judicial Process

The link between justice system inequalities and policing practices that affirm and intensify inequality has been central to the Brazilian criminal process, especially since 1871, and with the emergence of Inquérito Policial, the process of police-driven inquiry or inquisition, still fully in force in contemporary Brazil.[7] This police inquiry process is implemented by the civil police, who are a juridical police, quite distinct from the militarized police (who carry out armed operations on the streets and commit high rates of gun violence) or the municipal guard (who monitor shopping, touristic, and commuter spaces), or the federal police (who are an investigative branch of the federal government).

In the Brazilian Inquérito Policial practice, the criminal is identified first before the crime. Thus, guilt is assumed, whereas a liberal-juridical perspective begins with the presumption of innocence, investigates the facts of a crime, and keeps the file of suspects open, at least at first. In the Inquérito Policial process, the crime is constructed through the investigation process with the criminal anchored as the target of the inquiry. Neither judges nor the accused are permitted to interfere with the police inquiry process, which unfolds secretly to construct the case around the criminal. Perhaps surprisingly, this system was created in order to protect the accused, since it was assumed that the judge would simply absolve the powerful and punish those without privilege, and that the police, in nineteenth-century Brazil, would be more objective in generating a case, which would then be delivered to the judge.

The legal concept of Inquérito Policial was intended to separate the police from judicial matters and constituted an instrument whereby police could check judicial arbitrariness. It was determined that conflict between legally unequal parties would occur inquisitorially—that is, through secret and written legal procedures conducted by the executive power (police and government) and based on the formation of guilt. De Almeida Júnior (1920), an influential jurist practicing at the turn of the nineteenth century, offered a contrast between accusatory (liberal) and inquisitorial systems, presenting a combined alternative:

> The inquisitorial system contains elements that cannot be repelled, so much that between the 13th to 18th centuries it was a guarantee of justice and freedom. When the man of humble condition was exposed to the arbitrariness of the strong, rich and powerful, it was not easy for him to appear before the lordly justice to accuse without supplication, without embarrassment and without the fear and almost certainty of revenge; Canon Law preferred inquisitorial procedure to accusatory procedure and thus presented itself as the protector of the weaker persecuted party and the opponent of tyrannical strength; if abuses [within the inquisitorial system] perverted the institution, causing later evils greater than the benefits, this does not require the abolition of the system, but the creation of precautions for its use. (de Almeida Júnior 1920, 250–51)

This quote defends the canonical inquisitorial system for the protection it would give to the oppressed. But in reality, canon law tends to associate the secrecy of the institutional process of police inquiry and conflict management with the protection of good names—that is, persons of honor and privilege.[8] Actually, Inquérito Policial secrecy does not protect low status or weakness but mostly shields impunity and power. The result is a caste-like conception of social structure where legal inequality is explicit and even heralded as just. Inquisitoriality is a model of institutional management of conflicts between unequal parties, in which the arbiter of the process—be it the state or not[9]—is above society and its conflicts. Consequently, the truth must be ascertained confidentially and recorded in writing during the course of this procedure and, once the grounds for the accusations are verified (that is, once guilt is demonstrated by the police inquiry), the case file is delivered for trial and sentencing by the judge (L. Lima 1999). Any chance to challenge the gathering of evidence or interpretation of evidence, or the suggestion of a more plausible suspect or alternative narrative of motive and opportunity, is blocked by the veil of secrecy that is the prerogative of the civil/juridical police inquiry.

Another characteristic of the Brazilian criminal procedural system is the search for the "real" truth through the logic of the contradictory,[10] which imagines that the parties must necessarily diverge and that only the judge may act as a final truth finder. In Brazil, although the crime of false testimony is typified, there is no consequence for perjury committed by the accused. Truth, then, will depend only on the judge's assessment, on his "motivated free conviction" (Mendes 2012) about what are, or are not, facts and evidence.[11] These legal categories end up obfuscating material events and actions with a narrative being reconstructed in the investigation (Geertz 1997, 249–356). Inquérito Policial filters out conflicts managed by judges, separating them from those that must not leave the police sphere (R. Lima 2019; Misse 2010, 35–50). In practice, it eliminates the presumption of innocence, as it presents the Public Ministry (similar to the attorney general or public prosecutor) and the judge with a notarized public document of public faith, which identifies the authorship, circumstances, and materiality of the crime (Ferreira 2013).

Thus, in the same process, we will have the exercise of two judicial logics, the monological and inquisitorial, to form guilt in the inquiry and its contradiction, the *disputatio*, to challenge it in court: two competing regimes of truth to achieve the same "real" truth. The Inquérito Policial translates the results obtained in the police inquiry into judicial language, transforming social facts into legal ones, when they are interpreted and criminally characterized by the chief executive, who is an executive officer and holds at the administrative level a position equivalent to that of prosecutors and judges.[12] Then the judiciary accuses and prosecutes them.

As already mentioned, this judicial articulation operates under the logic of the contradictory, which is tolerant of contradictions, thus differing from scientific logic, founded on the provisional consensus on facts (Kuhn 2003). However, in Brazil such logic is not only in the judiciary; the types of knowledge of the legal field (constitutional, criminal, civil) are seen as isolated and autonomous sciences, with their own principles and authorized interpreters, called indoctrinators. Rui Barbosa's conception of equality, proper to a hierarchical state society, remains inscribed in our republican laws, which grant procedural privileges, such as the already mentioned special imprisonment and the forum prerogative for privilege of role,[13] coexisting naturally with the fifth article of the Constitution, which reads that we are all "equal before the law."

Legal Equality Models: The Production and Reproduction of Institutionalized Judicial Treatment Inequality in Brazil

To better explain the two ideas of legal equality and the paradoxes of their simultaneous coexistence,[14] consider two cases. In the first, equality by similarity can be viewed as a pyramid—where unequal and complementary segments in law are arranged in an orderly manner, on top of each other, in order to avoid conflict and ensure its harmony and complementarity. Here, equality means similarity, and not everyone can reach the top. The other model represents a distinct idea in which all unique individuals have the same rights but different interests and are therefore in permanent opposition and inevitable conflict. In this second case, order will consist in managing rather than eliminating difference. This last version of equality can be represented as a system of parallel pipes moving upward, in which the top is equal to the base, and thus everyone at the base can reach the top individually, according to their merit. Equality, here, means difference.

In the pyramid example, everyone, by definition, cannot have equal access to the summit. This cannot occur since there is no place for everyone at the top. The consequence is that the rules of the pyramid are general but of particular application.

Doing justice, here, means accepting the unequal reality of different segments and peoples. The aforementioned parallel pipes model, on the other hand, insists that the rules are for everyone, and doing justice means applying the law in an equal, universal, and uniform way.

Now, in the Brazilian case, the model is hybrid and seems to have a trapezoidal shape, like a parallel pipe embedded in a pyramid, or vice versa. Thus, the law produces inequality as it operates in a capitalist context of radical stratification and class distinction, one that legally and legitimately favors cartels and monopolies. The market naturally functions unequally among those already legally and economically unequal. So the market is actually more resonant with inquisitorial normalization of inequality than it is with liberal notions of freedom of choice and action. This parallel realm of inequity—the result of tutelage by institutions of social control over society—extends indefinitely over relationships, which become personalized and allow hierarchical exchanges not necessarily linked to classes. This legal treatment would cause disgust in an egalitarian and individualistic society.

The tradition of inquisitorial judicial processes in Brazil's populations not only highlights unequal treatment but ultimately categorizes citizens in multiple categories, to be dealt with as fundamentally distinct legal entities (Baptista 2013). This tutelary posture is the result of Brazil's colonial, imperial, and slave-owning history—a position that is submissive to theories of racial and geographic inferiority in the face of civilized Europe (Faria 2002). It is also strongly influenced by Catholic beliefs, averse to liberalism and individualism, explicitly hierarchical, and devoted to the superiority of a common good over individual interests. This constitutes a strong component of the education offered to elites since the empire, and which can be summarized in a text published by a Spanish priest in 1884, titled *Liberalism Is Sin* (Salvany 2016).

This deficit, within citizenship, plagues us and produces a civic world that makes citizens who are not covered by minimum rights suffer civil subjection and discursive exclusion (Cardoso de Oliveira 2018, 2020). Brazil's justice system procedures and police practices are based on the principle of secrecy, presumption of guilt and privilege, and inequality of status before the law. Our laws, therefore, support structures of antiliberal inequality, which stratifies segments of the population, prior to and overdetermining the market, which in turn intensifies and extends those inequalities and privileges.

NOTES

Parts of this discussion were taken from R. Lima (2013).

The data discussed here are the result of ethnographic research conducted on the criminal justice system on an ongoing basis, since the 1980s, in Rio de Janeiro, initially for a doctorate in anthropology at Harvard University (R. Lima 2019). The comparative methodology by contrast (Geertz 1997) led me to perform ethnographies with the police in Birmingham, Alabama, in the 1990s and the public defender's office in San Francisco, California, in the 1990s and in 2011–12, with funding from CNPq, CAPES, and the Fulbright Commission.

1   The moniker of the profoundly conservative but supposedly nonideological establishment at the core of the political spectrum.

2   Judicial truth, then, depends only on the judge's assessment, based on his "motivated free conviction," a legal category that makes officially explicit the judge's free discretion (Mendes 2012) about what are (or are not) facts and evidence. Moreover, as the judges are not civil servants but actually organs of the judiciary power, they are not accountable for their decisions (article 92 of Brazilian Constitution).

3   The canonical inquisition, or "prior investigation," is foreseen in the current Canonical Code, Canons 1717–21 (John Paul II 1983, 296–97).

4   Geertz (1978) distinguishes "models of," which concern the description of the observed facts, from "models for," of a normative character.

5   For the purposes of this text, inquisitoriality consists in the presumption of guilt established by official investigations, mostly written by judiciary police without knowledge produced by investigation, preliminary to the prosecution.

6   In this sense, it is not to be confused with the concept of "legal sensitivity" (Geertz 1997, 260–61), of a broader comparative nature.

7   Cardoso de Oliveira (2011; 2018, 34–63) refers to "two conceptions" of legal equality, to distinguish that which provides for uniform treatment from that which, according to him, provides for different treatment.

8   Canonical Code, Canon 1717, paragraph 2 (John Paul II 1983, 296).

9   See note 3.

10 The contradictory principle is in the Constitution and implies the right to respond to a civil or criminal charge. The logic of the contradictory, however, refers to the need for opponents in the criminal process to diverge obligatorily and systematically, leaving only the final decision to the judge. Therefore, contradictory and adversarial are not synonymous. Adversarial logic implies that "the truth is best discovered when two parties are competing, each conducting its own investigation of the facts, presenting different theories about the facts and the law and arguing their own case before the court. In this version of the process, the parties can always reach an agreement and ask the judge to terminate. And he must remain neutral, impartial, and aloof to increase the fairness (impartiality) of the procedures" (Hall 2009, 284). In Brazil, as the parties to public criminal proceedings on serious crimes cannot agree, it is only the judge who decides to close the case.

11 See note 5.

12 Criminal classification is preceded by processes of crimination (definition of a specific action as a crime) and incrimination (defining the authorship of the criminal action), framing it in articles of the Penal Code (criminalization). For more details, see Misse (2008).

13 The Brazilian Constitution of 1988 (arts. 29, 96, 102, 105, 108) and the Code of Penal Procedure (arts. 84, 86, 87) list a series of authorities that are entitled to privileged forum due to the prerogative of function (Brasil 1988). This means that, when accused, the case must be processed at a higher level than that of the

single judge—who is in charge of the instruction and judgment of ordinary cases. About forty thousand positions in the different municipal, state, and federal spheres hold this prerogative. The special prison, on the other hand, guarantees special conditions for the duration of the process, according to the status and occupation of the accused—for example, if they have higher education, if they are religious ministers, and so on—and without taking into account the seriousness of the charges (art. 295 of the Criminal Procedure Code).

14 Cardoso de Oliveira (2018, 34–63) discusses this issue widely, pointing to the imperfect configuration of a civic world in Brazil.

REFERENCES

Baptista, Bárbara Gomes Lupetti. 2008. *Os rituais judiciários e o princípio da oralidade: Construção da verdade no processo civil brasileiro.* Porto Alegre: Sérgio Antônio Fabris.

Baptista, Bárbara Gomes Lupetti. 2013. *Paradoxos e ambiguidades da imparcialidade judicial: Entre "quereres" e "poderes."* Porto Alegre: Sérgio Antônio Fabris.

Barbosa, Rui, ed. 1995. *Oração aos moços.* Rio de Janeiro: Edições Casa de Rui Barbosa.

Brasil (Office of the President). 1941. "Decreto-lei no. 3.689, de 3 de outubro de 1941." In *Código de processo penal.* http://www.planalto.gov.br/ccivil_03/decreto-lei/del3689 .htm.

Brasil (Office of the President). 1988. Constituição da República Federativa do Brasil de 1988. https://www.planalto.gov.br/ccivil_03/constituicao/constituicao.htm.

Cardoso de Oliveira, Luís Roberto, ed. 2011. *Direito legal e insulto moral: Dilemas da Cidadania no Brasil, Quebec e EUA.* Rio de Janeiro: Garamond.

Cardoso de Oliveira, Luís Roberto. 2018. "Sensibilidade cívica e cidadania no Brasil." *Antropolítica: Revista contemporánea de antropologia,* no. 44: 34–63.

Cardoso de Oliveira, Luís Roberto. 2020. "Civic Sensibilities and Civil Rights in a Comparative Perspective: Demands of Respect, Considerateness and Recognition." *Ius Fugit,* no. 23: 195–219.

Cavalcante Filho, João Trindade, and Frederico Retes Lima. 2017. "Jurisdiction, Prerogative and Privilege: Which and How Many Authorities Have Jurisdiction in Brazil?" *RDU, Porto Alegre* 14, no. 76: 176–97.

DaMatta, Roberto, ed. 2000. *A casa e a rua.* Rio de Janeiro: Rocco.

de Almeida Júnior, João Mendes, ed. 1920. *O processo criminal brasileiro.* 2 vols. Rio de Janeiro: Typ. Baptista de Souza.

de Carvalho, José Murilo. 2002. *Cidadania no Brasil: O longo caminho.* Rio de Janeiro: Civilização Brasileira.

dos Santos, Wanderley Guilherme, ed. 1987. *Cidadania e justiça: A política social na ordem Brasileira.* Rio de Janeiro: Campus.

Estrada, Gaspard. 2021. "Operation Car Wash Was No Magic Bullet." *New York Times,* February 26. https://www.nytimes.com/2021/02/26/opinion/international-world/car -wash-operation-brazil-bolsonaro.html.

Falcão Neto, Joaquim de Arruda. 1988. "Lawyers in Brazil." In *Law and Society,* edited by Abel Philip Lewis Richard, 400–442. Berkeley: University of California Press.

Faria, Luiz de Castro. 2002. *Oliveira Vianna: De Saquarema à Alameda São Boaventura, 41Niterói. O autor, os livros, a obra*. Rio de Janeiro: Relume Dumará.

Ferreira, Marco Aurélio Gonçalves. 2013. *A presunção da inocência e a construção da verdade: Contrastes e confrontos em perspectiva comparada*. Rio de Janeiro: Lumen Juris.

Figueira, Luiz Eduardo. 2008. *O ritual judiciário do tribunal do júri*. Porto Alegre: Sérgio Antonio Fabris Editora.

Fishman, Andrew, Natalia Viana, and Maryam Saleh. 2020. "Keep It Confidential: The Secret History of U.S. Involvement in Brazil's Scandal-Wracked Operation Car Wash." *Intercept*, March 12. https://theintercept.com/2020/03/12/united-states-justice -department-brazil-car-wash-lava-jato-international-treaty/.

Geertz, Clifford. 1978. *A interpretação das culturas*. Translated by Fanny Wrobel. Rio de Janeiro: Zahar.

Geertz, Clifford. 1997. "O saber local." In *O saber local: Novos ensaios em antropologia interpretativa*, edited by Clifford Geertz, 249–356. Translated by Vera Mello Joscelyne. Petrópolis: Vozes.

Hall, Daniel, ed. 2009.*Criminal Law and Procedure*. New York: Cengage Learning.

John Paul II. 1983. "Código de direito canônico." In *Constituição apostólica "Sacrae disciplinae leges" de promulgação do código de direito canônico*. Braga: Editorial Apostolado da Oração. http://www.vatican.va/archive/cod-iuris-canonici/portuguese/codex-iuris -canonici_po.pdf.

Kuhn, Thomas S., ed. 2003. *A estrutura das revoluções científicas*. Translated by Beatriz Vianna Boeira and Nelson Boeira. São Paulo: Perspectiva.

Lima, Lana Lage da Gama. 1999. "O tribunal do santo ofício da inquisição: O suspeito é o culpado." *Revista de sociologia e política*, no. 13: 17–21. https://doi.org/10.1590/S0104 -44781999000200002.

Lima, Roberto Kant de. 2008. *Ensaios de antropologia e de direito: Acesso à justiça e processos institucionais de administração de conflitos e produção da verdade jurídica em uma perspectiva comparada*. Rio de Janeiro: Lumen Juris.

Lima, Roberto Kant de. 2013. "Entre as leis e as normas: Éticas corporativas e práticas profissionais na segurança pública e na justiça criminal." *Dilemas: Revista de estudos de conflito e controle social* 6, no. 4: 549–80. https://revistas.ufrj.br/index.php/dilemas/article /view/7436.

Lima, Roberto Kant de, ed. 2019. *A polícia da cidade do Rio de Janeiro: Seus dilemas e paradoxos*. Translated by Otto Miller. Rio de Janeiro: S/N.

Marshall, Thomas H. 1967. *Cidadania, classe social e status*. Translated by Meton Porto Gadelha. Rio de Janeiro: Zahar.

Mendes, Regina Lúcia Teixeira. 2005. "Igualdade à Brasileira: Cidadania como instituto jurídico." In *Ensaios sobre a igualdade jurídica: Acesso à justiça criminal e direitos da Cidadania no Brasil*, edited by Maria Stella de Amorim, Roberto Kant de Lima, and Regina Lúcia Teixeira Mendes, 1–34. Rio de Janeiro: Ed. Lumen Juris.

Mendes, Regina Lúcia Teixeira. 2012. *Do princípio do livre convencimento motivado: Legislação, doutrina e interpretação de juízes Brasileiros*. Rio de Janeiro: Lumen Juris.

Misse, Michel. 2008. *Acusados e acusadores: Estudos sobre ofensas, acusações e incriminações*. Rio de Janeiro: Revan.

Misse, Michel. 2010. "O inquérito policial no Brasil: Uma pesquisa empírica." *Dilemas— Revista de estudos de conflito e controle social* 3, no. 7: 35–50. https://revistas.ufrj.br/index .php/dilemas/article/view/7199.

Noronha, Magalhães. 2002. *Curso de direito processual penal*. 28th ed. São Paulo: Saraiva.

Phillips, Dom. 2017. "Brazil's Leftist Hero Basks in Adulation as He Bids to Revive Political Fortunes." *Guardian*, September 2. https://www.theguardian.com/world/2017 /sep/02/lula-brazil-leftist-hero-basks-adulation-bids-revive-political-fortunes.

Romero, Simon. 2012. "Brazilian Corruption Case Raises Hopes for Judicial System." *New York Times*, October 9. https://www.nytimes.com/2012/10/10/world/americas/brazilian -corruption-case-raises-hopes-for-judicial-system.html.

Salvany, Félix Sardá y. 2016. *O liberalismo é pecado*. São Caetano do Sul: Santa Cruz.

Wilpert, Greg, and Brian Meier. 2019. "Lula da Silva's Second Conviction Another Travesty of Justice." *Wire*, February 13. https://thewire.in/world/lula-da-silvas-second -conviction-another-travesty-of-justice.

3

Armed Dominions / Domínios Armados

The Fabrication of Insecurity and the Governance of
Public Space by Criminal-Political Monopolies in Rio de Janeiro

ANA PAULA MENDES DE MIRANDA AND
JACQUELINE DE OLIVEIRA MUNIZ

The landscape of security, armed social control, and the extraction and circulation of capital in Rio de Janeiro is an Ouroboros of disputes over territory and public spaces by various armed groups (narco-trafficking gangs or factions, vigilante militias, and racketeering operations). These disputes rage over the collective exploitation and regulation of (il)legal markets in goods, land, and labor. The concept of armed dominions, presented below, offers up a new intersectional tool for mapping and understanding how criminal networks (including armed forces and police battalions operating beyond the framework of the law) operate in relationship to territorialized illegal and irregular economic activities through violent coercion. We understand this to be a mode of governing. In the spaces where these intersecting disputes occur, armed groups are virtually the only form of government: they are the state, not an antistate.

These coercive forms of armed governance emerged during—and even before—the period many analysts have labeled neoliberal. Their operations have little direct interest in free markets per se, however. Armed dominions control the movements of people and goods in their territories. They monopolize urban economies in a shifting intersectional and disputed (not shared in any positive sense) fabric, which some might describe as a paradoxical monopolization, but which we prefer to understand as an illegal autonomous government. The notion of armed dominions differs from that of parallel power, since the strategies of armed dominion require interaction, connivance, or even intimate collaboration (no matter how extralegal) with state agents in the regulation of illegal and informal markets. One can identify a territory under armed dominion via signs indicating the frontiers of what is essentially an illegal autonomous government. These signs typically include publicly legible acts of violence and the deterioration of public areas (marked by barricades, graffiti, armed checkpoints, etc.), signifying and implementing limits of access and mobility, revealing that one is entering (or leaving) an unstable, conflicted territory. The signs reveal practical knowledge that residents, users, and workers must incorporate in their transits to stay in these unstable and uncertain domains.

What Is Organized Crime in Brazil?

Human and social scientists in Brazil have dealt with criminality, criminal justice, public safety, and violence for over forty years now (Lima, Misse, and Miranda 2000; Muniz et al. 2018). Here, we present the concept of armed dominions (Muniz and Proença 2007) as a key to understanding the representations and practices generally lumped together under the rubric of organized crime,[1] most particularly their relationships with the expansion and transformation of conventional criminality. Territorial control and management, especially in racialized, criminalized, and/or marginalized urban areas, are part of an (il)legal, translocal, itinerant, and networked political economy. These political forms of sovereignty over territories, populations, and the economic means of regulating markets for goods and services are what makes the criminal groups operating in Rio de Janeiro recognizably unique.[2]

Armed dominions—and their mobile, political, and commercial technologies—are key to understanding the disputes for hegemony and the negotiations (violent or peaceful) between police, militia, and drug cartels in Rio de Janeiro. As an expression of autonomous government, they reveal links between the policy objectives, business strategies, commercial tactics, and the logistical needs for territorial maintenance of the various factions attempting to exert dominion over a given urban area (Miranda and Muniz 2018). The various factions (facções), or comandos, that dispute dominion are characteristically in direct confrontations with each other and with state security forces for territorial control of marginalized areas of Rio (Misse 2003; Dias 2013; Biondi and Marques 2010).[3] During the 1990s, comandos and street organizations administering crime economies emerged in the prisons of Rio and São Paulo. English-language media often refer to these groups as narco-cartels, but that is a Mexican and Colombian term that has been laid over a distinct Brazilian reality. These groups are called comandos or factions, terms that capture their concrete organization for low-intensity armed struggle. Wars were and are waged between these comandos and factions for political and economic control within the prisons, producing alliances and rifts between incarcerated criminalized organizations. These pacts and rivalries have become powerful structures for armed social control and surplus extraction, deploying ever-expanding operations outside prison walls, that can extend throughout all of Brazil.

It should be noted that the expressions *faction* and *comando* are emic categories employed by inmates, state security agents, and the media to identify and make visible different and contending groups in the context of criminalization discourses. These terms are allegorical, sensitive, and prescriptive. They assert power, legitimize exercises of authority, claim possession, and announce regimes of truth. The categories highlight forms of armed power that employ different ways of exercising governance. *Faction* signals a tactical unity of purpose and action. It exploits fragmentation through provisional and unstable alliances of disparate groups in disputes for economic supremacy through territorial struggle. *Comando* indicates a more strategic political unity of purpose and action. It concentrates decision-making and management, producing more or less homogenous subjects and assimilating rivals while attempting to exercise political-economic hegemony over the territory in question.

These two categories are different ways of governing autonomously, constructing and regulating illicit markets in their interfaces with the constituted public powers. Factions, comandos, militias, firms, and families are all variations of the same conceptual theme: armed dominion and governance at the local level. The various myths of origin and the reputations of these groups are supported by their central practice: the production of threats to sell protection. Whatever their names or degree of legality (or conviviality with public power), all of these groups make war to sell peace while instituting regimes of fear. Armed dominions use Rio as an immense stage for the dramatic production of insecurity and—as a result—projects for power.

The Protection Racket Economy: "'Tá dominado, 'tá tudo dominado"

Militias in Rio are often composed of off-duty or retired police and military officers. They often rival and even overlap with narco comandos/factions, fighting for control over and profiteering from urban neighborhoods and territories. They implement "protection rackets" and collect "informal taxes" in their illicit operations (Muniz and Proença 2007). Michel Misse points out (2011) that violent criminal activities are characterized by disputes over territories in which illicit commerce takes place: disputes over the sale of drugs, electric grid taps, off-the-books transport services, and so on. Misse also remarks on the presence of "militias" in Rio, which dispute territorial control. They also attempt to monopolize freight and automobile robberies, arms trafficking, clandestine surveillance operations, and murder for hire, often with the occasional participation of the police. Links between numbers games, militias, and factions have also been identified.[4]

All of these criminal arrangements strengthen individual and collective fear through (in)direct threats, and this is the political-economic foundation of the protection rackets that serve as the basis for the regulation of illegal markets.[5] Such a system cannot develop unless it is tolerated or even supported by local politicians and sectors of the state that give up territories and let the firms operate in relative peace.

The expansion of the militias is directly related to their knowledge of state bureaucracies and to the financing of electoral campaigns, which represent the possibility of exchanging favors, privileges, and advantages. Militias were initially treated as a lesser evil by politicians, police, the mainstream media, and part of the population. The 2008 Congressional Inquiry Committee into Militias in the Legislative Assembly of the State of Rio de Janeiro (ALERJ) made it clear (at least to the media and the population) that the militias are the most critical expression of armed domains in Rio. Composed of law enforcement agents, they work from within and on the fringes of the executive, legislative, and judiciary powers, in cooperation with or in opposition to justice and public security agencies. This is in line with the militia's political projects and business plans (Muniz and Almeida 2018).

Militias are the most sophisticated manifestation of a criminal government and its concomitant illegal practices of surveillance, regulation, and correction in the territories under militia control. Militias epitomize the dangerous relationships between police officers, politicians, government officials, drug dealers, and professional killers that make up capitalist enterprises of illegal exploitation and illegal employment of public goods and services. The original narrative—that the militias would be community self-defense leagues against drug traffickers—served as a political marketing strategy for legitimizing the alleged pacification of the territories under their armed rule.

In 2000, a chorus of "it's dominated, everything is dominated" (Abreu 1992) overtook Rio. Popularized at funk parties in the favelas, the expression became a reference to local politics. In a city that is a "purgatory of beauty and chaos," where state authorities face multiple and permanent states of crisis, the idea of being "dominated" reveals in what contexts order manifests itself, making explicit the popular Carioca saying that "those who can, rule, and those who are wise, obey" (SD Boys 2000).

This local view of power refers to Max Weber's analysis of the political situation in Europe at the end of the nineteenth century. Weber sought to demonstrate that the state—in terms of creating domination based on legitimated physical violence—produces a politics that manifests itself as a struggle for political power. In this way, Weber theorized that the modern state developed through the ambition to control the "use of physical force" ([1918] 1948). Thus, the concept of the state came to be associated with a "human community that, within a given territory . . . (successfully) claims for itself the monopoly over legitimate physical coercion" (78). The attempt to understand the meanings of domination in the dispute for territories in Rio de Janeiro presented here is inspired by Weber's perspective. We understand domination, as constituted by the ideas of force and violence, as structural parts of political disputes and the functioning of institutions.

One must understand the distinction between power and domination to understand the state's relationship to coercion. Since *power* is a sociologically imprecise term, Weber preferred to use the concept of domination. Domination means the making explicit of a relationship in which one of the parties imposes its will on the other. In the case of Rio, this imposition is made through an armed dispute over territories. For this reason, we felt we must deepen the original concept of armed domain (Muniz and Proença 2007) to designate criminal networks that exercise armed territorial control and act in illicit and irregular economic activities on a specific territorial basis through coercive violence—said violence being the main resource for the maintenance and reproduction of their practices. It is the construction and maintenance of these territorial domains—or rather, of a type of illegal government that aims to obtain legitimacy—that impacts public services and trade in dominated areas.

The illegal sale of goods and services is associated with a policy of coercing people and preventing merchants and service providers from freely operating in dominated territories.

This expanded notion of armed domain (Miranda and Muniz 2018) expresses the construction of a scenario of instability and fluidity, in which actors (police, militia, and drug dealers) move and become stronger in disputes for itinerant control of territories. Armed territorial control, monopoly over illegal/irregular economic activities, and violent coercion have become the main means of maintaining and reproducing local power in Rio de Janeiro. Illegal governments aim to obtain legitimacy through the provision of public services and control of commerce in dominated territories. In total opposition to the idea of a free market—but also totally free of state accountability, taxation, and human rights structures—the businesses in these armed dominions embody and deploy coercive management over access to, permanence within, and the movements of people around these territories. Through the mechanisms underpinning the construction and maintenance of armed domains, public space can be controlled without state agencies intervening in its regulation.

Armed Dominions Are Not Parallel Power Structures

Contrary to what one might expect, the actions of armed groups do not simply translate into increased numbers of homicides. Since these groups wish to remain relatively clandestine, they produce latent fear and diffuse threats in each territory. Less explicit coercion reduces operational costs (in armaments, ammunition, staff, etc.) and ensures that deaths are generally limited to certain situations. A public-private partnership model has been implemented for police and public safety, with public security agents often perversely serving as armed auxiliaries for or giving operational support to criminal governments. As a result, other urban services have been appropriated through intimidation. Armed dominions shape the spaces and situations to which the populations that circulate or live in them are exposed. They must be seen as a dynamic phenomenon, however, and not as a fixed and limited geographic space. These criminal networks and their associated state ties function as an itinerant form of government, regulating illicit and irregular commerce.

Armed dominion is thus distinct from the commonsense notion of parallel power. Democratic institutions that denounce violence both compete and coexist with armed dominions. Both structures are intertwined through pragmatic temporary alliances and feuds between individuals and institutions. Armed dominions are therefore best understood as the imposition of an illegal armed authority that exercises an autonomous government through coercion, as Muniz and Proença have outlined (2007) and as has been further detailed by Miranda and Muniz (2018). This government is connected to and networked with the formal government in the regulation of illegal and informal markets and the provision of essential services in dominated territories (Muniz and Proença 2007; Miranda and Muniz 2018). Armed dominions work together with state agents (and at the state's convenience) as often as they enter into conflict with them. Interactions between the two shape and are shaped by local actors' reputations, and it is the interrelationships between armed dominions and the state that institutes power: the one does not exist as an alternative or parallel to the other.

Violence is also a category that is of limited use in trying to describe what takes place in armed dominions. These territories are marked by certain visible signs (barricades, graffiti, etc.) that indicate violence and degraded public space, and which serve to warn of restrictions on mobilities and access.[6] The militias and comandos that govern armed dominions authorize the provision or prevention of services. They can cut power or block access to neighborhoods on a whim. Barricades, shootings, illegal power taps, and so on, all contribute to creating certain territories' reputations for violent crime. All markers indicate the presence of armed groups regulating and disputing territories with the police, becoming factors that help to constitute a constant feeling of insecurity and a reputation for violence, whether or not a given area generates more or fewer cases of violence (Roché 1993).

A Case Study: Energy, Theft, and Fraud

Our risk perception maps offer a dynamic and multifactorial approach to the notions of violence, risk, and armed dominions, which breaks with commonsense views of these phenomena.[7] They capture the procedural, multidimensional, and multicausal ways in which labor insecurity and victimization are perceived in each territory by electrical grid linemen. Our analysis of indicators of the presence of armed dominions was carried out at different times through a series of collection instruments: the Denunciation Hotline (Disque Denúncia) database;[8] guided tours to locations in the cities of São Gonçalo and Duque de Caxias; focus groups and semistructured interviews that resulted in the production of mental maps; and victimization surveys of electric company employees.

Our use of mixed instruments and methods produced a set of qualitative and quantitative data to criticize the methods used by the National Electric Energy Agency (ANEEL) to measure electricity theft. It made visible parts of the social phenomenon of risk that were not measured in available official data. By paying attention to the local signs of armed dominion revealed by this data, we could indirectly observe the capillary nature and functioning of the armed groups exercising domination over territories with high rates of electricity theft, as well as their interactions with state agents.

Our data reveal that there is a strong convergence between the presence of armed groups and the places that service providers understand to be of greater risk for carrying out their work. The relationship between these variables was validated by other sources and by data from the electric company and from other institutions (Disque Denúncia, Public Safety Institute, Instituto Brasileiro de Geografia e Estatistica [IBGE]), as well as data produced during the Labor Victimization Survey, of which our project was part.

We observed differences in how armed dominions operate in regulating the access of energy company employees to risky areas. According to the survey participants, militiamen and drug traffickers act differently toward electrical workers. To prevent power cuts, a designated militiaman comes and talks to the technician about the service work being performed. In areas dominated by traffickers, residents use the fact that they are in an area of risk to threaten technicians with reprisals. In these trafficker-dominated areas, threats are more diffuse.

In the focus groups, reports emerged of people with radios or cell phones who carry out illegal policing and monitoring of services provided by company workers. Drug traffickers are more noticeable in the areas where this occurs than militiamen, according to our interlocutors. The quantitative data from the labor victimization survey support our qualitative work about the frequency with which electric company workers encounter signs of armed dominion: over 80 percent of the workers encounter barricades or graffiti when on their rounds.

The possibility of being exposed to disputes between armed dominions, becoming targeted by traffickers or militia, or of having to silently watch violations against local residents are part of the quotidian fears of electric workers. In these locations, workers must be constantly alert to danger. They can suddenly find themselves in the middle of a firefight, for example. Practical knowledge guides them along their work routes. They constantly feel out the situation by talking to residents, drug gang lookouts, drug gang soldiers, local merchants, and whoever else might be willing to help them complete their tasks. The practices of workers in areas of risk are a prescription for survival in the field, informing workers how to identify signs of risks and bypass unpredictable and dangerous situations in their work routines.

Final Considerations

Our interpretation of the dynamics of violent urban criminality in Rio de Janeiro, based on the concept of armed dominions, has been guided by a multidimensional approach to an empirical phenomenon that does not rely upon or produce easily digested stereotypes. This has been possible because our understanding of the empirical facts has emerged through the observation and analysis of different forms of conflict, through which the plurality of factors that contribute to the existence of these conflicts may be identified. Conflict makes explicit confrontations between different subjects, revealing state "fictions" (Radcliffe-Brown 1970) and their effects, which transform said fictions into realities that directly affect day-to-day lives.

Armed dominions are illegal and extralegal ways of governing. They impose upon public space modes of surveillance and movement and access restriction for residents and workers, managing populations and territories and the flows of goods and services. They are a mobile and criminal management mechanism producing equally mobile controls over subject territories and temporalities. Armed dominions are a potential and concrete means of violence, used to undermine citizenship and the more or less inclusive limits of the political-legal pact. They profit from gray areas in which security institutions choose to operate (either institutionally or informally) with no effective guidelines as to the use of legal and legitimate force. In this fashion, armed dominions guarantee that autonomous criminal governments continue to function in spaces characterized by low institutional penetration and informal decision-making apparatuses that favor political partisan manipulation and the private appropriation of security and other public resources.

NOTES

1   *Organized crime* was used as a synonym for illicit drug trafficking, mainly marijuana, cocaine, crack, and derivatives.
2   We refer to both the city and the state of Rio de Janeiro.
3   *Comando* is one of the names given to the organized drug-trafficking groups. These terms vary from one place to another (Rio or São Paulo).
4   Jogo do bicho, or the animal game, is similar to the numbers game in the United States, and its organization is, historically, the closest that Brazil has come to creating a mafia-style group.
5   Protection taxes are commonly levied in militia areas. It is estimated that these groups raise some 300 million reais in taxes in Rio annually (de Lima 2020).
6   A barricade is created to establish order for the armed dominions (Ribeiro and Platero 2017). Graffiti acts as a signature for the armed group that controls a

particular region. Biblical passages are also used to delimit the borders of these groups.

7 Risk perception maps were the result of the Non-technical Energy Loss Diagnosis Project in São Gonçalo and Duque de Caxias (RJ), financed by the Research and Technological Development Program of the Electric Energy Sector (R&D). It was coordinated by Roberto Kant de Lima, Ana Paula Miranda, and Jacqueline Muniz between 2016 and 2018 (Miranda, Muniz, and Corrêa 2019).

8 The NGO Disque Denúncia (https://www.disquedenuncia.org.br/), inspired by the Crime Stoppers of the 1970s, is a hotline for crime reporting and human rights reporting created in the 1990s; it depends upon anonymous tips from the population.

REFERENCES

Abreu, Fernanda. 1992. "Rio 40 Graus." *Letras*. https://www.letras.mus.br/fernanda-abreu/580/.

Biondi, Karina, and Adalton Marques. 2010. "Memória e historicidade em dois 'comandos' prisionais." *Lua nova* 79: 39–70.

de Lima, Renato Sérgio. 2020. "A economia política das milícias." *Folha de S. Paolo* (blog), UoL, July 19. https://facesdaviolencia.blogfolha.uol.com.br/2020/07/19/a-economia -politica-das-milicias/.

Dias, Camila N. 2013. "A regulação dos conflitos pelo PCC no interior das prisões paulistas: Redução da violência física, interdependência e controle social." In *Prisões e punição no Brasil contemporâneo*, edited by L. Lourenço and G. Rocha, 77–98. Salvador: Edufba.

Lima, Roberto Kant de, Michel Misse, and Ana Paula Mendes de Miranda. 2000. "Violência, criminalidade, segurança pública e justiça criminal no Brasil: Uma bibliografia." *BIB* 50: 45–123.

Miranda, Ana Paula Mendes de, and Jacqueline de Oliveira Muniz. 2018. "Dominio armado: El poder territorial de las facciones, los comandos y las milicias en Río de Janeiro." *Revista voces en el fenix* 68: 44–49.

Miranda, Ana Paula Mendes de, Jacqueline Muniz, and Roberta Corrêa, eds. 2019. *Mapas de percepção de riscos: Metodologia multimétodo para análise de territorialidades afetadas pelo domínio armado*. Rio de Janeiro: Autografia.

Misse, Michel. 2003. "O movimento: A constituição e reprodução das redes do mercado informal ilegal de drogas a varejo no Rio de Janeiro e seus efeitos de violência." In *Drogas e pós-modernidade*, edited by M. Baptista et al., 147–56. Rio de Janeiro: EDUERJ.

Misse, Michel. 2011. "Crime organizado e crime comum no Rio de Janeiro: Diferenças e afinidades." *Revista Sociologia Política* 19, no. 40: 13–25.

Muniz, Jacqueline, and Rosiane Almeida. 2018. "Respondendo às balas: Segurança pública sob intervenção das palavras entrevista com Jacqueline Muniz." *Trabalhos em linguística aplicada* 57, no. 2: 993–1014.

Muniz, Jacqueline, Haydée Caruso, and Felipe Freitas. 2018. "Os estudos policiais nas ciências sociais: Um balanço sobre a produção brasileira a partir dos anos 2000." *BIB* 84, no. 2: 148–87.

Muniz, Jacqueline, and Domício Proença Jr. 2007. "Muita politicagem, pouca política os problemas da polícia são." *Estudos avançados* 21, no. 61: 159–72.

Radcliffe-Brown, Alfred R. 1970. "Preface." In *African Political Systems*, edited by Meyer Fortes and E. E. Evans-Pritchard, xi–xxiii. Oxford: Oxford University Press.

Ribeiro, Fernanda de S., and Klarissa A. S. Platero. 2017. "Barricadas, traficantes e favelas: Uma análise sobre as representações e percepções sobre a categoria 'risco' dentro dos espaços urbanos no Jardim Catarina." *Confluências* 19, no. 1: 4–22.

Roché, Sebastian. 1993. *Le sentiment d'insécurité*. Paris: Presses Universitaires de France.

SD Boys. 2000. "Tá dominado." *Letras*. https://www.letras.mus.br/sd-boys/500529/.

Weber, Max. (1918) 1948. *From Max Weber: Essays in Sociology*. Translated by H. H. Gerth and C. W. Mills. New York: Galaxy.

4

Rot Politics and the Cunning of Anticorruption /
Política de Podridão e a Ardileza da Anti-corrupção

The Polysemy of Corruption and the Emergence of
a Cross-Class Right in Brazil

SEAN T. MITCHELL AND THAYANE BRÊTAS

Corruption has been an extremely flexible political category in recent Brazilian political discourse. It can be stretched to mean everything from simple robbery by politicians to undue influence of private interests in politics; perceived erosion of sexual morality; the undermining of race, class, gender, and sexual hierarchies thought to be important to order; and the term through which deficiencies in health care, education, security, and other public services and goods are often explained and understood. Relying on field research in Rio de Janeiro and a reading of Brazilian scholarly literature about corruption, we show how the polysemy, ubiquity, and explanatory power of *corruption*—and consequently, of anticorruption—helped create the cross-class electoral constituency in Brazil that facilitated the election of the far-right president Jair Bolsonaro in 2018.

Brazilian corruption discourse is often used by poor and working-class people to explain why needed public services are deficient. Yet it is also often used to describe supposed deficiencies of Brazilians themselves—frequently by elites, and in ways that track closely with existing forms of exclusion and exploitation in Brazilian society. Undergirding this reactionary version of anticorruption politics is a set of racist, heteronormative, and repressive notions of "rot politics." Within this framework, certain people are more than just criminal, queer, or deceitful—they are rotten and morally disgusting, meriting punishment via invisibility, segregation, and/or death. Rot politics ties into the inquisitorial regime described elsewhere in this book (chapter 2), and other discussions of the colonial and racial logics of dehumanization.

Corruption as a Floating Signifier

Corruption is everywhere in Brazil. We don't mean the act of corruption, which, in its most straightforward usage, tends to refer to bribery, graft, and other kinds of unethical self-dealing by the powerful. There is plenty of that in Brazil, of course. But there is plenty of that all over. Consider the United States: vast amounts of corporate money are not poured into US elections or US news media for fun, after all. Corruption, in the straightforward sense we defined above, is one of the great motors of our staggeringly unequal global political-economic system, not some Brazilian specialty. But talk of corruption, concern with corruption, corruption discourse: at this Brazilians excel. Still, the meanings of *corruption* in Brazilian political discourse are highly variable. And the consequences of that variability are enormous.

In 2016, one of the authors of this chapter and colleagues carried out a survey in three large Brazilian cities: Rio de Janeiro, Recife, and São Paulo.[1] We surveyed 1,200 people in poor and working-class neighborhoods in those cities to learn about people who, in the first few years of the 2010s, were often identified as part of a so-called new middle class—some 35 million people who rose out of poverty during the years of economic growth and progressive social policy under PT (Workers' Party) governments (2003-16).

A full 45.7 percent of survey respondents in those neighborhoods reported that corruption was the biggest problem facing Brazil. They made this selection from fourteen options. The next biggest contenders after corruption were unemployment (17.4 percent), public safety/violence (8 percent), the health system (7.9 percent), education quality (4.45 percent), and social inequality (3.1 percent). Everything else—from economic growth to racism, inflation, and the environment—barely moved the meter.

However, ethnographic work in those neighborhoods has made clear to us that corruption was not only the largest problem in people's minds but also the key discourse through which these other problems were discussed and explained. Why were the schools bad? Politicians stole. Why couldn't you get a job? Because of corruption. *Corruption* in popular Brazilian political discourse acts as a kind of floating signifier: highly variable in its meaning, yet used to explain and talk about all other political ills. The flexibility of the category of corruption has made the category crucial to the process that brought the votes of many poor and working-class people into alignment with the votes of many of the rich in the 2018 election.

That 2016 survey was taken after PT president Dilma Rousseff was provisionally impeached under a spurious budgetary pretext. Although a hostile mass media did all that it could to tar Dilma with corruption during that impeachment process, she was a rare politician of national stature without any serious allegations of personal enrichment made against her at the time. But on a list of eleven questions about electoral politics that we asked people during that period, the one with the second highest level of agreement was whether "corruption was the main reason for Dilma's impeachment." Among the 1,200 respondents, this question came in at 3.55 on a Likert scale, where 1 was "strongly disagree" and 5 was "strongly agree." People's relatively strong agreement about Dilma's corruption was even more striking given that the statement from that list of eleven that elicited the highest level of agreement (3.65) was whether people felt that their lives had improved during the eight years of government under Dilma's PT predecessor, Lula. People also felt agreement (3.23) that life had improved under the PT governments, which included those of Dilma.

Poor and working-class urban Brazilians in 2016 generally saw their lives as having improved under PT governments, but they also saw corruption as the major problem facing them, and they saw the PT as guilty of corruption. In the 2018 elections, many poor and working-class urban Brazilians voted against PT presidential candidate Fernando Haddad and for the far-right Jair Bolsonaro. This trend was particularly pronounced in Rio de Janeiro, where all the working-class electoral areas favored Bolsonaro, a complete inversion of recent presidential electoral history, in which they had favored the PT (Richmond and McKenna 2020). Corruption is part of this story: the leader in all polls for that election was ex-president Lula until his dubious arrest by the ostensibly anticorruption judge Sérgio Moro rendered him ineligible. Leaked transcripts from Moro and the prosecutorial team leave no doubt that they were deliberately targeting the left while sparing the right and that they targeted Lula for political reasons (Greenwald, Demori, and Reed 2019) and in illegal collaboration with the US government (*Brasil Wire* 2021). But corruption was a crucial part of this story in another way. It is the very power yet flexibility of corruption discourse that allowed for the formation of a political coalition among people with vastly different political concerns and class positions.

Culturalist Corruption and Cruel Pessimism

There is an old Brazilian tradition that frames corruption as the nation's worst evil, a cancer, the pervasive problem at the heart of all other problems the country faces (Almeida 2019). In Raymundo Faoro's (1958) canonical analysis, corruption is deeply rooted in Brazilian culture, inherited from Iberian colonizers and their project of state formation. Because Brazilian bureaucracy was constituted through biased and personal arrangements, public and private spheres became confused in Brazil, and the country fell short of the ideal, impersonal, and rational modern capitalist state. In another famous analysis, by Sérgio Buarque de Holanda ([1936] 1979), corruption is rooted in the individualistic and informal character of Brazilian sociality (Avritzer and Filgueiras 2011; Filgueiras 2009). These moralistic and culturalist readings of Brazilian corruption retain wide popular and scholarly resonance.

Rio is fertile ground for culturalist diagnoses of corruption. Long-standing national stereotypes of the city cast it as a center of the jeitinho brasileiro (the Brazilian informal, tricky way) and malandragem (a term associated with informal street hustling). These ideas are widely held by many Cariocas (Rio residents) themselves. And these terms are used most often to mark racialized men of lower- or working-class backgrounds, men who supposedly prefer to resort to informal, personal, and illegal solutions to make a living.

Culturalist corruption discourse has many faces but, in its most reactionary variants, is more frequently used to describe the character of the relatively marginalized (and their allies) than to describe elites. This is true when poor, Black Cariocas are identified for their supposedly characteristic malandragem, leaving elite, white Brazilians unmarked, and it is true when countries like Brazil are singled out for their proclivity to corruption, sparing the reputation of sprawling, underregulated corporate tax havens, like the United Kingdom. Reactionary variants of corruption discourse tend to identify subalterns—and social policy intended to benefit subalterns—as intrinsic sources of corruption. Thus, they tend to be disdainful of the public sector as such.

In 2016–18 fieldwork and interviews with poor and working-class residents in the suburbs and favelas of Rio de Janeiro, the corruption-related discourses most often encountered differed from these more reactionary forms. These nonreactionary corruption discourses—we might call them critical corruption discourses—did not make the poor and marginalized the key objects of blame, or the public sector as such. Instead, they most frequently cast blame on the dishonesty of those holding power and resources and how that dishonesty diminished people's access to rights and to a better quality of life. And critical corruption discourses most frequently characterized the public sector as a victim of that corruption, rather than as a necessary source of corruption. This does not mean that poor residents of the suburbs and favelas did not believe in or invoke reactionary discourses. Each of these discourses crossed class lines to some degree. But critical corruption discourses were the most common. Consider these 2017 interview excerpts. They are typical of our large body of interviews from that period in that they offer corruption as an explanation for why public services are so poor and, consequently, for inequality, illiteracy, and poverty: "Ninety percent of the politicians here are corrupt. So, where there is corruption, the country doesn't grow. People will always live in poverty. Children won't learn anything. They'll always be illiterate. Here, on this street, if you look, there are many children who are illiterate, who should be in school, in a good school. There's no good reason why the country doesn't offer anything better for these children. You understand?"[2] In other instances, corruption provided a context for environmental degradation: "These days, nobody goes [to Bica beach, a once-popular beach in Rio's North Zone]. People don't go because of the pollution in Guanabara Bay. I know that money comes in for cleanup. I know because I read the newspaper a lot, and I watch television. Money came to Rio de Janeiro to clean it up, but the corrupt put the money in their pockets, right?" Elsewhere, and drawing on this same research, Mitchell (2018) has identified a form of affect that, drawing on Lauren Berlant (2011), he terms *cruel pessimism*. Cruel pessimism helped bring together reactionary and critical variants of corruption discourse.

In the first decade and a half of this century, poor and working-class people in Brazil had very good reason to anticipate significant social mobility. The dashing of those hopes—amid economic crisis and the rollback of the welfare state after the 2016 judicial coup against Dilma Rousseff—was coupled, for many people, not only with a renewed awareness of the venality of corruption but, crucially, a growing awareness of the hypocrisy of anticorruption. All this helped foster, for many recently optimistic people, an effect of cruel pessimism—the sentiment that projects of collective striving for the public good in Brazil are doomed to fail because of the moral failings, and the corruption, of Brazilians themselves. This reinforces a sense of unavoidable decline, similar to bacteria and fungi feeding on a fruit that rots in silence. This affect, of cruel pessimism, helps push people who were not reactionary in their political inclinations closer to reactionary variants of anticorruption politics.

Cruel pessimism was especially resonant in Rio because of the disconnect between the city's decline and its role as Brazil's international showcase. In the decades since the national capital was moved from Rio to Brasília in 1960, Rio has witnessed a general decline in economic and political importance. This has been accompanied by an aggravation of economic, social, and housing inequalities, as well as the rise of job insecurity, urban violence, and informal or illicit economic activity and housing construction. These trends were partially reversed during the boom years that made up much of the first period of PT governance (2003–16) and after the 2007 discovery of vast oil deposits off the coast near Rio. But industries located in Rio de Janeiro were hit especially hard by the penalties meted out because of Sérgio Moro's Lava Jato anticorruption investigation (Belluzzo 2018). Lava Jato did enormous harm to Brazil's economy (Alvarenga 2015; *CartaCapital* 2021), but Rio's economic decline has outpaced the nation's trajectory (Osorio et al. 2020).

Meanwhile, Rio is Brazil's main site for international tourism, conventions, and graft-ridden international mega events, such as the 2016 Olympics. These events are frequently used to justify "hygienist" interventions (chapter 26, this volume) that the city's poor and racialized communities have long been familiar with, many of which entail urban displacement and police brutality. These interventions—as many of our interlocutors in Rio have pointed out—frequently fail with time, with the urban poor reoccupying areas once targeted for aesthetic embellishments and cleansing projects.

Cariocas, poor and rich, tend to be keenly aware of these contradictions and frequently name them with that ever-slippery term *corruption*. During the first set of years that the PT held the presidency (2003–16), this helped conservative political and media figures to lay the groundwork for cross-class anticorruption and anti-left coalitions in Rio and Brazil, tethering anticorruption discourses to antipetismo (anti-PT sentiment). The ascent of a Brazilian far-right agenda that gained steam around 2014 had corruption as its most effective discursive tool, gluing together the heterogeneous masses through their mutual antipathy to corruption, even though corruption had different meanings to different constituencies (Ortellado and Solano 2016; Solano 2018; Hunter and Power 2019; da Silva and Shaw 2018; Messenberg 2017).

Corruption and Class in the Scholarship and Politics of Rio and Brazil

Débora Messenberg (2017) notes that, in 2015, the most powerful right-wing social media influencers (formadores de opinião) singled out the PT as having institutionalized corruption as a "governmental practice," ignoring the long-standing ubiquity of graft in Brazilian politics. Mass media did the same at the time, helping create a popular association between corruption and the left for many of our interlocutors in Rio. Also addressing the role of social media in (re)producing disputes and representations of corruption, André Luiz de Paiva, André Spuri Garcia, and Valderí de Castro Alcântara (2017) examined differences in representation and selective silences in the Twitter activity of two magazines, the left-wing *CartaCapital*, and the right-wing *Veja*. While *CartaCapital* is more active in reporting the involvement of private companies in corruption and less active when former PT president Lula is involved, *Veja* is more active when political institutions and Lula are involved, and they tend to leave private companies in investigations unnamed. Meanwhile, the interactions among Twitter users on such publications reveal—besides disputes between polarized political positions that the magazines represent—the recourse to morality and a call for moral cleansing in politics to defeat corruption in Brazil (de Paiva, Garcia, and Alcântara 2017).

Moral differentiation and condemnation of the other—in Rio, sometimes involving the portrayal of degradation or rotting (Cerioni 2020)—is crucial to various politicized Brazilian uses of the term *corruption* (Kalil 2018). One upper-middle-class Carioca interlocutor in a 2018 interview, for example, singled out LGBTQI+ people for promoting "moral corruption and degradation," in contrast to the cidadão de bem (upstanding citizen), another important category in these discourses.

Isabela Kalil (2018) examined interactions on social media and WhatsApp between 2016 and 2018, amid protests and other political events, and noted a connection between the discourse of anticorruption and the identity of the cidadão de bem, or upstanding citizen. This upstanding citizen is a figure that gets placed in direct opposition to those who are pro-corruption—a category that can include bandits of different sorts, those who defend them (9), or those who are seen as degrading moral values. Three key meanings of corruption emerge in these political discourses: first, politicians stealing public money—a discourse that more often ascribes blame to the public, rather than the private, sector. The second meaning relates to the degradation of family values and mores. For example, in her impeachment process, ex-president Dilma Rousseff's "sexuality, criminality, ideology, and policy proclivity" all became signs of her corruption in pro-impeachment discourses (Ansell 2018, 322). "Confusion between rights and privileges" constitutes the third meaning of corruption. Here corruption identifies the beneficiaries of social programs who are not understood to be contributing to society (2018, 10).

For antipetistas, especially of the middle class, the social spread of a culture of corruption was enabled by PT-era social programs, such as the conditional cash transfer, Bolsa Família, and the housing program Minha Casa Minha Vida. These programs were cast as impediments to the country's growth, re-producing a kind of nondesirable citizen that was lazy, opportunistic, prone to claiming victimhood, dependent on the state, and degrading moral values (Solano 2018; Ansell 2018). Relying on such archetypes, cidadãos de bem con-structed themselves as the precise opposite—self-made (typically white, middle-class) men—agentive, entrepreneurial, and dependent on the state for only the bare minimum (Solano 2018).

Returning to the analysis of poor and working-class Rio, pervasive experi-ences of unreliable or hostile authorities—articulated frequently through a discourse of corruption—produce a deep and cruel pessimism about state inter-ventions. For example, Police Pacification Units (UPP) were supposed to bring peace and social services to favelas scarred by violence and municipal abandon-ment. Yet residents of these favelas feared collaborating with the police because they correctly assumed that, when traffickers restored their power over the area, they would punish those residents who had worked with the UPPs (Zaluar 2017).

Tensions between these different corruption discourses come together to tell a larger story. The elite and middle-class accounts of corruption tend to push against the viability of a progressive public sector, while the accounts most com-mon among the poor and working class in Rio's favelas and peripheries tend to lament that corruption harms a progressive public sector. Corruption, here, is a floating signifier that, despite these different emphases, class positions, and in-terests, was able to bring widely different constituencies together in favor of a common anticorruption political program that, during the pivotal period of Brazilian history at the end of the 2010s, was successfully hijacked by the right.

The Necessity and Duplicity of Anticorruption

This chapter was written during a period when lifelong con artists, like Donald Trump, and lifelong associates of paramilitary extortion rackets, like Jair Bol-sonaro (Barrocal 2020), held presidencies in nations of hundreds of millions. That period, and the years that followed, are part of an era of yawning global wealth inequalities that have permitted the wealthy and corporations to subvert democracy and dictate policy in both wealthy and poor countries. And it is an era in which those policies may have a detrimental effect on the very viability of human life on planet Earth. There is no doubt that such an era screams for some sort of anticorruption politics. Yet, as has been demonstrated here, corruption is one of the most slippery of political categories, and anticorruption as a form of politics is readily turned to reactionary—and of course, corrupt—ends.

It was anticorruption politics that allowed demonstrably corrupt (Greenwald, Demori, and Reed 2019) figures to be extolled globally as heroes of democratic reform (e.g., Spektor 2016) and that enabled Sérgio Moro and insatiable gobblers of public funds, like the director of Dilma's impeachment, former congressman Eduardo Cunha (*CartaCapital* 2016), to corrupt Brazilian democracy. And it was anticorruption politics that helped bring together poor Brazilians and elite Brazilians into the political coalition that elected the extortion-racket-friendly Bolsonaro. Yet, for all of corruption's deceptiveness, and for all the easy corruptibility of anticorruption initiatives, corruption does denote something very real and very corrosive to democracy, and it is understood as a pressing issue by Brazilians across class lines, as our survey and ethnographic research show.[3] Yes, the world needs some sort of anticorruption politics. But as recent Brazilian history and the research here demonstrate, the meanings of corruption and anticorruption should never be taken at face value. Corruption is an uncannily slippery concept, and anticorruption has a persistent habit of becoming its ostensible opposite.

NOTES

1   The survey was carried out as part of a three-year collaborative grant from the National Science Foundation's Division of Behavioral and Cognitive Sciences, Cultural Anthropology Program. The project, with principal investigators Sean T. Mitchell, Benjamin Junge, and Charles Klein, is titled Collaborative Research: Social Mobility, Poverty Reduction, and Democracy in an Emerging Middle Class (Klein, Mitchell, and Junge 2018).

2   These and all other translations from the Portuguese are ours.

3   The survey and ethnographic research on which this chapter relies was carried out in 2016–18, before the election of Jair Bolsonaro and the start of the COVID-19 pandemic. Informal conversations suggest that attitudes about corruption may have shifted, especially among poor and working-class Brazilians, but we do not have systematic data.

REFERENCES

Almeida, Ronaldo de. 2019. "Bolsonaro presidente: Conservadorismo, evangelismo e a crise brasileira." *Novos estudos CEBRAP* 38, no. 1: 185–213.

Alvarenga, Darlan. 2015. "Impacto da Lava Jato no PIB pode passar de R$140 bilhões, diz estudo." *G1 Brasil*, August 11. http://g1.globo.com/economia/noticia/2015/08/impacto -da-lava-jato-no-pib-pode-passar-de-r-140-bilhoes-diz-estudo.html.

Ansell, Aaron. 2018. "Impeaching Dilma Rousseff: The Double Life of Corruption Allegations on Brazil's Political Right." *Culture, Theory and Critique* 59, no. 4: 312–31.

Avritzer, Leonardo, and Fernando Filgueiras. 2011. *Corrupção e controles democráticos no Brasil*. Textos para discussão CEPAL-IPEA 32. Brasília: CEPAL, Escritório no Brasil/ IPEA.

Barrocal, André. 2020. "Votos e bens de Bolsonaro e Flávio avançaram junto com milícias." *CartaCapital* (blog), July 1. https://www.cartacapital.com.br/politica/votos-e-bens -de-bolsonaro-e-flavio-avancaram-junto-com-milicias/.

Belluzzo, Luiz Gonzaga. 2018. "As consequências econômicas da Lava Jato." In *Operação Lava Jato e a democracia brasileira*, edited by Fábio Kerche and João Feres Júnior, 21–35. São Paulo: Contra Corrente.

Berlant, Lauren. 2011. *Cruel Optimism*. Durham, NC: Duke University Press.

Brasil Wire. 2021. "Lula's Arrest Is 'a Gift from the CIA,' Mocked Lava Jato Prosecutor." *Brasil Wire* (blog), February 9. https://www.brasilwire.com/lula-arrest-is-a-gift-from-the-cia -mocked-lava-jato-prosecutor/.

CartaCapital. 2016. "Eduardo Cunha: Da realeza fisiológica ao abandono dos antigos aliados." *CartaCapital* (blog), October 19. https://www.cartacapital.com.br/politica /eduardo-cunha-da-realeza-fisiologica-ao-abandono-dos-antigos-aliados/.

CartaCapital. 2021. "Lava Jato acabou com 4,4 milhões de empregos, aponta Dieese." *CartaCapital* (blog), March 17. https://www.cartacapital.com.br/cartaexpressa/lava-jato -acabou-com-44-milhoes-de-empregos-aponta-dieese/.

Cerioni, Clara. 2020. "Ampliar combate à corrupção depende de instituições fortes e vigilância social." *Casa Jota*, October 21. https://www.jota.info/casa-jota/combate -corrupcao-fortalecer-instituicoes-popularizar-vigilancia-21102020.

da Silva, Rita de Cácia Oenning, and Kurt Shaw. 2018. "Sentinels of Privilege and the Ressentiment of the Powerful: The New Right in Brazil." *Challenging Authoritarianism Series*, no. 3. War and Pacification Project, Transnational Institute.

de Holanda, Sérgio Buarque. (1936) 1979. *Raízes do Brasil*. Rio de Janeiro: José Olympio.

de Paiva, André Luiz, André Spuri Garcia, and Valderí de Castro Alcântara. 2017. "Disputas discursivas sobre corrupção no Brasil: Uma análise discursivo-crítica no Twitter." *Revista de administração contemporânea* 21, no. 5: 627–47.

Faoro, Raymundo. 1958. *Os donos do poder: Formação do patronato político brasileiro*. Rio de Janeiro: Editôra Globo.

Filgueiras, Fernando. 2009. "A tolerância à corrupção no Brasil: Uma antinomia entre normas morais e prática social." *Opinião pública* 15, no. 2: 386–421.

Greenwald, Glenn, Leandro Demori, and Betsy Reed. 2019. "How and Why the Intercept Is Reporting on a Vast Trove of Materials about Brazil's Operation Car Wash and

Justice Minister Sergio Moro." *Intercept* (blog), June 9. https://theintercept.com/2019/06/09/brazil-archive-operation-car-wash/.

Hunter, Wendy, and Timothy J. Power. 2019. "Bolsonaro and Brazil's Illiberal Backlash." *Journal of Democracy* 30, no. 1: 68–82.

Kalil, Isabela Oliveira. 2018. "Quem são e no que acreditam os eleitores de Jair Bolsonaro." São Paulo: Fundação Escola de Sociologia e Política de São Paulo.

Klein, Charles H., Sean T. Mitchell, and Benjamin Junge. 2018. "Naming Brazil's Previously Poor: 'New Middle Class' as an Economic, Political, and Experiential Category." *Economic Anthropology* 5, no. 1: 83–95.

Messenberg, Débora. 2017. "A direita que saiu do armário: A cosmovisão dos formadores de opinião dos manifestantes de direita brasileiros." *Sociedade e estado* 32, no. 3: 621–48.

Mitchell, Sean T. 2021. "Cruel Pessimism: The Affect of Anti-corruption and the End of the New Brazilian Middle Class." In *Precarious Democracy: Ethnographies of Hope, Despair, and Resistance in Brazil after the Pink Tide*, edited by Benjamin Junge, Alvaro Jarrin, Lucia Cantero, and Sean T. Mitchell, 79–89. New Brunswick, NJ: Rutgers University Press.

Ortellado, Pablo, and Esther Solano. 2016. "Nova direita nas ruas? Uma análise do descompasso entre manifestantes e os convocantes dos protestos antigoverno de 2015." *Perseu: História, memória e política*, no. 11. https://revistaperseu.fpabramo.org.br/index.php/revista-perseu/article/view/97.

Osorio, Mauro, Maria Helena Versiani, Alexandre Freitas, Marcelo A. Filho, Israel Sanches, and Joilson Cabral, eds. 2020. "A crise no Estado do Rio de Janeiro." *Jornal dos economistas*, no. 371 (July). https://www.corecon-rj.org.br/portal/jornal.php?a=2020.

Richmond, Matthew Aaron, and Elizabeth McKenna. 2020. "Revoltas regionais: Direitização eleitoral no Brasil e nos EUA." *Horizontes ao Sul* (blog), August 5. https://www.horizontesaosul.com/single-post/2020/08/01/REVOLTAS-REGIONAIS-DIRETIZACAO-ELEITORAL-NO-BRASIL-E-EUA.

Solano, Esther. 2018. "Crise da democracia e extremismos de direita." *Análise Friedrich Ebert stiftung* 42, no. 1: 1–27.

Spektor, Matias. 2016. "AQ Top 5 Corruption Busters: Sérgio Moro." *Americas Quarterly*, January 27. https://americasquarterly.org/fulltextarticle/aq-top-5-corruption-busters-sergio-moro/.

Zaluar, Alba. 2017. "Police and Gendered Labor Performances: Hypermasculinity and Policing as a Masculine Function / Performances de gênero no trabalho policial: Hipermasculinidade e policiamento como função masculina." Translated by Camila Gripp, Alba Zaluar, and David Rodgers. *Vibrant: Virtual Brazilian Anthropology* 14, no. 2.

5

Stateness / Estatalidade

*Reconceptualizing Bureaucratic-Technical State Effects
That Perform Agency, Governmentality, and Subjectivity*

ANA PAULA MENDES DE MIRANDA AND MARÍA VICTORIA PITA

What Do We Mean by Stateness?

Stateness represents a new concept created by the authors of the present chapter, which builds on and diverges from Foucault's notion of governmentality. We created the concept through a meticulous and historically grounded tracing of official data on crime, of public policies regarding crime, and of uses these two things have been put to. Our focus here is the knowledge production practices of state bureaucracies. To map state rationalities and discourses in detail, this chapter offers a case study of how statistics regarding deaths by stray bullets are bureaucratically constructed. *Stray bullets* is a Brazilian-specific category that encapsulates drive-by shootings, friendly fire, accidental weapons firing by police, and exchange of fire during police invasions of neighborhoods and consolidates it into a single statistical jumble. Put simply, if someone is shot to death and the state can't (or won't) identify the shooter, then the death is categorized as caused by a stray bullet (bala perdida). Data on stray bullets help constitute a form of state-sponsored knowledge (which we call here *state language*) reflecting bureaucratic decisions and ways of thinking about the world.

The concept was developed through research into state interventions and governmentality. The ways and means in which the stray bullet has become a legitimate category of how the state envisions its actions, violence, and citizens' claims in response to these actions are stateness. Stateness informs certain forms of unaccountability and violence, allowing them to persist, even as it renders other logics (particularly those critical of race) invisible. In performing these functions, it ensures that only certain kinds of citizen responses are understood as legitimate. In order to explain the rationales that orient agents, we have taken as our case study the introduction of the stray-bullet category in official statistics. Here we see it become a legitimate form of state knowledge. It is part of what we call the language of the state, which is simultaneously the result or effect of actions, decisions, or modes of thinking about the world of bureaucracies, revealing subject agency and documents as they are made, and also a way of strengthening the power of the state in its interventions.

An Ethnography of Official Statistics

The concept of stateness aims to address the state in its concrete manifestations, incorporated into categories and classification systems. It aims to analyze discourses and the knowledge produced by state agents, guided by an analysis of public policy and statistics on criminality.[1] Using a case study, this contribution focuses on the stray bullet and its transformation into a specific category in official records related to deaths. This analysis will highlight the tensions and conflicts between different rationalities that have an impact on the measurement and classifications of violent events. This approach leads to a discussion about the state, beginning with its interaction with agency (Ortner 2007) and governmentality (Foucault 1990, 2009).

The empirical basis for our argument comes from police sources on violent deaths—in particular, intentional homicides in the metropolitan areas of Buenos Aires and Rio de Janeiro. Our choice of object was made based on the authors' professional experiences with the Public Security Institute (ISP in Portuguese) and the National Board for Criminal Policy (Dirección Nacional de Política Criminal in Spanish) between 2003 and 2008. During this period, we conducted mixed-methods analysis (qualitative and quantitative) to understand the production of official data. We focused on how violence was represented in homicides, which are an extreme form of conflict management, and which are thus well represented in crime statistics. Searching for consistencies in these statistics and comparing them resulted in an ethnography of how they are constructed, allowing us to understand their reach and limitations (Miranda and Pita 2011; Pita and Miranda 2015).

Official statistics are produced using different technical, scientific, and political forms of knowledge that influence state actions and public policies. Data regarding violence is thus not just a translation of facts narrated by victims and/or alleged perpetrators in an unaffected and neutral manner via bureaucratic and legal procedures that search for just the facts. From the moment police reports are written, competing knowledge shapes the judicial process. To understand this process, it was necessary to incorporate the different logics involved in the process of identifying, naming/categorizing, and classifying facts. The implicit and explicit interests at stake in these operations and their concrete effects on the production of official data also factored into our analysis.

The dimensions that shape what might be called state rationality—with its technical, cognitive, and political dimensions (Pantaleón 2004)—are the product of more or less consistent and stable forms of technical know-how, combining with the (not always explicit) political interests of bureaucratic cadres, police and juridical institutions, social scientists and other specialists, and representatives of the state and federal executive branches. We must first clarify this universe's specificities. Its object is the demand for public security and the operation of the penal code. It operates, however, through a field of conflict, as information regarding public policies is traversed by different issues and interests: law-and-order campaigns that support or delegitimize governments; positive or negative assessments of police agencies; considerations about the success or failure of the public policies that have been.

This is not just a conflict about numbers: it is also a struggle about how to name (and therefore categorize and classify) facts and their treatment as legal and/or social events, particularly in their social narrations. Classifications are directly related to the ways in which professionals act in their day-to-day lives. Therefore, when looking at a report that systematizes police/crime statistics, one must understand that the numbers do not represent a scientifically constructed sample. Rather, they are the sum of what various legal and administrative institutions have deemed as relevant to register. In no way should they be understood as reflecting the demands of the population at large. These statistics are administrative reports designed to inform criminal case reports. They are also simultaneously used as police and justice system management tools. As such, their analysis can reveal how the police and justice systems function. In this manner, official records can be seen as cultural artifacts (Riles 2006): they are the material expressions of organizational processes and structures. Consequently, the production, circulation, and archiving of these documents can explain the values, relationships, and environments through which they were produced.

What Does Counting Mean? The Codification of a Term

Though the term is not new in Brazil and Argentina, the stray bullet has only recently become employed as a category in official data production. Looking at how this has occurred allows us to think about how the state has become incorporated (and, indeed, personified) into this classification system. In thinking about Rio de Janeiro, urban violence is represented in many different ways. Some of these narratives and images have been recorded in public memory as iconic events: the massacres of Candelária and Vigário Geral in 1993; the hijacking of Bus 174 in 2000; the murders of journalist Tim Lopes in 2002, Judge Patrícia Accioli in 2011, and city councillor Marielle Franco in 2018; and the expansion of the city's militias beginning in 2004.[2] All these have a factor in common: the tenuous boundaries between the world of crime and that of security institutions in Rio de Janeiro. In all these cases, we see the lawful and illicit intertwined in the construction and maintenance of armed dominions (Miranda and Muniz 2018). These dominions are forged by the constant presence of fear-producing threats, which create the business of providing security. The logic that operates the resulting business of security is ambivalent, alternating between visible and invisible actions that range from public assassinations to the surreptitious disappearance of people without a trace.

Constant shootings with varying motivations (e.g., state policy as part of the war on drugs, disputes between criminals, drug traffickers, and/or militias, etc.) tend to pull the general population of Rio into the crossfire. Shootings have become so common, in fact, that the Rio de Janeiro press inaugurated a new category—the stray bullet—to designate violence that ends up harming bystanders. Following a decision by the former state secretary of public safety,[3] the expression was incorporated by the state government and adopted as part of the official statistics from 2007 to 2012. In this use of the term, *stray bullet* was used to identify those situations in which shooting victims were people who had not actively participated in a firefight or shooting. It is necessary to differentiate the way in which the ISP defined the role of the Public Safety Department in those cases resulting in stray bullets, however. The ISP used *police operation* to designate a nonroutine but planned police action resulting in gunfire, while *confrontation* was employed to characterize armed reactions to the ordinary actions of the military or civil police.

In 2015, two veteran researchers in the field of public security conversed with the head of the civil police and the ISP president-director in order to formulate a clear concept of how to deal with cases involving stray bullets. An official survey resulted in changes in the civil police record system and the inclusion of "unknown origin, stray bullet" as a category indicating homicide and personal injuries resulting from presumed stray-bullet incidents. The objective of this was to provide a constant flow of information so that the ISP could produce official statistics related to the phenomenon. In practice, however, it proved to be impossible to produce accurate reports. The simple creation of the stray-bullet category in the state violence statistics system in no way compelled the police to use the category when filling out their reports. When they analyzed the data generated by the new system, ISP management found several inconsistencies and, as a result, decided not to publish any stray-bullet reports.[4] Nevertheless, the press continued to carry out informal monitoring employing the category. The subsequent emergence of two digital platforms (Fogo Cruzado, https://fogocruzado.org.br; Onde Tem Tiroteio, https://www.ondetemtiroteio .com.br/) to monitor Rio-based shootings has allowed city residents to register the locations where shootings have occurred, as well as something of their circumstances.[5]

The incorporation of *stray bullet* as a category employed in daily life transforms representations of violence, shaping conflicts into random or accidental phenomena. Its use pushes us to consider the state's civil responsibility, by omission or action, for harm done to society. Credence in the fiction that the state holds a monopoly on the legitimate use of force has the effect of exculpating the state on a judicial level. The idea, which has come to prevail in Rio, is that it is impossible to demonstrate the state's particular culpability with regard to public safety duties, given that the state cannot predict or avoid such inevitable and random events as stray bullets. The category effectively allows state agencies to protest their complete innocence, even though these presumptions are quite incorrect.

The expression's institutionalization in official and extraofficial monitoring agencies is our jumping-off point for analyzing the concept of stateness, ten years after we coined the term. The stray bullet is a unique invention, formulated to characterize situations of violence caused by the presence of firearms, but which don't result in any kind of penal action. The mass acceptance of this term demonstrates how governmentality relates to stateness in the creation of agencies and subjectivities. We must question how and why there is always someone in the path of these stray bullets and why the lives of these victims never become a political hot topic.

Understanding the incorporation of the discourse of stray bullets into the world of official documentation and policy analysis requires an assessment of the (in)security they cause among the general population. Although death by stray bullets is a rare occurrence in the official records that register homicides by firearms, the classification remains relevant due to the perception of urban violence as a shared problem (Machado da Silva 2004). The classification also allows us to construct a map of possible places where stray bullets might be encountered, which shapes how residents organize their daily routines, work, and social activities. The monitoring of stray-bullet cases related to children or adolescents, carried out by the Rio de Paz NGO, revealed fifty-seven victims, of which thirty fell in confrontations between police and criminals from 2007 to 2019. Most of these events occurred in favelas.

The randomness of stray bullets becomes doubtful when one observes that they systematically hit the residents of Rio's poorer neighborhoods. These lost bullets seem to have distinctly preferred destinations. Police, drug traffickers, and militias produce a type of violence that multiplies as part of the flow of licit and illicit goods. By highlighting the stray bullet as the center of the conflict, one produces invisibility for the confrontation. Everything ends up being presented as happenstance or as collateral damage, and the policies of police and other state security agencies are not questioned. Analysis of stray-bullet data, however, has altered the public and political debates about violence in Rio.

The official recognition of stray bullets as a statistical and empirical variable reinforced a narrative of symbolic and social detachment between the favela and other regions of the city since the war on drugs occurs only in favelas. On the other hand, when the stray bullets hit children, one can see other narratives emerge, constructed by residents of the slums. These accuse the state but also delimit identities. "We are workers," favela residents proclaim, in contrast to drug traffickers or militias, with whom favela residents sometimes maintain family or neighborhood relations. Juxtaposing stray-bullet incidents with claims to rights and identities helps humanize a population while emphasizing their ambiguities and agency amid the violence committed by a handful. The few cases of stray bullets identified in the upper- and middle-class South Zone of Rio, however, compelled the city's elite to momentarily abandon the idea that they live in zones of peace. The codification of stray bullets had the effect of spatial and social separation, constructed as a way to normalize urban violence. Its propagation as a category, however, has made any space in Rio potentially lethal. Perhaps this is the political reason why it has ultimately been abandoned as a category in official statistics.

Stateness, Agency, and Governmentality

Treating official statistics as legitimate knowledge produced by state officials—thus, the language of the state—means understanding the power of agency of bureaucracies and documents, which make the state's authority be what is. It is to understand how the addition of authority to the actions and decisions of certain individuals takes place in the exercise of politics. The analytical key is in the decision-making process, which is a determining factor in the imposition of order in conflict situations.[6] Stateness is the expression of performances through which public agents invest themselves with authority and, therefore, embody the state, which is materialized in official documents. Stateness is directly associated with the actions and representations produced by bureaucracies in their direct interaction with other social actors who manage and construct order in a given territory. Stateness must be thought of as beyond law as, in many situations, to do what is considered right and fair, it is necessary to disregard legal procedures. Contrary to what political theory would have us believe (that a strong state is by definition legal and holds a monopoly over the means of violence), history shows that strength often depends on practices that would be considered illegal today.[7] This is something that can also be observed when we analyze tax collection practices (Miranda 2015) or public order enforcement (Pita 2017; Tiscornia 2004).

This understanding of stateness impacts our analysis of public policies, which takes place in a broader context of studies of forms of governance. When one realizes that stateness reveals how public policy is exercised in practice, the idea that the state holds a monopoly over decision-making dissolves. In this way, the state "is a fiction of philosophers" (Radcliffe-Brown 1970, xxxiii). This does not mean it is powerless: rather, this fiction produces concrete effects. Social fictions are based on the imaginary, which acquires strength and materiality in the form of beliefs, norms of behavior, and moralities (Godelier 1998). Therefore, the state is neither an entity with its own, supreme individual will, nor is it a legal abstraction. Nor does what Michel Foucault labels *stratification*—"the gradual, piecemeal, but continuous takeover by the state of a number of practices, ways of doing things, and, if you like, governmentalities" (2010, 77)—adequately encompass the processes and agencies we see expressed in the phenomenon we describe above. The symbolic and physical diffusion of violence created by stray bullets and the way they are dealt with in Carioca society is not something that is constantly (re)produced by the processes and practices of government. Rather, it is the product of people, interest groups, bureaucracies, laws, and regulations that embody the authority of the state fiction. In other words, these agents and entities are invested with stateness.

To better envision this, let's return to statistics or the language of the state. Those involved in the production of a stray-bullet case—whether in the form of a complaint or a police or judicial investigation—help build data that become reality to policymakers and shape (and are shaped by) the values of those who produce the case. This last point is not a trivial matter since the construction of reality is linked to the population's presentation of its demands. In this context, it is possible to think of stateness as having agency in the sense that all decision-making processes are molded according to specific feelings, rationalities, and intentions. The agency of stateness is made possible through a technical dimension (scientifically legitimated through unified measurement processes), an expert cognitive dimension (which constructs taxonomical categories from practical police knowledge, linking this practical knowledge to legal codes), and a political dimension (produced by connecting the often conflicting perspectives and practices of bureaucrats, politicians, and social scientists who seek to define and impose certain ways of measuring and reading social phenomena). Understanding these dimensions is of fundamental importance, given that state classifications are the embodiment of conflicting power relations that are obscured and/or presented as a methodological problem, which leads the discussion to another type of debate: the technical debate.

In seeking to understand the methods by which the state produces and accumulates the knowledge that enables its operation, Foucault (2009) addresses the constitution of the police and a science of the state as a form of political knowledge centered on the mechanisms that enable the regulation of the population—"the science of good governance." He calls this science "governmentality" and understands it as a set of management techniques based on knowledge produced by political economy, whose objective is the control of the population through security apparatuses (dispotifs) in order to submit it to the prevailing interests of a given socioeconomic and spatial context. The concept of governmentality—and the problem of how to govern—is therefore related to governance, understood as the state's relations with social interests and the modes of production of order and obedience. Based on this problem of how one governs, we suggest that in order to analyze a public policy, it is necessary to prioritize the practical dimension of the different forms of intervention through which state agents regulate and codify behaviors and values. These forms reveal interests that may or may not be in line with social demands and guarantees of rights. Ultimately, this boils down to thinking about ways of "making the state" (Souza Lima 2012). Thus, without forgetting that the state can be thought of as a homogenizing fiction (or that it at least tries to be this), it is necessary to understand it in all its complexity, paying attention to the expression of forces present in social relations that open up opportunities for change.

The naturalization of violence in Rio's public security field has been a political project that fragments public demands.[8] This creates policies that seem to respond to urgent needs, but which lose sight of the fact that every project that seeks to construct social order does so not only through control but also through the delimitation of social identities. The institutionalization of the stray bullet demonstrates how, in practice, the state functions as a dynamic and conflicting set of relations between the classes, in which domination is not necessarily based on the means of coercion. A tension is exposed here between governmentality (the art of governing the other in the production of sovereignty) and stateness (the decision-making agency of subjects, based upon the state). The official monitoring of stray bullets is an example of how a public administration that defends a policy of armed confrontation tried to build a narrative that would justify who, where, and how these bullets found a final destination, arguing that they were completely random occurrences.

By pointing out that most cases happen in the same places—the poorest areas of Rio's metropolitan region—the argument in favor of randomness is dismantled. Even less random is the fact that these bullets are most commonly found in racialized bodies—for, of course, most of their victims are Black. The experiments in policies and forms of intervention in territories and in the government of populations (which include ways of classifying people, places, things, etc.) are part and parcel of socio-spatial colonization technologies. The procedural strategies that make up these technologies continuously rewrite an asymmetrical cartography of the city in social, economic, racial, and gendered terms. In this way, then, the fiction of the state produces effects that appear to create change while reproducing the same old results.

NOTES

1 *Criminality* is more appropriate, as it emphasizes the social ties between individuals and their practices, while *crime* is restricted to the legal dimension (Lima, Misse, and Miranda 2000).

2 In that year, six slums with militias were identified (Struck 2018).

3 It was the beginning of the pacification policy that originated the Unidade de Polícia Pacificadora (Miranda 2014).

4   Throughout this period, the same secretary of public safety was the responsible manager, who was exonerated in 2016.
5   It is noteworthy that these cases result in forms of activism in the slums that should be considered as references for the analysis of these processes.
6   The refusal to summon a public defendant is a crime in Brazil. In our perception, the decision not to act is a political expression, which represents resistance or fields of force inherent in becoming a state. This is evident when dealing with situations in which a police officer convinces a victim not to report an occurrence or to delay reporting.
7   Studies on stateness in political science analyze the strength of the state based on its capabilities to carry out the implementation of regulatory structures, focusing on macro dimensions. According to this conception, stateness can be present or absent when a state does not fulfill its functions (Altman and Luna 2012). By *history*, we refer to the process of expansion of national states, which was associated with practices such as piracy, mercenaryness, and the enslavement of others.
8   Police violence is a structuring factor in this policy, and the stray bullet is not a random event (Kucinski et al. 2015).

REFERENCES

Altman, David, and Juan Pablo Luna. 2012. "Introducción: El Estado latinoamericano en su laberinto." *Revista de ciência política* 32, no. 3: 521–43.

Foucault, Michel. 1990. *A microfísica do poder*. 9th ed. Rio de Janeiro: Graal.

Foucault, Michel. 2009. *Seguridad, território y población: Curso em Collège de France (1977–1978)*. Buenos Aires: Fondo de Cultura Económica.

Foucault, Michel. 2010. *The Birth of Biopolitics: Lectures at the Collège de France, 1978–79*. Basingstoke: Palgrave Macmillan.

Godelier, Maurice. 1998. *El enigma del don*. Barcelona: Paidós.

Kucinski, Bernardo, Christian Ingo Lenz Dunker, Coronel Íbis Pereira, Fernanda Mena, Guaracy Mingardi, Jean Wyllys, João Alexandre Peschanski, et al. 2015. *Bala perdida: A violência policial no Brasil e os desafios para sua superação*. São Paulo: Boitempo Editorial.

Lima, Roberto Kant de, Michel Misse, and Ana Paula Mendes de Miranda. 2000. "Violência, criminalidade, segurança pública e justiça criminal no brasil: Uma bibliografia." *BIB* 50: 45–123.

Machado da Silva, Luiz Antonio. 2004. "Sociabilidade violenta: Por uma interpretação da criminalidade contemporânea no Brasil urbano." *Sociedade e estado* 19, no. 1: 53–84.

Miranda, Ana Paula Mendes de. 2014. "Militarização e direitos humanos: Gramáticas em disputa nas políticas de segurança pública no Rio de Janeiro/Brasil." *Forum sociológico* 25: 11–22.

Miranda, Ana Paula Mendes de. 2015. *Burocracia e fiscalidade: Uma análise das práticas de fiscalização e cobrança de impostos*. Rio de Janeiro: Lúmen Juris.

Miranda, Ana Paula Mendes de, and J. de O. Muniz. 2018. "Dominio armado: El poder territorial de las facciones, los comandos y las milicias en Río de Janeiro." *Revista voces en el fénix* 68: 44-49.

Miranda, Ana Paula Mendes de, and María Victoria Pita. 2011. "Rotinas burocráticas e linguagens do estado: Políticas de registros estatísticos criminais sobre mortes violentas no Rio de Janeiro e em Buenos Aires." *Revista de sociologia e política* 19, no. 40: 59-81.

Ortner, Sherry B. 2007. "Poder e projetos." In *Conferências e diálogos: Saberes e práticas antropológicas*, edited by Miriam Pillar Grossi, Cornelia Eckert, and Peter Henry Fry, 45-80. Blumenau, Brazil: Nova Letra.

Pantaleón, Jorge. 2004. "Uma nação sob medida: Estatísticas, economia e planificação na Argentina (1918-1952)." PhD diss., Universidade Federal do Rio de Janeiro.

Pita, María Victoria. 2017. "Poder de policía y administración de grupos sociales: El caso de los vendedores ambulantes senegaleses en la Ciudad Autónoma de Buenos Aires." In *Territorios de control policial: Gestión de ilegalismos en la Ciudad de Buenos Aires*, edited by María Victoria Pita and María Inés Pacecca, 77-146. Buenos Aires: Editorial de la Facultad de Filosofía y Letras de la Universidad de Buenos Aires.

Pita, María Victoria, and Ana Paula Mendes de Miranda. 2015. "Alcance y limitaciones de las consultorías en materia de seguridad pública y derechos humanos: ¿Es posible resistir a las generalizaciones y a los productos estandarizados?—relato de una experiencia." *Civitas: Revista de ciências sociais* 15: 128-54.

Radcliffe-Brown, A. R. 1970. "Preface." In *African Political Systems*, edited by Meyer Fortes and E. E. Evans-Pritchard, xi-xxiii. London: Oxford University Press.

Riles, Annelise, ed. 2006. *Documents: Artifacts of Modern Knowledge*, 1-37. Ann Arbor: University of Michigan Press.

Souza Lima, Antonio Carlos de. 2012. "Apresentação: Dossiê fazendo estado." *Revista de antropologia* 55: 559-64.

Struck, Jean-Philip. 2018. "Acabar com o crime no Rio, uma velha promessa." *DW*, March 14. https://www.dw.com/pt-br/acabar-com-o-crime-no-rio-uma-velha-promessa/a-42964088.

Tiscornia, Sofía. 2004. "Seguridad ciudadana y policía en Argentina: Entre el imperio del 'estado de policía' y los límites del derecho." *Revista nueva sociedad* 191: 78-89.

6

Recolonial Militiarchy /
Miliciarquia Recolonial

The Political Evolution of Organized Crime

JOSÉ CLÁUDIO SOUZA ALVES

The concept of colonial militiarchy proposed here represents a specific reading of the sociohistorical spatial formation of Brazil—particularly state formation over time and its role in controlling populations, based on the interests of the ruling class. The correlation between capitalist accumulation and coercive technologies, in the various phases of extractivism in the colonial period, accentuated the basis of a state that made acting outside formal and legal limits the most significant dimension of its power. This enabled gains far greater than if it had remained stuck to conventional models. The use of armed groups—militias of free and poor men, in the colonial slavery order—configured the creation of a gray zone. It was within this space that the legal and illegal, the formal and informal was used to expand a structure of totalitarian power, capable of keeping territories and populations under control while maximizing economic, social, cultural, and political gains.

Colonial militiarchy structures the relationship between legal and illegal armed groups, under the control of the state. The coexistence of distinct forms of violence and exploitation is notably geared toward Black Brazilians and slum dwellers. Initiated during the colonial period, this violence continued to be practiced by current militias to the advance of today's extreme right.

This chapter traces the historical origins of militias (paramilitary vigilante protection and extraction operations), which became the dominant governing institution in Rio de Janeiro by 2020. These groups are more widespread and powerful even than the uniformed police, spanning the lower-middle-class and working-class areas of about half of the megacity's neighborhoods.[1] I argue here that, as the offspring of death squads created in the late 1960s (Barbara 2018), militias evolved as a political structure created by the state, not as a voluntaristic invention by community groups who came together to protect themselves. This conclusion, that the state created the militias, emerged from research on the impact of the historical legacies and accumulated social and economic capital of death squads and the overlapping influence of the long-term institutional and organizational relationship between police apparatuses, drug-trafficking cartels (known in Rio as comandos or factions), and militias themselves. The legal and illegal dimensions of the state, in its totalitarian and genocidal forms, represent a particular racial-colonial continuity that undergirds the seeming novelty of militias that only began to make headlines in the early 2000s. Militias, as an extension of colonial state logic, maintain forms of racially violent and hierarchical rule over the Black population of the peripheries (in particular, I focus on the enormous lower-middle-class and working-class neighborhoods of the Baixada Fluminense, which span the north of Rio de Janeiro and resemble in some ways the Bronx in New York).

Territorial rule over favelas and other Black and northeastern majority communities brings deaths and losses to the population. Violence, following the molds implanted by colonization in Brazil, is built by groups that control territories in a militarized way and establish an economic base through the monopolistic exploitation of services and goods, and is sustained by electoral-political projects that allow the extralegal or criminal careers of militia leaders and death squad commanders to ascend successfully into political office as heroes. This chapter also tracks the investigative intervention of Brazil's federal government in Rio de Janeiro, in the wake of the death-squad murder of Black queer city councilwoman and community leader Marielle Franco, and in the context of the electoral victory of extreme-right politicians directly linked to the death squads and militias. Over the last five decades, Rio (including the vast working-class community of Baixada Fluminense) very much became a laboratory for militia-based forms of racialized rule, revengefully and violently reestablishing supremacist and genocidal doctrines of control, a political system I label here with the neologism *recolonial militiarchy*.

Emerging Squads

Death squads—today acting in the form of militias and articulated by the interests of economic and political sectors of society—undergo constant evolution while attempting to maximize their gains. This regime of recolonial militiarchy is the result of what Rio-based anthropologist Michel Misse (2009) has labeled "the social accumulation of violence." This is a historical process particular to urban peripheries such as the Baixada Fluminense.[2] Such spaces have been used as a laboratory that refines the use of violence against vulnerable populations, creating forms of segregation and domination to which different social groups were subjected: Indigenous and Black peoples, slaves, poor nonenslaved, squatters, small landowners, rural workers, tenants, urban workers, voters, women, children, the LGBTQI+ community, and defeated political groups.

In the colonial period, the Portuguese invasion resulted in the genocide of the Jacutingas, an ethnic group that occupied the territory and that would become the first to be enslaved for cheap labor. The plantation master was a kind of sun king in his territory, establishing his mills and plantations in the valleys of Meriti, Sarapuí, Saracuruna, Jaguaré, and Pilar, and in the areas of Marapicú, Jacutinga, and the Ramos River starting in 1566 (Pereira 1977, 12). In the implementation of the colonial model of exploitation—with its production linked to environmental devastation—Black slaves from Africa came to constitute 62 percent of the region's population. Owned by their masters, they were only recognized as subjects when they were tried for crimes committed against their owners and sentenced to confinement or torture. The baron-farmers mediated many of their relations with violence and death. Dissonance in their practices, however, was due to the formation of Campo Negro de Iguaçu, a quilombo that existed between the Sarapuí and Iguaçu rivers for almost a century, starting in 1812. Its longevity reveals one of the genetic codes of the dominant class present there. Those who went to the press to condemn the existence of such threats to people, land, and slave owners were the same ones who guaranteed the quilombo's survival. It was there that they found the cheapest prices for the firewood extracted from the mangroves, used on a large scale in by the royal court in Lisbon. Those who economically supported the quilombo, buying the firewood that Black people extracted, were the same ones who demanded and financed the police expeditions that killed these people. Any resemblance to the war on drugs—as a public security policy today that results in thousands of murders across the country—is not an accident. Black people remain scapegoats for those securing their sources of illegal and cheap goods, services, and labor.

Over time, in the great outskirts of the city of Rio de Janeiro, in the region of Baixada Fluminense, this model of domination has morphed. Migratory waves in the 1950s and 1960s—which through exploited labor built and maintained Rio—brought thousands of people into an extensive and precarious urban network. Capitães do mato and expeditions against quilombolas (Black-led maroon republics of escaped enslaved peoples and Indigenous rebels) gradually gave way to a historical successor: the police apparatus and death squads.[3]

At the end of the 1950s, peasants began to be evicted from their lands by those who appropriated them for city-building projects. In eviction lawsuits, the use of force by the police apparatus was frequent, provoking armed resistance from peasants. On July 5, 1962—two years before the military coup—famine among urban workers, who had no access to peasant agricultural production, caused one of the biggest looting events in the history of the country. The looting hit approximately two thousand commercial establishments and caused the death of forty-two people in several municipalities of the Baixada (Torres and Menezes 1987). This event was at the origin of the death squads, when businessmen and merchants started to organize themselves to protect their businesses, using armed men. Across time, the violence that emerged from these groups continued against the Black population. The violence led the state toward the interests of private groups. The demands for land and food—fomenting the armed peasant struggle and urban looting—needed a response. The 1964 business-military coup was that answer. In just a few years, the dictatorship realized that revoking political mandates, intervening in unions and prisons, and torturing and killing leftists and opposition groups would not be enough. The urban dimensions and industrial development had reached a level that required more detailed control of the potential threats to the regime. Here, the rise of the murderous, illegal, and criminal scoundrel began, as a political project to control the peripheral and poor populations.

Police and Death Squads in the Militia Phase

Death squads came into existence alongside models of policing that we still have today. Their operation was based on three factors: (1) the participation of public security agents in the killings, (2) financing from businessmen and merchants, and (3) the political support provided by the business-military regime. After starting their actions in 1967, when the military police became an auxiliary force to the military regime, these groups killed thousands of civilians in the 1970s. They executed people on a scale never before seen in the history of the Baixada Fluminense or anywhere in the country. Expanding the control that the business-military dictatorship wanted to exert over the populations—especially the urban ones—these extermination groups were encouraged within the public security administration. Regardless of the legal and formal duties of the police, they justified these exceptional practices by arguing that they were providing protection and security for society. With the decline of the business-military dictatorial regime, the early 1980s brought changes to the structure of killing. In order to escape increasingly frequent denunciations in the media, security agents began to recruit civilians to form death squads, protecting them by manipulating the judicial system. Fraud ranged from failing to identify those suspected of murder to falsifying various aspects of the investigations and prosecutions. Beginning in the 1990s, city halls, city councils, and the state legislative assembly saw increases in assassinations (Alves 2020). The work of public prosecutor Tânia Maria Salles Moreira, in the city of Duque de Caxias, led to the arrest of twenty-seven members of these groups in an unprecedented operation in the region. Meanwhile, death squads—in the militia phase—had returned to being organized almost exclusively by members of the police.

In the mid-1990s, three areas in the Rio metropolitan region experienced the emergence of militia prototypes—namely, Rio das Pedras and Campo Grande (in the West Zone of Rio) and São Bento and Pilar (in the second district of Duque de Caxias). In these areas, urban land occupation and authoritarian leadership, especially regarding electoral participation, were central to maximizing control and profit. The early 2000s saw the configuration of militias along the lines that we still have today. The monopoly on goods and services by public security agents in these locations indicates a new level of organization of crime by the state. These businesses offer the sale of real estate, landfills, water, and access to natural gas as well as clandestine access to TV and internet signals, fuel, basic food, cigarettes, public works contracts, health care, and transportation (Grandin et al. 2018).

The term *militia* was used in popular media in 2005, in an attempt to understand a growing phenomenon. Quickly incorporated into journalistic language, it was heavily disputed, with positive connotations from politicians who could claim militias were a form of self-defense in the face of drug trafficking and the crimes linked to it. It was only in 2008, with the news of the kidnapping and torture of journalists from the newspaper *O Día* by the Batan favela militia in Rio (*O Globo* 2008)—and the report of the Parliamentary Commission of Inquiry of the Legislative Assembly of Rio de Janeiro on militias—that a more critical movement against them begin to emerge.

Organizational Structures of Militia Networks

Militias here are death squads, made possible by the social accumulation of violence in two large territories: Baixada Fluminense and Rio's favelas, where the relationship between the state police apparatus and the drug-trafficking factions makes surveillance expansive. Five factors explain how these militias succeeded previous death squad models: (1) they are composed of civil servants, operating in the state security area, rendering the journalistic jargon of statelessness and parallel power unjustified; (2) their members are trained in police operations based on public security policies from the war on drugs; (3) they establish territorial control as a form of operating, in the case of death squads, in a more fluid and diffuse way and, in the case of militias, more detailed and precise; (4) they have financing from business owners and entrepreneurs; and (5) they gradually concentrate political power through electoral victories.

The militia phase of the death squads is characterized by a flexible and changing network and organizational structure. It can resume a partnership with civilians, as in the case of Baixada in the 1980s. Civilians enlisted by militia leadership came from a drug-trafficking faction. Drug trafficking in the late 1970s in Rio de Janeiro led to the growth of large factions such as Comando Vermelho (CV) and their rivals, the Terceiro Comando (now called Terceiro Comando Puro, or TCP). To maintain drug sales, these groups were inclined to negotiate and pay bribes (arregos) to the police.

The dynamics of rising and expanding death squads, now in their militia phase, reached a new high by 2018 in fourteen cities in the state of Rio de Janeiro and twenty-six districts in the capital, affecting about 2.2 million inhabitants (Grandin et al. 2018). Federal intervention in public security in Rio, carried out by the government of President Michel Temer and led by the current minister of the Civil House of the Jair Bolsonaro administration, General Braga Netto, not only ignored the expansion of the militias but also did not provide any explanation for the murder of city councillor Marielle Franco and her driver, Anderson Gomes. This historic tragedy occurred at the beginning of the state's intervention and has not been explained. Investigations on the case—carried out by the State Prosecutor's Office in conjunction with the civil police—joined ongoing investigations into the use of funds from parliamentary offices of state deputies to finance the illegal real estate construction market controlled by the militia in the West Zone of the city of Rio de Janeiro. Investigations found

Flávio Bolsonaro, son of Jair Bolsonaro and currently a senator, was a participant in the Rio das Pedras militia. Adriano Magalhães da Nobrega—honored by Flávio Bolsonaro with the Tiradentes Medal, the highest commendation from the Legislative Assembly—became a fugitive and then was killed in a police operation in a rural area of the state of Bahia, in February 2020. Fabrício Queiroz, another advisor of Flávio Bolsonaro's office, had financial connections with Adriano Magalhães da Nobrega, was a member of a militia, and is currently in prison for his alleged role in the executions of Franco and Gomes. Militia growth is often accompanied by increasing relationships between members and elected officials in government.

Emerging from the colonial massacre, used in the enslavement of Indigenous peoples and Black Africans, employed in containing peasant and urban protests, and developed during the dictatorial period for the elimination of opponents, death squads are now being used during electoral campaigns and operate as militias. Illegal economic monopolies in peripheral areas and favelas, thriving on extortion, helped establish a recolonial militiarchy that is now launching itself into broader and more lasting projects of economic, social, and political domination. A decisive contribution to this was the widening socioeconomic gap, seen in the postdictatorship period beginning in 1985. The governments of Luíz Inácio Lula da Silva and Dilma Rousseff did not represent any significant change in the containment of these groups. In Rio de Janeiro and Baixada Fluminense, the Workers' Party (PT) failed to distance themselves from the killers but also approached them in search of votes and political support, reinforcing their totalitarian and transpartisan power. On the right and the left, the recolonial militiarchy flourished as a mediator across economic and political differences. Pentecostal evangelical churches, for example, find themselves in an unavoidable relationship with the dimensions of militia power, sheltering groups in exchange for favors.

The historical interest of ruling classes in maintaining social inequality helps solidify mechanisms that guarantee economic gains, which in this case are militias. Faced with an unprecedented economic crisis and deepened by a pandemic that killed 700,000 Brazilians between 2020 and 2023, the federal government's role in maintaining their economic interests through the support of militias seems even less tenable.

NOTES

1 A map of Rio's armed groups (Núcleo de Estudos da Violência 2020) indicated that militias controlled 25.5 percent of the neighborhoods in Rio, totaling 57.5 percent of the city's land area, where 33.1 percent of the population lived.

2   The Baixada Fluminense is a region composed of thirteen municipalities located west of the city of Rio de Janeiro. It is part of the metropolitan area, and it has a population of about 4 million residents.

3   Capitães do mato were vigilante militias sent out to crush rebellions of free Black people and poor slaves. These groups became part of the colonial structure, mainly during the seventeenth century, and coexisted during the growth of quilombos in Brazil. Rio's military police were originally the same people, now in uniform, that formed slave-catching squads in the nineteenth century and who worked as plantation captains for Rio's large landowners (Amar 2009, 518; Dantas 2004; Vallejos 1985).

REFERENCES

Alves, José Cláudio Souza. 2020. *Dos barões ao extermínio: Uma história da violência na Baixada Fluminense*. Rio de Janeiro: Consequência.

Amar, Paul. 2009. "Operation Princess in Rio de Janeiro: Policing 'Sex Trafficking,' Strengthening Worker Citizenship, and the Urban Geopolitics of Security in Brazil." *Security Dialogue* 40, no. 4–5: 513–41.

Barbara, Vanessa. 2018. "The Men Who Terrorize Rio." *New York Times*, May 22. https://www.nytimes.com/2018/05/22/opinion/rio-janeiro-terrorize-militias.html.

Dantas, Mariana L. R. 2004. "'For the Benefit of the Common Good': Regiments of caçadores do mato in Minas Gerais, Brazil." *Journal of Colonialism and Colonial History* 5, no. 2.

Grandin, Felipe, Henrique Coelho, Marco Antônio Martins, and Nicolás Satriano. 2018. "Franquia do crime: 2 milhões de pessoas no RJ estão em áreas sob influência de milícias." *G1* (Rio de Janeiro), March 14. https://g1.globo.com/rj/rio-de-janeiro/noticia/franquia-do-crime-2-milhoes-de-pessoas-no-rj-estao-em-areas-sob-influencia-de-milicias.ghtml.

Misse, Michel. 2009. "Sobre a acumulação social da violência no Rio de Janeiro." *Civitas revista de ciências sociais* 8, no. 3: 371–85.

Núcleo de Estudos da Violência. 2020. "Mapa dos grupos armados do Rio de Janeiro." Datalab Fogo Cruzado, NEV da Universidade de São Paulo. https://nev.prp.usp.br/mapa-dos-grupos-armados-do-rio-de-janeiro/.

O Globo. 2008. "Jornalistas são torturados por milicianos no Rio: Equipe de 'O Dia' foi Espancada por 7 horas na Zona Oeste." *O Globo Online*, May 31. Rio de Janeiro. https://extra.globo.com/noticias/rio/jornalistas-sao-torturados-por-milicianos-no-rio-equipe-de-dia-foi-espancada-por-7-horas-na-zona-oeste-519747.html.

Pereira, Waldick. 1977. *Cana, café e laranja: História econômica de Nova Iguaçu*. Rio de Janeiro: FGV/SEEC-RJ.

Torres, Rogério, and Newton Menezes. 1987. *Sonegação fome saque*. Duque de Caxias: Consórcio de Administração de Edições.

Vallejos, Julio Pinto. 1985. "Slave Control and Slave Resistance in Colonial Minas Gerais, 1700–1750." *Journal of Latin American Studies* 17, no. 1: 1–34.

7

Parastatal Sexarchy /
Sexarquia Parastatal

Mitigated Regulation and Prostitution's World Making

THADDEUS GREGORY BLANCHETTE AND ANA PAULA DA SILVA

The commercial sale of sex is not exactly legal in Rio de Janeiro. It is not illegal, either. One could say that regimes of permission, control, and punishment directed at sex work in the city are highly contingent upon the race/sex background or cis/trans identity of workers, clients, and even the collective identities of particular urban zones or worlds. This chapter delves into the history and sociology of prostitution in Rio de Janeiro,[1] exploring how the city has constructed a system that one of its major critics once labeled "mitigated regulation." We relabel this regulation regime as one of parastatal sexarchy. When we say *parastatal*, we mean "coalitions that can include government policymakers, NGOs, private security agencies, morality campaigns, and property developers . . . [that perform] the public functions of a state that has outsourced its functions into a parallel realm of reduced accountability and unregulated power" (Amar 2013, 18).

As part of a collective of sex worker activists in Rio, we use *parastatal* to emphasize the powerful dynamics of ambivalence and the structuring role played by the concept of arrego (discussed below), in opposition to the overused notion of corruption. The latter is frequently used to try to understand how and why a formally abolitionist state tolerates—and even profits from—illegal and irregular sex work. The prostitution sector and its workers, consumers, and world-making practices are simultaneously legalized but hyperpoliced in Rio, regulated but parastatized. The sector is bounded and its wealth extracted by a sex panic regime that fundamentally governs different class, gender, race, and trans-marked bodies by sexual categorization, medicalization, criminalization, and violence.

Through this regime, prostitution is simultaneously regulated, prohibited, and tolerated in Rio, confusing the typical understandings of sex work. In this chapter, we describe prostitution in Rio as parastatally regulated, since the policing apparatuses of the state extralegally (directly or indirectly, overtly, or, more often, covertly) manage the sale of sex through proxies or parastatal formations (Amar 2009). In this way, parastatal actors combine with police and sexual governance legislation to forcibly control and extract surplus from the city's sex workers. In order to set the scene for this discussion, we begin our analysis with notes from ethnographic fieldwork that took place during a historic time of struggle in Rio de Janeiro: the 2016 Olympic Games.

Copacabana, Rio de Janeiro: Day 9 of the 2016 Olympic Games

It is Saturday, August 13. I arrive on Copa at the Baccarat Termas at around 10:00 p.m.[2] The locker room is empty, in sharp contrast to how it was two years earlier at the World Cup. I change into the termas' obligatory bathrobe and flip-flops and head to the lounge. I sit down next to the bar, one of three men among two dozen women. Disco thumps over the loudspeakers. The women look bored. Two of them sit down next to me and begin caressing my thighs. I tell them that I won't pay for a programa (a trick), but that I'll happily talk about work. One woman, Tia, stays. She says it's been slow during the Olympics. She's surprised, because she'd heard stories of women making 14,000 reais at Baccarat during the Cup. "The owner even put in four more bedrooms," Tia says. "We're not using them."

Tia gets up, and a blonde woman in her thirties sits down. We chat. Bete confirms that business is slow. I say some places seem to be doing well, but she laughs and asks, "Where?" She's recently returned to prostitution after a divorce, hoping that the Olympics would pay her debts. A few girls are dancing, but most are sitting, doing the Tinder swipe. Two men speaking English enter and are mobbed. They extract themselves, ask for beers, and ignore the women, who drift back to the bar. An hour later, four more gringos stick their noses in, and the scene repeats. The men dive downstairs. It's now 12:30 a.m. with only twenty-five women and six men in the house. The women are frowning, peering at the door. This is at odds with the festive atmosphere of Baccarat during the Cup. I decide to leave.

Downstairs, I chat with the locker-room attendants, both Black women in their forties. They confirm that business has cratered and that the girls are unhappy. We're interrupted by a topless Black Brazilian man, draped in a robe tied around his waist (a form of dress forbidden in this termas). He's singing pagode and seems relaxed.[3] It is rare to see Black Brazilian men in upscale termas, and I have never seen them at Baccarat. The man chats with the attendants, using their first names. The women respond neutrally and concisely: "Yes sir. No sir. Your towel, sir." The man disrobes and stretches, exhibiting the sinewy physique of someone who does much physical activity but little formal exercise. "Now I'm headed to Bertolucci's and Chichi's." He declares, "Que noitada gostosa!"[4]

I leave and meet up with Ana Paula at Carangueijo's around 1 a.m. Carangueijo's is an open-air beachfront bar used by independent women sex workers to meet clients. It is not formally a brothel, but it is a prostitution venue in the sense that men and women meet and make deals there before going elsewhere for sex. Independent sex workers prefer it for finding clients because the bar's owner does not charge them for anything other than what they consume when they frequent the place. We count maybe five hundred women and men, total, at Carangueijo's and in the surrounding Fishbowl.[5] The women look tense. Few are walking away with clients. I talk to one sex-working friend. She's angry because the Games are worse than the Cup. I ask her why she doesn't go to Bertolucci's or Chichi's, two nearby venues where women must pay a hefty fee to enter. "Eu, hein?"[6] she snorts, scornfully. "I'm too grown-up to give my money to pimps." A half hour later, we walk down R. Prado Junior, following a sex worker as she weaves away from Carangueijo's with a client. She is babbling to him, although he doesn't appear to speak Portuguese: "There're a lot of whores at Bertolucci's, but I'm a natural whore. I don't pay pimps to work!"

Bertolucci's is a nightclub and strip joint where both men and women have to pay to get in. It rents VIP rooms out to couples for sex. It is booming compared to most places on Copacabana but is nowhere near capacity. We retreat back to Prado Junior for a snack at the Soup Aunty's cart.[7] As we're leaving, the Black Brazilian man from Baccarat walks out of Bertolucci's and up to the cart. He banters in a simultaneously friendly and menacing tone with Aunty, joking that he'll denounce her for health code violations.[8] Aunty tells him to go ahead, asking, "Are you gonna eat or keep talking shit, Fulano?"[9] The man laughs and strolls toward Chichi's, another club/strip joint/brothel. Auntie sniffs and jerks her head at the departing man's back. "Corporal Fulano's been a kick in the nuts ever since he was set to gather in the arrego," she explains to us.

Parastatal (Non)Regulation of Prostitution

Arrego—meaning giving something up or capitulating—is used as an interjection in Portuguese, possibly a lack of patience for a particular scenario (be it out of fear, irritation, or the perception of defeat). It can thus mean "giving up" or "I surrender." In its noun form, employed in the police regulation of informal Carioca commerce, it means "what is given up"—generally money to police—so that one is left in peace. *Arrego* is an emic term that floats above all sectors of Rio's economies—not just sex work. It's a word that illustrates the total social fact that is parastatal (non)regulation (chapter 26, this volume).[10] The arrego underpins the parastatal administration of Rio de Janeiro, but it is ambiguous with regard to the relationship between the formal state, the auxiliaries that administer the arrego, and the people and institutions that pay it. The arrego modulates a fraught situation without recourse to violence, permitting antagonisms to balance out and allowing supposedly contradictory worlds to occupy the same urban spaces without open conflict.

Without defending the arrego, we also hesitate to label it corruption. It seems to be a feature and not a bug of Rio de Janeiro's res publica. Nowhere is this clearer than in the field of sex work, where different versions of the arrego have been employed in managing prostitution since the late nineteenth century. While many people believe prostitution is legal in Brazil, it is more correct to say that it is not illegal (Blanchette and Murray 2017; Blanchette and Schettini 2017).

There are currently three main models of dealing with prostitution in the world: prohibitionist (criminalization or stigmatization of sex workers and clients), abolitionist (elimination of prostitution without harming sex workers), and regulationist (establishment of laws permitting sex work).[11] While all systems of dealing with prostitution demonstrate elements of these three models (diachronically if not synchronically), in Rio de Janeiro, they are simultaneously employed in a parastatal sexarchy. The system is parastatal in that it's based upon public-private partnerships that negotiate and collect the arrego and apply sanctions to sex workers according to a parahumanitarian "protection" logic. The parahumanitarian and parahuman are concepts derived by Paul Amar (2013), who locates them at the intersection of practices of paramilitarism and of "humanitarian rescue" dependency or debilitation-by-force. The arrego system is sexarchy because it establishes clear hierarchies between sexual behaviors and actors—hierarchies that, while not enshrined in laws or constitutions, are often enforced by police, judges, and social workers in a transsectorial institutionalization of hegemonic moralities that Dewey and St. Germain (2016) call, in the context of the United States, the alliance.

Brazil is formally abolitionist, having signed every international treaty seeking to eliminate prostitution while protecting the human rights of women. But prostitution in Rio is also regulated by the arrego system, with state and parastatal extraction of surplus from the commercial sexual economy. And, if you are a sex worker outside the confines of the arrego, you can meet violence and/or criminalization at the hands of the police or their auxiliaries/adversaries that rivals or exceeds that employed by any formally prohibitionist state.[12] These encounters aren't inevitable, but the chances increase to the degree a sex worker operates outside of this system, whose primary parastatal mediator is the pimp (i.e., the venue owner or manager). Brazil doesn't criminalize prostitution. Instead, its laws potentially criminalize everyone involved in prostitution, from clients to sex workers and their families. These laws stretch back to the 1940s but were prefigured in earlier nineteenth-century legislation (Blanchette and Schettini 2017). They are strategically (un)enforced to channel sex work into certain places and times and permit the state and its partners to extract surplus from prostitution. Sex work in Rio de Janeiro is thus situationally criminalizable. The state does not make any commitments, neither toward repressing prostitution, nor toward guaranteeing the human and labor rights of prostitutes. Typically, state agents operate in this sector through parastatal arrangements that ensure the family is not corrupted by segregating prostitution and prostitutes from proper society. This underlying dynamic has remained stable in Rio de Janeiro for more than a century in spite of the ever-shifting composition of the state, its partners, and what constitutes a family.

Early nineteenth-century Brazil had no laws regarding prostitution. The sexarchical organization of society was perhaps so well established in that period that specific sex work laws didn't even need to be passed: one was simply a "family woman" or a presumed harlot. "Laws regarding the protection of honor" (Caulfield 2000a) clearly defined the place of women and what rights they were due. The 1830 Imperial Criminal Code gives us a hint that a legal distinction between honest and dishonest women had already been established, given that rape of the first category was punishable by three to twelve years in prison, while rapists of women deemed dishonest only received one month to two years. *Honest woman* was a very exclusive category until the 1950s, and *whore* was the default for any woman unmarried and unaccompanied by a male protector in public (Caulfield 2000a; Vainfas 1985). The outlines of the modern parastatal sexarchy took shape in Rio during the late nineteenth and early twentieth centuries, following the abolition of slavery. This was a period in which open regulation of prostitution was proposed and rejected in favor of abolition (Schettini 2005). Republican elites looked to England and not France in qualifying sex work as a form of slavery. Mass male in-migration to cities and urbanization ensured that the sale of sex would continue to be lucrative in Rio, however. Such profits wouldn't go unharnessed.

While Brazil ballyhooed abolitionist virtue, the organization of sex work in Rio de Janeiro became increasingly de facto regulationist. The growth of an informal economy of sex work emerged alongside and in response to state regulations. Female boarding house owners became initial brokers in this parastatal system. In 1924, white slavery investigator Paul Kinsie interviewed a "Madame Sophie," who described how Rio's abolition worked:

> The law does not allow the girls to give half to the madame; but a woman can open a house any place in the city as a boarding house for girls. To do that you must get a license . . . that you pay every six months in advance. You can have as many girls in your house as you have rooms. . . . Each girl pays . . . board and room [every day].
>
> A girl comes to this house; she puts her name in the book; also her age, nationality, etc. I send the name to the Police Department. They put her on record. The same way as they put you on when you register at a hotel. . . . If the girl wants to be [medically] examined she can go, but she does not have to. She can have her own doctor or the free clinic. It is not compulsory. The only thing is this: The law says that we cannot take in girls under 22 years of age. What we do is, in case we get a girl say 16 years or 18 years of age, we always send her age in as 22 or 24. (Chaumont, García, and Servais 2017, 76–77)

In other words, most of the elements of the French-style regulation of prostitution were present on the ground in Rio in 1924. We can see this in the interactions between women, house owners, and police, even while those prostitution regulations were being formally rejected by the state in favor of abolition. House-owning madams extracted surplus from sex workers and turned a portion of this over to the police via the formal licensing of boarding houses. The madams were responsible for controlling prostitution as well as paying the state's agents, even though this third-party extraction of surplus from sex work was specifically prohibited by law.

The state thus created the legal fiction of female boarding houses and subjected them to the same sort of controls present in French brothels via the intermediation of the parastatal relationship between the house madam and the cop on the beat. In so doing, the state could simultaneously claim to be abolitionist while exerting de facto regulationist control over prostitution and its profits. Although the resulting system did not require obligatory medical exams or formal "internment" of prostitutes in brothels, all evidence indicates that parastatal controls kept a tight reign over sex-working women. Sophie's comment about hotels is telling: hotels during this period were understood to be "family" or "nonfamily," with improper women (and other suspect populations) banned from entering the first sorts of establishments. Restaurants, cafés, theaters, and other urban entertainments were likewise divided by custom. Even the famous Colombo Café, which served both family and bohemian clients, divided its working day into periods when suspect women were and were not welcome. Women who broke these unwritten rules could be arrested or worse (Engels [1884] 1985; Blanchette and da Silva 2009).

By the first decades of the twentieth century, urban hygienization projects motivated attempts to ban prostitution from the family region of downtown Rio. These were unsuccessful, but they did much to reinforce a parastatally hierarchized class, racial, and ethnic divide in Rio's sex markets. A new red-light district was established in the Mangue, a stretch of reclaimed marshland near what is today Rio's famous Sambódromo. The founding of this district illustrates the functioning of Rio's parastatal sexarchy. In 1920, King Albert of Belgium visited the city to commemorate the completion of two decades of intense urban hygienization. Historian Paulo Donadio describes Albert's visit as "an opportunity to showcase the country in Europe: he'd be a perfect representative of civilization who could attest to Brazil's progress" (2008, 31). As part of the preparations for the king's visit, the police collected the city's poorer prostitutes and dumped them in the Mangue—a "quarantine zone" for sex workers: "Instructed to 'clean up' the areas through which His Highness would pass, the police rounded up lower-class prostitutes on the allegation that they were 'bums' and kept them under arrest until the end of the royal visit, later gathering them all together in brothels around the nine streets of the Mangue. Here, a few kilometers away from the shores of Guanabara Bay, far from the modernized center of town, there began a series of experiments in police administration of prostitution" (Caulfield 2000b, 51).

Two prostitution-related institutions were founded in the Mangue: the São Francisco de Assis hospital (specializing in the treatment of venereal disease) and the Thirteenth Police Precinct (effectively a vice unit charged with registering and maintaining the records of prostitutes). In the words of Soraya Simões: "These measures made the Mangue appear to be the ideal place for situating carioca prostitution, contributing to the definition of the city's [new] moral spaces and to the hygienist view of the times, as well as to the control of syphilis and the other venereal diseases which haunted the city at the beginning of the twentieth century [. . . giving] it the reputation of being the 'natural region' for lower-class prostitution in Rio" (2010, 25). As a containment measure, the Mangue was only partially successful. Lower-class prostitution—especially that of nonwhite women (although also plenty of white European immigrants, many of whom were Jewish)—was more or less kept within its boundaries. Middle-class, upper-class, and cabaret-based sex work blossomed in the bohemian district of Lapa, however. During World War II, the city tried to close down prostitution but only succeeded in driving it temporarily underground or into new areas (Niterói, Praça Mauá). By the early 1950s, the Mangue was operating once again, and middle-class prostitution followed Rio's nightlife as bossa nova shifted the city's bohemian district from Lapa to Copacabana. This was the period in which the Fishbowl was established (Caulfield 2000b; Leite 1993; Blanchette and Schettini 2017).

This bifurcated model of sex work has continued into the present. As boarding houses closed and clubs, termas, motels, and apartment prostitution boomed in the mid-twentieth century, police attempted to keep the sale of sex limited to certain times and places. The Mangue shifted farther north, becoming today's Vila Mimosa in the 1980s and 1990s. Venues catering to the middle class, bohemians, and tourists moved south. Meanwhile, prostitution in the Centro (downtown) survived periodic waves of hygienization, becoming the densest concentration of venues in Rio, catering to both ends of the class and race spectrums. Luxury termas were located meters away from the cheap pay-by-the-hour "motels" or rental rooms jocosely called *fast fodas*.[13] By 2009, Rio had almost three hundred commercial sex venues—all illegal and almost all regulated through the arrego (Blanchette and da Silva 2011).

An example of the many ways in which Rio's sexual hierarchies have been parastatally organized over the past century can be found in the early 1970s in Praça Mauá, a red-light district that boomed following the temporary closure of the Mangue during World War II. In 1971 police forced sex workers indoors, under the rubric of "protecting fathers of families" from harassment by prostitutes. Women were registered by the police through bar owners, who were in turn made responsible for keeping their women off the streets. Extrajudicial fines were collected directly by police when the rules were violated. Recalcitrant bar owners were forced out of business; reluctant sex workers were arrested as bums.

Soon, Praça Mauá was once again safe for the delicate sensibilities of "fathers of families" (Baltar, Araujo, and Jacob 1971).

A key element of control of prostitution evident in Praça Mauá was the Vargas-era Lei da contravenções penais (LCP) and its provisions against vagrancy, a misdemeanor employed against sex workers before the end of military rule in the 1980s (Olivar 2013). Defining vagrancy as not being able to show legal means of support, the LCP empowered police to imprison bums for up to three months. The easiest way for a woman to prove her legitimacy under these circumstances was for her husband (i.e., any permanent male partner) to show up at the precinct, pay a fine, and bail her out. As a result, female sex workers often had to have male partners (called gigolos) who could pose as husbands, whom they'd pay to publicly perform sexual-affective relationships in order to get around vagrancy laws. The vagrancy clause of the LCP was enforced less often as it came under public scrutiny in the 1990s (though not removed from the books). Since then, police control of prostitution has had to rely more and more on parastatal partnerships with venue owners. As mentioned by our interlocutors in the beginning of this chapter, these are the pimps who are the owners or managers of sex work venues—clubs, termas, strip joints, fast fodas—that charge women to work.[14] There are many ways in which this can be done, but the most common is to simply make women pay a fee at the door for coming into the venue or to charge room rental fees. These venue owners and managers then pay some of this extracted surplus to low-ranking beat police via the arrego. This money is then passed on to precinct chiefs and their political allies and patrons (who are also often covert partners in the ownership of prostitution venues). Sex work venues are kept orderly and sex work largely restricted to certain times and places via the oversight of the beat cops, while the arrego transfers a significant portion of the surplus generated by sex work to state actors and agents.

As this brief history of the social control of prostitution should make clear, neither parastatal governance of sex work nor the arrego are particularly new extractive modes. The passing of the 1940s criminal code forced public (although informal) police regulation of prostitution underground, completely off the books. The term *arrego* is simply modern slang referring to the now-clandestine control and taxing of Rio's sex workers by police authorities—a form of extraction that never was legally formalized, but which was openly recognized by city authorities as being a police prerogative in the early decades of the twentieth century. Following the redemocratization of Brazil in the 1960s, the line between police, paramilitary, and parastatal agents increasingly blurred (chapter 16, this volume), making it ever less clear where these extracted resources ultimately wind up. This should not be seen as a bug but rather a feature. What we see when we find Corporal Fulano wandering the Fishbowl late at night, collecting the arrego, is not so much a new extractive mode as a very polished and perfected one. It is a mode that functions more or less like clockwork, collecting fixed fees even when—as at the Olympics—the sex industry is in a profound recession.

During the 2016 Olympic Games, gender scholar Gregory Mitchell and I had the opportunity to speak with a so-called pimp—a Carioca businessman who had invested in a downtown termas.[15] He gave us a concise description of how one legally operates a brothel in Rio, setting up a parastatal partnership with state agents:

> You need authorities as partners. You must choose your location carefully so that you won't anger these people. Before you open, you visit the precinct. You explain that you want open direct channels with the police in case you've any problems in your club. You invite them over. Soon, you'll be told how much needs to be paid to the precinct. They'll send someone to have a drink and pick up the arrego. You're expected to keep things quiet, to not employ minors, and so on. If there's a problem, you contact the precinct directly, and they take care of it.

The general outline of this system is quite consistent with that described by Madame Sophie in 1924. In 1967, Armando Pereira, a police inspector who had managed prostitution in Rio for over thirty years, remarked upon the contradictions and stability of this method of managing prostitution, describing it as "mitigated regulation": "Brazil has an abolitionist tradition. During the Republic, we didn't sanction laws or measures which would regulate prostitution. The European problem [of regulated prostitution] thus does not exist among us. . . . However, in practice, we have always adopted a mitigated form of regulation. We tolerate houses of prostitution. . . . There is no continuity in this policy . . . however. There have been periods in which all the houses are closed. Others in which [the police] fiercely persecute only streetwalkers. Still others in which they attack the numerous sex hotels" (Pereira 1967, 44). One can work without pimps in this mitigated prostitution, but it is dangerous because it is through venue managers and owners that most sex workers can gain some degree of police protection from violence. The 2014 FIFA World Cup gave us an example of what it means to be outside the arrego system. The city of Niterói (across the bay from Rio) announced plans to remove sex workers from the downtown area as part of the Porto Maravilha hygiene campaign. The women who worked in the Caixa federal building had been paying the police US$30,000–50,000 a month in arrego and demanded that removal be stopped. The police claimed nothing could be done, as eviction orders had come from high-ranking government officials. Consequently, they would not be picking up the arrego anymore. The women decided to stick it out.

On May 23, 2014, over two hundred police descended on the building, arresting dozens of women and allegedly raping one. Only sex workers were removed, and their property was left for other building residents to loot. The operation employed an improperly issued warrant but was widely reported as a blow against sexual exploitation, despite no charges being filed. The women dispersed to other sex work sites around greater Rio de Janeiro, most particularly in the parastatally managed Vila Mimosa, the direct descendent of the Mangue red-light district established by police in 1924 (Murray 2014; interview by Thaddeus Gregory Blanchette with woman arrested in the operation, September 23, 2014).

Conclusion: Parastatal Pimps and Police

For over a century, despite brothels and third-party profiteering from sex work being prohibited by Brazil's abolitionist laws, Rio's sex work venues have operated in relative tranquility, directly or indirectly regulated by the police and their parastatal auxiliaries. Our sex-working interlocutors are adamant: behind every pimp there is a cop. Although the paid-off police can generally be relied upon to make sure that violence in Rio's sex work venues is kept to a minimum, sex workers are under no illusions as to where the ultimate loyalty of the police lies—certainly not with sex workers.

This parastatal organization of sex work in Rio challenges typical views of sex work regulation as regulationist, abolitionist, or prohibitionist. In Rio, aspects of all three of these systems are conditionally activated as circumstances warrant. But the overall reproduction of the parastatal control of sex work has never been comprehensively challenged. In this sort of context, it becomes questionable what sex work solutions, such as the so-called Swedish model (i.e., criminalization of clients coupled with stigmatization of sex workers), could ever possibly achieve in Rio—other than to further entrench parastatal power and the system of arrego. The Brazilian state has long agreed that prostitution is a bad thing. This has not, however, prevented its agents from systematically and directly profiting from sex work through parastatal alliances with venue owners and managers. In the face of this system, only the systematic political organization of sex workers is liable to have an impact. But the continued strong stigmatization of sex work operates against that and in favor of the parastatal system.

NOTES

1 Sex worker activists (led by cisgender women, trans women, and travesti workers) in Rio de Janeiro tend to explicitly preserve and reappropriate the terms *prostitute* and *puta* to describe their labor. They argue that to use only the term *sex worker* is to eliminate the gendered history (women and trans) of the struggle, give in to respectability politics, and adopt an unproductive class-versus-gender binary. Rio's activists also tend to think that the term *sex worker* can tend to privilege male sex workers (since the term *worker* is a male-gendered noun in Portuguese) in a context where cisgender hetero and gay men have not invested much in the collective struggle to de-police sex work.

2 In this chapter, *I* refers to Thaddeus Blanchette. Baccarat Termas is a sauna brothel (Mitchell and Blanchette 2021).

3 A 1980s subgenre of samba.

4 "What a delicious night out!"

5 The traditional red-light district in Copacabana.

6 "Who, me?"

7 A woman who sells soup on the corner of Prado Jr. and Min. Viveiros de Castro.

8 Aunty's cart is part of the informal economy.

9 A generic name, like Joe Blow, used to protect anonymity.

10 A social fact is a phenomenon with pervasive effects in many domains of life (legal, social, cultural, political, etc.; Mauss 1950). We understand *parastatal* following Amar's (2013) definition, and in the way outlined by Blanchette et al. (chapter 26), in this volume.

11 Ignoring New Zealand's decriminalization approach, which remains an outlier.

12 In Rio, it is never clear where the dividing line between these categories lies.

13 A play on the English term *fast food*, *fast foda* literally means "fast fuck."

14 These are not pimps in the sense popularized by American cinema (Blanchette and da Silva 2017).

15 The term for pimp—*cafetão*—was never employed by the man himself, but rather by the women who worked in the venue he partially owned.

REFERENCES

Amar, Paul. 2009. "Operation Princess in Rio de Janeiro: Policing 'Sex Trafficking,' Strengthening Worker Citizenship, and the Urban Geopolitics of Security in Brazil." *Security Dialogue* 40, no. 4–5: 513–41.

Amar, Paul. 2013. *The Security Archipelago: Human-Security States, Sexuality Politics, and the End of Neoliberalism.* Durham, NC: Duke University Press.

Baltar, T., P. C. Araujo, and A. Jacob. 1971. "Praça Mauá abriga em 11 boates mercado de sexo para os homens do mar." *Jornal do Brasil* 7–8 (March): 40.

Blanchette, Thaddeus Gregory, and Ana Paula da Silva. 2009. "As American Girls: Migração, sexo e status imperial em 1918" [American girls: Migration, sex and imperial status in 1918]. *Horizontes Antropológicos* 15: 75–100.

Blanchette, Thaddeus Gregory, and Ana Paula da Silva. 2011. "Prostitution in Contemporary Rio de Janeiro." In *Policing Pleasure: Sex Work, Policy, and the State in Global Perspective*, edited by Susan Dewey and Patty Kelly, 130–45. New York: New York University Press.

Blanchette, Thaddeus Gregory, and Ana Paula da Silva. 2017. "Sympathy for the Devil: Pimps, Agents and Third Parties Involved in the Sale of Sex in Rio de Janeiro." In *Third Party Sex Work and "Pimps" in the Age of Anti-trafficking*, edited by Amber Horning and Anthony Marcus, 15–48. New York: Springer.

Blanchette, Thaddeus Gregory, and Laura Murray. 2017. "Discretionary Policing, or The Lesser Part of Valor: Prostitution, Law Enforcement, and Unregulated Regulation in Rio de Janeiro's Sexual Economy." *Criminal Justice and Law Enforcement Annual: Global Perspectives* 7, no. 2: 31–74.

Blanchette, Thaddeus Gregory, and Cristiana Schettini. 2017. "Sex Work in Rio de Janeiro: Police Management without Regulation." In *Selling Sex in the City: A Global History of Prostitution, 1600s–2000s*, edited by Magaly Rodríguez García, Lex Heerma van Voss, and Elise van Nederveen Meerkerk, 490–516. Leiden: Brill.

Caulfield, Sueann. 2000a. *In Defense of Honor*. Durham, NC: Duke University Press.

Caulfield, Sueann. 2000b. "O nascimento do Mangue: Raça, nação e controle da prostituição no Rio de Janeiro, 1850-1942." *Tempo* 9 (July): 43–63.

Chaumont, Jean-Michel, Magaly Rodríguez García, and Paul Servais, eds. 2017. *Trafficking in Women, 1924-1926: The Paul Kinsie Reports for the League of Nations*. Vol. 1. Geneva: United Nations.

Dewey, Susan, and Tonia St. Germain. 2016. *Women of the Street: How the Criminal Justice-Social Services Alliance Fails Women in Prostitution*. New York: New York University Press.

Donadio, Paulo. 2008. "Tem rei no mar." *Revista de História*, July 7.

Engels, Friedrich. (1884) 1985. *The Origin of the Family, Private Property and the State*. New York: Pathfinder Press.

Leite, Juçara Luzia. 1993. "A República do Mangue: Controle policial e prostituição no Rio de Janeiro (1954-1974)." Master's thesis, Universidade Federal Fluminense.

Mauss, Marcel. 1950. *The Gift: The Form and Reason for Exchange in Archaic Societies*. London: Norton.

Mitchell, Gregory, and Thaddeus Blanchette. 2021. "Tricks of the Light: Refractive Masculinity in Heterosexual and Homosexual Brothels in Rio de Janeiro." *South Atlantic Quarterly* 120, no. 3: 609–29.

Murray, Laura. 2014. "Victim Management and the Politics of Protection: Between 'Fazer Direito' and 'Direitinho.'" *Revista Ártemis* 18: 28–41.

Olivar, José Miguel Nieto. 2013. *Devir puta: Políticas da prostituicao de rua na experiência de qautro mulheres militantes*. Rio de Janeiro: Eduerj.

Pereira, Armando Santos. 1967. *Sexo e prostituição*. Rio de Janeiro: Gráfica Record Editôra.

Schettini, Cristiana. 2005. "Lavar, passar e receber visitas: Debates sobre a regulamentação da prostituição e experiências de trabalho sexual em Buenos Aires e no Rio de Janeiro, fim do século XIX." *Cadernos Pagu* 25: 25–54.

Simões, Soraya. 2010. "Identidade e política: A prostituição e o reconhecimento de um métier no Brasil." *Revista de antropologia social dos alunos do PPGAS-UFSCar* 2, no. 1: 24–46.

Vainfas, Magali Engels. 1985. "Meretrizes e doutores: O saber médico e a prostituição na cidade do Rio de Janeiro, 1845-1890." Master's thesis, Universidade Federal Fluminense.

8

Nonbinary Governance Epistemologies /

Epistemologias de Governança Nãobinárias

Entangled Circuits of Violence, Crime, and Governmental Syncretism

FERNANDO BRANCOLI

Previous research on large-scale narco organizations and protection rackets has analyzed the capacity of such actors to provide public goods and to actually govern urban areas such as Greater Rio de Janeiro (Crawford 1999; Rodrigues 2018). Since the 1970s, such studies have articulated concepts such as parallel state, hybrid governance zones, and nongovernance areas while pointing out relationships between drug traffickers, militias, and government actors. These concepts maintain a strict binary notion of order—between the nonstate actors and crime-ridden populations, on the one hand, and the state on the other. Such conceptions posit a unitary, rational, and easily identifiable concept of the state actor (agents of law, bureaucracies, uniformed police, and elected officials). Paramilitary groups, within these expressions, represent exogenous agents, who might articulate with recognized state institutions but who only penetrate the state or hybridize with the state during instances of exceptional corruption, rather than as a hegemonic mode of rule. The problem with this binary notion of rule that cleanly splits state from nonstate is that it masks, and thus props up and legitimizes, systems of radical unaccountability and systematic violence. This fosters blame against Black and working-class populations—as almost naturally spawning the criminal worlds of the nonstate while being engaged by the formal, visible state only in moments of coercion, punishment, or extermination. Also, this binary epistemology of governance is a political-economic regime. It permits the invisibility of the superprofits milked from illicit commerce, drug trafficking, tax avoidance, gun running, and money laundering by agents of the state, institutions, and by the elite. While the spectacle of policing and violence renders hypervisible (Amar 2013, 219) the Black bodies of youth mowed down during police invasions or crammed into prisons, their punishment maintains the binary illusion that the state maintains a strict blue line between itself and (racialized) disorder and barbarism. But in this chapter, I elevate the concept of a nonbinary crossroads epistemology for understanding the true formations of rule. I spotlight the regular and nonexceptional operation of this kind of entangled governance. Starting from decolonial epistemological premises, my research suggests that it is more useful to understand the relationships between paramilitary groups and government forces as a complex constellation of powers, knowledge, and interests that constitute parastatal (Amar 2013, 18–29) or nonbinary state formation.

The decolonial premises are seen neither as a rupture with the preceding colonial era nor as its abolition, since "the end of colonialism as a political relationship did not imply the end of colonialism as a social relationship, or as a mentality and mode of authoritarianism and discrimination" (B. Santos 2004). Recognizing the complex knowledge-power connections that underpin all academic activity, postcolonialism offers a critique of its political purpose, which is to oppose asymmetrical global power distribution. In this sense, the postcolonial perspective must actively contribute to the implosion of dominant colonial/ Western discourses that naturalize disparities between nations, classes, races, and peoples. Homi Bhabha points to postcolonial sensibilities that, instead, "deploy the cultural hybridity of their borderline conditions to 'translate,' and therefore reinscribe, the social imaginary of both metropolis and modernity" (1994, 6). Gayatri Spivak supports this effort to promote subalternity as a locus of enunciation from which the postcolonial may arise, arguing that the margins and peripheries are the preferred loci of enunciation for identifying and subverting power and knowledge systems (see B. Santos 2004). Although she began by specifying the subaltern as "subsistence farmers, unorganized peasant labor, the tribals and communities of zero workers on the street or in the countryside" (Spivak [1988] 1994, 84), she later offered more broad frameworks for oppressed populations. Frantz Fanon's project, likewise, was larger than ending colonial occupation, but transforming the psychology and culture of Manicheanism that emerged from it: "It is rigorously false to pretend and to believe that this decolonization is the fruit of an objective dialectic which more or less rapidly assumed the appearance of an absolutely inevitable mechanism" (1964, 170). Aside from misunderstanding the reproduction of colonialism in the postcolonial period, structurally and culturally, Manichean understandings of state/nonstate binaries largely underestimate spaces that exist within the formal boundaries of a state without at all becoming subject to it (Scott 2008).

Rather than positioning political agents on one side of a state/nonstate binary, I intend to signal the regular basis by which governing actors ignore this binary and are actually protected from accountability by those who believe that the binary or blue line between state and nonstate actually exists. In order to highlight a key node in this nonbinary regime dynamic, my research focuses on former military police officers who become leaders of armed militias. Do they really then become nonstate or antistate actors? Or does this crossroads move simply amplify their political and economic hegemony as governance agents, but in an intensely unaccountable and illiberal way that creates dependence and systematic insecurity, racial/religious/patriarchal terror rather than citizenship? I will map these actors through a cartography, based not on identifying sets of actors as state or nonstate, but by identifying particular practices by which each mobilizes social capital, police capital, and crime capital. Criminal governance takes place intentionally and productively (in a recolonial sense) at this crossroads. I argue that only in this nonbinary way is it possible to perceive how the spaces are constituted where social and political actors—the corrupt policeman or thief with a social conscience—meet and interact systematically, especially in popular or working-class neighborhoods.

This chapter presents the concept of nonbinary governance as a methodological and epistemological alternative that illuminates practices of criminal control and governance in spaces in the Global South. For this, I articulate reflections taken from the literature and cultural studies of Rio de Janeiro, focusing on the dynamics of parastatal governance syncretism and presenting the political consequences that the lens of nonbinary governance brings to the table. I explicate the results of ethnographic research and semi-structured interviews as well as inquiries involving various fields of knowledge in the city of Rio. The period when research and writing were conducted was tumultuous, during the 2020–21 COVID-19 pandemic. This period brought paradoxical messages for the residents of Acari, one of Rio de Janeiro's largest favelas, who saw President Bolsonaro on national television defining the pandemic as a "little flu" and asking the population to reject the media's "hysteria." Though he dismissed calls for social isolation, a few days later, unidentified vehicles drove through the community's streets blasting a different tune: a nightly lockdown and obligatory use of masks for all residents leaving home (Briso and Phillips 2020). In some neighborhoods, loudspeakers also announced that food and medicine would be distributed to those who had lost their jobs due to the crisis but warned that any breach of the rules would have serious consequences.

This chapter's foray into nonbinary governance within decolonial studies offers both a compelling and precarious lens, notably devoid of gendered considerations but rich in potential for nuanced discourse. Drawing from robust analyses by scholars such as Mark Goodale (2006) and Nancy Scheper-Hughes (1995) as well as case studies from the Brazilian context by Michel Agier (2015) and Maria Hita and John Gledhill (2010), this work challenges traditional governance frameworks, exploring a spectrum of formal and informal actors and ethical considerations. The notion of the parastatal (Amar 2013) serves as a fitting conceptual framework for understanding the multilayered, often contradictory, nature of governance. As we delve deeper into the convoluted realms of violence, crime, and governmental syncretism, it becomes evident that further interdisciplinary research is necessary to transcend conventional binaries and foster more comprehensive dialogues.

Images of the vehicles circulated on social media and in the press in April, weeks after residents had shared a video through WhatsApp groups. Police confirmed reports of threats in Acari and opened an investigation. Some public security experts claimed that the vehicles had been hired by paramilitary groups (Sobreira 2020), while others said it was part of a new strategy for local social movements to inform people about the pandemic. In other favelas, however, the messenger's identity was clearer. In Cidade de Deus, drug gangs hung banners on several streets, threatening residents who held parties or left home for reasons other than emergencies. The groups even signed the message, making it clear who was giving the orders. In the Vila Brasil neighborhood of Itaboraí, a city in the metropolitan region of Rio de Janeiro, criminal groups erected barriers as a public health measure to block outsiders, including police, from entering.

Crowded conditions, precarious infrastructure, and almost no state support made favelas like Acari—one of the poorest in Rio de Janeiro—particularly vulnerable to the coronavirus. By mid-July there were more than 3,800 confirmed COVID-19 cases in Rio's favelas, including 105 in Acari, according to one count by community media outlet Voz das Comunidades. In Rio, Afro-Brazilians predominantly reside in the favelas. As in the United States, COVID-19 dispro-portionately impacted Black communities in Brazil (Batista et al. 2020).

For armed groups, the COVID-19 threat brought an opportunity to assert control. An estimated 1.4 million people reside in Rio's underprivileged areas, and more than three-quarters of these neighborhoods live under the influence of armed groups. Armed groups, whose control dates back at least to the 1970s, previously focused on more limited parastate governance such as the illegal collection of security fees. Today, they administer work permits, conduct drug sales, sell real estate, and control vehicle traffic in and out of the communities. They also assert political power by using territorial control to elect politicians and by occupying spaces within institutions.

The 2020 COVID-19 pandemic galvanized these political dynamics by mak-ing room for unprecedented changes in how they operate. Amid disputes be-tween state governors and the president, militia groups—made up mainly of retired police officers—have positioned themselves as better connected to poor communities and their problems than politicians. Combining the health emer-gency with the use of force, paramilitary actors began to control more aspects of everyday life in the favelas during the pandemic, from the operation of small businesses to the ability of residents to leave their homes. Militias have even controlled access to doctors at the city's public hospitals (J. Santos and Fachin 2020). In contrast to traditionally more covert activities, these actions put the militias on full display. And yet they have little fear of police sanctions, in part due to their complex intersections and interactions with state power. This relationship occurs in the context of a variety of political objectives, as state agents recognize the effectiveness of militias in controlling peripheral areas, for example. Through this type of interaction between governments and militias, regions that have historically been neglected by official institutions may still be under informal control—for example, to ensure votes or political influence. The political impacts of this reality remain unpredictable.

Despite the pandemic reinforcing the dynamics of city area control by crimi-nal groups, the control and oppression of poor communities in Rio dates back decades. At the same time that political actors are quick to describe such groups as external entities and completely disconnected from the state's structures, critical academics have reinforced the dimension of symbiosis or hybridism among them. In both cases, the analyses start from ontological assumptions in which the state is a unified, rational, and easily identifiable actor, threatened by alien agents. This chapter presents conceptual reflections that try to overcome the binomial state-nonstate of these cases. Perpetuating interpretations of the state as a normalizing and pacifying element by extension justifies actions that are often violent and that would have (at least discursively) the objective of bringing the state into the poor communities.

The federal government's dismissal of COVID-19 created a political vacuum and opportunities for a constellation of actors to assert authority. State governors were the first to contradict the president, and several states (Rio de Janeiro and São Paulo, among others) quickly implemented isolation measures. When Bolsonaro threatened to open the entire country by decree, the Supreme Court upheld the autonomy of governors and mayors to take their own measures. Despite states' actions, the president's denial of the problem's seriousness still had an effect. Research shows that adherence to physical distancing measures was below average in the areas where Bolsonaro won the most votes in the 2018 election (Batista et al. 2020). The government's refusal to swiftly provide economic assistance to the unemployed also forced a significant proportion of Brazilians to leave their homes for work. As elsewhere, the poor, working class, and communities with inadequate public services and sanitation were left most at risk. These disputes—together with the ensuing health emergency when Brazil emerged as the epicenter of the pandemic in the Americas—enabled armed groups with historical ties to the state to impose themselves as the purveyors of solutions for poor communities. The COVID-19 crisis did not create this dynamic, but it may have deepened it.

Favelas and Narratives of Crime in Rio de Janeiro

Unlike many cities in the Global North, such as Paris and London, where the poor generally live in remote peripheries, in Rio the properly paved, planned, and registered middle-class neighborhoods (called the "asphalt" zone) and the favelas sit in close proximity. This complex coexistence has always laid bare the city's structural racism and inequality. Many residents of the favelas, mostly Afro-Brazilians, go down every day to the wealthier (flatter) streets for work.

Former soldiers, mostly descendants of enslaved Africans, first occupied Rio's favelas in the late nineteenth century (Valladares 2015, 2). Almost since the inception of these communities, narratives of the favelas as spaces of violence proliferated. Mainstream media depictions constructed favelas as areas of nongovernance where the absence of the state promoted these difficulties. The first police raids, starting around the 1920s, targeted armed groups formed by residents. The state has long justified police presence as a response to violence while abandoning favela residents when it came to providing basic public services, such as sanitation services or job creation programs.

The favelas returned to the Brazilian political imagination in the 1970s amid an increase in drug trafficking. As a port city, Rio is an important export point for narcotics, mainly cocaine en route to Europe. Vying for greater control of the favelas, over the next decades these groups grew out of their previous organizational amateurism and used their new economic power to swap pistols for rifles and machine guns. Economic objectives always served as the primary purpose behind the group's actions and strategies. At the same time, gangs aimed to secure their relationship with the local communities where they operated, including by distributing food and medicines and recruiting residents as informants.

Impoverished residents often found themselves in a complicated relationship with these groups. Drug-trafficking gangs used indiscriminate violence to maintain control, including kidnappings and torture of alleged spies and traitors. At the same time, due to the complete lack of state support, many residents found themselves dependent on the gangs' occasional material aid. In the 1980s, the predominant narrative shifted from the favelas being described as a stateless space to gangs constituting a parallel state. State forces used this logic to paint drug traffickers as enemies to be eliminated in a war for territorial control. Gangs never came close to having the organizational capacity of a state, yet the discourse served to justify increasingly violent police actions. If favelas are filled with exogenous enemies, not citizens, legal guarantees do not apply.

Although the media and government officials widely adopted the parallel state concept, the boundaries between actors have always been porous. Police forces have cut deals with drug dealers regularly, through either kickbacks or illegal arms sales. Local politicians have used gangs' influence and territorial control to guarantee votes by, for example, preventing opponents from campaigning in the area. This kind of exclusive political access instrumentalized armed groups while continuing to neglect the poor communities they controlled, helping pave the way for a new type of armed group to emerge.

Militias, Pacification, and Pandemic

Amid profound public security changes in Rio in the early 2000s, armed groups flexed their governance capacities and their relationships with state agents, and a new kind of criminal group—and accompanying political discourses—emerged. Formed mainly by former police officers and military firefighters, the militias initially justified their presence in favelas as a force to drive out drug traffickers. They quickly became a greater threat. Meanwhile, promising a new strategy to clamp down on crime in the favelas, the government of Rio rolled out pacification practices in 2008 that permanently installed joint army and police forces in poor communities. The tactic was also part of the city's preparations to host two mega events: the 2014 FIFA World Cup and 2016 Summer Olympics (Brancoli, Amar, and Rodrigues 2017). These Pacifying Police Units (UPPs) have been highly criticized for criminalizing poor, Black communities while failing to deliver on crime-reduction promises and disregarding demands for structural responses, like building schools or improving health care infrastructure. Among the UPPs' vocal critics was Rio city council member Marielle Franco, whose 2018 assassination is believed to have been carried out by militia operatives with ties to President Bolsonaro. On her Facebook page just days before her murder, Franco spoke out about Acari, denouncing police violence and the apparent killings of two men, whose deaths media outlet the Intercept later described as "shrouded in mystery" (Demori et al. 2018).

The implementation of UPP was eminently political. The program targeted favelas that tourists frequented and where traditional drug traffickers operated. This was, in part, due to the emergence of the militias. As pacification policies targeted drug traffickers, militias prospered, being accused of crimes like kidnapping, extortion, taxing local commerce, and charging security fees. Even drug trafficking, which the militias initially claimed to oppose, came to feature in their activities. Unlike the traditional gangs, militias also have political objectives, organizing to elect members of Congress and lending support to certain mayors. This experience is directly derived from the drug-trafficking groups' attempts at political control in the 1980s, but with much more sophistication and organization.

This was the backdrop to the COVID-19 outbreak in Rio de Janeiro in March. As the pandemic hit, some community groups organized mutual aid initiatives to support residents in need. In Acari, military police offensives reportedly disrupted these solidarity efforts on at least two occasions. Militias, meanwhile, imposed lockdowns, enforced the use of masks, and dictated when local stores could open and under what circumstances—measures with an underlying interest in collecting illegal fees. They have also reportedly leveraged political connections to attempt to influence health norms and to issue early warnings about possible police operations. Facing an economic crisis for the past five years that's only set to worsen with the pandemic, the government of Rio de Janeiro has shown little political will to change this scenario. The government's police pacification operations target traditional drug-trafficking groups while systematically sparing militias of similar scrutiny. In doing so, state police have tacitly signaled that militias may be important players in implementing isolation measures. There are no public documents indicating why govern-ment organizations chose not to actively confront the militias. However, given the facts presented in this chapter, it is not difficult to assume that this is a logical choice driven by the police forces' direct relationship with these armed organizations. Militias would be favored by government forces in this regard precisely because they embrace the same constellation of interests.

Hybridism, Symbiosis, and Nonbinary Conceptualizations

The literature on criminal governance by nonstate actors is long and had its genesis in scenarios of armed conflict (Crawford 1999). In the Brazilian context, as previously shown, studies began in the 1980s, focusing on the dynamics of public security erosion caused by drug trafficking. A comprehensive review of the literature points out that criminal groups in Brazil are historically ana-lyzed starting from their relationship with the state, with divisions such as insurgent, bandit, symbiotic, predatory, and split (Magaloni, Franco-Vivanco, and Melo 2020). The relational distinction to state institutions is at the cen-ter of governance practices, with *insurgent* at the most antagonistic pole, with recognized actors in a violent relationship marked by confrontation, and *split* pointing out the scenario in which militias and states divide governance in certain scenarios. This becomes a fragile negotiation and attempt at nonaggres-sion. Again, formal institutions are presented as channels emanating from a unified actor, the state, which—being easily identifiable—is usually presented as the solution to governance crises. If security dilemmas are all caused by the absence or the malfunctioning of the state, the crisis resolution would involve merely restructuring it.

Critical perspectives insist that criminal groups and states have close relationships, even using references to symbiotic practices to describe the proximity of criminal groups to more legitimate actors (Rodrigues 2018; Ferreira 2019). Although such reflections are an improvement on previously mentioned work, they still have important ontological limitations. They start from the principle that the distinction between state and criminal groups is easy to make, in addition to being epistemologically important for the understanding of gov-ernance practices in those spaces. In Rio de Janeiro, in the specific case of the militias, journalists, academics, and politicians describe militias as practicing hy-brid governance or contaminating the state. During the pandemic, for example, one of Brazil's largest newspapers, *O Globo*, used this contamination narrative to describe militia governance in the greater Rio municipality of Duque de Cax-ias. Residents claimed that the militias paid bribes to police officers to ensure they would not interfere in their decisions to force local stores to open or close. This framing presents nonstate actors as a hindrance to the proper functioning of institutions while depicting the state as a permanent, rational, and easily defined entity that needs to be cleansed of harmful external components. This argument is similar to contemporary discussions around policing in the United States that identify bad apples in police ranks as the problem while downplaying structural issues. In Brazil, this analysis ignores the complex relationships between the different actors.

Nonbinary governance is intended as an epistemological and conceptual alternative for understanding the dimensions of governance in vulnerable spaces in Rio de Janeiro and other areas in the Global South. The concept tries to cover the constellation of actors who establish connections to govern a vulnerable area. These practices combine the supply of public goods, illegal tax collection, and a strong component of coercion through violence and moral control of the population. The epistemological distinction is that we do not try to reinforce the dividing dimension between state actors and nonstate actors. It is a matter not of affirming that, legally, these actors are not divided into formal categories but of pointing out that this legalistic division clouds and erases essential characteristics and movements. In this sense, beyond trying to carry out a positivist cartography of the involved agents, focus is better placed on the fluid practices of those involved, reinforcing how characteristics such as *legal* and *illegal* circulate in this context.

The formulation of nonbinary governance is the result of reflections provided by the literature and questions of cultural studies in Rio de Janeiro, mainly the dynamics involving crossroads and syncretism. Historically, crossroads have been perceived as spaces where different social and political actors with contradictory subjectivities—such as the corrupt policeman or the thief with a social conscience—meet and interact, especially in popular neighborhoods (Simas and Rufino 2019, 56). This framing helps illuminate the current models of governance involving armed groups, governments, and the police in the Rio de Janeiro story. The crossroads, therefore, is the space par excellence for the deconstruction of binary and consolidated elements, calling for reflections to be based on a portrait of the practices of individuals, with reinforcement of their ambivalent movements and not on an obsession with locating them in fixed concepts.

The crossroads are strongly linked to the dimensions of syncretism in Rio de Janeiro. The concept is used mainly in religious contexts to denote how religions originating on the African continent combine practices, knowledge, and symbols of Christianity. At first, syncretism was understood as capitulation or subterfuge, insofar as such sacred practices were centered on the enslaved Black population, who would try to annex white dynamics as a form of protection. It was seen as a movement of aggregation and sophistication (Verger 1999; Simas and Rufino 2019). Gods come together not as a way of hiding the true nature of the African divine but as a way of gathering entities and their powers. Syncretism, as pointed out by Nei Lopes (2010, 2015), is seen as typical of Rio de Janeiro and the Global South, where nonbinarism becomes an epistemic practice, and the sophistication of the analysis lies in understanding the circulation of different actors through different spaces. Like Abdias do Nascimento (2004), I do not understand syncretism to be the consequence of the consolidation of two prior variables. The syncretism of crossroads, in this situation, demonstrates how ephemeral and socially manufactured the borders and demarcations imposed on these realities are.

Through the use of terms such as *interstitial* and *in-between-ness*, transdisciplinary anthropology and cultural studies have supported research into spaces of liminality and hybridity (Bhabha 2015; Fernandéz y García 2017). Rather than focusing only on the conflict between the Global North and South, Bhabha suggested that we should instead focus on the fault lines themselves, on border situations and thresholds as sites of enactment and contestation of identities.

While I recognize the importance of these novel methods and their political impact, the debate on syncretism and crossroads provided here raises further issues. In this perspective, I consider these concerns as part of a complex epistemic system founded on Indigenous knowledge. The crossroads are portrayed here not as a point of convergence for two sides but as a central node that produces paradoxes and invisibilities while maintaining a regularized system of violence, domination, superprofits, and unaccountability.

I propose in this chapter that these epistemological reflections, traditionally centered on cultural and religious studies in Rio de Janeiro, can be expanded to other areas, such as analyses of public security and global studies. More than rescuing the values of the engaged communities, it is about recognizing the sophistication of these analytical tools and their conceptual possibilities.

Looking at armed groups with a fixed understanding not only denotes a colonial dimension of analysis but also tends to simplistic conclusions that ignore that they were "in fact made up of rogue active and retired police officers in league with evangelical church operations, and which sometimes routed trafficking cartels, sometimes joined forces with the traffickers to establish absolute, extortive control over the areas" (Amar 2013, 193). Crossroads governance offers a more nuanced way to understand criminal governance in Brazil, especially in relation to the responses to the COVID-19 pandemic in Rio. In this network of power and influence, police agents–turned–paramilitary operatives interact with lawmakers, and actors can have fluid roles. In the case of the Duque de Caxias militias that allegedly bribed police officers to turn a blind eye to parastate governance during the pandemic, the former police officers making up the militia acted with the benefit of historical institutional knowledge and connections. Militias operate illegal companies in the region in partnership with active-duty police officers who should be fighting such criminal activities (Simões 2020). Becoming militia agents does not strip officers of their ties to the state; rather, they continue to operate with data, contacts, and even material, such as weapons and vehicles, from their former roles.

The analyses related to criminal governance in the Global South permeate a series of distinct groups: militias in Latin America, warlords in Africa, and fundamentalist groups such as the Islamic State in the Middle East. Despite presenting different local situations, this contribution indicates that certain perspectives are marked by obsessions in classifying such actors, with the state as the central element for this cartography. Grasping how such realities manifest in communities demands eschewing an understanding of the state as a monolithic actor that sometimes has contaminated pieces. Conditioned by networks of different interests, the distinctions between state and nonstate authorities are not always clear. The use of concepts such as nonbinary governance, based on reflections on syncretism and normative fluidity, allows research to gain sophistication by focusing on the practices of agents and not on state formalisms. The presentation of the state as a regulating and problem-solving element is avoided, pushing away conclusions about state reconquering of spaces and state building.

NOTE

A shortened version of this contribution was published in the Essays section of *NACLA Magazine* in September 2020.

REFERENCES

Agier, Michel. 2015. "Do direito à cidade ao fazer-cidade: O antropólogo, a margem e o centro." *Mana* 21: 483–98.

Amar, Paul. 2013. *The Security Archipelago: Human-Security States, Sexuality Politics, and the End of Neoliberalism.* Durham, NC: Duke University Press.

Batista, Amanda, Bianca Antunes, Guilherme Faveret, Igor Peres, Janaina Marchesi, Pedro Cunha, and Leila Dantas. 2020. "Análise socioeconômica da taxa de letalidade da COVID-19 no Brasil." *Núcleo de operações e inteligência em Saúde (NOIS)*, May 27.

Bhabha, Homi. 1994. *The Location of Culture.* New York: Routledge.

Bhabha, Homi. 2015. *Debating Cultural Hybridity: Multicultural Identities and the Politics of Anti-racism*. London: Zed.

Brancoli, Fernando, Paul Amar, and Thiago Rodrigues. 2017. "Global Cities, Global (In) Securities: An Introduction." *Contexto internacional* 39, no. 3: 467–76.

Briso, Caio Barretto, and Tom Phillips. 2020. "Brazil Gangs Impose Strict Curfews to Slow Coronavirus Spread." *Guardian*, March 25. https://www.theguardian.com/world /2020/mar/25/brazil-rio-gangs-coronavirus.

Crawford, Adam. 1999. *The Local Governance of Crime: Appeals to Community and Partnerships*. Oxford: Oxford University Press.

Demori, Leandro, Carolina Moura, Juliana Gonçalves, Yuri Eiras, and Bruna de Lara. 2018. "Who Killed Eduardo, Matheus and Reginaldo?" *Intercept*, March 21. https:// theintercept.com/2018/03/21/marielle-franco-death-brazil-violence-police/.

dos Santos, Gislene Aparecida. 2019. "Estudos pós-coloniais e antirracismo." *Revista gestão e políticas públicas* 9, no. 2: 340–53.

Fanon, Frantz. 1964. "Unity and Effective Solidarity Are Conditions for African Liberation." In *Toward the African Revolution: Political Essays*, translated by Haakon Chevalier. New York: Grove.

Fernández y Garcia, Marta Regina. 2017. "Rethinking Peace-Building Practices through the Somaliland Experience." *Review of African Political Economy* 44, no. 151: 85–103.

Ferreira, Marcos Alan S. V. 2019. "Brazilian Criminal Organizations as Transnational Violent Non-state Actors: A Case Study of the Primeiro Comando da Capital (PCC)." *Trends in Organized Crime* 22, no. 2: 148–65.

Goodale, Mark. 2006. "Toward a Critical Anthropology of Human Rights." *Current Anthropology* 47, no. 3: 485–511.

Hita, Maria Gabriela, and John E. Gledhill. 2010. "Antropologia na análise de situações periféricas urbanas." *Cadernos metrópole* 12, no. 23: 189–209.

Lopes, Nei. 2010. "Religiões afro-brasileiras: Um novo olhar." *Afro-Hispanic Review* 29, no. 2: 197–210.

Lopes, Nei. 2015. "Religiosidade na diáspora: Continuidade e permanência." In *Seminário Internacional Diversas Diversidades*, edited by Rolf Malungo Ribeiro de Souza, 81–108. Rio de Janeiro: Cead/UFF.

Magaloni, Beatriz, Edgar Franco-Vivanco, and Vanessa Melo. 2020. "Killing in the Slums: Social Order, Criminal Governance, and Police Violence in Rio de Janeiro." *American Political Science Review* 114, no. 2: 552–72.

Nascimento, Abdias do. 2004. "Teatro experimental do negro: Trajetória e reflexões." *Estudos avançados* 18: 209–24.

Prandi, Reginaldo. 2001. "Exu, de mensageiro a diabo: Sincretismo católico e demonização do orixá Exu." *Revista Usp*, no. 50: 46–63.

Rodrigues, Thiago. 2018. "Symbiotic Interactions: On the Connection between Drug-Trafficking, the Legal Economy and State Power in Brazil." *KAS International Reports*.

Rufino, Luiz. 2019. *Pedagogia das encruzilhadas*. Rio de Janeiro: Mórula Editorial.

Santos, Boaventura de Sousa. 2004. "Do pós-colonial: E para além de um e outro." Opening lecture at the VIII Congresso Luso-Afro-Brasileiro den Ciências Sociais, Coimbra, Portugal.

Santos, João Vitor, and Patricia Fachin. 2020. "Não há poder paralelo. 'Tanto a milícia quanto o tráfico têm relações diretas com o poder do Estado.' Entrevista especial com José Cláudio Alves." Instituto Humanitas Unisinos. https://www.ihu.unisinos.br/categorias/159-entrevistas/599202-nao-ha-poder-paralelo-tanto-a-milicia-quanto-o-trafico-tem-relacoes-diretas-com-o-poder-do-estado-entrevista-especial-com-jose-claudio-alves.

Scheper-Hughes, Nancy. 1995. "The Primacy of the Ethical: Propositions for a Militant Anthropology." *Current Anthropology* 36, no. 3: 409–40.

Scott, James C. 2008. *Seeing Like a State: How Certain Schemes to Improve the Human Condition Have Failed*. New Haven, CT: Yale University Press.

Simas, Luiz Antonio, and Luiz Rufino. 2019. *Fogo no mato: A ciência encantada das macumbas*. Rio de Janeiro: Mórula Editorial.

Simões, Mariana. 2020. "Milicianos invadem área ambiental e formam máfia da areia no Rio de Janeiro." *Agência pública* (blog), May 26. https://apublica.org/2020/05/milicianos-invadem-area-ambiental-e-formam-mafia-da-areia-no-rio-de-janeiro/.

Sobreira, Gabriel. 2020. "Carro da lapada: Criminosos anunciam toque de recolher em Acari." *O Dia*, April 24. https://odia.ig.com.br/rio-de-janeiro/2020/04/5904264-carro-da-lapada--criminosos-anunciam-toque-de-recolher-em-acari.html.

Spivak, Gayatri C. (1988) 1994. "Can the Subaltern Speak?" In *Colonial Discourse and Postcolonial Theory*, edited by Patrick Williams and Laura Chrisman, 66–111. New York: Columbia University Press.

Valladares, Licia do Prado. 2015. *A invenção da favela: Do mito de origem a favela*. Rio de Janeiro: Editora FGV.

Verger, Pierre. 1999. *Notas sobre o culto aos Orixás e Voduns na Bahia de Todos os Santos, no Brasil, e na Antiga Costa dos Escravos, na África*. São Paulo: Editora da Universidade de São Paulo.

9

Militianization /
Milicianização

Dark Innovation at the State-Crime Frontier

BENJAMIN LESSING

In the early 1980s an innovation in the organizational technology of crime, born in the dungeons of Brazil's military dictatorship, spread beyond the prison walls and transformed Rio de Janeiro. Comando Vermelho (CV) was Brazil's first facção (organized crime or trafficking organization). With these comandos or facções came a sophisticated, prison-based network whose capacity quickly eliminated or subsumed the autonomous donos (bosses) who then ruled over the city's favelas and illicit markets (first street gambling/bookie operations like jogo do bicho, then retail drugs). The CV's initial hegemony—it controlled the vast majority of Rio's favelas by the mid-1980s—soon collapsed into internecine conflicts with rival factions and open confrontations with state forces that continue to this day. But the faction model—splitting up Rio's favela territory among a handful of prison-based groups—proved incredibly resilient. This model has now taken over Brazil, spreading first to São Paulo (with the rise of the Primeiro Comando da Capital or PCC, Sao Paulo's largest organized-crime cartel) and thence to virtually every state in the federation. This chapter focuses on field research I conducted in recently factionalized states (Amazonas, Ceará, Rio Grande do Norte). This in turn has led to new reflections and speculation on Rio's second great criminal innovation: the advent of milícias. These are mafia-like groups that transformed Rio in the early 2000s, conquering large swaths of territory and indelibly marking the city's politics.

In this chapter, I introduce and develop the concept of militianization (milician-ização) and reflect on its implications. At its simplest, militianization denotes the spread of milícias, the second of the two basic forms of criminal organization that operate in and exert territorial control over Rio's favelas. Although milícias rose in opposition to the first form—the powerful, prison-based drug syndicates known as criminal factions (facções criminosas)—the two have many things in common. Both were born in and remain strongly associated with Rio de Janeiro, and, like the factions before them, milícias have brought seemingly irreversible reorderings of both criminal activity and daily life in the favelas under their control. Most importantly, just as occurred with factions, milícias and milícia-like groups have started to appear in other states beyond Rio.

As such, the history of the factions' spread from Rio to every state in Brazil is likely to hold clues to how militianization might proceed. For decades, local officials, experts, and even scholars from other states asserted that factions were "a Rio thing" (coisa do Rio de Janeiro), confidently proclaiming that their own prison systems and favelas were and would remain free of factions. Despite these denials, factionalization proceeded, slowly at first, and picked up speed after 2006. By the time interfaction violence erupted across prisons and peripheries in the north and northeast in 2016, making further denial impossible, Brazil became almost entirely factionalized. Hence the urgency of thinking, writing, and talking about militianization now. It is not enough to simply hope that milícias will remain a Rio thing. At best, scattered hints of milícias beyond Rio may offer clues for halting or at least slowing the process of militianization; at worst, they suggest that the spread of milícias has already begun.

The urgency of exploring militianization conceptually—rather than simply descriptively, journalistically, or even normatively—lies in the concept's slipperiness. Defining the milícias themselves can be a challenge: shadowy armed groups led by rogue and even active-duty police officers whose structure, size, and modi vivendi have constantly shifted over the last two decades. Definitions and typologies matter for the drafting and enforcement of anti-milícia law and jurisprudence. Nonetheless, it is a debate which—if the broader literature on organized crime with its endless profusion of definitions is any guide—will not be settled soon or easily (Varese 2010).

More importantly, militianization as a concept takes us beyond the milícias per se. Like factionalization before it, militianization occurred first in Rio, quietly gestating for years before quickly transforming the city's periphery, and now shows clear signs of replication and adaptation. How does militianization start? Which conditions enable it, and which inhibit it? How does it play out over time? What are its mechanisms of reproduction, and when—if ever—does it die out on its own? How do we know it when we see it? What are its observable implications, and what less visible effects should we be on the lookout for? Above all, what does this process act on? *Militianize*, like *transform*, is a transitive verb that acts upon its object. Part of its value as a concept is in inviting us to think about the direct objects it can affect: how physical territories, communities, economies, political systems, and society itself might become militianized. One must ask what each of these would mean, and how they might be detected, contained, ameliorated, and possibly inoculated against.

The Rise of the Factions

We cannot understand militianization or milícias without considering the rise of the factions, for two reasons. First, the milícias arose as a response, defining and presenting themselves as fundamentally distinct from, opposed to, and better than the factions. Second, the factions not only took over Rio de Janeiro's favelas but ultimately spread to cities throughout Brazil. How did this happen?

In the 1970s, an innovation in the organizational technology of crime occurred within the dungeons of Brazil's military dictatorship. In the early 1980s, it spread beyond the prison walls and transformed Rio de Janeiro. Though initial hegemony gave way to internecine conflict by the 1990s, the underlying faction model—control over the criminal underworld and urban periphery by a handful of prison-based groups—would remain largely unchanged. This faction model—initially seen as unique to Rio—spread to São Paulo with the rise of the PCC in the 1990s and early 2000s, and to the rest of Brazil thereafter, albeit with variations in structure and outcomes.

Rio's (and Brazil's) first faction, CV, was born of the disastrous decision by Brazil's military dictatorship to house political prisoners together with common criminals (Amorim 1993; Lima 1991; Penglase 2008). The CV gleaned techniques of collectivist practice, protest, and organization from the militants, imposing a rough but welcome social order in Rio's chaotic prison system, which it soon consolidated control over. It then expanded outward, coming to dominate some

75 percent of Rio's favela communities by the 1980s, relying on its capacity for collective action and mutual aid to quickly eliminate or subsume the incumbent, autonomous donos (bosses) and illicit markets (first jogo do bicho, then retail drugs).

To be sure, the rise of this astonishingly resilient criminal organization—likely the longest-lived nonstate armed group in Brazil's modern history—is important in its own terms, central to the drama of Rio de Janeiro for almost a half century. But it also heralded a broader, transformational innovation in the organizational technology of crime. Like the disruptive technologies that tech companies dream of developing, the CV's prison-based model of coordinated criminal activity allowed it to sweep away competitors and for a time enjoy near hegemony in Rio. But more importantly, this model could be imitated, improved on, and adapted to local circumstances.

The first replications were in Rio itself, with the consolidation of the Terceiro Comando faction from an assortment of enemies of the CV's founders, and the subsequent rise of Amigos dos Amigos (ADA). By the mid-1990s, Rio's prisons and favelas were effectively divided up among groups and would remain so with only minor changes for decades. At this time, factions were seen as exclusive to Rio, fueling conjectures as to which of Rio's many unique features—steep hills, especially corrupt police, loss of national capital status—was responsible. Scattered reports from prisons in São Paulo and Bahia of home-grown factions, inspired by the CV, were dismissed by officials there as scaremongering and exaggeration. The incipient groups were portrayed as just new configurations of the inmate gangs that had long existed. Nothing like the spectacular prison breaks, confrontations with police, and turf wars seen in Rio had occurred anywhere else. Factionalization seemed to be a one-off.

Then, in 2001, the first mega-rebelião struck São Paulo—synchronized riots in twenty-three prison units across the state—publicly confirming the until-then only rumored existence of the PCC and leaving no doubt that it was more than just another predatory inmate gang. Indeed, the PCC's own founding statute echoed the CV's motto of "Peace, Justice, and Liberty," making clear its debt to the older Rio faction, with which it declared itself in a coalition to "revolutionize the country [from] within its prisons." Several of the PCC founders had spent time in Rio's prison system (the order for the megarebellion was given from Rio's Bangu prison complex) and likely absorbed firsthand the CV's organizational practices, habits, ideologies, structure, and strategies.

Astoundingly, however, the myth of factionalization as a one-off lived on for another half decade. São Paulo's officials launched a crackdown on the PCC, centering around a harsh new maximum-security custodial regime known as

Regime Disciplinar Diferenciado (RDD), which permitted extreme and extended solitary confinement of PCC leaders. By 2002, officials bragged about how the PCC was a failed and dismantled organization. In reality, the PCC was consolidating its power within São Paulo's rapidly expanding prison system at the same time that it was—like the CV before it but in less violent and visible fashion—coming to exert authority over vast tracts of the urban periphery. The results of this process were paradoxical: on the one hand, the PCC launched a second mega-rebelião in 2006, involving not only ninety-six prisons in São Paulo and neighboring states, but also waves of violent attacks on the streets, bringing the largest city in South America to a standstill for days. On the other, the PCC was laying down its lei do crime (law of crime), prohibiting unauthorized killings throughout its sphere of influence, contributing to a massive and sustained drop in homicides that continues to this day, making São Paulo the least violent state capital in Brazil (Biderman et al. 2019; Willis 2015; Feltran 2010).

From a conceptual point of view, the PCC did not merely extend the faction model to another city—it vastly expanded the idea of what a faction is, how it might grow, and ultimately what factionalization might look like. Internally, the PCC developed a unified, decentralized, and flattened-hierarchical structure, de-emphasizing personal power in favor of consensus. At the same time, its institutionalized job posts, replicable management structures, and staggering bureaucratic capacity allowed it to expand quickly, eventually encompassing branches throughout Brazil (Lessing and Willis 2019; Paes Manso and Dias 2018).

The process in Rio and São Paulo produced two almost polar-opposite realities in terms of factionalization: in the former, seemingly endless conflict, not only among factions but between the CV and the state; in São Paulo, a remarkable pax monopolista (Biderman et al. 2019) led by a single, hegemonic faction. Today, most of Brazil's other states fall between these two extremes, with multiple factions dividing up favela territory and maintaining a tense standoffishness that reaches neither Rio's levels of violence nor São Paulo's stable peace.

The Rise of the Milícias

Ironically, while the faction model born in Rio a generation earlier was consolidating in São Paulo and taking over the rest of the country, in Rio itself a new technology of criminal organization was gestating. Like the factions, milícias did not arise ex nihilo, but rather grew out of older traditions, while introducing important innovations that contributed to their transformational power. Whereas the factions built on long-standing inmate codes of behavior, milícias built on traditional police-linked vigilante death squads known as esquadrões de morte and grupos de extermínio. These groups performed social cleansing of indigent, homeless, and otherwise marginalized populations in working- and middle-class neighborhoods, sometimes selling their services to local small businesses. But the more direct progenitor of the milícias is the so-called polícia mineira of the Rio das Pedras favela in the sparsely populated Zona Oeste (Western Zone) of Rio de Janeiro. There, at some point in the 1980s, as the CV was beginning its rapid takeover of the city's favelas, a group of resident police officers—apparently at the behest of local businessmen—banded together to expel the drug trade from the community. For the next twenty years, their rule was seen as a rare and largely positive exception to the drug traffickers' dominance of Rio's favelas (Burgos 2002).

An early sign that the Rio das Pedras model was replicable came in the early 1990s, when Campo Grande (another Zona Oeste region) fell under the control of similar police-linked groups. In some sense, it was this early replication that created the idea of milícias as a type. To this day, there is still debate about how to define milícias, but a few key characteristics stand out. First, these groups wield the same kind of community-level armed authority, based on a local monopoly on violence, as do factions.[1] However, milícias are, almost by definition, not tráfico (drug trafficking); indeed, keeping out tráfico has been the milicias' primary raison d'être. That said, in Rio, *tráfico* is more of a synonym for the factions and their members (who do traffic drugs) than a description of drug trafficking per se. Thus, while it is quite possible to observe drug consumption, possession, and even trafficking in milícia-controlled neighborhoods, conceptually, rule by milícia remains a stark alternative to rule by factions. A third common feature follows: presumably in lieu of drug profits, milícias rely on protection fees and taxes paid by residents, often on informal or semilicit but widely used goods and services like cooking gas, pirated cable TV and internet, and unlicensed public transportation. Putting these pieces together, the basic logic of the milícias comes into focus as an alternative technology of criminal governance.

In this model, corrupt police, rather than extracting surplus profits from the local factions' retail drug business, instead directly administer and tax the local civilian population by amassing sufficient armed force to permanently wrest control from the traffickers. The genius of this innovation is captured in a now-famous scene of the film *Tropa de elite 2*, as an epiphany befalling the corrupt police officer Rocha as he goes to collect the weekly arrego (bribe) from the local faction (Padilha 2010). When the traffickers reveal that drug profits are virtually nil, and so they have been taxing residents' use of pirated internet (gatonet) to survive, Rocha realizes he can eliminate the middleman and make a fortune. This fortune, in turn, can fund soldiers, and hence secure new territories and tax bases.

If taxing civilians is so lucrative, why don't factions do it? For traffickers, taxing civilians is a dangerous game: they rely on the complicity of residents to minimize their exposure to police. Residents' willingness to pay factions for protection may also be low because whatever protection factions can offer against low-level street crime, they not only cannot prevent but ultimately attract militarized police incursions and shootouts. For these reasons, factions tend to offer quotidian governance to residents for free, a loss leader if you will, in order to maximize drug profits. These profits, in turn, are the basic revenue supporting the governance activities of factions. Milícias, in contrast, can charge more for governance, enough that they can and—supposedly—do forgo the profits of the drug trade. They can charge more because they provide a form of protection that the factions cannot: protection from the police. Militarized police incursions occur with far greater frequency in favelas belonging to factions than to milícias.

Milícias initially drew little attention even as, in the late 1990s and early 2000s, milícia leaders began to seek and sometimes win electoral and political power. Then, between 2003 and 2006, milícias rapidly expanded both within the Zona Oeste and into areas of the city and greater metropolitan region with no tradition of such groups. The revelation in 2006 that some ninety-two favelas in Rio had been taken over by milícias laid bare the most significant reconfiguration of power in these communities since the rise of the CV. Milícia leaders replicated the legitimizing discourse of the factions, crafting a positive public image of a Comando Azul to oppose the Comando Vermelho. Composed of active-duty, reserve, and retired police officers—as well as firemen and military officers—milícias supposedly liberated and protected communities from tyrannical drug traffickers (Cano and Iooty 2008). In classic paramilitary fashion, milícias thus presented themselves as righteous vigilantes, protecting allegedly vulnerable and thankful citizens. Indeed, Rio's then-mayor César Maia publicly termed them ADCs, or Community Auto-defense forces reminiscent of Colombia's AUC (Autodefensas Unidas de Colombia). For milícia supporters, the state's apparent inability to permanently retake favela territory from the factions made the milícias—with their strong links to police and their respect for law and order—a viable second-best solution, or as Mayor Maia put it, "a far lesser problem" (Bottari and Ramalho 2007).

The election to Rio's state legislature and municipal city council (Câmara de Vereadores) of actual milícia members like Nadinho, Jerominho, and Coronel Jairo drew concern from some quarters but also insulated milícias from prosecution. Repeated efforts in 2007 and 2008 to convoke a congressional investigatory commission (Comissão Parlamentar de Inquérito, CPI) were sys-tematically blocked by milícia-allied legislators. The heyday of milícia public relations success came to an end only in May 2008, when a team of reporters from the *O Dia* newspaper were captured and tortured by a milícia linked to state legislator Coronel Jairo. The horrific details and ensuing media firestorm abruptly shifted public and political opinion from acceptance to skepticism and alarm. This in turn allowed the CPI investigation to move forward. The CPI resulted in expulsions of milícia members from the legislature and some arrests, while providing the first systematic assessment of milícias' territorial control and illicit activity.

Since then, milícias have learned to keep a low public profile, "no sapatinho" (discreetly) in the words of residents living under their rule in the post-CPI pe-riod (Cano and Duarte 2012). Nonetheless, militianization proceeded apace. By 2014, milícias dominated 148 favelas in twenty-eight of Rio's neighborhoods. Per-haps even more ominously, milícias spread to another twenty-three of Rio state's ninety municipalities. Tellingly, Rio's famed pacification or Unidade de Polícia Pacificadora (UPP) strategy—in which the state reoccupied hundreds of favelas with specially trained community police battalions, leading to a 66 percent re-duction in armed confrontations—almost totally ignored the milícias.[2]

Territorial Expansion and Militianization

We are now in a better position to think about militianization as a process or set of processes. A few key points jump out. Since milícias depend on territory even more than factions, one fundamental dimension of militianization is territorial expansion. Yet unlike the factions, milícias have deep and friendly ties to the police and other forces. Thus, militianization also occurs, perforce, within the state's coercive apparatus. Finally, given milícias' heavy involvement in electoral politics—far more thorough than the factions—militianization must also be understood as occurring within the political realm.

The period of rapid milícia expansion (2002–8) is illustrative, if only because militianization occurred, along all dimensions, in a relatively overt fashion. There was a large and rapid increase in milícia territory, apparently conquered through brute force. In practice, such conquests occurred as a fait accompli in the wake of massive police interventions that weakened the incum-bent faction—a clear-cut form of militianization of the state's coercive force. Above all, this period constitutes a high-water mark for the militianization of politics: visible, effective, and enjoying relative public legitimacy. Elections were militianized in ways that were shockingly transparent: milícia leaders openly ran for and won office, obtaining vote shares in the communities they controlled that were high enough to make an autocratic dictator envious (Bottari and Ramalho 2007; Hidalgo and Lessing 2011). The resulting existence of a milícia bloc in the state legislature was at best an open secret. The bloc was effective in channeling state resources to sympathetic officials and preventing state scrutiny of milícia power and activities even as their territory expanded (Cano and Iooty 2008; Cano and Duarte 2012; Hidalgo and Lessing 2011), as repeated scuttling of the CPI exemplified. All of this occurred in a context in which milícias were widely seen and often publicly characterized as the lesser of two evils.

In the wake of that CPI and the reversal of public opinion that sparked it, militianization too has begun to occur no sapatinho. Milícias continued to expand, but generally avoided outright military confrontation.[3] Militianization may also be taking on new direct objects. In Rio's Zona Oeste, the Silicon Valley of milícia technology, a new configuration has taken hold in which milícias essentially rent out their drug markets to local branches of the Terceiro Comando Puro, which appears far more willing to work with milícias than the CV. At a minimum, this suggests that the arrego—a payment factions make to corrupt police in order to operate freely—has become militianized. But reports of new organizational forms, narco-milícias, often populated by soldiers recruited from the factions (sometimes at gunpoint), suggests that the factions themselves may become militianized.

It is tempting to say that the militianization of politics now takes place mostly under the surface. Certainly, milicianos have learned to cultivate long-term relationships with friendly and trusted candidates rather than run for office themselves. But the idea that the militianization of politics has abated is belied by the rise of Jair Bolsonaro. In the most obvious sense, Bolsonaro has militianized politics simply through the multiple (possibly criminal) linkages he and his family have with actual milicianos.[4] The militianization of politics in Brazil goes beyond specific milícias. It is an entire mode of politics, and whatever its less tangible reworking of discourses and the contours of power, it also heralds concrete and immediate effects on state and society. The potential for a militianization of the police at national scale is quite real: witness the recent efforts by the Bolsonaro government to isolate and possibly expunge police forces of antifascist (i.e., critical of his government) elements. As for society, one key tenet of bolsonarismo is the glorification of a kind of armed vigilantism by all good citizens. Both forms of militianization jibe with the milícias' public-facing, trafficker-fighting pretext but have far deeper and more harrowing implications.

Factionalization, Militianization, and State (Non)Formation

We should look to factionalization for clues about the forms that militianization may take and the mechanisms through which it may operate. But factionalization itself may also be an important contributor to or even trigger of militianization. Just as it is impossible to imagine factions rising in the absence of an abusive and expanding incarceration system (which they were a direct response to), it is hard to imagine milícias without factions (at least as a potential threat). There were factions before milícias, but it is hard to imagine milícias without factions. Part of what makes something a milícia, after all, is its difference from, opposition to, and purported preferability to the factions.

Recent scholarship on the PCC (Dias 2009; Feltran 2018), and on prison gangs in general (Lessing 2010, 2017; Skarbek 2011), finds that mass incarceration not only instigated the rise of factions but actively fosters its growth both within and beyond the prison walls. In parallel fashion, the factionalization of Brazil may not just be laying the groundwork for the rise of milícias beyond Rio, but materially facilitating their expansion and consolidation. Here are some possibilities for how this might happen:

1   Factions organize retail drug markets and the criminal underworld more broadly. In contexts of corrupt police, this can streamline and centralize arrego processes and possibly make lucrative the kinds of agglutination of corrupt police actors into something approaching milícia cadres.
2   Factionalization normalizes the idea of the periphery divided up into territories held by nonstate actors—this is part of why the lesser evil argument makes sense.
3   Factionalization contributes to public security crises, including the kinds of orchestrated bus burnings and attacks on public infrastructure once unique to Rio, perfected by the PCC in São Paulo, and now occurring throughout Brazil (Penglase 2005; Adorno and Dias 2016; Lessing 2020). These crises open up space for milícias to effectively present themselves as the lesser evil.
4   These crises also lead to potential increases in spending on police armament and technology, some of which nascent milícias—that is, corrupt elements within the police—may be able to appropriate for their own ends.

These potential mechanisms, especially the last, point to a final lesson we can adapt from the study of factions (narco organized crime) and milícias, concerning the role of the state. All too often, analysis stops at the aphorism that organized crime flourishes where the state is weak or absent. This conventional wisdom obviously contains some truth: we do not see powerful mafia organizations reaching out from Scandinavia to conquer the world. Many attribute the relative success with which the United States has fought organized crime over the last half century compared with, say, Italy, at least partially to more robust state capacity (Reuter 1995). Yet the most powerful criminal groups often arise in places where the state is relatively strong (witness the PCC in São Paulo). And often it is the very actions taken by states—including, but not limited to, militarization of the police and mass incarceration—that provide the raw materials for criminal organizations' growth. At a minimum, states and criminal groups can grow symbiotically (Willis 2009; Lessing 2020), if not through active cooperation.

From this perspective, the rise of milícias may be less a story of state absence than a pathology of state formation. Milícias co-opt police forces and can make use of broader state resources, draw power from elections and their spoils, and, if this analysis is correct, depend at least partially on the existence of factions, which are themselves emboldened by counterproductive punishment in the form of mass incarceration. Since brute, hardline repression has so abjectly failed to contain the factions—indeed, has almost certainly helped them consolidate and propagate—our operating assumption should be that it will have similarly empowering effects on militianization.

NOTES

1 In this, both types draw on an even older tradition in Rio of donos do morro, local nonstate leaders with clear authority over favela communities. That said, the factions and the milícias after them brought a significant increase in the level of armed force.

2 Pacification was a new model of policing deployed to clean out the trafficking factions from favelas and marginalized communities in the years leading up to the 2016 Olympic Games in Rio. The only milícia-dominated favela to be pacified was Jardim Batam, which police occupied in the wake of the *O Dia* episode.

3 A major exception to that rule is the very violent war between milícias and the CV for Praça Seca that has convulsed the far Zona Oeste from 2020 to 2022.

4 Lest we forget, on the day of the assassination of Rio City councilwoman Marielle Franco, her killers met and left for the scene of the crime from the condominium where Bolsonaro's home is located.

REFERENCES

Adorno, Sérgio, and Camila Nunes Dias. 2016. "Cronologia dos 'Ataques de 2006' e a nova configuração de poder nas prisões na última década." *Revista brasileira de segurança pública* 10, no 2: 118–32.

Amorim, Carlos. 1993. *Comando Vermelho: A história secreta do crime organizado*. Rio de Janeiro: Record.

Biderman, Ciro, João M. P. de Mello, Renato S. de Lima, and Alexandre Schneider. 2019. "Pax Monopolista and Crime: The Case of the Emergence of the Primeiro Comando da Capital in São Paulo." *Journal of Quantitative Criminology* 35: 573–605.

Bottari, Elenilce, and Sérgio Ramalho. 2007. "A força eleitoral das milícias." *O Globo*, February 11.

Burgos, Marcelo B. 2002. *A utopia da comunidade: Rio das Pedras, uma favela Carioca*. Rio de Janeiro: Editora PUC-Rio and Edições Loyola.

Cano, Ignacio, and Thais Duarte. 2012. *No sapatinho: A evolução das milícias no Rio de Janeiro (2008–2011)*. Rio de Janeiro: Fundação Heinrich Boll/LAV.

Cano, Ignacio, and Carolina Iooty. 2008. "Seis por meia dúzia? Um estudo exploratório do fenômeno das chamadas milícias no Rio de Janeiro." In *Segurança, tráfico, e milícias no Rio de Janeiro*, edited by Justiça Global, 48–103. Rio de Janeiro: Fundação Heinrich Boll.

Dias, Camila Caldeira Nunes. 2009. "Efeitos simbólicos e práticos do regime disciplinar diferenciado (RDD) na dinâmica prisional." *Revista brasileira de segurança pública* 3, no. 5: 128–44. https://edisciplinas.usp.br/pluginfile.php/1724570/mod_resource/content/0/Efeitos%20simb%C3%B3licos%20e%20pr%C3%A1ticos%20do%20%20Regime%20Disciplinar%20Diferenciado%20%20%28RDD%29%20na%20din%C3%A2mica%20prisional%20%20-CAMILA%20DIAS.pdf.

Feltran, Gabriel. 2010. "Crime e castigo na cidade: Os repertórios da justiça e a questão do homicídio nas periferias de São Paulo." *Caderno CRH* 23, no. 58: 59–73.

Feltran, Gabriel. 2018. *Irmãos: Uma história do PCC*. São Paulo: Companhia das Letras.

Hidalgo, F. Daniel, and Benjamin Lessing. 2014. "Endogenous State Weakness: Paramilitaries and Electoral Politics." Paper presented at NBER Summer Institute, July. https://scholar.google.com/citations?view_op=view_citation&hl=en&user=mrP5bi8AAAAJ&citation_for_view=mrP5bi8AAAAJ:YsMSGLbcyi4C.

Lessing, Benjamin. 2010. "The Danger of Dungeons: Prison Gangs and Incarcerated Militant Groups." In *Small Arms Survey 2010: Gangs, Groups, and Guns*. Geneva: Small Arms Survey. https://www.smallarmssurvey.org/resource/small-arms-survey-2010-gangs-groups-and-guns.

Lessing, Benjamin. 2017. "Counterproductive Punishment: How Prison Gangs Undermine State Authority." *Rationality and Society* 29, no. 3: 257–97.

Lessing, Benjamin. 2020. "Conceptualizing Criminal Governance." *Perspectives on Politics* 19, no. 3: 1–20.

Lessing, Benjamin, and Graham Denyer Willis. 2019. "Legitimacy in Criminal Governance: Managing a Drug Empire from Behind Bars." *American Political Science Review* 113, no. 2: 584–606.

Lima, William da Silva. 1991. *Quatrocentos contra um: Uma história do Comando Vermelho*. Rio de Janeiro: ISER.

Padilha, José, dir. 2010. *Tropa de elite 2*. Brazil: Zazen Produções.

Paes Manso, Bruno, and Camila Nunes Dias. 2018. *A Guerra*. São Paulo: Todavia.

Penglase, Ben. 2005. "The Shutdown of Rio de Janeiro: The Poetics of Drug Trafficker Violence." *Anthropology Today* 21, no. 5: 3–6.

Penglase, Ben. 2008. "The Bastard Child of the Dictatorship." *Luso-Brazilian Review* 45, no. 1: 118–45.

Reuter, Peter. 1995. "The Decline of the American Mafia." *Public Interest* 120 (Summer): 89.

Skarbek, David. 2011. "Governance and Prison Gangs." *American Political Science Review* 105, no. 4: 702–16.

Varese, Federico. 2010. "What Is Organized Crime?" In *Organized Crime: Critical Concepts in Criminology*, edited by Federico Varese, 1–35. New York: Routledge.

Willis, Graham Denyer. 2009. "Deadly Symbiosis? The PCC, the State, and the Institutionalization of Violence in São Paulo, Brazil." In *Youth Violence in Latin America*, edited by Gareth A. Jones and Dennis Rodgers, 167–81. New York: Palgrave Macmillan.

Willis, Graham Denyer. 2015. *The Killing Consensus*. Berkeley: University of California Press.

Part II
Space

10

Elactivism / Vereativismo

Merging Contradictory Antistate Social Leadership Roles and Elected Councilwoman Positions

MONICA CUNHA AND LEONARD CORTANA

In many countries, years of democratic processes have created a basis for civil society and human rights defenders to call out abuses of process by the state. With the succession of conservative parties coming into power all over the world, on both local and national levels, many social leaders have made the step to enter electoral politics after years of spurning elections to focus on grassroots organizing. In Brazil and more particularly in Rio de Janeiro, a resurgence of right-wing and illiberal populism seeks to empower police forces in favelas, ban critical race theory in school curricula, and restrict LGBTQIA+ rights. In response, community organizers have set in motion a paradigm shift, moving to take over elected offices and assume roles as agents of the state to embed their local activist practices in public policies and new logics of governance that promote racial and social equality.

Here, we focus on the mobilizations of Black mothers (and allies) of victims of police killings. These mothers have been among the most prominent figures to make this switch from grassroots organizer to elected municipal representative or state official. Carioca scholars have specifically highlighted the work of a group of mothers, their discursive strategies, and the larger movement of activists and political subjects in the favela. This movement, which features street protests, gives mothers a loudspeaker to reinscribe their sons' personal stories. Narratives produced in those moments are not only stories of resistance but, crucially, acts of reexistence. Their political role goes far beyond fighting for the justice of their sons. They reinscribe new values into favela communities and fight against the categories created through being Black or favelado (de Araujo, Biar, and Bastos 2020).

The concept of elactivism/vereativista encapsulates a political praxis. *Elactivism* means more than just the election of an activist. The term signals the persistence of an act of reexistence; that is, when members of mobilized community activist groups redeploy their grassroots experience as a campaign for elected office, all while keeping strong ties with their communities. We insist on avoiding words such as *rupture* or *transition* when describing the passage from community mobilization to institutional politics. Vereativismo, a term we coin in Portuguese, represents this merging of roles of vereadora (elected municipal council officials), and ativismo (activism). And in recent years some of the vereativistas, or elactivists, have carried their mission all the way to the federal congress.

After the 2016 impeachment of progressive president Dilma Rousseff, Brazil's first female head of state, Marielle Franco wrote about her peculiar place in politics in an essay about her election to Rio's municipal council. She stated, "The historic election, with 46,000 votes, of a Black feminist councilwoman from the favela, who assumes a left-wing political agenda, appears to be a contradiction in this period of the coup. Therefore, we should reflect on the importance of occupying state spaces of power through elections and even in the fight against authoritarian meritocracy, bringing more diversity to alter the male and white presence of these environments" (Franco 2017, 121). In her words, the task of the new generation of political leaders that vereativistas embody so eloquently will be to transform this contradiction into a corroboration, reaching political leaders, the media, and, maybe most importantly, those from communities that the vereativistas have worked with over the years.

Monica Cunha (coauthor of this chapter) won a historic election and became one of the first woman activists from the social movement of mothers of youth killed by state violence. For this among many other reasons, we engaged in elactivism-vereativismo to highlight her political experience and fight against the many alleged assumptions attached to elected activists. Vereativistas do not abandon their communities but rather bring the people they represent to formal political institutions, inviting them to attend the council's public working sessions and to share much-ignored life stories of those living in favelas.

Vereativistas also reveal the uncomfortable power dynamics that many would rather sweep under the rug—for instance, showing the complicity of people from the Zona Sul (South Zone) in normalizing the poor conditions and inequality experienced by favela dwellers. Of course, the vereativista will not automatically be trusted when they assume their official role in government. They have to gain the trust of their communities—which are not used to seeing these figures in elite institutions, partly due to racist, sexist, and classicist assumptions—on- and offline. By sharing our personal experiences and expertise as an activist and city councillor (Monica Cunha) and a scholar-filmmaker researching activism in Rio de Janeiro (Leonard Cortana), we aim to show that what we call modernity in politics is much more than increasing diversity in institutional spaces but instead shaping a new way of making politics in the collective imaginary.

IN THE ELECTIONS OF October 2, 2022, I (Monica) won a seat in the municipal council of Rio de Janeiro after twenty-two years of working as an organizer at the street level and supporting social movements. This Movimento Moleque, which I founded, brings together mothers whose children were threatened, attacked, or killed by the police and began in 2006 when I witnessed my son Rafael's poor treatment in the Rio de Janeiro Department of General Socio-educational Action (DEGASE), an institution hosting teenagers charged with minor crimes, where he was detained after a robbery.[1] Upon being released from DEGASE, he was killed by police officers.

My experience and the emotional strength I carry from the experience of losing a son to state violence guides me to fight for social justice and is part of my agenda. The anthropologist Juressa Freire, in her ethnographic research on Black mothers' social movements in the Baixada Fluminense, describes how emotions became a resource for them to generate solidarity, which sensitizes the other and engages the group of mothers in a shared narrative (Freire 2011). As a leader of the movement, I have worked to transform grieving into contestation. It is commonly said that showing emotions and developing empathy in traditional politics can be interpreted as weakness. But as a vereadora, I allow empathy—for the people I represent—to be my guide.

In 2020, at the peak of the COVID-19 pandemic, I started my campaign. I contacted all the people I collaborated with as social leader. I discussed this via video chat with several nodes of organizing across Rio de Janeiro among groups of Black youth, mothers, families, social workers, artists, and community leaders.[2] I listened carefully to their ideas, hopes, and expectations. Many offered their support and deployed communication strategies or raised funds for my campaign. We had a small budget, but we entered the race. As a vereativista, I knew that if I wanted to gain the trust of my community, I should involve them from the very first day of my campaign in every step of the electoral process.

I chose the slogan "Vamos chegar de bonde" (a very Carioca expression that literally means "We will all arrive together in the same streetcar" but roughly translates as "We must all progress together") for my campaign for Rio City Council. Funkeiro musical performers of the Rio de Janeiro–originated musical style of funk (distinct from the US genre of the same name) use this expression, "Vamos chegar de bonde," when they prepare to come together for the party. It is an expression close to us and has already transformed our presence in the campaign into a celebration. *Bonde* also refers to the importance of increasing the presence of Black women on the council. Think of Marielle Franco. She was the only Black woman in the Congress at the time of her election. When they executed her, we did not have anyone to keep up the fight. A Black woman alone on the City Council has her voice undermined, but with many other Black voices in general and Black women's voices in particular, they cannot overthrow us. Angela Davis, in a lecture in Salvador de Bahia, said, "When a Black woman moves, the whole structure of society moves with her."[3] It has become my mantra. Whenever I discuss a text and propose a law, Black women in the forefront will observe how to conduct politics and support me.

The mission of a vereativista is broader than bringing people into space, showing people from the favela that a woman from a community organizing tradition—with whom they can exchange a beer after a soccer game—is also fit for the role of councilwoman. In Rio de Janeiro, the voting landscape is changing. In 2022, Renata Souza, also from the same party, PSOL,[4] was the third highest vote getter in the Rio de Janeiro state elections. She gained many votes in the Favela da Mare, where she grew up with her family. Dani Monteiro was elected in 2018 with 27,000 votes. In 2022, she doubled her score with 50,000 votes after running a brilliant campaign empowering Black youth and giving more positive visibility to hip-hop. This marks a real achievement for all the work on the ground that we have done with other community organizers to fight against favela dwellers' internalized racism. Before this, many community members, including Black women themselves, did not feel confident in voting for these community-based candidates, fearing that they will not be able to achieve as much in office as the traditional political elites.

Bringing the south and north sides of Rio together (the wealthier, whiter South Zone and the more working-class, Black, and mixed-race North) must be informed by racial equity. For instance, our movement has created the café das fortes, a moment of dialogue where mothers discuss themes and focus on implementing antiracist initiatives. We City Council members should reproduce these accessible spaces of encounter and dialogue whenever and wherever possible. Similarly, we have implemented these forms of dialogue and community engagement in schools in Favela da Maré that integrated this mix of emancipatory pedagogy, political accountability, and public engagement in the curriculum. These vereativismo paradigms function to turn the government's image of the favela inside out—as only a place where people die and have no voice. I have collaborated with Dani Montero, elected state councillor, and Henrique Vieira on the federal level to ensure that popular views, via these vereativismo dynamics, are heard and appreciated by leaders in formal political institutions. Assassinated Rio city councilwoman and Black lesbian favela leader Marielle Franco's fight significantly influenced my choice to run for elected office, but I do not consider myself a mere semente (seed or sprout stemming from Marielle's legacy).[5]

As a vereativista/elactivist, I must keep spreading influence inside and outside the country's borders. I have traveled to Europe and the United States to meet other human rights defenders and connect with Black leaders in Latin America and the United States. Global practices can foster relationships among Black scholars and leaders from other parts of the world, allowing them to discuss and learn from people of the favela. Those who have entered traditional politics may leverage their ability to organize such events more quickly and push their message into the digital world. Rio de Janeiro may offer the world engagement paradigms for organizing and public policy innovations.

I (LEONARD CORTANA) MET Monica Cunha in February 2019 when I shot my documentary *Marielle's Legacy Will Not Die* (Cortana 2019),[6] which examines the memorialization of assassinated councilwoman Marielle Franco in Rio de Janeiro. This film is based on my dissertation, which draws on case studies of assassinated antiracist and feminist activists from South Africa, Colombia, France, and the United States. I dove into archives, read cases of torture, and even got access to many autopsy reports. I became desensitized to violent crimes, especially gun violence and mass shootings. The only time I broke through this desensitization during my four years of fieldwork happened when I heard Monica's speech at the release of Marielle Franco's master's thesis. I was moved by Monica's descriptions of the conditions of favela dwellers and their resistance, and by admiration of such a powerful movement leader's voice.

From Colombia to Brazil, the United States, and France, I observed the same racist and xenophobic reactions from political elites who felt threatened by the presence of leaders who were not afraid to speak truth to power. In Colombia, even some more progressive media fell into the trap of biased assumptions, asking the same type of questions to the vice-president-to-be, Francia Márquez: "As a Black woman, how do you feel about the treatment of the Black population?" "How will your previous experience as a housekeeper influence public policies on domestic work?" "How do you react to all the caricatures published on Twitter of you as King Kong?" They chose to prioritize such questions of (mis)representation and the domestic sphere rather than questioning Marquez about her political and environmental vision for society or policy prescriptions, despite her decades as a movement leader and her having won the prestigious Goldman Environmental Prize.

This misrepresentation of the political paradigms and engagement strategies of Black women activists in Brazil is common practice among the political elite, who depict traditions and paradigms of grassroots organizers as incompatible with the skills and duties of an elected officeholder. But these elected activists argue that, far from being a contradiction, the merging of grassroots organizing skills and electoral official duties embodies modernity in politics and continuity in practices and values. These figures combine personal experience and expertise while representing the population's interests. They adapt grassroots practices to an institutional praxis that is often very far away from the reality of the ground.

Afro-Brazilian and Indigenous artists have strategies to counter any attempts to undermine the legitimacy and dignity of newcomers to electoral politics. Isabel Cristina Ramírez Botero (2022) demonstrated this in her analysis of street murals and political flyers, as a strategy of visibility of political forces historically marginalized in Colombian politics. These visual markers were reused both domestically and internationally to spread the broader vision of Francia Márquez's political agenda when she ran for vice president of Colombia.

The visual elements of Monica Cunha's campaign for Rio de Janeiro City Council in 2022 followed a similar strategy. Many of her posters included images of favelas to link her political identity to those communities. Other images and campaign videos portrayed her collaboration with institutions like universities, City Council working groups, and prominent figures of Brazilian politics like President Lula and governor candidate Marcelo Freixo.

To a certain extent, *vereativista* speaks to Jennifer Nash's (2021) recent work *Birthing Black Mothers*. She argues that the US liberal left tends to participate "in the crisis frame [that] has transformed Black mothers into a distinct form of Left political currency during the era of Black Lives Matter (BLM)" (4). We can see similar strategies in Rio de Janeiro, where the leftist politics of Black motherhood tend to capitalize on tragic representation instead of highlighting the favela as a source of intellectual production and street occupations. Among many other examples, Tereza Campello, former minister of Social Development and the Fight against Hunger from 2011 to 2016 during the government of President Dilma Rousseff, capitalized upon the vulnerability of Black women as a metaphor for the disastrous economic management of the country during Temer's and Bolsonaro's governments. The famous quote from Maria Carolina de Jesus (2014, 5)—"who has gone hungry and learns to think of the future and the children"—is an excellent reference to reposition the Black mother's narrative. Vereativismo is a chance to fight this constant epistemicide. Cunha's speeches reassign Black motherhood as political praxis.

Vereativismo also fights against the prejudice that comes simultaneously from the urban social periphery and the heights of Congress in the federal capital—an assumption that people emerging from grassroots activism leave their communities behind. Part of the work of the vereativista is to build continuous and durable bridges with local communities and remind them that they also may belong in the formal political arena. Monica Cunha, for example, worked to delegate and train new mothers for specific tasks when she traveled and attended meetings. When she spoke at a panel at San Diego State University, I saw her organizing logistics to support a mother who had just lost her son to police violence, keeping her company on the first night.

Black feminist philosopher Djamila Ribeiro (2017) extensively reflects on these dynamics in her landmark essay *O que é lugar de fala?*, where she theorizes the importance of a new praxis of political representation in Brazil—a praxis where people analyze their positionality while representing others. With a Black youth being assassinated every twenty-three minutes by the police and the health challenges highlighted by the federal government's disastrous management of the 2020 COVID-19 pandemic, Cunha starts her mandate with full awareness of her lugar de fala (presence). After decades of activism, she has shaped a proper discourse with other mothers to answer the criminalizing stigma of being a mae de bandido (a narco-criminal/bandit's mother). Their presence in the space—not as Black women from the favelas but as Black mothers who have built a political identity that delegitimizes the killings of their sons—will also pressure City Council members who are used to speaking for them and portraying these women without their presence in the room or speaking in their own voice.

After the global wave of protests following the 2020 murder of George Floyd, racial justice advocates expressed their concerns that favoring illusory, nonthreatening diversity and inclusion policies functions largely as performative allyship rather than substantive change. From a transnational perspective, vereativistas have the power to challenge the normalization of neoliberal diversity and inclusion practices that bring faces of diversity into landscapes where they have not usually been seen toward frameworks of reparation. A practical example in the context of Rio de Janeiro is the politics of affirmative action. Historically marginalized groups enter the university with grants and privileged access, thanks to public policy innovations pushed by activists and implemented in early 2000 by the Lula government. If the policies showed that many political leaders benefited from the affirmative action policy, their presence in the university should not be the only end goal. After almost two decades of affirmative action in Brazil, the discourse of meritocracy continues to undermine the legacy of slavery and the persistence of systemic racism against Black students entering the university (Coelho et al. 2019).

Cunha, along with Black student unions, insisted on the urgency to diversify the national curriculum, including in it the celebration of Black resistance figures and a history of slavery and postslavery that goes beyond white redemption. One may highlight, for example, the role of enslaved Black people as engineers during slavery, as does the Museu Afro in São Paolo.[7] Or perhaps it will feature figures like Dandara—female leader of Palmares, the massive maroon republic of self-emancipated slaves in Brazil in the 1600s—on the cover of history books. Such an action would follow the lead of the massive samba group Mangueira, who featured Dandara and other Black and Indigenous historical leaders in their award-winning 2019 Rio Carnival performance.[8] It is in this context that Monica Cunha's goal is most relevant—to challenge pat-on-the-back diversity policies and introduce a reparation framework through grassroots and formal political avenues.

Elactivista/vereativista recenters debates about political representation and democratic processes. The coining of this term in English and Portuguese is justified by the need to underline the continuity of paradigms of activism, as organizers transition into electoral office and official institutional roles within the state. Vereativismo opens up the possibility of collaboration between the city and the state. Far from being translations of identity politics frameworks, elactivism/vereativismo highlights the necessity of embracing a politics of presence, reaffirming the institution's role as a public forum open to everyone. Through a transnational perspective, this concept opens a path to reflect on the emergence of Black leaders in global politics, aligned with the Ubuntu philosophy, "I am because we are" (Paulson 2020).

NOTES

1 *Moleque*, in Portuguese, is a term that means boy or teenager, and in Brazil has become racialized to signify a Black boy and often connotes a delinquent youth. The Movimento Moleque was born on December 10, 2003. Organized by the mothers in partnership with other NGOs, they have had an impact on Rio de Janeiro in several conferences and colloquiums, and in debates about young people in conflict with the law and the socioeducational system. It seeks to promote networks of fathers and mothers, through training courses and workshops.

2 Some excerpts of these communications and poster quotes can be found on Monica Cunha's Instagram account, @Monicacunhario.

3 Angela Davis delivered the lecture "Atravessando o tempo e construindo o futuro da luta contra o racismo" at a conference at the Federal University of Bahia on July 26, 2017.

4 The Social and Liberty Party (PSOL) is a left-wing political party created in 2004 after a split with the Workers' Party (PT). In 2022, the party endorsed the precandidacy of Luiz Inácio Lula da Silva (PT) for the presidency. Monica Cunha ran for the first time in Rio de Janeiro's elections in that party in 2020.

5 Many Black women who ran for election after Marielle Franco's execution were called *sementes* (seeds), among them, Renata Souza, Dani Monteiro, Monica Francisco, and Taliria Petrone.

6 The film *Marielle's Legacy Will Not Die* (Cortana 2019) follows activist movements spreading the intersectional legacy of Afro-Brazilian activist and politician Marielle Franco in Rio de Janeiro, at the first anniversary of Franco's execution. Monica Cunha is one of the main characters.

7 The Museu Afro houses an extensive permanent exhibit on the history of slavery in Brazil.

8 Estação Primeira de Mangueira, one of Rio's oldest and most traditional samba schools, won the 2019 Rio Carnival competition with their performance titled "History for Lulling Adults." The performance paid tribute to Marielle Franco and all unsung Black figures of resistance in Brazilian history.

REFERENCES

Botero, Isabel Cristina Ramírez. 2022. "Estética de la visibilización: La propuesta visual de la campaña de Francia Márquez." *Revistas Uniandes* 11. https://revistas.uniandes.edu.co/index.php/hart/article/view/3604.

Coelho, Ingrid Mesquita, Rosemary Amanda Lima Alves, Daniel Cerdeira de Souza, and Eduardo Jorge Sant'Ana Honorato. 2019. "Preto lá faz faculdade? Uma revisão da literatura sobre racismo nas universidades brasileiras." *Revista intersaberes* 14, no. 32: 381–95.

Cortana, Leonard, dir. 2019. *Marielle's Legacy Will Not Die*. Tornado Cine Festival.

de Araújo, Etyelle Pinheiro, Liana de Andrade Biar, and Liliana Cabral Bastos. 2020. "Engagement in Social Movements and the Fight for Justice: A Study on the Narratives of Black Mothers." *Trabalhos em linguística aplicada* 59, no. 3. https://doi.org/10.1590/0103181383618111202011113.

de Jesus, Maria Carolina. 2014. *Quarto de despejo: Diário de uma favelada*. São Paulo: Atica Press.

Franco, Marielle. 2017. "A emergência da vida para superar o anestesiamento social frente à retirada de direitos: O momento pós-golpe pelo olhar de uma feminista, negra e favelada." In *Tem Saída? Ensaios críticos sobre o Brasil*, edited by Winnie Bueno, Joanna Burigo, Rosana Pinheiro-Machado, and Esther Solano. Porto Alegre: Editora Zouk.

Freire, Juressa. 2011. "Quando as emoções dão formas às reivindicações." In *Cultura e sentimentos: Ensaios em antropologia das emoções*, edited by Maria Claudia Coelho, 168–96. Rio de Janeiro: FAPERJ.

Nash, Jennifer. 2021. *Birthing Black Mothers*. Durham, NC: Duke University Press.

Paulson, Steve. 2020. "'I Am Because We Are': The African Philosophy of Ubuntu." *To the Best of Our Knowledge*, Wisconsin Public Radio, September 30. https://www.ttbook.org/interview/i-am-because-we-are-african-philosophy-ubuntu.

Ribeiro, Djamila. 2017. *O que é lugar de fala?* Belo Horizonte: Editora Letramento.

11

Analytics of Raciality / Analítica de Racialidade

Political-Symbolic Processes of Racial Power

DENISE FERREIRA DA SILVA

Fear of police terror has long been a daily facet of economically dispossessed people of color in urban spaces of North America, Europe, Latin America, and elsewhere. This chapter addresses the conditions of possibility of the form of racial injustice manifested in police brutality. It challenges the centrality of the logic of exclusion—the view that race is only politically and socially significant when race identification is explicitly or implicitly used to justify discrimination—in the understanding of race injustice. It explores the political-symbolic processes that have produced the mechanisms of racial power of which police brutality is a most dramatic example. To elaborate on this critique of the logic of exclusion, I discuss newspaper coverage of an episode of police terror in a favela of Rio de Janeiro. Newspaper coverage of the Chacina de Vigário Geral reveals the operation of meanings produced in an analytic of raciality, encompassing the various instances of manufacturing the modern concept of the racial—the science of life, the science of man, and the sociology of race relations.

Over ten years ago, my cousin Marlão was shot to death by undercover police officers in front of his house in the early hours of a night of terror that left nine dead in my neighborhood. Though I was emotionally worn out by yet another demonstration for the lives of those who live on the margins of justice, fear prevented me, at the time, from breaking the code of silence that contributes to police terror going unchecked in Rio de Janeiro's favelas. However, the mother of a nineteen-year-old who was killed on his doorstep while leaving to buy milk in the morning—having no one else to fear for, since she had already lost her two other sons at the hands of the police—broke the code of silence to bring her child's murderers to justice.

Reading the *New York Times* coverage of the murder of Amadou Diallo—the West African street vendor killed by undercover police officers in the foyer of his Bronx apartment building—in 1999 was another painful reminder.[1] As I followed the coverage, I realized that, instead of apologies and promises, the return to Africa of another body killed at the hands of law enforcement agents should invite reflection upon the commonality that only Blackness produces. Reports of police terror are perhaps the only sign those from the outside have of what takes place in this moral and legal no-man's land, where universality finds its spatial limits. These deaths—Marlão, Amadou, and the young Black males and females killed by police bullets across the continent—challenge us to inquire into the fundamental effects of the power signified in their shared Blackness. My argument here is that to grasp the power effects of raciality manifested in police brutality demands an approach that goes beyond the view of race as a mechanism of exclusion. To elaborate this argument, I undertake an archaeological exercise that situates this dominant view—which I will call the socio-logic of exclusion—within the larger field of production of meanings of the racial as a modern category of being.

I begin by discussing the prevailing legal conceptions of racial injustice. My argument is that the hegemonic strategy of race subjection in Brazil has been informed by another construct of the scientia racialis, the notion of miscegenation (mestiçagem, race mixture), whose primary effect has been to construct Black and mestiço (mixed-race) Brazilians as pathological social subjects, and their bodies and the urban spaces they inhabit as signifiers of illegality. With this, I hope to contribute to an approach for amending the effects and power of the racial, which goes beyond the exhaustive cataloging of race injustice characteristic of works informed by the social logic of exclusion.

Beyond the Socio-Logic of Exclusion

Following the critical legal scholarship strategy that uses the social to challenge law's claims of uncommitted universality, the critics of the liberal legal construction of racial injustice seem to suggest that the recognition of racial (social) subjugation in itself would render judicial processes just. While this claim is fundamentally correct, it inherits a problem imposed by the logic of racism. It is critical to challenge the prevailing civil rights discourse, which constructs race injustice as discrimination, in which racism appears as a deviation from neutral and universal principles and adopts color blindness as the fundamental means to achieve racial justice (Crenshaw et al. 1995). Against this view, students of critical race theory (CRT) advance a race-conscious legal perspective to address how racial power informs legal discourse and strategies. What this race-conscious legal scholarship accomplishes is a recuperation of the social basis of race injustice occluded in both the *Plessy* and *Brown* decisions. Not only does a race-conscious scholarship recuperate and support "a radical tradition of race consciousness," which was shunned with the conception of racial justice as color blindness; it also curbs attacks on affirmative action that oppose it to the *Brown* principle. Legal scholarship using CRT targets the perpetrator perspective, informing liberal constructions of race injustice that leave unaddressed how representations of race have organized US social formation (Freeman 1978). While recognizing the limits of this individualized—as opposed to historical, structural, and institutional—view of racial injustice, CRT scholarship seems to retain a primary focus on exclusion. For instance, in his critique of remedies deployed to ensure the adoption of the *Brown* decision in defiant school districts, Derrick Bell (2004) retains the view that racial power manifests primarily as discriminatory (i.e., segregationist) acts and policies.

Using CRT, considerations of the relations between the racial and justice are ultimately limited to whether and how racism—as ideas and practices that exclude based on attributed racial difference—plays a role in social encounters, processes, and structures affecting the political and social rights of individuals of color. The limitations of its project reside in its sharing the liberal legal construction of racism, the view that if one's racial difference is not explicitly found to determine unfavorable social thoughts or actions, exclusionary ideas, and behavior, it cannot be proven to be the ultimate cause of the ensuing harm to that person's rights. Precisely this construction, identified here as sociological—guiding both liberal and CRT constructions of race—renders certain claims of racial injustice (e.g., denunciation of police terror) either inarticulate or unheard because they fail to meet the criterion of racial invocation.

It seems to me that to address the most elusive and insidious modes of racial injustice, we need to expand the investigation of the material effects of the racial beyond the sociological archive (the accumulation of quantitative and qualitative evidence of exclusion). I locate these forms of racial injustice in the socio-logical construction of Blackness, as a social category that refers to a domain outside the terrain of the legal. Blackness simultaneously retains the construction of whiteness as the signifier of the form of consciousness to which the principles underlying the normative schema of universal justice are indigenous. The most crucial effect of this socio-logical construction has been to produce Blackness, and the place of residence of Black people, as natural (preconceptual and prehistorical) signifiers of social pathology.[2]

The logic of exclusion itself was first introduced in the sociology of race relations in the early twentieth century, stemming from investigations of Africans, Asians, and Native Americans in the United States, which assumed their original outsideness to the space of Anglo-Saxon modernity, immediately signified in their bodies.[3] A central consequence of these early sociological studies was to write about subaltern conditions as an effect of their racial difference. In this movement, Blackness was constructed to signify this ambiguous territory, which, while located within the boundaries of universality, would consistently signify that which belongs to the outside. Unlike the United States, where racial difference organizes accounts of the national subject, Brazil's mode of racial subjection is organized around the idea that miscegenation constituted the condition of possibility for the emergence of the national subject, the mestiço (mixed-race individual), whose particular combination of whiteness, Blackness, and, to a lesser extent, Indianness enabled the construction of a modern tropical social space (da Silva 1998). Placing Blackness outside the domain of justice can be captured when one traces the meaning attributed to Blackness in accounts of the Brazilian social subject.

Historical and Social Ends of Mestiçagem

Since the late nineteenth century, racial power has been exercised, at the level of the symbolic, through two main strategies. Racial difference, which prevails in the United States, is a strategy of particularization that indicates how one would present physical and cultural conditions. Hybridity or miscegenation (the result of racial mixture), which prevails in Brazil, was deployed as a signifier of containment, which indicated the harmful effects caused by a violation of these fundamental laws. Miscegenation is unquestionably the central component of the hegemonic narrative of Brazilian national subjectivity, the notion of racial democracy. Like racial difference, miscegenation is also produced by the analytics of raciality; that is, it is a productive strategy whose primary effect has been to enable the production of Black Brazilians as subaltern social subjects. Like racial differences in the United States, miscegenation has also been placed at the center of knowledge projects that adapted the strategies of intervention deployed in various moments of the analytics of raciality to reveal the alleged truth of Brazilian cultural and social conditions. Unlike in the United States, this centrality resulted in racial subjection in Brazil operating independently of (if not against) the logic of exclusion. Examining various social scientific articulations of miscegenation can help us to understand how, in the late twentieth century, the bodies and social spaces inhabited by Black Brazilians were constructed as signifiers of illegality.[4]

To understand racial subjugation in Brazil, one should notice how the duality of the national subject has enabled both meanings of miscegenation—as a teleological and eschatological signifier—to become available to produce statements about modern Brazil.[5] The ideal subject of the nation's history appropriated Blackness and Africanity to write the teleology of the Brazilian historical subject while the Brazilian social subject is represented in the eschatological figure of the mestiço, the slightly tanned European subject, mired in moral pathology and destined for obliteration. The teleological version was articulated early, in the works of Silvio Romero (1978, 1988) and other late nineteenth-century nationalists. But only in the 1930s, in anthropological studies and in particular sociologist and anthropologist Gilberto Freyre's (1946) oeuvre, would miscegenation be consolidated as that condition providing the particularity of the Brazilian national subject. Miscegenation is written to produce Brazil's difference as the result of the unique Portuguese ability to mingle with other races, to assimilate them without losing an essentially European character. However, even as Freyre's and others' positive versions of miscegenation did not erase the initial version of the national text, in which Blackness and Africanity were appropriated in the writing of the ideal (historical) Brazilian subject, the eschatological meaning of miscegenation was deployed to produce the actual (social) subject.[6] The mestiço was described as mentally inferior and lacking free will and all other traits of populations of a nation capable of realizing the ideals of progress, liberty, prosperity, and sovereignty.

Later, from the 1950s onward, sociological constructions of racial subjugation in Brazil—while rejecting both the negative and positive takes on miscegenation—retained, even if by omission, the view of miscegenation as a degenerative process. This view contributed to the writing of the mestiço, the actual Brazilian subject, as an embodiment of the zone of illegality. In works by the Paulista school of race relations in the 1950s, this construction (produced by anthropologists) attributed the current economic dispossession and pervasiveness of crime among descendants of former slaves to their cultural incapacity. This has resulted in a naturalization of criminality (as an effect of cultural poverty) and a silencing of race under the concept of class. Since the late 1970s, the Carioca school of race relations has rejected this previous construction. These works examined and explained racial differences operating in Brazil as a mechanism of social exclusion, and attributed the economic dispossession experienced by Blacks and mestiços to the operation of racial mechanisms of exclusion, discrimination, and racial inequalities. Nevertheless, the Carioca school did not confront and disentangle the naturalization of economic dispossession and criminality (as expressions of moral inferiority) produced by the early anthropologists and by the Paulista school. The most perverse consequences of Brazil's strategy of race subjection have been the production of this double (ambiguous) subject, where markers of Blackness in the body of the mestiço, the Brazilian body, and the body of the poor become indexes of whether they inhabit that domain of the good, legal, and just.[7]

Writing the Domain of Illegality in Rio de Janeiro

A few years after my cousin's murder in the early 1990s, I went back home—my first trip since I had moved to the United States—to discover that Rio remained the same. Near the end of my visit, at my neighborhood's bus stop on a wintry gray Carioca morning, I learned of yet another instance of police terror. This time it happened downtown. Seven children and teenagers were executed by the police while sleeping on the steps of the Church of Candelária. The victims of the Chacina da Candelária (slaughter or massacre of Candelária) were street children, those who most dramatically signify the excess, the overflow of alleged danger, dispossession, and moral degeneration from poor neighborhoods claimed by Rio's economic elites. Surprisingly, I noticed fewer attempts to write these kids out of their childhood and imprison them on the other side of morality. However, this was an exception. A little over a month later, when I had returned to the United States, Rio woke up to another Chacina. In an economically dispossessed neighborhood not much different from my family's, the night of August 30, 1993, was a night of police terror that left twenty-one residents dead, several wounded, and many whose lives may still be colonized by fear.

Continuing coverage of the Chacina de Vigário Geral investigation by a major newspaper, with a mostly middle- and upper-middle-class readership, is telling. For a long time in Rio, a discourse has prevailed of constructing poor neighborhoods as zonas de violência (zones of violence) and therefore rendering the majority of enlightened (middle- and upper-middle-class) Cariocas deaf, insensitive, or unable to articulate an effective political/civic counterdiscourse. The configuration of Rio de Janeiro's space is but an indication of Blackness as a constructed signifier, indicating an unbecoming of cultural qualities that threaten Brazil's claims to modernity. The enlightened Cariocas referred to some diffuse phenomenon called a violência (the violence). People in the neighborhoods of the poor identify it, with a mix of fear, loathing, revolt, and resignation, as o bicho (the animal). As I reflect upon these terms, I am sure I understand both. Each identifies a distinct symbolic region of the city. Each refers to a distinct moral zone of the city space, a site of invisible demarcations that distinguish the terrain of the legal—the sacred domain of justice—and the zonas de violência. It is a strange place where the poor (Blacks, mestiços, and "blackened" whites stigmatized by their proximity to Black populations)—the enlightened would wonder—seem to find it fit to live. But beyond their correspondence with the geo-economic configuration of the city space, they also indicate distinct ways of being Carioca.

The kind of racial injustice expressed in police terror in these neighborhoods—regardless of whether it targets drug dealers or other residents—is hidden by a perverse logic. It assumes that since they have been written outside the domain of legality, residents are also placed there and are therefore rightful victims of police terror. Police terror is also rendered elusive because the placing of the neighborhoods and their residents on the other side of legality obscures the line separating terror from the necessary (drastic) routine police operations to protect these communities. Its raced character is made perverse and elusive because poor is a category that combines the effects of class and race subjection, thereby hiding both. The category poor—when used in self-identification—refers to those Black, mestiço, and blackened white Brazilians whose consciousness sociology writes as unable to adopt the values required to survive and thrive in capitalist societies. Nevertheless, while this incapacity has been associated with miscegenation (and Blackness), its raced character is diffused because, among enlightened Brazilians, the logic of exclusion, the requirement of racial invocation, also prevails. Self-identification of the subaltern Brazilian as poor indicates silencing of race at the expense of class. Moreover, it also points to that form of injustice that can only be captured by the concept of the racial, that is, in these circumstances when most basic human rights are violated only because Blackness remains a signifier of in-humanity; when the acts of terror against people of African descent are overshadowed by the violência said to be proper to the poor and the places they live.

The second Chacina is a most painful example of this form of racial injustice. In the early 1990s, not even Rio's incumbent socialist/populist state administration—elected by the poor and which committed itself to the protection of their human rights—could destroy this logic. Actually, it helped to render it even more perverse. In seven days, the newspaper struggled to provide closure to the Chacina—that was adequate to anyone but the few cops who were put in jail and the community residents who lost their relatives, friends, and neighbors. How was that version produced? On day two, the paper quoted state authorities, the police command, politicians, the governor, the community, and organizations of the enlightened Carioca civil society, many of which seemed certain that the Chacina was an act of revenge. Most mass killings that have made it into the news generally involved teenagers and young adults who were (or could have been) involved in drug dealing. Hence, for most of the enlightened Cariocas, these episodes could be explained as unfortunate but understandable since—whether due to the routine work of police officers or extermination groups—there was always the possibility that victims were or could become drug dealers and would then be outside the domain of the legal.

Many believed, however, that in the early 1990s, Rio's violência seemed to be out of control (out of its Indigenous grounds) thanks to an incompetent state administration. From the third to sixth day, the coverage emphasized that the Chacina represented a police and state crisis of authority. A state representation of the opposition recalled that the governor had various opportunities to show more concrete action to resolve the shameful situation. He did nothing, and now it was clear that there was a crisis of command in the state. This view was shared by the president of the Rio de Janeiro State Federation of Neighborhood Associations, who insisted that what happened in Vigário Geral was not an isolated case. For the president of the Rio de Janeiro State Supreme Court, it indicated that certain degenerate social subjects had penetrated the state itself. He insisted, "We are in a social war between the layer of bandits which integrate the police and the other that practice[s] all sorts of crimes. . . . We will do everything in the Court's power to punish both the ones who killed the police officers and those responsible for these deaths" (Gonçalves and Garcia 1993).

Much of this probably reflected the newspapers' and Rio's middle-class bias against an administration that they described as populist and, on many occasions, accused of being soft on criminals. But those most affected by crime only partially shared in this interpretation. The president of the federation of favela resident associations publicly raised alarm about the tense moment, claiming that the city, state, and federal administrations were responsible for this situation, and "we will report what happened to international human rights groups. We do not trust the Brazilian authorities; they don't do anything" (Garcia 1993). Indeed, an examination of the quotes supporting the crisis of authority argument suggests the preferred interpretation. The seven-day coverage also produced an image that violência was dangerously out of control and could affect morally upright and hardworking people everywhere. The sentiment was reflected by the press secretary of the Organization of Brazilian Catholic Bishops, arguing that "the cold-blooded killing shows that the avalanche of violência in this country has reached its maximum and now seems uncontrollable" (O Globo 1993a).

Expectedly, closure of the events required demarcating boundaries of the zona da violência, accomplished by grouping an evangelical family and other victims with drug dealers and bad cops. As part of this strategy, the newspaper recounted the constant shootings in the neighborhood (and those taking place in other favelas), the fear of witnesses who refused to collaborate with the investigations, the existing war with the neighboring community (a rivalry between drug dealers that, the paper insisted, represented community residents), and the state of the community school building—situated between the two enemy favelas and riddled with bullet holes (O Globo 1993b). With this strategy, the paper wrote off the community as just another favela, the sort of place where violência is indigenous and not a novelty brought about by police vengeance. The paper gradually explained to enlightened Cariocas why working residents could very well be the victims of police terror: they lived in the domain of the illegal (O Globo 1993c). Moreover, in the absence of any other points of reference that explained the historical and structural processes out of which Rio's favelas had been created—or how and why the drug traffickers were able to control the communities via terror—the only explanation left was that something intrinsic and unique to the favela residents had put them in this predicament. But to construct this place, the favela, as the embodiment of violência was not sufficient.

The closing of the zona da violência also needed to address why, this time, only working people, and more importantly an evangelical family, were the victims. The answer here was as simple as one might fear. On the third day, the newspaper advanced the hypothesis that the family was killed by mistake because they knew the former local drug lord (who was in jail) and because they lived in a suspicious house that once belonged to him. On the following day, the paper added that this house was used to hide the dealers' heavy weaponry and that the family had connections with the former drug lord. It was finally on the fifth day that the paper began building the version that would provide enlightened Cariocas with the desired closure. On the one hand, short reports reinforced the crisis of authority and the dangerous liaisons theses. The authority problem became an institutional, internal one. The Chacina was supposedly committed not by the police as an institution but of certain bad cops (some favela residents themselves) working with the drug traffickers by supplying weapons, ensuring the transportation of drugs, and organizing themselves into extermination squads. As the state, via its law enforcement institutions, was identifying, separating, classifying, and punishing them, it disentangled itself from the problem, and only the small group of allegedly bad cops was placed in the zona da violência. On the other hand, the paper also included a short report suggesting that the evangelical family also inhabited the same domain: "There are two possibilities that connect the death of the police officers with the later killings: revenge or continuity of crime. In the first hypothesis, it is admitted that some of the police officers were achacadores [cops working with/for the drug traffickers]. They were trapped and killed. The extermination squad believed that the trap was created by the evangelical family. In the second hypothesis, the officers were protecting the local dealers who, with the connivance of the killed family, had failed to pay drug suppliers" (O Globo 1993d). Quite simple. The evangelical family could have been responsible for the death of the working, law-abiding residents.

This closure was analogous to the perversity and elusiveness of the form of injustice expressed in police terror. It constructed the poor and the favela as embodying that kind of social consciousness that exists only in material deprivation and crime. The explanation for the troubling deaths of documented working people and the morally elevated family revolved around their belonging to the zona de violência, the domain of illegality. At least one of the officers killed on the first night belonged to the domain of illegality. He, along with the other officers, had been trapped by the drug lord seeking revenge for his relatives. On the second night, the bad cops invaded the community, killing the evangelical family because they lived in a suspicious house that they had bought from the former drug lord who was also their godchild. The final version wrote them in the space shared by the police, terrorists, and drug dealers. The community was depicted not as a typical favela but as the headquarters of Rio's organized crime.

On the seventh day, lengthy reports claimed that the community hid weapons used by a large criminal organization and that, once the enlightened and their human rights organizations left, life as usual would return to the favela. Drug dealers walked about unabashedly with their AR-15 and 9 mm pistols in daylight, and a new drug lord was in command. In the following week of coverage, the paper reported that the same group of police officers was also responsible for the Chacina da Candelária. Finally, enlightened Cariocas could reacquire their peace of mind as the episode was explained away as indigenous to the other side of the invisible curtain, the zona de violência, and to the poor who live there. While they would continue to be concerned with crime, violência remained something foreign to the region they inhabited, despite the daily risk of encountering it in banks, on beaches, in stores, and on highways. For those living in the favelas and other communities of the poor, o bicho remains a palpable entity evident in the constant fear of stray bullets, in the dead bodies found in bloody corners and alleys, and in the wet faces of those who find themselves victims of the form of racial injustice of which drug trafficking and police terror are only the most dramatic manifestations.

In the post–civil rights era in the United States—when the practices and ideas that produced and justified the subjugation of African Americans had been exiled from the domain of justice—it seems necessary to investigate the extent to which Blackness itself has retained that which was once defined as proper to the minds of certain unenlightened and prejudiced white minds. The CRT critique of liberal legal scholarship has produced powerful challenges to the thesis of universality, with the argument that law and judicial procedures are inherently exclusionary, even in the absence of legal segregation. This is because principles, procedures, and judicial decision-making are informed by the majority's cultural values and therefore are biased in favor of its interests. Just as emancipation recuperated Southern morality, the civil rights movement has recuperated US morality. Yet once again, Black people carry the burden of retaining that which defined the boundaries of justice, moral qualities that exclude them from the terrain of the legal. Our (Brazilian) predicament does capture a form of injustice specific to race subjection. This is a dimension we share with many African Americans who perhaps will never leave the inner cities to come into contact with the institutions and people who may use racial invocation to produce racial injustice. They can, at any moment, face police terror and other forms of racial injustice that consistently and stubbornly escape the logic of exclusion.

NOTES

An earlier and significantly distinct version of this chapter was previously published as "Towards a Critique of the Socio-logos of Justice: The Analytics of Raciality and the Production of Universality," *Social Identities* 7, no. 3 (2001): 421–54, https://doi.org/10.1080/13504630120087253.

1   In the years since Amadou Diallo was shot forty-one times by members of the New York City Police Department's now discontinued Street Crime Unit, the murder of George Floyd in Minneapolis, and the killing of Breonna Taylor in Louisville, there have been many other episodes of police brutality for which the police officers

were not charged or were acquitted (and whose names are too many to enter here but who should be remembered and cited as often as possible).

2   For a thorough analysis of this signifying process, see Spillers (1987).

3   For the full presentation of this argument, including a full description of the analytics of raciality, see da Silva (2007).

4   Elsewhere, I elaborate on this argument through an analysis of this modality of state violence, which I call racial violence. The main trait of this mode of subjugation is registered by how the social scientific construction of Blackness as a signifier of violence allows for the collapsing of justice (the demand for judicial review of a killing) as law enforcement (self-preservation) (da Silva 2009, 2017).

5   For a full presentation of this argument, see da Silva (2007), in particular chapter 10.

6   An early articulation of this version is in the work of another practicing anthropologist, Raymundo Nina Rodrigues. His ethnographic and (physical) anthropological investigations were pursued out of concern with the costs of the failure to institute effective mechanisms of segregation. Uncontrolled physical miscegenation, Nina Rodrigues argued, would prove to be harmful to the Brazilian mentality. In his critique of the first Republican Penal Code's universal application of the principle of free will, Nina Rodrigues ([1894] 1957, [1900] 1935) argued that miscegenation required a distinct criterion of penal responsibility. The problem, he argued, was that Brazil had neither the moral superiority nor the homogeneity presumed in the principle of free will. Deploying the science of man, he noted that Black "mental inferiority" and the "various degrees of moral and intellectual" degeneracy of mestiços suggested that the application of the penal code should be based on distinct degrees of penal responsibility. The Brazilian population, he argued, "lack[s] physical and moral energy, [suffering from] apathy, and the want of foresight" (Nina Rodrigues [1900] 1935, 134–35). His solution was to limit this unwanted effect by constructing mestiços (the majority of the Brazilian population) as legally (juridically) incapable modern subjects.

7   The original article (da Silva 2004) was written in 1999 and published in 2001. A few years after its publication, as the Brazilian government during the first Luiz Inacio Lula da Silva administration was responding to the recommendations of the Durban Conference on Racism, the Carioca school of race relations' approach would be assimilated as the official discourse on the Brazilian racial situation (da Silva 2004).

REFERENCES

Bell, Derrick 2004. *Silent Covenants:* Brown v. Board of Education *and the Unfulfilled Hopes for Racial Reform.* New York: Oxford University Press.

Crenshaw, Kimberlé, Neil Gotanda, Gary Peller, and Kendall Thomas, eds. 1995. *Critical Race Theory: The Key Writings That Formed the Movement.* New York: New Press.

da Silva, Denise Ferreira. 1998. "Facts of Blackness: Brazil Is Not Quite the United States . . . and Racial Politics in Brazil?" *Social Identities* 4, no. 2: 201–23.

da Silva, Denise Ferreira. 2004. "An Introduction: The Predicament of Brazilian Culture." *Social Identities* 10, no. 6: 719–34.

da Silva, Denise Ferreira. 2007. *Toward a Global Idea of Race*. Minneapolis: University of Minnesota Press.

da Silva, Denise Ferreira. 2009. "No-Bodies: Law Raciality and Violence." *Griffith Law Review* 18, no. 2: 212–36.

da Silva, Denise Ferreira. 2017. "1 (life) ÷ 0 (blackness) = ∞ − ∞ or ∞ / ∞: On Matter beyond the Equation of Value." *Re-visiones* 7. http://www.re-visiones.net/index.php/RE-VISIONES/article/view/217.

Freeman, Alan David. 1978. "Legitimizing Racial Discrimination through Antidiscrimination Law: A Critical Review of Supreme Court Doctrine." *Minnesota Law Review* 62, no. 73: 1049–119.

Freyre, Gilberto. 1946. *The Masters and the Slaves*. New York: Knopf.

Garcia, Renato. 1993. "Investigação provoca conflito entre polícias Civil e Militar." *O Globo*, September 3.

Gonçalves, Renato, and Liana Garcia. 1993. "Grupo matou para vingar PM envolvido em extermínio." *O Globo*, September 4.

Nina Rodrigues, Raymundo. (1894) 1957. *As raças humanas e a responsabilidade penal no Brasil*. Salvador: Livraria Progress.

Nina Rodrigues, Raymundo. (1900) 1935. *O animismo fetichista dos negros bahianos*. Rio de Janeiro: Civilização Brasileira.

O Globo. 1993a. "Ruas se transformam em praça de guerra." August 31.

O Globo. 1993b. "OAB dará parecer sobre indenização." September 2.

O Globo. 1993c. "Policia Interroga PMs suspeitos." September 3.

O Globo. 1993d. "Chacina: Cinco PMs já estão presos." September 4.

Romero, Silvio. 1978. *Teoria, crítica, e história literária*. Rio de Janeiro: Livros Técnicos e Científicos Editora.

Romero, Silvio. 1988. *História da literatura brasileira*. Rio de Janeiro: Garnier.

Spillers, Hortense. 1987. "'Mama's Baby, Papa's Maybe': An American Grammar Book." *Diacritics* 17, no. 2: 64–81.

12

Black Brotherhood Urbanism /
Urbanismo Confrarial Negro

*Forms of Urban Expansion Designed by Mutual Aid
Societies of Freedmen and Slaves*

MARCOS COUTINHO

Mutual aid societies of Black freedmen and enslaved individuals, particularly Bantu-speaking groups from what we call Angola and Mozambique today, came together to collectively build municipal welfare and self-governance organizations known as brotherhoods or confraternal organizations during the eighteenth century. These collective organizations emerged in the cities of coastal Brazil to build and maintain churches, and, in turn, these churches maintained a spectrum of social, political, welfare, and cultural functions. These brotherhoods designed and built the churches and the squares around them and provided services and architectural guidance to the nearby ports housing clusters of Black residents and workers. As they did so, they shaped the forms, directions, spatial meanings, and uses of rapidly expanding urban residential and public spaces.

The fabric of cities like Rio de Janeiro and Salvador de Bahia was fundamentally shaped by the design imaginaries, functional needs, and self-organized labor of Black urbanites, even those still enslaved. The Black brotherhoods, together with quilombos and terreiros, constituted spaces of both resistance against hegemonic powers and internal struggles for more equality between men and women. In Bahia (Salvador), reports reveal the activism of Black women who were members of the brotherhood. The female presence is an important factor in such associations in Brazil, since women came to occupy high positions in their brotherhoods as providers and scribes (Quintão 2002). The Black confraternities, in turn, waged several disputes with civil and religious authorities during the colonial period, mainly involving issues related to their autonomy and freedom (Soares 2002). However, the historical period covered here (the first half of the eighteenth century) reveals no such accounts that Black women held administrative, consultative, or decision-making positions within these religious associations (Santana 2013).

Religious brotherhoods are Catholic associations formed by (faithful) laypeople within traditional interpretations of Catholicism, based around the worship of a saint, represented by a corresponding relic or image (or both). The brothers were not priests or monks and therefore did not need to be celibate (or married). The churches of brotherhoods are not ordinary religious buildings (e.g., monasteries or convents); they are churches built by their followers, without assistance from the state or the church itself. They are not linked to a diocese and, therefore, are semiautonomous, being managed not by a parish priest but by an administrative board whose head is the provider or judge. They had autonomy regarding the church's administration and the choice of priest. Generally, the brothers lived near the houses of worship of which they were members. *Brothers* here refers exclusively to free Black people, the only ones capable of owning goods and making wills.

Black brotherhood, here, challenges the traditional idea that urban modernity and contemporary city geography were colonial by-products—images of social hygiene imposed from above by Iberian or French planners. I aim to show the Black brotherhoods' role in urban expansion to resist white hegemonic narratives of the contemporary city's formation. This will also help historians and readers in imagining the Black individual in spaces not solely defined by subalternity or reification. The churches built and operated by Black mutual aid societies promoted and made essential historical contributions to the expansion of Rio de Janeiro during the first half of the eighteenth century and continue to shape the fabric of Rio today. During this period, members of the Black urban community realized that the construction and operation of these churches would enable maintenance and control of certain parts of the city. They served as hubs for Black collective life, not limited to the construction and expression of collective identity. This chapter recovers the role played by the Rio de Janeiro brotherhoods of Our Lady of Rosário and Saint Benedito, Saint Domingos, Saint Elesbão, and Saint Efigênia, and Our Lady of Lampadosa. I offer a synchronic and diachronic approach that aims to epistemologically and historically restore the memory of Afro-Brazilians as central players in the production of urban space.

In recent decades, eighteenth-century Afro-Brazilian mutual aid societies (long before abolition was declared in Brazil in 1888) have been interpreted in academic literature as mere instruments for maintaining colonial order, within which enslaved peoples and Black freedmen were surveilled and disciplined by the church and state. Scholars tended to depict these church societies as serving two sociocultural functions: (1) to facilitate catechetical pastoral service, and (2) to enable the control of populations with African origins (Boschi 2019). My work—inspired by Black urban researchers and antiracist movements in Rio de Janeiro—hopes to reappraise Black agency through archival recovery. This is a project that struggles against institutional academic racism as well as a collective effort of remembering and restoring historical agency and Black memory in Brazil (Collins 2016; Kilomba 2012). Patricia Hill Collins and Grada Kilomba, as well as others like Djamila Ribeiro, represent multiple voices of Black female activism. If we attempt to break with epistemic colonialism and other forms of academic oppression, we cannot do so without the use of Black authors, especially those who work and advocate for feminism, historical reflection, trauma-informed thinking, and antiracism within the Afro-American and Afro-Brazilian communities.

In the rest of this chapter, I will focus on the degree to which Afro-Cariocas created and occupied places and roles beyond that of enslavement.[1] The chapter concludes by examining the leading roles of the following brotherhoods: Our Lady of Rosário and Saint Benedito (IRSB), Glorious Saint Domingos (IGSD), Saint Elesbão and Saint Efigênia (ISEE), and Our Lady of Lampadosa (INSL). Together, these groups constitute critical players in the expansion of urban territories in the city of Rio de Janeiro during the eighteenth century. Nireu Cavalcanti offers an in-depth study of the colonial city, approaching his work with the lens of both a historian and architect. *O Rio de Janeiro setecentista* (Cavalcanti 2004) rebuilds our image of colonial urban space in Rio de Janeiro, highlighting the Catholic Church and its institutions (religious orders, third orders, and lay brotherhoods).

Churches as Factories of City Building

The term *fábrica de igreja* (church council) refers to the administrative and legal governing structure in charge of managing all assets and activities intended for church conservation and maintenance, organizing and supervising both festivals and solemn processions, and exercising liturgical rites and services (Bluteau 1712, 3–4). In Portuguese, the word *fábrica* invokes urban construction since it also means *workshop* or *factory*.[2] I utilize the original phrase *fábrica de igreja* to maintain its original meaning, lost in the English translation *church council*. *Fábrica* also was used to refer to the religious building of the mutual aid society (Lajo 1990, 80). The interpretative scope of the term *fábrica* is expanded here to also designate the construction and preservation (not by the state) of religious houses (of all sizes), as well as other buildings and urban facilities that make up broader understandings of the church. Black collective organizations asserted control over these "factories" or self-run governing facilities.

The urban church council/fábrica represented one of the most efficient instruments of geomorphic transformation in colonial Rio. These brotherhood churches could be classified into three distinct categories:

- Large council seats: A model operated by the great Catholic orders with religious houses, usually consisting of monasteries or convents. These monastery-convent complexes played a notable role as beacons or hubs of urbanization that mapped the shape of city expansion.
- Medium fábricas or confraternities: These types of church facilities were built under the command of third parties and lay brotherhoods. The churches had vast lay or secular functions that would now be considered state duties (e.g., intervening in physical transformation, plotting, and enabling new suburbs to be built).
- Small fábricas or devotional chapels: The final category includes chapels, hermitages, shrines, and any other Catholic entities with a simplified architectural-religious structure. These structures reflect the devotional-contemplative character and artistic influence of its craftsmen. In addition, the small brotherhood shrines took over the sites of prayer that had emerged in spiritually and socially strategic points within the city. These eventually flowered into grander ecclesiastical constructions, erected on or around the small shrines (Cruls 1949, 78–79).

Afro-Brazilians became owners of these sacred properties—buildings that, in addition to places of counter-hegemony, became spaces for free speech and collective self-organization.

Afro-brotherhood Quadrilateral: Black Protagonism in the Production of the Eighteenth-Century Urban Space

Black Brazilians came together in the organization, construction, and maintenance of brotherhood churches and through this shaped the course of Catholicism in Brazil and mobilized resistance to white hegemony in the urban context. This historical process created literally a place of speech that acted as the social locus that authorized (or denied) the entry of certain marginalized groups into spaces of citizenship based on their own experiences (Ribeiro 2019, 53–79). Following the lead of feminist Black Brazilian activist scholar Djamila Ribeiro, we recognize this historical *lugar de fala* (place of speech) to critically contextualize who is consistently placed as the individual who is able to speak and who is seen as universal in a Eurocentric cisheteropatriarchal society, which blocks possibilities for identifying specific experiences and, thus, differentiates the discourses according to the social position of distinct speakers' positions and histories. In this context, it is important today to displace the universal speaking position of urban history as a top-down European imposition, and to historiographically and geographically open places of speech in Rio and across Brazil for how Black brotherhood churches offered other possibilities of existence, functioning as a repository of diasporic collective identity, speech acts, and collective cultural expression, and as places where normative discourses were disrupted (Mombaça 2017). Black brotherhoods were one of the main means of humanization and integration of Black communities in Portuguese-Brazilian colonial society. In this view, it is possible to think of such brotherhoods as places of speech (see introduction, this volume) insofar as they behaved as mechanisms of interlocution and momentary interruption of the hegemonic matrix, acting in favor of the existence of discriminated groups in other places beyond the servitude and reification.

These church facilities hosted meetings and elections to choose the board of directors of brotherhoods while serving to camouflage Bantu and African spiritual and religious traditions and collective-cultural practices considered heterodox (i.e., prohibited and purged by the Catholic hierarchy) at the time. In this way, the brotherhood churches served as spaces of autonomy. Having an important role in the formation of a Black consciousness—made possible through building identities and leaderships—the brotherhoods became a natural stage of struggle for more autonomy within an oppressive system and, consequently, in the expansion of emancipatory movements of Black people in Brazilian society (Souza 2014). These mutual aid societies could choose their own priests and forge social alliances and design strategies (Reis 1992). Through these brotherhoods and the infrastructure that sustained them, Black Brazilians had institutional avenues to offer knowledge, create a place for speech and articulated consciousness, and, eventually, to launch insurgencies (Ribeiro 2019).

It was in the eighteenth century that the IRSB (1700), the IGSD (1706), the ISEE (1745), and the INSL (1748) began to cultivate political spaces and disrupt colonial hierarchy (Alcoff 2016, 217). Land donated to these brotherhoods for the construction of churches was also used to construct new homes outside the city's urban limits. The city expanded as the faithful sought to beautify saints' churches, restructuring streets to offer more access to this new space (Cavalcanti 2004, 206). Brotherhood church councils oversaw processes of accumulation and subdivision of Black land. These settlements were gradually organized and populated and made up the urban periphery, consisting of Afro-brotherhood planning blocks or Afro-confrarial (Afro-fraternal) quadrilaterals. This term, *quadrilaterals*, is my own and refers here to the space that makes up a church's perimeter. It is a concept that allows us to give a name to the physical infrastructure that Black populations built and which contributed to their growing agency. Churches were built and contributed to this physical structure after freedmen settled in the city's Rossio. The quadrilateral stretched from east to west in Rio de Janeiro, from Rua da Vala (currently Uruguaiana) to Rua da Lampadosa (today's Avenida Passos), and from north to south, from Rua Larga de São Joaquim (now Av. Marechal Floriano) to Rua do Piolho (now Rua da Carioca). An eviction order was received from the Cabido da Sé (Governing Council of the Diocese).[3] In this case, the brotherhood mobilized its political position as an outsider within (racially excluded from white political institutions but part of this religious institution) and, in doing so, created places of power (Collins 2016). Individually or institutionally, the brothers were able to receive benefits from the Christian charities—despite the hierarchical dependence inherent to such an economic model (Sennett 2003, 152–57). Equipped with social aid, solidarity, and charity, these brotherhoods eventually consolidated and drained land in the port-adjacent marshes and floodplains. Black settlements were installed in Campo da Cidade and Rossio, public streets located beyond the Rua da Vala and once covered by ponds and swamps (Coaracy 1965, 61–62). The first Afro-Carioca communities to receive recognized allotments were the IRSB, in 1700, and the IGSD, in 1706.

Built in a border area between the city and the countryside, the IRSB was the first beacon that emerged around an urban neighborhood and formed a kind of eighteenth-century suburb. By appropriating allotments, the brotherhoods exercised symbolic control, offering an identity based on notions of territory. The Brotherhood of Nossa Senhora do Rosário and São Benedito dos Homens Pretos played an important role in the fight against the usurpation of churches. Their churches were transformed into a cathedral in 1734 by the Corpo Capitular ou Cabido (religious advisors), which took advantage of legal loopholes and filed several petitions to the city council of Rio de Janeiro and the Mesa de Consciência e Ordens in Lisbon. In their complaints, they reported abuses committed by the brotherhood church administration.

The history of Black brotherhoods in the city of Rio de Janeiro, to date, does not point to singular prominent Black historical leaders or figures who attempted to safeguard the institution. What exists are reports of collective action by the brothers. And one of the most famous was the strategy to circumvent the Cabido during a Mass celebrating the arrival of the royal family in Rio de Janeiro in Black churches and the city's cathedral in 1808. Prevented by the Cabido from welcoming the emperor and his court at the entrance to the church, the brothers set up a strategy and managed to circumvent the order, being the first to kiss the monarch's hand before the Padres Capitulares (Council of the Bishop and the Diocese). This can be seen in a painting by Armando Martins Viana, presently at the Historical Museum in Rio de Janeiro.

Exercising control over a territory offered some claims to sovereignty for the brotherhoods. But their own spaces were being encroached upon more generally. Territory, here, must refer not only to political-structural control but identity/affective and symbolic power as well (Haesbaert 1997, 41–42). Territory can be understood through appropriation (symbolic-cultural) and domination (political-economic), and appropriated territory can create objective (territorial) and subjective (symbolic, identity-based, and affective) characteristics of lived spaces. Territorial identities develop over time into social groups, which offer symbolic control over the spaces that they live in (through stories, laws, etc.). More concretely, territory takes on a political-disciplinary character, with the appropriation and ordering of space as a way of dominating and disciplining individuals from the Black brotherhoods (Haesbaert 1997, 42).

The (IRSB) had matured into a territorialized sociopolitical organization, sometimes usurping the functions of the Cabido da Sé. This brotherhood of autonomy lasted more than sixty years, between 1737 and 1808 (Ribeiro 2019, 84–85; Quintão 2002, 127–68). The IRSB exercised a double function: it centralized and drew in Black populations toward the church and its services in the earlier years. Later, it facilitated urban decentralization through the allocation of lands and construction of housing and services in the new eighteenth-century suburbs, which became the city center as Rio expanded. The brotherhoods attracted residents and institutions, including those from the more urban areas of the city. The fábricas profoundly impacted the layout of urban space in Rio, transcending the formalism of a walled port city and moving toward a more open layout (Santos 2015, 17–41).

The IGSD was the second Afro-brotherhood to receive land in Campo da Cidade in 1706 and built a church in 1713 (Fazenda 1921, 431). They renamed the area Campo de São Domingos, which became a new city neighborhood. The presence of the IGSD attracted a population that remade the land and divided it into farms and houses, with streets and squares in between (Coaracy 1965, 62–64). But the brotherhoods were later evicted. The reports are inconclusive, but they do reveal that the brothers, in addition to facing prejudice, had been evicted due to the independence that characterized their institutions (Quintão 2002, 129). The arrival of the Cabido at the cathedral represented a particularly intolerant chapter of the brotherhoods' existence. The church decided that there was no more room for Black worshippers and began to stifle Black activism and associations. The tensions subsided only when land was donated to Black populations on floodplains.

The construction projects of the IGSD drained the swamplands, creating a dry region between the slave market in Valongo Wharf (in the port zone) and the expanding urban settlements. The IGSD's property, since its foundation, included the church and the Saint Domingos Cemetery. This space existed until the 1940s, when the city government subjected the church to aggressive urban gentrification and eviction campaigns (Cruls 1949, 228–29).

The IRSB and IGSD also took on the role of incubator for other brotherhoods, offering shelter and protection to Africans who were not yet in a position to organize their own space. The fruits of this incubation are the Church of Saint Elesbão and Saint Efigência (ISEE), independent of IGSD since 1745, and the Church of Our Lady of Lampadosa (INSL), emancipated from the IRSB in 1748. These are the pioneers and protectors of the expansion of the Afro-brotherhood and its institutions. The INSL had been founded before 1740 on the devoted initiative of enslaved people from Lampedusa Island (part of present-day Italy), who came from Abyssinia by way of Egypt. The historical accounts that describe Black presence on the island report the transfer of segments of this population to Rio de Janeiro, later forming the Irmandade de Nossa Senhora da Lampedusa at the beginning of the eighteenth century. They arrived in Rio de Janeiro and initially lodged at the Church of Nossa Senhora do Rosário and São Benedito dos Homens Pretos. Taking Nossa Senhora da Lampadosa as their patron saint and protector of their blissful journey, they founded a brotherhood and, years later, built their own church. This is the only Black brotherhood made up of Ethiopians,

Christians, and free people in Rio de Janeiro (Torres 1997, 21–24). The brotherhood remained at the IRSB until 1748, when, by donation, it received a piece of land in Campo de São Domingos, closing its church in 1772 (Mauricio 1946, 213–16). Small yet influential brotherhood churches attempted to impact memory and history by naming streets, lanes, and fields around them while planning new urban perimeters.

Final Considerations

The gradual accumulation of land and mobilization to protect these settlements helps explain the social, political, and physical geography of the city in the modern era (Fridman 2017, 15). In describing the urbanization process of Rio de Janeiro during the eighteenth century, equal recognition should be given to Black churches and brotherhoods, and their accomplishments should stand out in the city's memory and its popular and scholarly historiography.

This chapter reflects today's ethical commitment to ensuring the visibility of Black agency in processes of urban expansion that have been epistemologically and historiographically sidelined. Afro-Brazilian groups' achievements have been erased, the places and built spaces they made not recognized, and their humanity discounted. History has shown that such erasures and invisibility can kill, in the past and in the current moment. When a Black brotherhood claimed the right to have a voice and to express itself, it was, in fact, claiming the right to its own existence (Ribeiro 2019, 64). To recognize these achievements and claims, this chapter provides counterconcepts and an alternative urban history of Rio, and of Black history in global modernity, in order to challenge colonial memory, creating space for agents capable of speaking for themselves and occupying places other than those of enslavement.

NOTES

1   Carioca is the original Tupi Indigenous term for the inhabitants of what is now central Rio de Janeiro, which residents of Rio continue to call themselves. Afro-Brazilian or in this case Afro-Carioca are terms that remain current, including among Black activists in Brazil and Rio, whereas in the North American context, the prefix is less common in the twenty-first century.

2   The term *fábrica da igreja* is still used today to designate legal entities to which all assets and rights related to conservation, maintenance, and repair of a religious building belong. It also includes the expenses related to worship.

3   Cabido da Sé, Capitular Corps, or Capitulares refers to clerics who assist the bishop in governing the diocese—in particular, advising on various matters of diocesan life.

REFERENCES

Alcoff, Linda. 2016. "Uma epistemologia para a próxima revolução." *Revista sociedade e estado* 31, no. 1: 129–43.

Bluteau, Raphael. 1712. *Vocabulario Portuguez e Latino*. Coimbra: Real Collegio das Artes da Companhia de Jesus.

Boschi, Caio Cesar. 2019. "Confraternidades negras na América portuguesa do Setecentos." *Revista estudos avançados* 33, no. 97: 211–33.

Cavalcanti, Nireu. 2004. *O Rio de Janeiro setecentista: A vida e a construção da cidade da invasão francesa até a chegada da corte*. Rio de Janeiro: Zahar.

Coaracy, Vivaldo. 1965. *Memórias da cidade do Rio de Janeiro*. Rio de Janeiro: José Olympio Editora.

Collins, Patricia Hill. 2016. "Aprendendo com o outsider within: A significação sociológica do pensamento feminista negro." Translated by Juliana de Castro and Joaze Bernardino Costa. *Revista sociedade e estado* 31, no 1: 99–127.

Cruls, Gastão. 1949. *Aparência do Rio de Janeiro*. Rio de Janeiro: José Olympio Editora.

Fazenda, José Vieira. 1921. "Antiqualhas e memórias do Rio de Janeiro." In *Revista do Instituto Histórico e Geográfico Brasileiro*. Rio de Janeiro: Imprensa Nacional.

Fridman, Fania. 2017. *Donos do Rio em nome do rei: Uma história fundiário do Rio de Janeiro*. Rio de Janeiro: Garamond.

Haesbaert, Rogério. 1997. *Des-territorialização e identidade: A rede "gaúcha" no Nordeste*. Niterói: EDUFF.

Kilomba, Grada. 2012. *Plantation Memories: Episode of Everyday Racism*. Chico, CA: AK Press.

Lajo, Rosina. 1990. *Léxico de Arte*. Madrid: Akal Press.

Mauricio, Augusto. 1946. *Templos históricos do Rio de Janeiro*. Rio de Janeiro: Laemmert.

Mombaça, Jota. 2017. "Notas estratégicas quanto ao uso político do conceito de lugar de fala." *Buala*, July 19. http://goo.gl/DpQxZx.

Quintão, Antonia Aparecida. 2002. *Lá vem o meu parente: As irmandades de pretos e pardos no Rio de Janeiro e em Pernambuco (século XVIII)*. São Paulo: FAPESP.

Reis, João José. 1992. "Différences e résistence: Les Noirs à Bahia sous l'esclavage." *Cahiers d'études africaines* 32, no. 125: 15–34.

Ribeiro, Djamila. 2019. *O que é lugar de fala*. São Paulo: Pólen.

Santana, Analia. 2013. *Mulheres negras do Rosário do Pelourinho: Memória, identidade e poder*. Florianópolis: Seminário Internacional Fazendo Gênero.

Santos, Paulo F. 2015. *Formação de cidades no Brasil colonial*. Rio de Janeiro: Editora UFRJ/Iphan.

Sennett, Richard. 2003. *Carne e pedra*. Rio de Janeiro: Record.

Soares, Mariza de Carvalho. 2002. Império de Santo Elesbão na cidade do Rio de Janeiro." *Revista topoi* 3, no. 4: 63–78.

Souza, Marina de Mello. 2014. *Reis negros no Brasil escravista: História da Festa de Coroação de Rei Congo*. Belo Horizonte: Editora UFMG.

Torres, José Pereira. 1997. *Venerável Confraria de Nossa Senhora da Lampadosa*. Rio de Janeiro: Edições Diáspora.

13

Anti-White Patriarchal Ultramodernity /

Ultramodernidade Anti-blancopatriarcal

Peripheral Dissent and Gender Battles in São Gonçalo

OSMUNDO PINHO

The City of São Gonçalo

I developed the critical concept of ultramodernity during my publicly engaged fieldwork in Jardim Catarina, a popular working-class neighborhood in the city of São Gonçalo. São Gonçalo includes more than a million residents, located within the state of Rio de Janeiro and within the Greater Rio region but outside the municipality. São Gonçalo is an industrial zone, on the other side of the vast and heavily polluted Guanabara Bay. The urban settlement is characterized by working-class communities and plagued by terrible public services and neglected infrastructure. Governance is often implemented by intersecting institutions of right-wing evangelical congregations, paramilitary militias, and police brutality. My research revisits discussions on the modernization of Brazilian society and on the theoretical status of modernity. I revive and resituate the continued relevance of these terms and the norms and modes of discipline they deploy, in the context of a racialized class society defined by poverty, as well as by passionate battles around sexuality and gender. In this scope, ultramodernity is the way to define how subjectivities and cultural practices incorporate the contradictions of modernity, namely its promises of universal emancipation, vis-à-vis the raw materiality of race and gender structures.

With a population of 1,084,839 inhabitants (compared to the 2004 estimate, 889,828), São Gonçalo has a large concentration of poor and Black populations with less education and access to services and urban resources in comparison with other racial groups (IBGE 2023).[1] And as we know, the formation of peripheries is characterized by the abuse of economic power and by a strategy that offers space for housing for the popular classes (Zaluar and Alvito 2003; Burgos 2003; Alvito 2001). For instance, residents came to occupy Jardim Catarina (JC) through the acquisition of lots sold after the dissolution of agricultural properties (Cordeiro 2004).

Favelas emerge as urban spaces integrated into necessarily subordinate economic and political centers of the city and market. They also represent the periphery of public space, citizenship, and political expression—all of which are informed by anti-Blackness (Caldeira 2000). The favela "ensures that the gendered black subject is an impossible subject, one whose impossible gender, impossible blackness, impossible being, inhabits the very impossible co-ordinates of time and space that make the nation possible. The nation is possible because the gendered black subject, qua subject, qua citizen, is an oxymoron" (Vargas 2012, 5).

This subordinate integration should not be thought of in cultural terms, as if the favela residents were constituting a kind of alternative and parallel space. Rather, these spaces emerge through differentiated access to markets and in terms of spatial allocation regulated by clientelism or violence of the state and parastatal forces (Zaluar and Alvito 2003; Souza 2003; Brandão 2004; Alves 2003). Residents are fully aware of their peripheralization and maintain a desire for access to citizenship and work, but the nature of their work leads to subjugation in a very concrete sense, as many interlocutors pointed out to us in the field.

Peripheral Subjects and Ultramodernity

The processes of social individualization can help us to reposition questions about the universalization of modernity and about modern individualism seen from a context of urban poverty.[2] Exemplary narratives can be highlighted here to discuss these tensions, offering the testimony of two young men with very similar material conditions but completely different trajectories. One self-declared white and queer (referred to as V. from here on), and the other Black and formerly a drug dealer (referred to as C. from here on). Together they reflect the contradictions between the desire for individualization—"to be someone"—and the material constraints and structures of inequality (Dumont 1992, 1993; Giddens 1993, 2002).

Starting to work at sixteen and finishing high school at twenty-two, V. enjoyed opportunities to better his and his family's material well-being through his active self-insertion in the labor market. His mother, an evangelical, condemns his sexual orientation, while his father left the family when V. was just a few months old. These features bring him closer to the biography of many other boys from JC but distinguish him from other queer residents of the nearby city of Rio de Janeiro—such as those portrayed by Carmen Dora Guimarães (2004).[3] The people with whom V. became emotionally and sexually involved in JC are distant in geographical and symbolic ways from the more privileged and globally visible universe of queer worlds in the touristic South Zone of Rio de Janeiro (Gontijo 2004).

C. was a twenty-four-year-old Black man who finished high school with difficulty. Despite being a former funk baller, thief, and drug dealer, C. acted as a youth leader in his community and had active social projects and dreams of studying social sciences.[4] C. tried to make himself distinct—following a trajectory entirely different from V.—by emphasizing aspects of hegemonic masculine violence. C. aspired to be respected and feared, and retroactively looked for ways to transform himself to achieve his goals. He labeled himself as a bandit, thief, neurotic, and sinistro, among other epithets, and was able to make rational decisions given his life circumstances. Both C. and V. are modern subjects and live the contradictions of modernization as radical ultramodernity (Pinho 2006, 2007). They are not malformed characters coming from another age but rather modern and rational beings. They embody ultramodernity imposed on Black and poor populations.

When theorizing about Brazilian modernization—and about the social construction of subcitizenship—one must question inequality. In this field of debate, the issue of universalization presents itself as singular to Western culture. Is Brazilian modernity incomplete, anomalous, or divergent because of its peripheral characteristics in a global system? Or as Partha Chatterjee puts it, is our modernity (of peripheral and postcolonial countries) in fact a modernity of the "already colonized" (2004, 58)?

From a certain angle, this feeling of inadequacy or exteriority has been emphasized by what Jessé Souza calls the "sociology of inauthenticity," for which we would not have been able to "institutionalize the individualistic and bourgeois values of Western Europe" (2003, 236). For Souza, Brazil is in fact a fully modern country, insofar as the value codes of the modern West, especially individualism, are the only legitimate and valorized codes. The specific aspect of Brazilian modernization refers to the selective nature of access to central goods, which defines a negatively regulated citizenship, with social actors positioned as urban and rural pariahs. This exclusion is rooted precisely in the differential relationship with this world of modern values, under the influence of the market and state—fully modern institutions in the Brazilian context (Souza 2003).

This is precisely what we observed, from an ethnographic point of view, in Jardim Catarina. The historical formation of peripheral neighborhoods, including the JC, may be seen through the history of their production as precarious social spaces, but also through the history of the relationship between this precariousness and the aspirations of consumption and integration into the world of goods.

Gender Battles in Jardim Catarina

The gender system operating in popular or working-class environments is often assumed to be relatively more traditional, according to heteronormative standards. I would prefer to explain this difference, which appears to be an irreducible cultural difference, as a materially structured one (Monteiro 2002). I do not want to assume a culturalist opposition, as in some established approaches biased by the idea of a culture of poverty, which requires that poor and/or Black people be characterized as nonmodern and imprisoned within traditional ways of life or living as opposed to a supposedly egalitarian middle class (Duarte 1986; Fry 1982; Lewis 1968). Simultaneously, I consider categories of race and gender as materialized through the performance of subjects (Crapanzano 2002). In this manner, I embrace an idea of structure as an articulated unit of objective contradictions (material and symbolic). This structure is reproduced through the human agency that replicates itself in the social forms experienced as determined but in fact contingent structures, such as race and gender. At the level of experience, then, structures of race and gender produce racialized or gendered individuals and bodies (Butler 2003).

In Jardim Catarina, a particular and localized battle along gender lines emerged. Asymmetries and gender oppression were pervasive among the lives of women—a trend openly discussed in that context with fervor and detail. Men, in turn, while acknowledging asymmetrical aspects of gender relations, offered pragmatic arguments centering around sex, rather than gender—that is, focused on the practices, not in the values.

In the popular urban culture of Rio de Janeiro, funk music is a preferred language for the expression and articulation of sexuality, the body, gender, and desire. One of the gender polemics present in the cultural universe of funk, but also clearly present in JC, had to do with the dispute between two women, the fiel and the amante (roughly translating as the faithful and the mistress) and the way in which men stand between the two. The unfolding of this distinction, in real time, can be very telling. On one occasion, I attended a barbecue for V.'s birthday, as V. was one of our main collaborators in the field. The backyard party was lively, dominated by pagode (a kind of samba music) and funk music. One of the husband's friends was attending the party, accompanied by a woman who we later learned was his lover (i.e., mistress on the side) and not his wife. All the women at the party were furious, condemning the man in question and by extension all the husbands present. The men were amused by the situation and seemed to support the unfaithful husband. The tension became clearer when the DJ started to play a certain funk track with the following chorus: "there must be a lover / there must be a lover / every real man must have a lover" (DJ Wally and MC Mascote 2022). The group of men, at the end of the yard, enjoyed themselves while the women responded to the provocation as they spoke among themselves. Meanwhile, the woman accompanying the husband seemed to enjoy herself apart from the tension, playing a kind of indifferent and amoral role expected for a lover.

If patriarchal ideas circulated in the locality, women were not passive victims and interacted precisely at this point of friction, between faithful and lover subjectivities, which also imposed contradictions on men. In a focus group, one man reported the following: "I started dating one of my girlfriend's best friends, then we dated, [for] like three months, more or less. She didn't know I had a girlfriend, and every time I arrived at our dates, I would stay a few moments and then leave to meet the other girl. I used to say I was feeling sick, so I could spend some time with the other. But there was a time when she started getting really aggressive so that I would leave her and stay with my girlfriend" (men's focal group, ages nineteen to twenty-four years, interview with author, 2004).

Race, gender, and sexuality, in the modern milieu of poverty and class exploitation, seem to be the operative elements in the concrete plane of existence of that systematic subordinate contradiction. Sex and race come together in the body, socially produced and represented, and it is in the body, as a sociological and discursive artifact, that the reproductive structures of subjection are articulated. Not that race and gender, as social practices, are not, in fact, structural practices, in the sense of being external and preexistent to the action of the individual agents; but the fact is that those practices and discourses of gender and race, as mechanisms, produce a strong connection between the formation of subjects and structures for unequal social reproduction (Arilha, Unbehaum, and Medrado 2001; Bruschini and Pinto 2001; Mattos 2006).

Disputes about the meaning of the body, gender, and sexuality appear in the context of ultramodern racialized peripheries insofar as they reveal the contradiction between, on the one hand, egalitarian values performed as a pretense of autonomy and reflexive agency, and, on the other hand, patterns of unequal social reproduction. Despite appearances, the young men's conduct is not traditional or premodern but is structured as a set of autonomous and plural subjects who are fully capable of reflexivity in relation to women.

Anti-Black Moral Panic

The ideas I have been discussing in this chapter are based on field research carried out over a couple of years in Jardim Catarina. I tracked and analyzed these contexts as I reflected on the theoretical status of modernity, in relation to systems of patriarchy, heteronormative masculinity, and white supremacy. I was devoted, indeed, to understanding how gender and sexuality are so important to structuring racialized notions of modernity.

The recurrent moral panics and the attacks on sexual and reproductive rights and a reactionary revival of masculinist discourses of law and order were, and still are, mediated by a globally pro-family respectability politics and recurring cycles of moral panic directed against Black social life (Pinho 2014). In speaking about the securitization of panic discourses, Paul Amar points out specific racialized and gendered techniques, which he labels parahumanization. His use of *para-* represents an "attempt to systematize the pervasive transnational vernacular use of terms like *shadow, shade, ghost, specter,* or *phantom,* which expressly capture the illiberal dimensions of security governance today . . . [in] vernacular terms that speak of shadow states and parallel governance . . . [or] '[p]hantom' developments. . . . Those in power also speak of shadows and phantoms . . . [to] racialize and sexualize suspect populations, . . . seeing peoples of subordinate classes as inherently suspect" (2013, 18).

Discussing sexualized racialization in the context of moral panic, Pinho (2018) refers to the relationship between discourses on Afro-Brazilians and the street, and how these generated panic as in the case of the notorious arrastão affair. Arrastão refers to a "dragnet" practice whereby groups of young people run across the beach on days when it is teeming with visitors and quickly snatch and steal items en masse:

These began in 1992, when Benedita da Silva, the first black woman candidate for governor of Rio de Janeiro, was ahead in the election polls. On another lovely summer Sunday, reports of arrastões appeared and then multiplied. A whole web of connections with deep historical meanings was resurrected in this moment, crystalizing in the arrastões, which were mostly a media phenomenon manifesting the fears of "dangerous," black/brown urban crowds that have terrorized whiter public subjects throughout the history of post-abolition Brazil. The arrastão is therefore a central trope in the production of contemporary urban Brazil's moral panic, helping to articulate the young black male body with crime; "favela"; and, of course, funk music. (Pinho 2018, 164)

De-Africanization politics, well known in Brazilian history, consisted of racialized campaigns that offered hypersexualized and primitive portrayals of Blackness and maleness in distinct historical contexts, such as colonial Bahia. In modern times, moral panic discourses circulate, as de-Africanization politics, in order to render these subjects paradoxically hypervisible, to justify campaigns of anti-Black violence (Amar 2013, 144–45, 231).

My contribution highlights the relation between poverty and the concrete nature of effective ultramodernization. Peripheral modernity—that suffered by sectors of Brazilian society subordinate to urbanization and modernization—is of course central to the discussion. This debate—on race and gender—acquires a particular significance when seen as a key element in understanding how Brazilian social reproduction managed, throughout the twentieth century, to produce the racial inequalities we know. For some, the Brazilian racial problem would be a by-product of cultural delay, or a symbolic residue of backwardness and the past. In this logic, social existence is asphyxiated by progress, by the evolution of capitalism, and by modernization itself (Fernandes 1978). It seems to me that in the third decade of the twenty-first century, the long-awaited modernization has already arrived but has failed to bring redemption to the wretched of the earth (Fanon 1961).

Ultramodernity: Peripheralizing Contradictions of Modernity

Ultramodernity, as a distinct concept, offers a way to analytically incorporate the structured process of forming subjectivity amid contradictory relationships within the market, the state, and corresponding racial formations.[5] In the same way that nation-states organize themselves along the problematic and contradictory relationships between center and periphery, other social entities are also peripheralized and integrated in a subordinate way under the economies of a global world. This subordinated economic integration is made basically effective in many cases through consumption (real or desired) and not through production. This represents a clear position that a large percentage of the Brazilian residents of Jardim Catarina find themselves in. To trace the implications of these overlapping processes, this chapter has discussed the formation of peripheral subjects, such as the self-contradictory process of subjectivation mediated through relative material deprivation. The contribution assesses ultramodernity as a potentially contradictory condition structured through the subjects and objectified in social order (Rubin [1975] 1993; de Almeida 2020; Mora 2018).

Immersed in the ideological environment of modernity, the seduction of markets and the commodification of everyday life cannot be avoided. In those contexts, consumer goods connect local young people's way of life to that of other young people from different social conditions. Just as they are coerced by the normative value of equality and individualism as an ideology, the contradictions that underlie the reproduction of race, class, and gender inequality are acted out daily. Modernity, at its extremes, puts them before extreme choices, sometimes between life and death. Everything the system promises (integration and citizenship via consumption) must be denied them (through racism and poverty) in order to preserve the profile of their uneven renewal (Telles 2003). Race, gender, and sexuality in the modern environment of poverty and class exploitation seem to be the operative elements, on a concrete level, of this subordinate contradiction, defining, for each contingent and structured intersection, the particular forms of oppression and contradiction within the ideals of universalization and equality of modernity.

NOTES

The research on which this work was based was carried out as part of a broader project, "AfroRio Século XXI," based at CEAB (Center for Afro-Brazilian Studies) at Candido Mendes University between 2002 and 2004 (Heringer and Pinho 2011). Thank you to the entire team at the center, especially Rosana Heringer, its director at that time, as well as Carla dos Santos Mattos and Herculis Toledo, who played a fundamental role in the fieldwork. I also thank Renato Emerson dos Santos for dialogue and support at the beginning of the research in São Gonçalo.

1   Between 28 and 30 percent of household heads in São Gonçalo, for example, received incomes below the monthly minimum wage (IBGE 2023).

2   Universalization of modernity as discussed in sociology by Giddens (1989) and classically by Weber ([1904] 2003).

3   In the case of Guimarães, the group was middle class and queer, well traveled, sophisticated, and, according to the author, all white. They articulated their desires for individualization using the surrounding conditions and possibilities that their class status afforded them. The author draws attention to how the actors' queerness interacts, in a way that is not necessarily subordinate, with "different domains of power." Thus, the class position is an "instrumental crossing point" for power relations (Guimarães 2004, 60).

4   I learned with horror that a few years after my departure from Rio, C. returned to drug trafficking and was killed.

5   As I discussed for the rolezinho phenomenon and for the funk and pagode known as ostentação (Pinho 2015, 2018).

REFERENCES

Alves, José Cláudio Souza. 2003. *Dos barões ao extermínio: Uma história da violência na Baixada Fluminense*. Duque de Caxias: APPH/CLIO.

Alvito, Marcos. 2001. *As Cores de Acari: Uma favela Carioca*. Rio de Janeiro: FGV Editora.

Amar, Paul. 2013. *The Security Archipelago: Human-Security States, Sexuality Politics and the End of Neoliberalism*. Durham, NC: Duke University Press.

Arilha, Margareth, Sandra G. Unbehaum Ridenti, and Benedito Medrado, eds. 2001. *Homens e masculinidades: Outras palavras*. São Paulo: Ecos/Editora 34.

Brandão, André Augusto. 2004. *Miséria da periferia: Desigualdades raciais e pobreza na metrópole do Rio de Janeiro*. Rio de Janeiro: Pallas.

Bruschini, Cristina, and Celi Regina Pinto. 2001. *Tempo e lugares de gênero*. São Paulo: Fundação Carlos Chagas/Editora 34.

Burgos, Marcelo Baumann. 2003. "Dos parques proletários ao favela-bairro: As políticas públicas nas favelas do Rio de Janeiro." In *Um Século de Favela*, edited by Alba Zaluar and Marcos Alvito. Rio de Janeiro: FGV Editora.

Butler, Judith. 2003. *Problemas de gênero feminismo e subversão de identidade*. Rio de Janeiro: Civilização Brasileira.

Caldeira, Teresa P. R. 2000. *City of Walls: Crime, Segregation and Citizenship in São Paulo*. Berkeley: University of California Press.

Chatterjee, Partha. 2004. *Colonialismo, modernidade e política*. Salvador: EDUFBA/CEAO/Fábrica de Idéias.

Cordeiro, Ana Márcia Soares. 2004. *Espaços da política: A associação de moradores como lócus da mediação entre as práticas cotidianas locais e o estado*. São Gonçalo: UERJ/FFP/Departamento de Geografia.

Crapanzano, Vincent. 2002. "Estilos de interpretação e retórica de categorias sociais." In *Raça como retórica a construção da diferença*, edited by Yvonne Maggie and Claudia Barcellos Rezende. Rio de Janeiro: Civilização Brasileira.

de Almeida, Heloisa Buarque. 2020. "Gênero." *Enciclopédia mulheres na filosofia*, July 16. https://www.blogs.unicamp.br/mulheresnafilosofia/genero/.

DJ Wally and MC Mascote. 2017. "Tem que Ter Uma Amante." YouTube video, posted November 16 by DJ Wally Oficial. https://www.youtube.com/watch?v=V_JIRkXW4Uw.

Duarte, Luiz Fernando D. 1986. *Da vida nervosa: Nas classes trabalhadoras urbanas*. Rio de Janeiro: Jorge Zahar Editor.

Dumont, Louis. 1992. *Homo Hierarchicus: O sistema de castas e suas implicações*. São Paulo: EDUSP.

Dumont, Louis. 1993. *O individualismo: Uma perspectiva antropológica moderna*. Rio de Janeiro: Rocco.

Fanon, Frantz. 1961. *The Wretched of the Earth*. Paris: François Maspero.

Fernandes, Florestan. 1978. *A integração do negro na sociedade de classes*. Vol. 2, *No limiar de uma nova era*. São Paulo: Ática Press.

Fry, Peter. 1982. "Da hierarquia à igualdade: A construção histórica da homossexualidade no Brasil." In *Para Inglês ver*. Rio de Janeiro: Zahar Editores.

Giddens, Anthony. 1989. *A constituição da sociedade*. São Paulo: Livraria Martins Fontes Editora.

Giddens, Anthony. 1993. "Modernity, History, Democracy." *Theory and Society* 22, no. 2: 289–92.

Giddens, Anthony. 2002. *Modernidade e identidade*. São Paulo: Editora Schwarcz-Companhia das Letras.

Gontijo, Fabiano. 2004. "Imagens identitárias homossexuais, carnaval e cidadania." In *Homossexualidade: Produção cultural, cidadania e saúde*, edited by Luís Felipe Rios et al. Rio de Janeiro: Abia.

Guimarães, Carmen Dora. 2004. *O homossexual visto por entendidos*. Rio de Janeiro: Garamond Universitária.

Heringer, Rosana, and Osmundo Pinho, eds. 2011. *Afro-Rio seculo XXI: Modernidade e relações sociais no Rio de Janeiro*. Rio de Janeiro: Garamond.

IBGE. 2023. "Brasil / Rio de Janeiro / São Gonçalo." Instituto Brasileiro de Geografia e Estatística. https://cidades.ibge.gov.br/brasil/rj/sao-goncalo/panorama.

Lewis, Gordon K. 1968. *Growth of Modern West Indies*. Vol. 130. New York: NYU Press.

Mattos, Carla dos Santos. 2006. "No ritmo neurótico: Cultura funk e performances 'proibidas' em contexto de violência no Rio de Janeiro." Master's thesis, Universidade do Estado do Rio de Janeiro.

Monteiro, Simone. 2002. *Qual Prevenção: AIDS, sexualidade e gênero numa favela Carioca*. Rio de Janeiro: Editora Fiocruz.

Mora, Mariana. 2018. *Política Kuxlejal: Autonomia Indigena, el estado racial e investigação descolonizante em comunidades Zapatistas*. Mexico City: Centro de Investigaciones y Estudios Superiores en Antropología Social.

Pinho, Osmundo. 2006. "A vida em que vivemos: Raça, gênero e modernidade em São Gonçalo." *Revista estudos feministas* 1, no. 14: 196–98.

Pinho, Osmundo. 2007. "A fiel, a amante e o jovem macho sedutor: Sujeitos de gênero, na periferia racializada." *Saúde e sociedade* 16, no. 2: 133–45.

Pinho, Osmundo. 2014. "The Black Male Body and Sex Wars in Brazil." In *Queering Paradigms IV: South-North Dialogues on Queer Epistemologies*, edited by Elizabeth Sarah Lewis et al. Oxford: Peter Lang.

Pinho, Osmundo. 2015. "Putaria: Masculinidade, negritude e desejo no pagode baiano." *Maguare* 29, no. 2: 209–38.

Pinho, Osmundo. 2018. "Black Bodies, Wrong Places: Rolezinho, Moral Panic, and Racialized Male Subjects in Brazil." In *Panic, Transnational Cultural Studies, and the Affective Contours of Power*, edited by Micol Siegel. New York: Routledge.

Rubin, Gayle. (1975) 1993. "O tráfico de mulheres: Notas sobre a 'economia política' do sexo." Edited and translated by Christine Rufino Dabat, Edileusa Oliveira da Rocha, and Sonia Corrêa. Recife: S.O.S Corpo. https://repositorio.ufsc.br/handle/123456789/1919. (Soscorpo.org is a feminist activist organization and website run by its headquarters based in Recife, Brazil.)

Souza, Jessé. 2003. *A construção social da subcidadania: Para uma sociologia política da modernização periférica*. Belo Horizonte / Rio de Janeiro: Editora UFMG/IUPERJ.

Telles, Edward. 2003. *Racismo à Brasileira: Uma nova perspectiva sociológica*. Rio de Janeiro: Relume Dumará.

Vargas, João H. C. 2012. "Gendered Antiblackness and the Impossible Brazilian Project: Emerging Critical Brazilian Studies." *Cultural Dynamics* 24, no. 1: 3–11.

Weber, Max. (1904) 2003. *A ética protestante e o espírito do capitalismo*. São Paulo: Pioneira / Thomson Learning, Impresso.

Zaluar, Alba, and Marcos Alvito, eds. 2003. *Um século de favela*. Rio de Janeiro: Fundação Getulio Vargas Editora.

14

Quilombo Portness / Quilombismo Portuário

Living Memory and the Porousness of Racial Capitalism in Rio de Janeiro

JOÃO GABRIEL RABELLO SODRÉ AND AMANDA DE LISIO

Despite popular perception, racial capitalism and attendant processes of accumulation by dispossession, theft, and exploitation of indentured or enslaved labor fail to create a neatly closed or coherent system. Brazil is, fortunately, illustrative of this failure or "unfulfilled future" (Purbrick 2017, 267). Whereas Ann Stoler (2013) highlighted the connection between race and imperial ruination—a connection that made racialized people and geographies susceptible to ruin—in this work, we focus on the portside vicinities of Rio de Janeiro. We argue that the specific future envisioned by modern capitalist advancement is always already in ruin. We see Rio's port district as the major site for the transatlantic slave trade. Once a hub for rebel communities (quilombos) of freed and escaped enslaved people, ports are now imagined as epicenters of tourism, heritage preservation, and rampant real estate speculation for continued capitalist expansion via the sports mega event. In this chapter, we interrogate and conceptualize the singular and collective struggle for social justice enacted and embodied within the port of Rio de Janeiro as a simultaneous site of racial capitalism as well as a hub of resistance, which we describe as the quilombo portness of this zone. As Jessica Cattelino, Georgina Drew, and Ruth Morgan contend, "water flourishing is more than a mode of being. . . . It is inherently substantive in its politics, and it is part and parcel of sovereignty and citizenship" (2019, 145). We therefore posit Rio's port area as a place of connection, grown from the social uses of water for global capitalist expansion and colonialism. This process has fostered a response by Afro-Brazilians, as they—the residents of the area—use the waterfront as a place of action, community, and contestation.

Quilombo portness represents resistance to the violent processes of urbanization in Brazil and speaks to the failure of modernization (Costa and Gonçalves 2019, 66–69). We identify and analyze how these port-adjacent urban spaces have persisted as important sites for political and intellectual intervention that realize and reimagine freedom from within the boundaries of a nation predicated on enslavement.

Officially established as a slave trade port in the colonial period, the wharves of Rio de Janeiro have long served as the gateway to a set of precarious and informal residential communities—whether referred to as favelas (slums) or quilombos (self-governing settlements of escaped Black slaves or freedpeople and their descendants, often mixing with Indigenous communities). Portuguese settlers and later the Brazilian imperial state headquartered in Rio de Janeiro cultivated the development of coastal and port settlements throughout the eighteenth and nineteenth centuries in order to ensure a population density that would stand against foreign invasion by sea. As Lilia Moritz Schwarcz and Heloisa Starling write, "the need to populate the land went hand in hand with the desire to exploit for profit. And nothing could be more profitable than the monoculture of sugarcane" (2015, 40). Although the Portuguese had limited knowledge of the territory of the New World, the coastline was relatively well known, and "they understood the need for it to be populated, if only to prevent the foreign invasions that were starting to occur along the coast" (Schwarcz and Starling 2015, 40). The persistence of communities composed of fugitive enslaved and impoverished freedpeople helped connect the struggle for freedom with the struggle for land. This is what is meant when one refers to Rio de Janeiro as a "porous city" (Carvalho 2013, 10–14) or "cidade quilombada" (Neder 1997). Transformations are simultaneously momentary and connected through a lineage of spatial resistance: "By exercising power in their street and local area, which then became known across the city, Afro-descendants conferred value on the most disparaged spaces of the city and made their own geographic knowledge. This construction of black geographies challenged official mappings and discourses of the city—the city as a landscape of power—oriented around its brand-new monuments and avenues" (Leu 2020, 130–31). The forced arrival of enslaved African people and their containment within the area known as the Valongo in 1774—combined with the construction of the Valongo Wharf in 1811—cemented the port district of Rio de Janeiro as a major transit site for the transatlantic slave trade. Racism and resistance to racism thus defined the urban landscape as much as it illustrated the relational violence inherent to modernization, which produced a condition of Blackness that was susceptible to or predicated on struggle (McKittrick 2011, 949).

Raquel Rolnik asserts struggle, not domination, in her definition of Black territories. In her conception, Rolnik (1989, 2) sees these territories not as confined to the experience of exclusion and the exercise of white domination but for the transmission of collective memories and the creation of lived geographies of survival and fortitude. The port district of Rio de Janeiro has made the porousness of the urban landscape in Brazil especially pronounced as a major site for the transatlantic slave trade and tandem focus of modernization: "The persistence of racialized geographies in the center of the urbanized downtown area repeatedly thwarted the dominant geographies that the Republican and municipal government sought to impose" (Leu 2020, 118).

Within a nation with more enslaved African people than any other nation in the Americas and the last to abolish slavery in the Western Hemisphere, the significance of the port area of Rio de Janeiro—as a microcosm of the cidade quilombada or a place representative of the porosities of colonial expansion, death, and life inherent to Rio de Janeiro—cannot be overstated. It is for this reason that we specifically discuss Afro-Brazilian memorialization processes within the Valongo Wharf as well as Quilombo Pedra do Sal to contrast the imaginaries and associated construction catalyzed by the 2014 FIFA World Cup and 2016 Olympic mega events.

Maroon (or quilombo, in Portuguese) communities fought for their autonomy, particularly with respect to production, before the abolition of slavery in 1888 in Brazil. They continue to exist as an important site for residence and celebration. Within Rio de Janeiro, there is an attempt to recognize urban territories nearest the historic port as a quilombo or a sacred space for Black cultural heritage. Attentive to colonial porosity, maroonage scholarship and activism (see Stern 1987; Joseph 1990; Miki 2012) have started to favor a broader conceptualization of quilombo to better recognize insurgence or rebel communities within the urban landscape—not merely relegated to rural or less inhabited territories. Quilombolas tied their struggle to the Constitution of 1988, including Article 68, which guaranteed land to quilombo communities (Mitchell 2017, 35), as well as subsequent actions in the 1990s and early 2000s that sought to more specifically address the structural racism inflicted on Black populations (Paschel 2018, 117), including Decree no. 3,551 of August 4, 2000, which established the registration and protection of immaterial culture and tradition that are part of Brazilian cultural heritage; Municipal Ordinary Law 5,781 of July 22, 2014; and Municipal Complementary Law 149 of December 15, 2014, which created a special area of cultural interest for the Quilombo Pedra do Sal in Rio de Janeiro (Mattos and Abreu 2012). This chapter uses porousness and quilombismo to examine the historic strategies of so-called fugitive communities within Rio de Janeiro to obtain formal recognition and claim official title to their land.

As such, we are especially fascinated by the contradiction between supposedly hegemonic global capitalist expansion and the local response to familiar processes of demolition and displacement that come to define everyday life for predominantly Black and low-income communities in Rio de Janeiro and throughout much of the world. Within Rio de Janeiro, this could also be examined through the rebel or insurgent activities characteristic of the favela. *Favela* and *quilombo* are defined and used differently by local people and state authorities—and in the case of the latter, inform an entire set of legislative and bureaucratic processes. We argue that the port of Rio de Janeiro—in spite of the recent attempts to redevelop and modernize the area through the spectacular sports mega event and attendant tourism, such as the Museu do Amanhã (Museum of Tomorrow)—is still quilombo and favela. To do so, we examine the significance of each term locally as well as their careful articulation within more globally oriented activism. We first present a historical overview of the port before we move into an actual discussion of quilombo and favela. In the end, we propose the introduction of a new language to describe local resistance to newly contoured and rearranged processes of capitalism. In doing so, we propose the concept of quilombismo portuário, defined as Afro-Brazilian territorial resistance that is unique to Rio de Janeiro (and Brazil more broadly) but also connected to other portuary (port) activities throughout the world that disrupt and challenge the flow of international capital.

Port of Rio de Janeiro: A Brief History

Between 1550 and 1888, at least an estimated 5 million enslaved African people were trafficked to Brazil (Araujo 2016, 1). Founded in 1565—and the capital of Brazil from 1763 until 1960—Rio de Janeiro has never experienced major destruction from war, fire, earthquake, or hurricane (Carvalho 2013, 1). As the most renowned city in a nation eager to be recognized as modern and cosmopolitan, Rio de Janeiro has served as a showcase or laboratory for numerous urban strategies. Between 1774 and 1831, the Valongo Wharf, a segment of the port in Rio de Janeiro, served as a major transit site for enslaved people (Rabello Sodré 2020). In 1843—after the entry of enslaved African people in Brazil became illegal in 1831, but before the definitive ban occurred in 1850—the Valongo Wharf was rebuilt to receive Princess Teresa Cristina Maria de Bourbon, the bride of the future Emperor Dom Pedro II. It was again transformed by Pereira Passos, an engineer appointed as mayor of the capital and architect of ambitious urban reform in the area (1902–6).

The Valongo Wharf is currently the only historical and archaeological site in Brazil recognized internationally as a place of memory of enslaved African people and the Atlantic slave trade as well as the continued cultural and political resistance of the Black population to violence and exclusion (Instituto de Pesquisa e Memória Pretos Novos, http://pretosnovos.com.br/; Pereira 2007). Most notably, Cemitério dos Pretos Novos was discovered in the Gamboa neighborhood, buried beneath the concrete of a nineteenth-century home, at 36 Rua Pedro Ernesto. It is estimated that between twenty thousand and thirty thousand newly arrived African people (referred to as pretos novos) were buried at this site—although the official record has 6,122 people buried between 1824 and 1830—mostly due to disease contracted in the forced migration from Africa to Brazil (Pereira 2007, 136). It has since been converted into a small museum, Instituto de Pesquisa e Memória Pretos Novos, founded on May 13, 2005, and maintained by Merced dos Anjos, who once lived in the house wherein the burial site was discovered.

While the slave trade declined with the emergence of the first antitrade legislation in 1831, Rio de Janeiro continued to be dependent upon the port as a major site of capitalist expansion. With the abolition of slavery in 1888, Rio de Janeiro and the port, specifically, became known as a hub for labor and economic exchange. People who occupied the site worked the dock, supported the coffee economy (1840–1930)—which boomed in the nineteenth century—and/or engaged in sex work. Even as export economies shifted from coffee to sugar, cotton, tobacco, cocoa, and rubber, the demand for industrialized labor in the port area remained relatively unchanged.

With the introduction of the first railroad in Brazil from Rio de Janeiro to Petropolis (inaugurated on April 30, 1854), the once sparsely populated neighborhood—considered a transient site housing people commonly referred to as nomadic—soon became a densely populated urban neighborhood (see also Corrêa 2016). To accommodate all those who came to work and live in the area, cortiços (tenement housing) became the common solution for immigrant families, freed and emancipated people, and migrant communities from the northeast or rural Brazil. Since most employment was located downtown and transportation was expensive, most of the population concentrated in the center wherein poorly serviced and inadequate infrastructure led to an inevitable decline in public health and rise in infectious disease (yellow fever, smallpox, and tuberculosis).

The rhetoric of urban reform soon targeted so-called dangerous classes, increasingly equated with the poor, as protection against the threat of disease. With the eviction of one famous cortiço, Cabeça-de-Porco (Pig Head), in 1893—home to an estimated four hundred to two thousand people at the time of demolition, and with speculation that four thousand once inhabited the site—it is believed that salvaged materials from the wreckage were used to build on the adjacent hillside, which was the origin of the favela (Vaz 2002, 54-57).

In response to a population boom and related public health crises, ideologies related to social hygiene—often racist and reliant upon pseudoscience—fostered the need for urban reform (Carvalho 2013). Medical authorities focused on biomedical treatment and behavioral reform that legitimated urban renewal (Schwarcz 1993). Oswaldo Cruz, a young Brazilian doctor with experience at the Pasteur Institute in Paris, led a series of public health strategies to eliminate the *Aedes aegypti* mosquito (which carried yellow fever) as well as the bubonic plague and smallpox epidemic. With support from newly elected president Rodrigues Alves (1902–6), Mayor Pereira Passos (1902–6) intervened to reform Rio de Janeiro in accordance with European-modernist imaginaries that prioritized the circulation of capital to and from the port area (Carvalho 2013; Passos 1906). Effectively, "modernization, to the elite of the early twentieth century, was to remove from the city center all traits of Africanity and poverty, pushing the population to favelas and the suburbs" (Diniz 2006, 16). In response, an antimodernization riot initiated by rebellion against a mandatory vaccination campaign signaled to authorities that reform would not occur as effortlessly as previously perceived. In fact, "by the end of the century, the neighborhood of Saúde became a stronghold for African customs and traditions brought from Bahia. . . . These included songs and dances, festivities, food dishes, rites, and beliefs" (Alencar 1981, 20). With income from activities such as Afro-Brazilian religious ceremonies and food sold predominantly in the street, a fortunate few secured enough prestige to escape law enforcement (Carvalho 2013). Afro-Brazilian heritage and tradition became synonymous with the port— even as only a fraction of the population was able to remain and understand, through the scholarship of Jeffrey Needell (1987), Jaime Larry Benchimol (1990), and Teresa Meade (1997), that reform worsened realities for the urban majority, particularly those of African origin (but also Indigenous and immigrant communities), while demolition debris spurred the growth of favela communities in the port and eventually throughout the entire Greater Rio de Janeiro area.

Urban intervention in racialized communities is certainly not novel or unique to Rio de Janeiro (evident throughout histories of economic development that has been sutured to racial capitalism). So-called security politics and samba politics are used to legitimize and corroborate strategies of securitization within communities that are simultaneously mentioned to symbolize the rich music and dance culture synonymous with Brazilian national identity (Amar 2013, 140; McCann 2014b). According to Paul Amar, "security politics claimed to ignore race while turning black communities into zones of unending police and trafficker warfare, racketeering, and impunity," whereas "samba politics" tended to "celebrate race while favoring small-scale entrepreneurship and photo opportunities rather than any structural changes in the economic, state, or legal spheres" (2013, 140, 141). For example, the Favela-Bairro (Slum-to-Neighborhood) Program—funded by the municipal government and the Inter-American Development Bank—attempted to regularize favela communities to replace "violent, degraded urban barriers with open spaces of dialogue, tourism, and amusement" (Amar 2013, 160). The program was an attempt to have such spaces adopt a liberal-progressive vision that referenced and commodified the favela as a site integral to samba—notably in the case of the Serrinha favela. In this context, the rhetoric perpetuated Vargas-era mythologies of Brazil as a racial democracy yet served to appropriate Afro-Brazilian heritage and tradition to incorporate informally titled land into the more formal system of capitalist circulation (Rolnik 2019, 202).

In a similar fashion, prior to the 2014 and 2016 mega events, the Unidades de Política Pacificadora (UPP)—advertised as a more humane response to crime and violence—occupied favela communities in the tourist-oriented South Zone to further securitize communities that mostly need protection from the state, not its increased presence. Careful analysis of the impact of pacification police in the favela detail the continuum on which disadvantaged, historically Black communities and the police (especially the rank and file), maintain their antagonistic relationship (Vargas 2018, 196). Both the Favela-Bairro Program and the UPP challenge the idea that formalization and regularization hinder or effectively dismantle violence within the favela or improve everyday life for the urban majority. It is more accurate to describe these strategies as enacted in service of racial capitalism—to coerce labor and reconfigure the urban landscape for future real estate speculation, irrespective of people. While accumulation by dispossession (Harvey 2003) is certainly evident, we are also interested in strategies of resistance that protect and maintain bodies of land and people within the everyday.

Porousness of Racial Capitalism: Favela and Quilombo in the Porto Maravilha

Favela, a term extensively incorporated into the English language, is complicated to define. Providência, popularly regarded as the first official favela in Brazil, was founded by soldiers who were formerly enslaved people that had been recently freed and drafted for the War of Canudos. These freed peoples returned from the war in 1897 and were promised land for settlement. At the time (and still), *favela* referred to an extremely durable weed found on the battleground and to signify communities that populate the hillside.

Since the establishment of the first favela, these semiperipheral urban communities have proliferated throughout Brazil as a solution to displacement and the need for housing. The Instituto Brasileiro de Geografia e Estatística (IBGE) defines *favela* as a "subnormal agglomeration" that has "at least fifty-one housing units (shacks, houses . . .) which lack, in their majority, [access to] essential public services, being located or having been until recently located in third party (public or private) property, following a disorganized and dense setting" (IBGE 2010). Bryan McCann (2014a) has elaborated upon this definition to add that the popularly imagined vision of an intricate hillside neighborhood can be dramatically different (e.g., some with a grid plan, some flourishing in deindustrialized flat lands, etc.). He writes, "Favelas are not defined by a clear set of physical characteristics; rather, they are defined by their history" (26). They can emerge from highly localized construction by a few people, transition into a favela from a government-sponsored housing project, or result from persistent demand, as is the case within the portside area of Rio de Janeiro. There is much variance internally too. Within the same favela, there is often limited consensus on property, regulation, and government intervention. Maybe the only common characteristic consistent across favela communities is the violence and exclusion experienced via familiar processes of development and the impermanence, neglect, and precariousness these communities are subjected to. To borrow from McCann, "they began as unplanned and unserviced settlements nurturing an informal real estate market and progressed through stages of consolidation and diversification without ever being fully incorporated into the surrounding formal city" (2014a, 26).

This too, we argue, is a key characteristic for quilombo communities. To illustrate our argument, we zoom into the port region of Rio de Janeiro. There are favela communities in the port (Providência is one example). But Pedra do Sal is classified as a quilombo. Quilombo or maroon communities are not exclusive to Brazil, but Brazil is regarded as the nation with the largest number of them (Klein and Luna 2010). While the colonial use of *quilombo* implied runaway enslaved people, the term received added nuance with time. Twentieth-century Black scholar Abdias Do Nascimento (1980) proposed the notion of quilombismo as a political and ideological project to affirm Black African liberation. It served as a "project of socio-political reorganization . . . with the ethical purpose of guaranteeing a human condition of Afro-Brazilian masses" (Lopes 1996, 215). The 1988 Brazilian Constitution codified into law and assigned a broad definition of *quilombo* to formally designated quilombo communities. Specifically, Article 68 in the 1988 Constitution claimed, "the definitive property rights of remnants of quilombos that have been occupying the same lands are hereby recognized, and the state shall grant them title to such lands" (Brazil 1988, translation by author; also see Rosenn 2017).

Although perceived at the time as largely symbolic—a gesture to celebrate the centennial of the abolition of slavery—communities soon started to invoke their quilombola status. In fact, the momentum led to a series of decrees that sought to improve the quality of life for people of African descent in Brazil. The 2010 Racial Equality Statute asserted "quilombola communities must receive adequate investment to obtain their right to health, including environmental protection, adequate sanitation, health, and food security" (Brazil 2010). Quilombo, as a political classification conferred in law, became a legal tool that confronted the type of land conflict endemic to rural Brazil and urban communities, such as the favela. Newly found relevance propelled the dynamism of the term, proposing that "quilombo is a form of organization, of struggle, over a space conquered and maintained through generations" (Leite 2000, 335). Becoming an actively used term, "quilombo, in current times, corresponds, to this part of Brazilian society, to a right to be recognized and not exactly merely a past to be commemorated" (335).

The transition of *quilombo* from a colonial word for runaways to a modernized term of resistance has become a nationwide phenomenon. Communities in northeastern Brazil, for example, sought "new emphasis on self-ascription and subjective perceptions of sameness and difference," which allowed for "the ethnic identification of indigenous Brazilians to be seen as flexible and contextual" (French 2009, 68–69). In Alcântara, the association with quilombismo by rural Afro-Brazilian communities represented an attempt to secure needed land titles to combat agrarian reform (Mitchell 2017, 23–53). Quilombolas—and their connection to Afro-Brazilian identity and communal land ownership—advanced the struggle against displacement.

Damião Braga, the leader of the quilombola movement at urban quilombo Pedra do Sal in Rio de Janeiro, has addressed the racial discrimination and processes of gentrification that resulted from the construction of Porto Maravilha. Braga has emphasized the racialized nature of the urban expansion, arguing that "Porto Maravilha, when aiming at establishing the new, cannot expel the old, and the old in this case are us. There is no larger reference in the area than the afro-descending population" (quoted in Corrêa 2016, 14). Braga has denounced the lack of popular participation in the distribution of wealth obtained by the state—communities and democratic processes circumvented through the creation of a public-private partnership to oversee construction in the area. With respect to the histories embedded within the port district, despite the effort to recognize the area as a heritage site—that is, via legislation that legally recognized Pedra do Sal as a quilombo in 2005 (Corrêa 2016, 12)—the result is the familiar "de-corporealization of blackness" (Cramer 2016, 2) and continued disregard for Afro-Brazilian people still within (and tantamount to) these local geographies and celebrated in local histories. For Braga, "one cannot protect patrimony without protecting the people, and these people are us, quilombolas" (Corrêa 2016, 15). He later elaborated, "The law says it is the responsibility of the state to preserve the area's heritage, but they haven't done anything, other than putting a plaque to say 'Pedra do Sal.' We see it as institutional racism" (McLoughlin 2015). To invest in and display a placard to memorialize a site of Afro-diaspora without accompanying public policies to address the people implicated in and impacted by the private intervention in the public domain is not only unhelpful but also demonstrative of the prevalence of state-sanctioned systemic racism.

In the port of Rio de Janeiro—specifically Pedra do Sal—communities resisted demolition through association with Afro-Brazilian tradition and, as a result, sought quilombo recognition. Pedra do Sal embodies the work of quilombos to protect heritage and tradition and maintain needed land for congregating, "to tell and sing their stories, after a long day of hard work at the port, in capoeira circles, at the sound of drums" (Lima 2018, 107). If the port is a sinew of global capitalism, as discussed in the work of Laleh Khalili (2020), a tightly engineered landscape to facilitate capitalist expansion only made possible through historic processes that enslaved and indentured people to labor, quilombo portness, or quilombismo portuário is, then, the lived-human insurgence needed to provide bodies of people with bodies of land. From a broader political perspective, it is also a legally conferred interruption to the otherwise extractive relationships to property and land that are tethered to capitalism.

Conclusion

Morro da Providência, the first official favela in Brazil, is now at the forefront of the newest real estate financial complex in Rio de Janeiro. The reconstruction of the area was initiated through a public-private partnership that followed the 2016 Olympic bid—an event that, as it has been known to do elsewhere in the world, shielded the project from routine democratic-bureaucratic processes. And it did so, at first, without recognition of the people already established on the supposedly abandoned land: "cities around the world have awakened to the new paradigm of sustainable development, where the new frontier is the occupation of vacant spaces" (Porto Maravilha 2011).

Far from vacant, communities within the port area are forced to contend with legacies of racial capitalism that demand and enshrine economic disparities. Through reconstruction, Porto Maravilha attempted to cement hegemonic processes of urban development via the commodification of land and accumulation by dispossession. Despite the difficult realities of those discursively constructed as marginal, people within the favela or quilombo—excluded from the image of tourist-friendly Porto Maravilha—still created opportunities to legally maintain their right to their land and to their resistance against neoliberal global economic interests.

The debate on favela citizenship in Rio de Janeiro is now interconnected with quilombola landownership. On March 14, 2018, after speaking at an event for youth activism, the Black queer councilwoman Marielle Franco and her driver, Anderson Pedro Gomes, were murdered in Rio de Janeiro. The tragic assassination of the thirty-eight-year-old elected official from a small but active progressive party created a wave of transnational attention directed at state-sanctioned violence in low-income communities—particularly, violence against queer Black women. Franco dedicated her career to favela activism (see Franco 2014), but it was her sudden and politically motivated death that made her denouncement of state violence impossible to ignore.

In March 2020, with her murder still largely unresolved, a museum memorial opened to commemorate her lifework, the Instituto Marielle Franco, in the historic and hotly contested port area of Rio de Janeiro. In addition to the Instituto Marielle Franco, the port became home to an aquarium, Ferris wheel, and the Museu do Amanhã (Museum of Tomorrow). The development inspired increased surveillance and attempted erasure of sexual minorities (De Lisio and

Rabello Sodré 2019). The intricate financial scheme favored real estate speculation and the obfuscation of activities and histories that seek to advocate for Black heritage (Rabello Sodré 2020).

Full erasure is never possible within porous cities. We reserve optimism for the world envisioned and enacted within communities that already contend with apocalyptic devastation yet continue to persist and resist. As Marielle Franco stated not long before her assassination in an interview with a major newspaper, "the favela is not a problem, it is a solution" (*O Globo* 2018). The statement echoes the idea that so-called marginal communities are not passive, primitive, and/or undesired. Rather, they are active in the construction of their shared cities. Despite the effort to raze, erase, or regularize low-income communities, the global preponderance of real estate speculation will make her statement radiate worldwide.

REFERENCES

Alencar, Edgar de. 1981. *Nosso sinhô do samba*. Rio de Janeiro: Funarte.

Amar, Paul. 2013. *The Security Archipelago: Human-Security States, Sexuality Politics, and the End of Neoliberalism*. Durham, NC: Duke University Press.

Araujo, Ana Lucia. 2016. "Slavery and the Atlantic Slave Trade in Brazil and Cuba from an Afro-Atlantic Perspective." *Almanack* 12: 1–5.

Benchimol, Jaime Larry. 1990. *Pereira passos: Um haussmann tropical—a renovação urbana da cidade do Rio de Janeiro no século XX*. Rio de Janeiro: Secretaria Municipal de Cultura / Departamento Geral de Documentação e Informação Cultural.

Brazil (Office of the President). 1988. Constituição da República Federativa do Brasil de 1988. http://www.planalto.gov.br/ccivil_03/constituicao/constituicao.htm.

Brazil (Office of the President). 2010. Law 12.288—Statute of Racial Equality. https://adsdatabase.ohchr.org/IssueLibrary/ESTATUTO%20DE%20LA%20IGUALDAD%20RACIAL%20(Brazil).pdf.

Carvalho, Bruno. 2013. *Porous City: A Cultural History of Rio de Janeiro (from the 1810s Onward)*. Contemporary Hispanic and Lusophone Cultures. Liverpool, UK: Liverpool University Press.

Cattelino, Jessica, Georgina Drew, and Ruth Morgan. 2019. "Water Flourishing in the Anthropocene." *Cultural Studies Review* 25, no. 2: 135–52.

Corrêa, Maíra Leal. 2016. *Quilombo Pedra do Sal*. Belo Horizonte: FAFICH.

Costa, Sérgio, and Guilherme Leite Gonçalves. 2019. *A Port in Global Capitalism: Unveiling Entangled Accumulation in Rio de Janeiro*. London: Routledge.

Cramer, Lauren M. 2016. "Race at the Interface: Rendering Blackness on WorldStarHipHop.com." *Film Criticism* 40, no. 2. https://doi.org/10.3998/fc.13761232.0040.205.

De Lisio, Amanda, and Joao Gabriel Rabello Sodré. 2019. "FIFA/IOC-Sanctioned Development and the Imminence of Erotic Space." *Bulletin of Latin American Research* 38, no. 3: 1–14.

Diniz, André. 2006. *Almanaque do samba: A história do samba, o que ouvir, o que ler, onde curtir*. Rio de Janeiro: Jorge Zahar Editor.

Do Nascimento, A. 1980. "An Afro-Brazilian Political Alternative: Memory. The Antiquity of Black African Knowledge." *Journal of Black Studies* 11, no. 2: 141–78.

Franco, Marielle. 2014. "UPP—a redução da favela a três letras: Uma análise da política de segurança pública do Estado do Rio de Janeiro." MA thesis, Universidade Federal Fluminense, Niterói. https://app.uff.br/riuff/bitstream/1/2166/1/Marielle%20Franco.pdf.

French, Jan Hoffman. 2009. *Legalizing Identities: Becoming Black or Indian in Brazil's Northeast*. Chapel Hill: University of North Carolina Press.

Harvey, David. 2003. *The New Imperialism*. London: Oxford University Press.

IBGE. 2010. *Censo demográfico 2010—aglomerados subnormais: Primeiros resultados*. Rio de Janeiro: Instituto Brasileiro de Geografia e Estatística. https://biblioteca.ibge.gov.br /visualizacao/periodicos/92/cd_2010_aglomerados_subnormais.pdf.

Joseph, Gilbert M. 1990. "On the Trail of Latin American Bandits: A Reexamination of Peasant Resistance." *Latin American Research Review* 25, no. 3: 7–53.

Khalili, Laleh. 2020. *Sinews of War and Trade: Shipping and Capitalism in the Arabian Peninsula*. London: Verso.

Klein, Herbert S., and Francisco Vidal Luna. 2010. *Slavery in Brazil*. New York: Cambridge University Press.

Leite, Ilka Boaventura. 2000. "Os quilombos no Brasil: Questões conceituais e normativas." *Etnográfica* 4, no. 2: 333–54.

Leu, Lorraine. 2020. *Defiant Geographies: Race and Urban Space in 1920s Rio de Janeiro*. Pittsburgh: University of Pittsburgh Press.

Lima, Monica. 2018. "História, patrimônio e memória sensível: O cais do valongo no Rio de Janeiro." *Outros tempos—pesquisa em foco—história* 15, no. 26. https://doi.org/10.18817 /ot.v15i26.657.

Lopes, Nei. 1996. *Dicionário Banto do Brasil*. Rio de Janeiro: Secretaria Municipal de Cultura.

Mattos, Hebe, and Martha Abreu. 2012. "Relatório histórico-antropológico sobre o quilombo da Pedra do Sal: Em torno do samba, do santo e do porto." In *O fazer antropológico e o reconhecimento de direitos constitucionais: O caso das terras de quilombo no Estado do Rio de Janeiro*, edited by Eliane Cantarino O'Dwyer, 23–63. Coleção Antropologias 7. Rio de Janeiro: E-papers.

McCann, Bryan. 2014a. *Hard Times in the Marvelous City: From Dictatorship to Democracy in the Favelas of Rio de Janeiro*. Durham, NC: Duke University Press.

McCann, Bryan. 2014b. *Hello, Hello Brazil: Popular Music in the Making of Modern Brazil*. Durham, NC: Duke University Press.

McKittrick, Katherine. 2011. "On Plantations, Prisons, and a Black Sense of Place." *Social and Cultural Geography* 12, no. 8: 947–63.

McLoughlin, Beth. 2015. "Pedra do Sal Quilombo Celebrates Ten Years with Procession and Bid at World Heritage Status." *Rio on Watch*, December 14. https://rioonwatch.org /?p=25826.

Meade, Teresa A. 1997. *Civilizing Rio: Reform and Resistance in a Brazilian City, 1889–1930*. University Park: Pennsylvania State University Press.

Miki, Yuko. 2012. "Fleeing into Slavery: The Insurgent Geographies of Brazilian Quilombolas (Maroons), 1880–1881." *Americas* 68, no. 4: 495–528.

Mitchell, Sean T. 2017. *Constellations of Inequality: Space, Race, and Utopia in Brazil.* Chicago: University of Chicago Press.

Neder, Gizlene. 1997. "Cidade, identidade e exclusão social." *Tempo* 2, no. 3: 106–34.

Needell, Jeffrey D. 1987. *A Tropical Belle Epoque: Elite Culture and Society in Turn-of-the-Century Rio de Janeiro.* Cambridge: Cambridge University Press.

O Globo. 2018. "Canal Brasil disponibiliza 'Cidade Partida' com Marielle Franco: 'Favela não é problema. Favela é solução.'" March 16. https://oglobo.globo.com/rio/canal -brasil-disponibiliza-cidade-partida-com-marielle-franco-favela-nao-problema-favela -solucao-22496089.

Paschel, Tianna S. 2018. *Becoming Black Political Subjects: Movements and Ethno-Racial Rights in Colombia and Brazil.* Princeton, NJ: Princeton University Press.

Passos, Francisco Pereira. 1906. "Melhoramentos da cidade: Projectados pelo prefeito do Districto Federal: Dr. Francisco Pereira Passos." Report. Rio de Janeiro: Oliveira Lima Library, Catholic University of America.

Pereira, Júlio César Medeiros da Silva. 2007. *À flor da terra: O cemitério dos pretos novos no Rio de Janeiro.* Rio de Janeiro: Garamond, IPHAN.

Porto Maravilha. 2011. "Porto Maravilha—Summary." https://www.thegpsc.org/sites/gpsc /files/2._porto_maravilha.pdf.

Purbrick, Louise. 2017. "Nitrate Ruins: The Photography of Mining in the Atacama Desert, Chile." *Journal of Latin American Cultural Studies* 26, no. 2: 253–78.

Rabello Sodré, João Gabriel. 2020. "Subaltern Spaces and Diasporic Imaginaries in Rio de Janeiro's Valongo Wharf." *Tinta Journal,* Second Series 1. https://tinta.spanport.ucsb .edu/digital-issues.

Rolnik, Raquel. 1989. "Territórios negros nas cidades brasileiras." *Estudos Afro-Asiáticos* 17: 29–41.

Rolnik, Raquel. 2019. *Urban Warfare: Housing under the Empire of Finance.* New York: Verso Trade.

Rosenn, Keith S. 2017. *Brazil's Constitution of 1988 with Amendments through 2017.* Constitute Project. https://www.constituteproject.org/constitution/Brazil_2017.pdf?lang=en.

Schwarcz, Lilia Moritz. 1993. *O espetáculo das raças: Cientistas, instituições e questão racial no Brasil, 1870–1930.* São Paulo: Companhia das Letras.

Schwarcz, Lilia Moritz, and Heloisa M. Starling. 2015. *Brasil: Uma biografia.* London: Penguin.

Stern, Steve J. 1987. "Introduction: New Approaches to the Study of Peasant Rebellion and Consciousness: Implications of the Andean Experience." In *Resistance, Rebellion, and Consciousness in the Andean Peasant World, 18th to 20th Centuries,* edited by Steve J. Stern, 3–25. Madison: University of Wisconsin Press.

Stoler, Ann Laura. 2013. *Imperial Debris: On Ruins and Ruination.* Durham, NC: Duke University Press.

Vargas, João H. Costa. 2018. *The Denial of Antiblackness: Multiracial Redemption and Black Suffering.* Minneapolis: University of Minnesota Press.

Vaz, Lilian Fessler. 2002. *Modernidade e moradia: Habitação coletiva no Rio de Janeiro, séculos XIX e XX.* Rio de Janeiro: 7Letras.

15

Fractalscopic Quotidian / Cotidiano Fractaloscópico

The Square as Social Project, the Social Project as a Space in Everyday Life

MARCELO CAETANO ANDREOLI

In examining the dialogue between everyday experience and territories of ex-perience, this chapter creates a language for recognizing and valuing practices of the contemporary city that point the way out of neoliberal modes of seeing and being. Here, I challenge specific epistemologies through a case study that unfolded during the construction and popular reoccupation of a public square in one of Rio de Janeiro's most violently policed areas. This crime-ridden site is also a critical space for popular culture and community self-organization.

The field research I carried out for this chapter was on a small square in the Complexo do Alemão that was built in cooperation with community members and students from the Architecture and Urbanism course at UFRJ (the Federal University of Rio de Janeiro). The Complexo do Alemão neighborhood is located in central-northern Rio, with at least seventy thousand inhabitants. Since 2000, the area has been a hotspot of security crises, police invasions, and occupation by the navy and armed forces. It has also served as a laboratory for the Unidade de Polícia Pacificadora (UPP, or Police Pacification Unit). The UPP is a security policy program created and implemented by State Public Security Secretary José Mariano Beltrame. This program sought to implement community-oriented policing, in contrast to militarized policing, in order to reclaim territories controlled by gangs of drug dealers. Santa Marta was the first community where UPP was established, in 2008. After some years, this program failed to reduce traditional police abuse and police-sponsored corruption in these territories and added fuel to the war between drug traffickers controlling Rio's favelas and the police.

Rio's social and physical landscapes can be seen as fractals. Usually, this term is deployed negatively to describe the chaotic, broken, or segregated terrain of the city, marked by radical asymmetries, contradictions, and antagonisms. But I push against assessing the neighborhood from the outside, by looking from within the fractal to see the outside world. I propose that Rio should be seen as more than a disjointed and segregated city of hills and asphalt but, instead, as a composition of multiple, coproduced phenomena that resemble a kaleidoscopic image. This kind of Rio necessarily brings us to the notion of daily life. Despite its common use, few use the quotidian as an alternative epistemology. The fractal geometry of Rio produces new knowledge, and it fosters new ways of seeing. This production relies on a reimagining of the everyday. My focus here is on mapping daily (quotidian) organic movements of production and coproduction in urban territories of sociability. This allows us to analyze and consider practices that are outside mechanisms of state discipline and are not necessarily limited by the privatizing and commodifying forces of the market but are far from separate from these phenomena.

This chapter rethinks favelas through a small initiative: the case of a public square constructed in 2015, which will help us understand the principles of mobilization and investigate the concept of the right to the city (Lefebvre [1972] 2019). With the increase in the number of projects initiated within favelas over recent decades (Ximenes and Jaenisch 2019; Vaz and Jacques 2006), it is critical to highlight the content of such interventions, which may be classified into three major strategies: (1) technocratic practice, vertical and mediated by aseptic state action; (2) missionary practice, defined by a colonial and voluntarist action of those who propose to save these territories; and (3) artistic practice, most of the time reduced to the color of the facades (Kapp et al. 2012). Regardless of the method used, interventions have consistently revealed a growing distance between the external observer/interventionist and the people who inhabit the affected territories.[1] Observing such practices is the basis for seeking alternative paths—not shortcuts, but exit routes that illuminate other possibilities of intervention, mainly guided by the exchange of different types of knowledge.

Different from those spatial interventions mentioned by Silke Kapp et al. (2012), the Praça para Alemão Ver (Square for a German view) represents another form of urban architecture in favelas. This is mainly because of its participatory process of design and construction, and also its symbolically saturated name.[2] The square proposes a new view of the favela as an archipelago of precariousness within the city, which constantly reaffirms the dichotomous vision of the city divided between hills and asphalt (Ventura 1994). This square demands another view of urban planning, where projects are addressed not as vertical impositions but as local projects that center resident belongings in the built infrastructure.

To confront this set of urban divisions, it is necessary to identify the autonomous practices that emerge from daily exchanges and conflict (B. Santos 2019). A fractaloscopic quotidian refuses to believe that the favela's desire is to become and remain asphalt. The favela instead seeks to be recognized through territorial rights. This perspectival shift helps us rethink the image of the split city and the fight for the right to the city in its expanded dimension (Lefebvre [1972] 2019).[3]

This contribution is structured in three parts. First, Lefebvrian arguments are introduced that can illuminate a practice, especially with regard to contradictions of space and instrumentalization by neoliberal logic. Next, the chapter narrates the experience of the Praça para Alemão Ver square in Complexo do Alemão, given its capacity to build dialogue between knowledge and territory. Finally, the square is discussed as a process and product, demonstrating its transformative potential through design and construction. Opportunities for encounter and territorial appropriation are significant for realizing the right to the city (Lefebvre [1972] 2019), building bridges, and offering opportunities for the elaboration of spatial invention aimed at the decolonization of the imaginary (Miraftab 2016).

We Need to Talk about Space

The spatial dimension is understood here as the arena of production and reproduction of the dynamics that structure and build society. It is the stage for disputes and tensions highlighted by urban critical theory (Lefebvre [1966] 2008; Soja 1993; Brenner, Marcuse, and Margit 2012; Harvey 2011). Starting from these premises, I search for a path to praxis architecture, which is purposefully destabilizing. The social transformations experienced in the early 1960s focused on combating dogmatic rationalism and valuing multiplicities.[4] Reflections on space gain new perspectives based on theories that no longer conceive time and space as unrelated dimensions but as a constructed dialectic (Soja 1993). The understanding of human space contributes to the objectification of nature (Buber 1957). But space is a sociopolitical and ideological product, whose conformation occurs starting from a series of historical and natural changes. It is, therefore, impossible to conceive of scientific thought about space and the urban phenomenon without "progressive and regressive procedures (in time and space), without multiple cuts and fragmentations" (Lefebvre [1966] 2008, 52). A linear conception of the production of space has been replaced with a dialectical one.

Space goes beyond the juxtaposition of its components, as it is configured through deliberate social action and relationships. Constant dynamism and expansionism assume a geographical character, transforming space into a mechanism capable of strengthening capital accumulation, labor exploitation, and the physical reshaping of our lived world (Harvey 1989). Urban critical theory understands the current condition of cities, perceived not only as the result of technocratic rationalities but also by the "continuous (re)construction as a place, means and result of historically specific socio-power relations" (Brenner 2010, 21). The historical development of capitalism depends on a very specific form of spatial re-production rooted in notions of private territory. Consequently, the fundamental agent of spatial reconfiguration in a globalized context can be found by those who manipulate the market (Gill 2000). The market redraws aspects of the social sphere through micro- and macroeconomic impositions, which are related to political and constitutional initiatives of a financial and monetary nature. The favela emerges as a necessary and at the same time marginal territory within the system that produces it, whose subjectivities are constantly captured and oriented toward a condition of subordination. In other words, there is a labor market that relegates part of the population to poverty, since it cannot afford to live anywhere but within the relatively affordable favelas.[5]

Space, here, becomes an "inseparable set of systems of objects and systems of action" (M. Santos 2009, 51). These systems feed a movement of constant transformations, whose social knowledge has an "endemically contextual" character (Brenner 2010, 21). Through sociohistorical arrangement, favelas represent a very particular spatial-economic production in Brazilian cities (Maricato 2015), articulated by ambiguity and the negotiation between the local and the global. Seen from this perspective, the favela's production of space requires an analysis of the relationship between everyday ways of moving and surviving the city, on the one hand, and on the other, the global market process. The observation of the quotidian as an analytical category is located exactly on this frontier, which recognizes alienating forces of the market and confronts them based on the concrete experiences of residents (Bondía 2002).

A Square within Everyday Life

The space of favelas and of the Complexo do Alemão are characterized by contradictions found within everyday life.[6] Inevitably, the quotidian becomes an analytical key and presents itself as the social by which all other plans are organized. Daily life organizes, regulates, and disciplines bodies by the very repetition of spaces. Still, it is in everyday life that the possibilities of transformation are observed through the suspension of alienated life, transforming it into a space of resistances and challenging logics of commodification. Situating an analysis based on the quotidian also leads us to understand that "deviations" within the city contribute to its overall growth and state governance (Lefebvre [1972] 2019). For example, informal markets may seem to violate zoning and seller license laws, but these spaces are essential for working-class inhabitants of the city, who depend on affordable goods to contribute to the formal economy. Of course, we do not aim to celebrate informal markets as a solution to rampant inequality; it is a strategy, and one that enables the reproduction of state-sponsored inequality.

The Complexo do Alemão's population density motivates a desire for public space. The Praça para Alemão Ver was a territorial symbol that challenged this condition of open space scarcity. The idea was to reclaim free and open spaces, where traditional coercive forces—military police or gangs of drug dealers—would not limit the range of possible community-led activities.

Praça para Alemão Ver was built in Avenida Central, one of the most important streets in Complexo do Alemão. It was designed and built by residents, students, teachers, and professors of the Alternative Urbanization Project (PUA) between July and September 2015. This initiative was the result of internal demands from some members of the community, especially in the figure of the Instituto Raízes em Movimento. The objective of PUA's proposal was, at first, to inspire alternatives for the residual spaces left by the Growth Acceleration Program (PAC).[7] The plan quickly ran into a problem. There is no empty space in the favelas, and constant disputes (most of the time tacit) only lead to private appropriation of land:

This dispute over space clearly shows that there is no "empty space" in favelas. In one way or another, favela spaces are potentially spaces for private construction, whether for private housing or rented housing, and the rights to "build" on them are from the immediately neighboring owner. These actions that show the predominance of the private over the collective dimension have very old cultural roots, originating from the relationship established between these residents and a city that in almost no time welcomed them and accepted them as effective and legalized members. The permanence of favela residents in adequate places in the city has always been guided by a certain illegality and individual effort, except for modest interventions by the public authorities. The vast majority of Rio's favelas are the result of the individual efforts of their residents. (Benetti 2017, 98)

The plan was redesigned, and the initial scope was reduced. The entire Avenida Central was modified for strategic action, understanding that a collaboratively built square could represent an effective effort to affirm the right to the city. The square faces challenges in a territory already inundated with many violent forces. The mobilization of various groups who worked on this project was critical in expressing their right to the city, which refers to the social and political capacity to make and rebuild spaces for the reproduction of life (Brenner, Marcuse, and Margit 2012).

The nursery and the headquarters of Instituto Raízes em Movimento became the starting points for thinking about this square as a space for articulation between inside and outside, with a direct connection to the street. Effectively, when looking at the square, the disputes and tensions that formulated this project predictably function according to privatist logic. With the combination of residents and students, the square rose in the face of all its contradictions, not only as a formal act but, above all, as a political posture that is able to demonstrate power through open and participatory methodologies. This square does not represent a turning point in the history of Complexo do Alemão, and we are aware of its scale. However, as a method and articulation between actors, this square renews hopes for actions closer to everyday concerns.

Conclusion: An Always Open Possibility

In this chapter, a reading of critical urban theory was approached through the conceptual construction of space, demonstrating how the quotidian can be mobilized. Believing that each individual and each social group produces its own system of meanings, the square Praça para Alemão Ver on Avenida Central represents a deviation from more hegemonic actions that are perpetuated from a distant governing body. Recognizing the power stimulated by discontent within the territory, this square confronts the neoliberal logic for two reasons: (1) it was carried out with respect to the logic and representations of the residents themselves; and (2) it mobilizes cooperative and participatory logics that relocate knowledge to build an effective relationship of territorial intervention. This expands narratives and proposes the materialization of this fractal encounter of optics in a concrete and specific project.

The intention of this chapter is to shed light on a social project built cooperatively in Complexo do Alemão. This was important not because of the result but its process. Participants were able to work in an unstable territory, with pre-existing violent forces, to claim their right to the city. Of course, it seems odd to explore this concept in a favela, a territory that has ostensibly been denied such rights in the first place. The fractoloscopic context of Rio de Janeiro—a city not split in two but having many tangential elements simultaneously coexisting—helps clarify political possibilities while taking aim at top-down projects that minimize the freedoms of everyday life.

The actions of residents confront the state's historical insufficiencies in providing space and assist the effort to decolonize our everyday perceptions (Miraftab 2016). Within a field of uncertainties, spatial structuring is defined according to the dynamics of the surrounding areas, which disregard common spaces. Contrary to this movement, Praça para Alemão Ver is a strategic possibility for rethinking the territory from the inside with support from the multifaceted dynamics of everyday life. The implications of such a space are uncertain and imprecise: "There is no guarantee that tomorrow the square will continue to be a square and that the agreements that made it possible will be maintained over time" (Benetti 2017, 101). The guarantees that support the permanence of other spaces in the city do not act in a regulatory manner and differ from this experience of the square.

NOTES

1 Used here to reaffirm space, territory's spatial fixation is necessary for the construction of a deep subjectivity (Lefebvre [1974] 2013; Soja 1993).

2 The cable car in Complexo do Alemão is possibly the most representative example of a failed project in recent years because it has not improved mobility, as promised by the planners. It simultaneously led to forced evictions and negatively impacted the informal housing market.

3 The split city is an expression that defines the contrast between two worlds: favela and asphalt. It was addressed initially by Zuenir Ventura (1994). To think about the Lefebvrian concept of the right to the city in this context is to reaffirm favelas as a singular territory, in which the community works to build space collectively.

4   Some movements are notably important in this period, as we can highlight: anthropological and ethnological thinking from the perspective of Claude Lévi-Strauss; the industrial archaeology that seeks to understand the birth of material and technical culture; studies related to strengthening associative social movements; the urban ecology debates that gain relevance given the alternative possibilities for obtaining energy; the review of studies of orthodox Marxist theories in the European context; and, finally, the study of mass culture in the face of the paradox of technical knowledge socialization and the manipulation of the social body.

5   Orthodox Marxist theories used to explain this exclusion from a class perspective, but, more and more, we can see in Brazil an intersectional marginalization, simultaneously impacting populations distinctly depending on gender, class, and racial composition.

6   Although a few initiatives have attempted to reconstruct this history of urban interventions and projects in favelas, with emphasis on the Favela-Bairro and Morar Carioca programs, these territories still remain historically forgotten.

7   The Growth Acceleration Program (Programa de Aceleração de Crescimento, in Portuguese) was an important initiative of the federal government in 2007, freeing up funds for investments in infrastructure. The priority areas for investment were sanitation, housing, transportation, energy, and water resources. The state had little dialogue with most demands from communities and was unable to reflect objectively on the breadth of the territory.

REFERENCES

Benetti, Pablo. 2017. "Costuras urbanas na Avenida Central do Morro do Alemão." In *Praça pr'alemão ter: O germinar de uma praça verde no Morro do Alemão*, edited by Pablo Benetti and Solange Carvalho, 89–101. Rio de Janeiro: Instituto Raízes em Movimento / CEPEDOCA.

Bondía, Jorge Larrosa. 2002. "Notas sobre a experiência e o saber de experiência." *Revista Brasileira de Educação* 19: 20–29.

Brenner, Neil. 2010. "O que é teoria crítica urbana." *E-metropolis* 3, no. 1: 20–27.

Brenner, Neil, Peter Marcuse, and Mayer Margit. 2012. *Cities for People Not for Profit: Critical Urban Theory, and the Right to the City*. New York: Routledge.

Buber, Maurice. 1957. "Distance and Relation." *Psychiatry* 20: 97–104.

Gill, Stephen. 2000. "The Constitution of Global Capitalism." Paper presented at the International Studies Association Annual Convention, Los Angeles.

Harvey, David. 1989. "From Managerialism to Entrepreneurialism: The Transformation in Urban Governance in Late Capitalism." *Geografiska Annaler. Series B, Human Geography* 71, no. 1: 3–17.

Harvey, David. 2011. *Rebel Cities: From the Right to the City to the Urban Revolution*. London: Verso.

Kapp, Silke, Ana Paula Baltazar, Rebekah Campos, Pedro Maghâes, Lígia Milagres, Patrícia Nardini, Bárbara Olyntho, and Leonardo Polizzi. 2012. "Arquitetos nas favelas: Três críticas e uma proposta de atuação." Paper presented at the IV Congresso

Brasileiro e III Congresso Ibero-Americano Habitação Social: Ciência e tecnologia "Inovação e Responsabilidade," Florianópolis, Brazil.

Lefebvre, Henri. (1966) 2008. *A revolução urbana*. Belo Horizonte: UFMG.

Lefebvre, Henri. (1972) 2019. *Espaço e política—o direito à cidade II*. Belo Horizonte: UFMG.

Lefebvre, Henri. (1974) 2013. *La producción del spacio*. Madrid: Alcobendas.

Maricato, Ermínia. 2015. *Para entender a crise urbana*. São Paulo: Expressão Popular.

Miraftab, Faranak. 2016. "Insurgência, planejamento e a perspectiva de um urbanismo humano." *Revista brasileira de estudos urbanos e regionais* 18, no. 3: 363–77.

Santos, Boaventura de Souza. 2019. *O fim do império cognitivo*. Belo Horizonte: Autêntica.

Santos, Milton. 2009. *A natureza do espaço*. São Paulo: Editora Universidade de São Paulo.

Soja, Edward. 1993. *Geografias pós-modernas: A reafirmação do espaço na teoria social crítica*. Rio de Janeiro: Zahar.

Vaz, Lilian Fessler, and Paola Berenstein Jacques. 2006. "Contemporary Urban Spectacularisation." In *Culture, Urbanism and Planning*, edited by Javier Monclus and Manuel Guardia, 241–54. Barcelona: Routledge.

Ventura, Zuenir. 1994. *Cidade partida*. Rio de Janeiro: Companhia das Letras.

Ximenes, Luciana Alencar, and Samuel Thomas Jaenisch. 2019. "As favelas do Rio de Janeiro e suas camadas de urbanização: Vinte anos de políticas de intervenção sobre espaços populares da cidade." Paper presented at Anais XVIII Enanpur, Natal, May 27–31.

16

Involved With as Police Method /
Envolvido-Com e Proximidade Punitiva

Selective Guardianship and Itinerant Controls in the Streets of Rio

JACQUELINE DE OLIVEIRA MUNIZ, FATIMA CECCHETTO,
AND RODRIGO MONTEIRO

The excerpt below, taken from our ethnographic fieldwork, illustrates the use of the phrase *involved with crime*, which we have repeatedly encountered during our decades of ethnographic fieldwork in favelas and among the police in Rio de Janeiro. It comes from our fieldwork in Fallet, a favela, in 2016–17. Here, we suggest the term *involved with* as a possible explanation for police violence. Responses by interviewed officers demonstrate that they completely understand not only the utility of the expression *involved with* but also its function as a marker of death:

AUTHOR/INTERVIEWER: Those that died were residents?
RESPONDENT: All residents. All on the same day, but not at the same time.

A: What was the explanation that the police gave?

R: There was no explanation.

A: Why did they die?

R: They died because they [the police] wanted to kill.

A: Could they have been called *involved*?

R: Some could have been called *involved*. I can't talk about it in public.[1]

This chapter unpacks the moral and philosophical bases of the view that those involved with crime—and, indeed, even those who are socially or physically adjacent to them—deserve death. *Involved with crime* articulates a police epistemology anchored in a form of social common sense that has come to dominate discourses about violence in Rio and which informs a methodology for policing (Cecchetto, Muniz, and Monteiro 2018, 2020). The category *involved with crime* is thus ultimately rooted in beliefs that the police spring from the same moral, cultural, and physical origins as the populations they surveil, categorize, judge, and punish. Police see themselves as having made a conscious choice to become right-living humans—cops and not bandits. *Bándido* is an emic moral category employed in Brazilian Portuguese to mark those involved with crime and thus deserving of death, as our commentator, above, expresses it. Police see themselves as having clawed their way out of the same physical and social milieu that produces *bandidagem* through heroic acts of self-discipline and sacrifice (Muniz 2014). This, they feel, earns them both human rights and a duty to employ their classificatory eye, formed by life at the margins, to take in who is and is not involved with crime at a glance and thus appropriately determine, in moments of conflict and crisis, who is deserving of death.

Involved with crime is not a new expression in Rio de Janeiro.[2] It is an accusatory category, broadly and flexibly applied, that can cast as criminal every interaction in any dimension of social life, from the world of politics to the "underworld of crime."[3] The tag *involved with crime* mobilizes diffuse forms of vigilance and extended control over and among social groups, especially the subaltern. Those thus tagged are stigmatized as involved with criminal behavior, a mark that makes them killable. In this fashion, being *involved with crime* unites stereotype and condemnation. It authorizes violation and violence by those with authority—legal or illegal, legitimate or illegitimate. Simply standing next to someone who is *involved with* is enough of a reason for one to enter into Rio's voluminous violent death statistics.

The category reveals the weight of the stigma that young favela dwellers carry for living in areas under the extensive and continued armed dominion of the police, militias, and criminal groups, whose armed disputes target these youths for discriminatory and violent practices (see chapter 3, this volume). Beginning with the notion of a regime of fear (with its concomitant states of exception and control and surveillance technologies), we try to understand police construction of the criminal, focusing on three aspects: its structural dimensions, its contexts of application, and its effects on relationships.

The research upon which this text is based has been underway since 2017. Its fieldwork took place in favelas in Rio de Janeiro (the Complexo do Alemão and the Morro do Fallet), Niteroi (Preventório and Vila Ipiranga), and São Gonçalo (Complexo do Salgueiro and Jardim Catarina), where we conducted interviews, focus groups, and informal conversations with youths, precinct officers, and "beat cops" of different sexes, genders, and colors.[4]

Policing as Knowledge Production for Control

Policing is an itinerant mode of knowledge production for controlling, classifying, and labeling subjects and their worlds. In its "boots-on-the-ground" aspect, it also produces obedience to rules of social play or, indeed, any play involving citizenship. A mode of coercive distribution, policing is both a potential and concrete resource that sustains the status quo. It is a mobile device for the vigilance and regulation of a dynamic reality composed of flows of ideas, memories, images, people, reputations, services, things, and merchandise. Finally, it is a technology of governance at a remove over the movements of various populations in and through distinct territories.

Policing, for Rio's PMs (Polícia Militar, Militarized Police), is "maintaining things within the norm."[5] It involves travel through places to "maintain order" from above, according to multiple (and sometimes conflicting) orders, while being embedded within and beside social groups to be controlled. Police move among subjects to keep them in their physical, social, and symbolic "proper places." Policing moves from acting in the name of the law to above and beyond law to guarantee "aggressive coverage" of what is believed to be the frontiers of the "morality of society," patrolling citizens' "good behavior." "To serve and protect," a motto widely employed by the PMERJ's "brave warriors," is seen as an "obligation" that goes beyond one's professional duty.[6] It is narrated as a mission experienced as fate: a predestined vocation in pursuit of an ideal. In the words of one of our police interlocutors, it is a calling "in the fight against evil, which not all can understand." In their official hymn, the PMs of Rio sing in unison refrains exhorting and evoking the mystique of being a policeman, which is cast as "a reason for being" that is felt as superhuman, trained to "face death, to be proud of your strength, to face whatever may come" (Muniz 1999).[7]

This heroic mandatory mode of being of the PMs synthetizes the moral philosophy they learn in the streets with the "school of life." This encompasses a distinctly disenchanted philosophical view toward human beings who, failing as "right-living humans," insist on "maintaining their privilege of having the right to human rights." It prescribes the basis of what police must know, consolidated as a sociology of dismay in the face of "this [Brazilian] society." Its origin myth is rooted in Brazilian common sense that parallels the more conservative visions of the country's elites that were consolidated during the apex of late nineteenth-century racist social Darwinism: "Portugal sent scum to populate Brazil: prostitutes, murderers, and thieves; degenerates who mixed with the lewd *Indians* and libidinous Africans."

The colonial origins of this worldview legitimize the need to maintain unequal and disciplinary tutelage over the population at large, exerted by strong, firm, and superior authorities who have a "carte blanche to act." In this understanding, Rio is a hypocritical society with low self-esteem that violates its own principles and rules while not respecting the value of the policeman, who unveils "the falsehood of human behavior." This police socio-logic often implements a fearsome, persecutory, and corrective criminology classificatory label, or tag: involved with crime. In the narratives of our police informants, it is human nature "to lie and hide things from the police." Given this, and somewhat contradictorily, police must thus trust their gut feelings based on the impressions created by appearances (and the games of race, gender, sexual orientation, social class, abode, consumption, etc.) in their policing.

This criminology of reverse social mobility is manifest in a police know-how of where, when, and how to set up the mobile barriers that control access to goods and services and define the paths of subjects and their social trajectories within and between the citadels that constitute Rio. In the representations and practices of the city's inhabitants (of all classes and types), there is a map of prestige structured by a strong moral and economic hierarchy that opposes the boroughs of the South and North Zones, along one axis, and the "favelas and the asphalt" along another.[8] This cartography serves as a sort of moral GPS for the PMs, intuiting the "economic condition" and the "individual's rank" in the social, political, and cultural markets. There is no lost qualifying trip. There is a discriminatory symphony that disharmonizes characters, biotypes, and places with an out-of-tune interaction between police and favela population.

This know-how provides a tutorial on how, "in the wonderful city, the purgatory of beauty and chaos," one identifies those who are involved and their degree of involvement.[9] One identifies and filters the various shades of Blackness, poverty, socioeconomic adequacy, and moral conformism into corresponding shades of acceptance by the police and authorities. The praxis of the beat cop is thus produced by the intersection of this mandatory mode of being and know-how. It expresses what police should be, know, and do in their process of applying social controls. This praxis is constantly updated in police experiences of the "heterogeneous city" (Gago 2018) by means of vertical and horizontal suspicion and surveillance of subjects, practices, places, and so on. The mechanisms of police involvement with the city render a portrait of unequal populations, creating selective barriers that demarcate who can and cannot mix in any given situation, time, and place. Hierarchy and social inequality are thus naturalized.

Policing dangers and uncertainties demand attention to detail, understood as police intuition, to be able to see what is suspicious at a glance. Police classification schemes are rooted in folk knowledge and informal practices shared with precarious subjects living in deteriorated areas understood to be "police turf" (Reiner 1991). This situation has been aggravated as the police have increasingly become weapons of warlike policies directed against internal enemies in Rio over the past three decades (Muniz 2012; Monteiro 2016).

The philosophical know-how-to-be, sociological need to know, and criminological know-how of the PMs are linked in a sacred struggle against evil that constantly tests their virtue (Muniz 1999). The police see themselves as engaged in a fatalistic crusade against a greater evil that is expressed in the violent, the criminal, and the disorderly—an enemy that is within us, corroding an order idealized as uniform and harmonic. Conflict, its nature and expressions, is the great villain fought by the PM who, Janus-like, oversees passages and regulates war and peace. Social disorder and conflict are seen as negative, manifest in the confrontation of divergent passions, intentions, and interests in the public arena. Conflict is seen as promoting the construction of a veritable Tower of Babel in society, inducing individuals who are fundamentally unequal in rights to commit deviations because they aspire to what they cannot be and to what they should not have. It is left up to the PM to repeatedly engage in an eternal moral battle in favor of "right living," in accordance with informal rules of politics, power relations, self-protective corporate convenience, and the limitations imposed by pragmatically having to live with the city's autonomous criminal governments.

The PM mode of knowing is an amalgam of distinct theories of the individual and society. It stipulates a common human nature characterized by a universal moral and psychological existence while it shifts its explanations from the most singular aspects to the most generalized attributes of the subjects and social realities it encounters (Muniz 2012). In search of deciphering human thought processes, police knowledge seeks to plumb our depths (de profundis). It seeks to reveal the meaning of what is said by an inquisitorial kidnapping of speech to trap those suspected of involvement (or, as in the case of our interlocutor in the Fallet, to co-opt witnesses into confirming involvement). This know-how of control is described by police as always correct, exemplified by the nitty-gritty of reality: life as it's lived, dramatized in each alley, on each corner, along every urban passageway.

Policing as Sacrifice for Citizenship

This is a prescriptive knowledge of our salvation from ourselves. It's a moral philosophy employing a curative, correctional messianism. Those who are supposedly born to be PMs have a catechizing mission to give security to society. This requires compulsory sacrifices for the police and involuntary sacrifices for everyone. The police—portrayed and portraying themselves as having low income and coming from the same social peripheries as the "bandits" they hunt—declare that they have experienced the same sacrificial citizenship as those who live on Rio's socioeconomic peripheries. Their ability to rise above what our anonymous commentator on the police stories blog (casodepolicia.org 2010) describes as being "the victim of an unequal society" earns them the merit of having rights as right-living citizens. The police exhibit this sacrifice with pride in their public policing behavior, which is often an ostentatious exhibitionism highlighting exaggerated, noisy, masculine behaviors that would be a clear call for police surveillance were they to be performed by anyone else.[10]

This kind of policing must occur without whining or falling into narratives about social (in)justice. The police portray themselves as coming from the favela or from areas of the "asphalt" that are similar in socioeconomic terms. The PMs see themselves as having the same initial moral substance as the populations they police: the careers of both bandit and cop were equally open to them at the beginning. The PMs believe it their job to demand from their co-citizens repeated demonstrations that they are bettering themselves so that they can better others—a requisite to cross the barriers they impose. The PM, "as a right-living human" originating in the lower, darker classes of Rio, is the polar opposite of those involved with crime: as non-right-living humans (and thus nonhumans) who chose the route the PM pulled himself away from through a conscious exercise of will.

The constant practice of stopping and frisking those suspected of being involved with crime is legitimized by the police as a necessary measure for defending society from traumas and blemishes. The Carioca stop-and-frisk is more than a procedure: it's a mode of being in and of making the city; a police civic morality. The liberty of those "good citizens" at the top of the social order is created by blocking the liberty of those below. The defense of "each one's liberty" or "of each one's capitalism" is anchored by police praxis supposedly through the "traditional values" discourse that saturates popular neoliberalism. The Carioca stop-and-frisk points to the "favela-style" mannequins who parade the signs of involvement. Body aesthetics, clothing, and accessories advertise the *involved with*.

This is the task of the police-as-good-guys. One must be a "true man" and exhibit an ostentatious heteronormative masculinity supported by one's comrades at arms and other right-living men (Cecchetto 2004). A hard-core PM, stripped of his territorial and moral origins, demands to be recognized as a self-made convert from a life of vice and racially mixed degradation. He presents himself as the pinnacle of the right-living man, an example to which other men must be bent (and even broken, if necessary) through therapeutic coercion.

Labeling Is Necessary; Policing, Not So Much

The police worldview produces a voracious appetite for order that wraps everyone in suspicion, seeking to account for sins in the uniqueness of each individual who is captured and classified as involved. Nothing is left out. This classificatory appetite, however, constantly generates leftovers that require confinement in carefully labeled packages. For the PMs, labeling is necessary, and policing is inaccurate. Policing demands that one overcome classificatory uncertainties that arise in the imponderables of social life. If one accepts the postulate that the police are only for those who need police, then duly inspecting and stamping social passports to regulate dispositions and support a given moral and socioeconomic framework becomes the police's central responsibility. In this scenario, the classificatory eye of the PM is expected to reduce social complexity and generalize itself through causal overdetermination that establishes the civilizing stages of involvement, the social (and even physical) evolutionary types of those involved, and the horizon of possibilities for (dis)involvement. Thus PMs cultivate an accumulative memory of physical and moral "types" to produce this expansive technology of social control.

This police ability to read and process social markers as social passports is a casuistic knowledge. Its regulating disposition is rooted in a late nineteenth-century social evolutionary morality. It reduces social complexity and generalizes itself through a causal overdetermination that establishes civilizing stages of involvement, types of involved actors, and their horizon of (dis)involvement. Military police commonly say they know a "guy who looks like that" when they scan people with their vigilant, classificatory eye. They employ an accumulative memory, rooted in their social upbringing, to produce expanded social control. This linear evolutionary approach to police surveillance is enormously convenient. It justifies selective tutelage for everyone, according to each individual's evolutionary "progress," increasing or decreasing in accordance with the PMs who rule each street corner. It justifies distinct treatment according to differentiated social filters to protect the unequal from themselves.

This PM-bricoleur rationality combines elements of deterministic thinking to give their labeling the status of truth. Geographic determinism morally typifies places based on natural elements (climate, environment, etc.). Biological determination is used to typify individuals' moral species according to their "natural characteristics" (race, gender, sexual orientation, etc.). Cultural determination lends itself to labeling social realities as closed and exclusionary worlds. The police, favela, South Zone, street, gay, and other worlds are presented as "worlds apart," antisocial, "with their own kings, laws and habits."

The PM way of seeing and knowing pretends that it is the ever-seeing eye of the Benthamian panoptic in order to affirm a calculating, competitive nature, expressing a monopolistic ambition to control the streets. This is a praxis that sums up and plays pretend, concealing its ways of accounting because it is applied to the present, the now of its performance, and the immediate moment of the performance of others. It occludes the fact that police solutions are always finite and provisional because policing produces controls over the world and not structural changes in the world. This knowledge for control does not change the wills of those who are involved: it can only change the chances of a given individual being able to be involved.

This now-you-see-it-now-you-don't form of knowledge conceals the fact that overwhelming strength and/or extreme violence do not produce a change of conscience in those who are policed. They can only change the opportunities of being *involved with*: the alternatives facing those who are under police surveillance and who are subject to police intervention. The knowledge that it hides is knowledge-in-debt. Therefore, police knowledge must torment and lecture, performing a pedagogy of transactions ranging from the most oppressive subjection to the most courteous obedience. This is a knowledge that masks its deceits to produce a revealing truth regarding involvements: an excavated truth that can only be found through the mighty blows of its sword.

Police knowledge results in a sociology born in disenchantment. General distrust and previous suspicion are part of the sociability devices that feed a circuit of asymmetrical exchanges between the PM and the involved, moderated by the latent expectation of illegal and illegitimate use of potential and concrete force. The resulting reciprocity oscillates between the coldness of indifference and the heat of affect, resulting in a constant bargaining made up of accusatory provocations in looks, gestures, and words. They—both PMs and favela residents, those "who are from the margins of society"—supposedly understand each other through these transactions. Police thus employ verbal insults and disdain that, when they are employed by those who are involved, are seen as deserving of neck slaps, confiscations, and the destruction of documents and personal property.

Here we see a disgruntled sort of knowledge that postulates that to survive life and weather professional consequences, one's suspicion of all and sundry is completely justified. This is a view that one must be constantly alert to others while being, essentially, the same as others. "The street teaches" is what this view preaches. All must take a side in the networks of involvement, and PMs need their knowledge of seeing to take in and comprehend all sides of the language of involvement. This requires distrust of the limitless, the infinite composed of an almost unimaginable level of detail: "the street baffles." In the face of this, one has to "remain distrustful and doubt the other's intentions."

The have-to-know-how-to-do that identifies what is within and without the ever-desired "normality" develops in police a prodigious memory, capable of gathering and curating an enormous collection of people, objects, places, and situations. Their stories are narrated as epics that describe in detail individuals, their names and nicknames, places, and the "mechanism of events." Through analogies and extrapolations, the unknown is connected to that which has already been mapped. Through this cognitive path, the PMs reduce the number of possibilities understanding opens up to a finite set of interpretative keys that orient their field of surveillance and intervention. This is a pragmatic knowledge, motivated by a project of utilitarian and finalistic power: the production of truth in the service of suspicion.

Lower-rank PMs are quick on the trigger in assigning nicknames to better label what goes on in the streets. They are compulsive classifiers and sardonic commentators of daily life. Clichés about individuals, their identities, and their paths create wrappers and stuffing: juridical, psychological, and criminalistic conceptions about human practices. Through metaphors and concepts, this vigilante-cum-comptroller knowledge appropriates allegories that are useful and functional to policing. The PMs learn they need to know how to be "reasonable," placing themselves between what "the law says," what is demanded in the name of "social peace," and what is understood as creating security. This classification system incorporates qualifiers such as *ganso* (lit. "goose" but means "suspect"), *ronca* (lit. "snorer" but means stool pigeon), and *X9* (which means "traitor" or "informant"). Its coverage and flexibility are such that it can modulate and mediate encounters, producing units of meaning. *Involved with* is born, as a classification through maneuvers within the context and scope of police actions, stretching opportunities for the control of spatial mobility and reiterating the belief in the existence of a police monopoly over this: "That's what we're here for."

Called to act in the face of emergencies, people, objects, and situations, this immediate knowledge is manifested by a presentist appropriation of temporality. An intense experience of what is imminent and unpostponable for oneself and for others is preordained for those who police the city in search of the involved. It contributes to a chronology of the immediate that privileges the time in which developments occur. This, in turn, rebounds to "the moment of truth": the here-and-now of concerns, fears, and insecurities.

A knowledge constructed and shared from itinerant and extended vigils is a knowledge of circulation, a calculus of presentism experienced in the vagaries of patrol and in the future of events. The surveillance of others and of oneself situates the senses and attunes them to watching—especially to watching for those who move in illegal, clandestine, or informal manners in the expanded grammar of the streets. Itinerant fences of involvement are raised in the city's dynamics.

The involved, who experience the city in and through their involvement, negotiate these stopping and frisking points as the limits of their physical and symbolic territories. They exert, in their own way and regions, the control over the entries, permanencies, and exits that is performed by the police in the city as a whole. The representations and practices of the multiple cities cut out by these subaltern powers are visited (invited or not) by PMs on their rounds. In daily work, police officers cross symbolic boundaries, enter other worlds, and seek—through the technology of (dis)involvement—to translate their senses to police the distinct orders that these realities make visible. *Involvement with* is, in this way, a method of policing.

The phenomenology of police action uses the world of emotions as a resource that is always at hand. This emotive knowledge is charged with disparate affections in the emergency of action. It is open to contradictions and paradoxical reactions, making use of disproportion and of outbursts in order to maneuver the tempers of others. "Abuse of authority" and "contempt for authority" are currencies of exchange in interactions between the police and the policed. These terms refer to the dramatization of exaggerations of control and the excesses of guardianship. When one deals with situations that involve feelings such as hatred, indignation, fury, scorn, and fear, an economy of affection is developed that can "keep self-control strong" in order to restrain the emotional state of the involved. How far does one go with cold and civilized tolerance, which is read as indifference? How does one "not accept provocations and not lose the moral high ground of the police"? How does a "PM keep his head"? The "PM doesn't come from Mars, from Policeopolis!" He comes from the same place as the involved, where emotions are tactical resources of reaction, resistance, and confrontation. Before being a policeman and "having authority," the PM was a "macho man" and also "a worker revolted at his status." He has a hot head and a pained heart, coupled with a nervous trigger finger that can (and, he believes, should) "exchange tit for tat" with those who are abusive and provocative. This is a painful form of knowledge that hurts and makes hurt. The theatricality of the PM's distemper and political incorrectness at these moments, on the part of those who wander by and watch from all sides, is not wanted anywhere. "The police doesn't have the society it deserves!"

Setting the Report

Policing corresponds to the production of a substantive truth of involvement as a method in Rio de Janeiro—a truth originated of commonsense moral rules, redefined by a process of particularization, which singularizes each encounter with the police, to discipline the situational truths brought by those involved. The practical knowledge of the PM, of a political and coercive nature, (re)affirms an order and its will to know to be able to produce controls, even if diffuse and indirect. Its persecutory classification function aims to control in order to know, to know in order to control. One suspects in order to get to know and to continue suspecting who was, is, or will be *involved with*. There is an instrumentality that answers a cognitive intention—to survey, to know. Their main mission is to control and only then understand, selectively including and excluding the subjects, their worldviews, and their practices. The Carioca-police-have-to-be-and-do reveals an unlimited appetite for power—power to order, power to label, power to tutor, power to govern without being governed; a desire, a taste, a power, emancipated from society and against the state.

NOTES

1 Excerpt from ethnographic fieldnotes on a discussion with a boy, Fallet favela, 2017.

2 The city of Rio de Janeiro, or simply Rio. *Involved with crime* is in italics to highlight the category and its wider uses, which go beyond simple involvement with crime. *Involved with police*, for example, is also employed as a stigmatizing marker by agents in conflict with the legally constituted powers of the state. Here we are concentrating on the police and media's use of the tag, but readers should always remember that it has wider applications in the urban violence of Rio de Janeiro.

3   Quote marks are generally used to highlight emic expressions taken from field material.
4   Beat cops are low-ranking military police officers responsible for policing.
5   Polícia militar, or military police, which are the city's principal police force.
6   Polícia Militar do Estado do Rio de Janeiro, the Military Police of the State of Rio de Janeiro.
7   Rio de Janeiro military police hymn (Hinos e Marchas Militares, n.d.).
8   The South Zone, with its famous beaches, good urban infrastructure, and relatively few favelas, is the realm of the tourist, the white, the upper and middle classes: it is the picture-postcard Rio. Meanwhile, the North Zone is marked by poor urban infrastructure, greater numbers of favelas, greater poverty, darker populations, and a distinct absence of tourism.
9   A common and sardonic way of describing Rio de Janeiro, immortalized by singer Fernanda de Abreu (n.d.) in her composition "Rio 40 graus."
10 For an example of this sort of ostentatious performance, see the video of the 2011 Santa Teresa tram accident, as filmed by the neighborhood's residents, beginning at the 7:45 mark (Goulart 2011).

REFERENCES

casodepolicia.org. 2010. Commentary on *Suspeito para Sempre* blog. Accessed March 3, 2021. Link no longer active.

Cecchetto, Fatima. 2004. *Violência e estilos de masculinidade*. Rio de Janeiro: Ed. FGV.

Cecchetto, Fátima, Jacqueline Muniz, and Rodrigo Monteiro. 2018. "Basta tá do lado—a construção social do envolvido com o crime." *CRH* 31, no. 82: 99–116.

Cecchetto, Fátima, Jacqueline Muniz, and Rodrigo Monteiro. 2020. "Envolvido(a)-com o crime: Tramas e manobras de controle, vigilância e punição." *Revista de estudos empíricos em direito* 7, no. 2: 108–40.

de Abreu, Fernanda. n.d. "Rio 40 graus." *Letras*. Accessed September 23, 2023. https://www.letras.mus.br/fernanda-abreu/580/.

Gago, Verónica. 2018. *A razão neoliberal: Economias barrocas e pragmática popular*. São Paulo: Ed. Elefante.

Goulart, Vico. 2011. "Acidente Bonde Santa Tereza Rio de Janeiro Completo." YouTube video. Accessed September 24, 2023. https://www.youtube.com/watch?v=BjenvNXP_iM.

Hinos e Marchas Militares. n.d. "Hino da polícia militar do Rio de Janeiro." Letras. Accessed September 23, 2023. https://www.letras.mus.br/hinos-marchas-militares/546104/.

Monteiro, Rodrigo A. 2016. "A pacificação e suas tramas conflitos em torno da construção de normas sociais em duas favelas cariocas." *Sistema penal e violência* 7: 127–36.

Muniz, Jacqueline. 1999. "Ser policial é, sobretudo, uma razão de ser: Cultura e cotidiano da polícia militar do Estado do Rio de Janeiro." PhD diss., IUPERJ, Universidade Candido Mendes.

Muniz, Jacqueline. 2012. "O fim da inocência: Um ensaio sobre os atributos do saber policial de rua." In *Desafios à segurança pública: Controle social, democracia e gênero*, edited by Luis A. Francisco de Souza, Bóris Ribeiro de Magalhães, and Thiago Teixeira Sabatine, 13–41. Marília: Cultura Acadêmica.

Muniz, Jacqueline. 2014. "Jogando o jogo democrático da segurança pública: Procedimentos, transparência e responsabilização policiais." In *Tensões contemporâneas da repressão criminal*, edited by Ana Claudia B. de Pinto, Jean-François Y. Deluchey, and Marcus Alan de Melo Gomes, 147–57. Porto Alegre: Livraria do Advogado Ed.

Reiner, Robert. 1991. *The Politics of Police*. Toronto: University of Toronto Press.

Part III
Subject

17

Pentecostal Repertoires and Narco-warfare Grammars / Repertórios Pentecostais e Gramáticas do Narco-conflito

Fabricating and Inhabiting Religious-Criminal Subjects in an Urban Drug War

CESAR PINHEIRO TEIXEIRA

Urban violence is explored here through an ethnography composed of formerly convicted individuals, police officers, Pentecostal evangelicals, and actors linked to NGOs. This study brings together counterintuitive social logics that would seem to be opposed. Pentecostal evangelicals have been positioned as countering narco-trafficking violence and working to morally redeem and rescue urban communities. But outside of that, traffickers and evangelicals share investments in certain grammars of subject production—that is, of shaping the identity and moral value of certain people within these communities. I begin by thinking about criminal subjection as a conceptual tool, analyzing three major logics of action: policing of crime as war that renders subjects killable, a Manichean religious worldview that Satanizes or cleanses, and a neoliberal logic of producing employable workers through NGOs. When the three intersect, they constitute a field of solutions to violence. Adopting criminal subjection as part of a larger conceptual framework helps focus and capture an essentialist representation of criminalized populations, central to the continued deployment of urban-based violence. Criminal subjection is part of a broader network of everyday repression in Rio.

Urban Violence as a Grammar of Subjectivity

"It is very complicated. It is very difficult to get a second chance. They do not trust us. They think that we are still criminals and that we will die like this," a former general manager of a Rio drug-trafficking group told me, as we ate lunch at his home. At the same time, the evening television news dramatically announced the arrest of a man suspected of having committed rape. Upon hearing the news, the ex-trafficker began a speech filled with outrage, harshly criticizing the suspect and following up with a series of stories from the time the manager was still a criminal—about how he killed many rapists. It all seemed very similar to what the same newscast often said about criminals themselves—about how they deserved to be killed—so I decided to provoke my interlocutor by drawing a parallel. I asked if everything he said a few minutes earlier about "getting a second chance" could also be applied to people like the man accused of being a rapist. The proposed exercise failed miserably and, therefore, illuminated how much he ignored the grammar at play. The ex-trafficker replied without hesitation, "No. You do not understand. I am a person who has not had a chance in life. This guy is a monster. It is very different. The only way to deal with these guys is to just kill them. There is no other way."[1]

This episode reveals a set of mechanisms that shape the geography of urban violence in Rio de Janeiro. This discourse provides a glimpse of movements of ontological approximation and distancing which, in turn, define the limits between biopolitics and necropolitics. The line—that distinguishes those who must die from those who may live—is not totally defined by rigid structural criteria, even if produced historically in a systematic pattern. It is built, deconstructed, and reconstructed by different actors. It is based on unique repertoires of action whose limits and possibilities are set by what I call a moral grammar of subjectivity.

These repertoires of action are similar to a stock of knowledge or collective action repertoire. These are beliefs, ideas, metaphors, images, languages, and other schemes for understanding the world and informing behavior and practice. The stock of knowledge "serves as an interpretive scheme of its past and present experiences, and also determines its anticipation of things which are yet to come" (Schutz [1970] 2012, 86). On the other hand, the more practical dimension of repertoires is also essential (Tilly 1978). The worker's strike, for example, could be thought of as a repertoire of collective action emerging in the nineteenth century. In my work, repertoires are thought of as stocks of knowledge and practice that structure a given field of possibilities and its forms of action.

Previously, I traced grammatical repertoires used by alleged criminals, police officers, Pentecostal evangelicals, and actors linked to NGOs to better explain the many forms (and interconnections) of violence in Rio (Teixeira 2011, 2012, 2015, 2016, 2023; Freire and Teixeira 2016; Teixeira and Brandão 2019). The policemen kill enemies, nonhumans, and monsters. Evangelicals announce to sinners the way out of crime through religious conversion. Social projects and NGO workers seek to reduce the consequences of social inequalities in the criminals' lives, expanding their range of opportunities. But this is not a static image. In some situations, for example, the Pentecostal repertoire is mobilized by police and social workers, just as Pentecostals and social workers also trigger, in certain situations, other repertoires. Those accused of crimes mobilize these diverse principles of action—either to understand and deal with their own trajectories (when, for example, they decide to stop their alleged activities) or to understand and deal with the actions of others, such as the so-called vacilões (screw-ups).[2]

A thorough examination of these repertoires, and the factors that regulate their mobilization, offers a more empirically relevant picture of urban violence. All repertoires find possibilities and limits for their activation in daily life and can be mobilized in an appropriate or inadequate, competent or incompetent, effective or ineffective manner. The Pentecostal repertoire, for example, can be quite effective in the process of public "symbolic cleansing" (Machado da Silva 2008) of former drug traffickers who converted to Pentecostalism. On the other hand, this repertoire is unlikely to have the same effect when considering and converting rapists or with regard to whistleblowers of drug-trafficking activities (so-called 69s/xisnoves or snitches) (Corrêa 2022).

As mentioned, the mobilization of these repertoires is regulated more generally by a grammar of subjectivity. It regulates the possible movements on a continuum between total identification and total differentiation—when the other cannot even be classified into categories such as *human* (Freire and Teixeira 2016). These representations are fundamentally about subjectivity—the interior, mind, soul, heart, and other categories that define what a certain person is believed to be. As part of this research object—not as a concept—subjectivity represents that point from which someone's actions begin. It serves the actors as a tool for operating in the world: to kill, to convert, to include, in short, to judge and deliberate about the actions of others and of themselves. The intention, here, is not to carry out a Foucauldian exercise of deconstructing subjectivity as essence and reconstructing relations based on the critique of power and its circulation. Instead, I investigate the ways in which actors build, deconstruct, and reconstruct the borders between the policies of life and death based on a complex set of practical essentialisms (Herzfeld 1997) that make up Rio's context of urban violence and which function as bio- and necro-legitimacy criteria.

Circuits of Criminal Subjection

An important part of this game can be seen in the historical transformations of the criminal and how they are connected to practices within the justice system and police. Criminal subjection works as a very specific device for the criminalization of poverty (Misse 2022). It separates and distances people, dividing them, in essence, into criminals and noncriminals. This strongly guides police necro-policies, legitimizing the deaths of thousands of people through narratives such as the war on drugs and resisting arrest, and popular jargon such as "a good criminal is a dead criminal." In the end, the criminal subject is the one who must be killed.

Criminal subjection is strongly rooted in state practices, especially in the processes of defining criminal activities and ways of dealing with them. It is, therefore, an essentialist representation of the criminal, woven and updated in the relations between state, law, and society. However, the context of urban violence in Rio de Janeiro is composed of other essentialist representations of characters considered deviant and dangerous who escape, partially or completely, from this state-rooted (juridical) image that characterizes criminal subjection. In Rio de Janeiro, the so-called world of crime, for example, also produces its own subjections, embodied in characters such as the enemy, the rapist, and the snitch. These figures are considered abject and killable or treatable and recoverable. In my work, therefore, I deal with a wider and more complex circuit of subjections, which does not end with criminal subjection.

This circuit includes a synthesis of practices—of governmentality (Foucault 2008b), biopolitics (Foucault 2008a), and necropolitics (Agamben [1995] 2002; Mbembe [2003] 2018). The general objective is to understand how different actors circulate within it, through the mobilization of different repertoires of action that situationally define the limits between the legitimacy of certain deaths and the legitimacy of certain lives. Bio-legitimacy (Fassin 2000) and necro-legitimacy (lives that are not, for example, amenable to mourning; Butler 2015) are justified by different repertoires of action and transform the boundaries that define the limits of policies pertaining to life and death.

Describing the entire circuit in this text is an impossible task, so I introduce a case—one more fully described and analyzed in Teixeira (2023). During my fieldwork in 2011, I met a Pentecostal pastor who worked for an NGO as a conflict mediator in some favelas in Rio de Janeiro. He was hired by the NGO due to his vast experience in evangelizing residents, especially drug traffickers. In this context, the pastor became friends with the owner of a large slum in Rio, who also shared his Pentecostal faith. During one of our conversations, the pastor talked about a case that he had recently witnessed and that would make evident how Pentecostalism would be able to intervene in the world of crime. A young man went unarmed into a slum near his own occupied by a rival faction. He repeatedly screamed, "We are the fucking bosses! I'm going to kill everyone here!" The traffic security guards (soldiers) who witnessed the scene soon captured him and took him to the chief (boss), asking if they could kill him. For them, this represented a mere formality, since death was considered certain in a situation like this—when an alleged criminal enters enemy territory and threatens his rivals with death.

There is extensive literature, especially of an ethnographic nature, on crime, which sheds light on the practices and values mobilized in different criminal experiences.[3] With regard to retail drug trafficking in Rio de Janeiro, the criminal repertoire is produced from experiences in three distinct dimensions, which are constitutive of this criminal activity: commerce, war, and the management of collective life (Teixeira 2023). It helps actors when they act as workers in an illegal market, as participants in armed conflicts, and as managers of local collective life.

War is an important localized term that is constantly circulated when referring to urban violence (Leite 2000). From the perspective of retail drug trafficking, there are at least two major enemies to be fought in the war: rival traffickers who seek to expand the boundaries of their businesses by occupying other territories (and here we can point out other criminal factions and the militias), and the police when acting to suppress the illegal drug trade by invading the slums, seizing weapons and goods, and killing criminals. War, therefore, is a type of possible situation in the world of crime in which enemies are seen as killable beings. At the limit, they can even be seen as monsters—bearers of a radical otherness and different from those who are considered "true criminals," who act in full compliance with the "ethics of righteousness" (Grillo 2013). By making evident the moral complexity of the world of crime, the criminal repertoire relativizes the more general essentialist representations of the criminal. This happens when one can distinguish, for example, the "formed criminals" (morally judicious in their actions, who would not be "so different" from people who live "out of crime") from "loose animals" (who would act without moral limits, closer to representations of a "monster") (Zaluar 1985).[4]

First of all, enemies in war are killable because it is assumed that the other will be capable of killing to achieve their goals. Therefore, the enemy's status as killable has to do, at first, with anticipation of the disposition that the other would also have to kill. But in addition, and more importantly, the enemies are also represented by the criminals as morally inferior beings. Criminals of rival factions would not respect the ethics of crime, being permissive toward thieves, traitors, rapists, and other vacilões. Those who do not respond with mortal force to vacilões are considered disloyal, dishonest, and dishonored—becoming, in a way, themselves vacilões. Other rivals, such as militias (paramilitary vigilante groups and racketeering operations) and the police, also enter the same field of representations for different reasons. The militias are accused of economically exploiting the residents, which would never be done by those considered true criminals, since there would not be an identification with the place and its residents.[5] The police, in turn, are considered hypocrites when they act in a repressive manner. "Criminals in uniforms" would not deserve respect, as they would not be loyal even to the principles that govern their institution and their world. In general, the enemy is an essentialist representation of the rivals.

Returning to the case narrated by the pastor: after taking the captured enemy to the boss, the boss surprised everyone by carrying out an evangelical reading of the situation that did not lead to death. According to the pastor, the boss questioned the soldiers using a different understanding of *criminal*. During the conversation, the boss said, "Are you crazy? Can't you see he is not alone? Can't you see that the devil is with him? Do you think I am going to give the devil an easy way out like that? I will not lose my salvation because of that. You can let him go" (Pentecostal pastor, interview with the author, Rio de Janeiro, 2011).

Pentecostal Repertoires and the World of Crime

The rise of Pentecostalism among the working class in Rio sheds light on the relationships established between evangelicals and criminals (Vital 2015), which are characterized by the moral authority of the former over the latter (Teixeira 2008). In general, Pentecostals make up a collective widely recognized as capable of interfering in the dynamics of local conflicts—either by mediating internal conflicts or by removing the criminals from the world of crime (Teixeira 2011).

The existence of a religious transit among criminals matches the more general transformations of the Brazilian religious field—with the poorest tending to shift away from religions of African origin and Catholicism and toward Pentecostal denominations, which have mostly become right-wing in their political and social doctrines (Vital 2015). The actors argue that their old religions could not promote the protection and spiritual assistance that Pentecostalism offers to those who are in situations of poverty, risk, and vulnerability. The criminals—as well as the majority of the population that resides in underprivileged urban areas and in the slums of large cities—would tend to adopt a Pentecostal grammar (Novaes 2003) as a form of social navigation. Through it, they interpret events, guide their relationships with others, and build on a repertoire of practice. It is in this context that the "evangelical drug trafficker" may exist (Vital 2015). They become part of the world of crime while simultaneously mobilizing the Pentecostal repertoire.

The spiritual battle—a narrative that describes a world divided between God and the devil—can be considered one of the main elements of the Pentecostal repertoire.[6] On the one hand, God acts to save the souls of sinners through conversion, and on the other, the devil acts to dominate people through sin and temptation. In a very general way, learning to use the Pentecostal repertoire means learning to read the world through the possible movements on this mythical board, recognizing the agency of God and the devil in the concreteness of everyday life. For the boss in the pastor's story, the boy was not a morally inferior being—a killable enemy who sought to confront him in his own territory—but a soul used by the devil, who wanted to deceive him and make him lose his salvation.

In this specific case, the grammar of subjectivity is operated by its practitioners as a complex game of ontological distancing and approximation, put into practice through the repertoires of intersecting crime and Pentecostal practices. The repertoire used by the boss allows him to deal with the enemy's distance, embedding him within the actions of another being whose outsider status is even more radical: the devil. The latter provoked the boss, authorizing the boy's death. Through the death, the devil would be able to conquer both the boy's and the boss's souls. If the boss was guided by the repertoire of crime and annihilated the boy, he would run the risk of being overcome and manipulated by the devil. The Pentecostal repertoire allowed the devil's otherness to deconstruct the enemy, making the man someone no longer likely to be killed. This is certainly not an isolated case. Criminals do not always kill enemies, even allowing them to be taken to evangelical recovery and social work in some situations (Teixeira 2016; Teixeira and Brandão 2019; Machado 2014).

This is important, as it shows that the Pentecostal repertoire is not used in a homogeneous and generalized way.[7] Just as the Pentecostal repertoire can reduce the dynamics of the production of death, it can also expand it (Vital 2015; C. Rocha 2021). The same pastor proudly reported how, with the help of a criminal, he had destroyed several altars to saints scattered throughout the slum, in addition to invading Candomblé and Umbanda territories and expelling religious leaders.[8] The Pentecostal repertoire produces its own ontological distances when it associates certain actors with an absolute evil, therefore legitimizing practices of annihilation of the other. This is important, as it shows how the boundaries between the policies of life and death move according to a moral grammar of subjectivity, a field of possibilities in which repertoires can be activated—whether to relativize a certain ontological distance, saving the life of someone who could be considered an enemy, or to produce a certain ontological distance, annihilating those considered as agents of evil.

These are not the only repertoires available in the context of urban violence in Rio de Janeiro. There is also the repertoire of neoliberal social work (Teixeira 2015, 2023; Lia Rocha 2012; Amar 2018), the civic-affective repertoires mobilized by movements of mothers who denounce police brutality (Araújo 2015; Luciane Rocha 2016), and the police repertoire that historically fuels criminal subjection (Misse et al. 2013; Teixeira 2023; Teixeira and Freire 2016). These repertoires of action influence each other and render dynamic the field of possibilities, expanding, reducing, or transforming the range of actions. For the construction of this text, I opted for an analysis that privileged only a few points of intersection between the repertoire of crime and the Pentecostal repertoire in Rio de Janeiro. Other cultural contexts may be composed of their own repertoires or repertoires similar to those indicated here, which may also make evident the moral grammar of subjectivity that regulates the boundaries between the legitimacy of life and death in urban conflicts.

NOTES

1 Based on fieldwork conducted in 2010–11 in a neighborhood in the North Zone of Rio de Janeiro.

2 *Vacilão* is a category generally used in the peripheries and slums of Rio de Janeiro, which describes actors whose action hurts shared morals. In the so-called world of

crime, the vacilão category can denote a more intense moral judgment, framing actions that seriously harm shared morality or that do so very frequently.

3 An excellent bibliographic review on the ethnography of crime in Brazil was made by Aquino and Hirata (2018).

4 *Monster* is a commonly used term in Brazilian Portuguese. It serves to qualify someone both negatively ("That killer is a monster!") and positively ("That woman plays a lot of guitar—she is a monster on that thing!").

5 In general, traffickers identify more with the community than do the militias.

6 Cecília Mariz (1999) carried out a remarkable bibliographic review on the subject.

7 Although, with this, I am not claiming that it is mobilized only to counter expectations.

8 These altars are small buildings that are a critical part of Afro-Brazilian Candomblé and Umbanda religious practice.

REFERENCES

Agamben, Giorgio. (1995) 2002. *Homo sacer: O poder soberano e a vida nua I*. Belo Horizonte: Editora UFMG.

Amar, Paul. 2018. *O arquipélago da segurança: Estados de segurança humana, políticas de sexualidade e o fim do neoliberalismo*. Rio de Janeiro: Editora UFRJ.

Aquino, Jania Perla Diógenes de, and Daniel Hirata. 2018. "Inserções etnográficas ao universo do crime: Algumas considerações sobre pesquisas realizadas no Brasil entre 2000 e 2017." *Revista brasileira de informação bibliográfica em ciências sociais—BIB* 84, no. 2: 107–47.

Araújo, Fábio. 2015. *Das "técnicas" de fazer desaparecer corpos: Desaparecimentos, violência, sofrimento e política*. Rio de Janeiro: Lamparina.

Butler, Judith. 2015. *Quadros de guerra: Quando a vida é passível de luto?* Rio de Janeiro: Civilização Brasileira.

Corrêa, Diogo. 2022. *Anjos de fuzil: Uma etnografia das relações entre pentecostalismo e vida do crime na favela Cidade de Deus*. Rio de Janeiro: EdUERJ.

Fassin, Didier. 2000. "Entre politiques du vivant et politiques de la vie: Pour une anthropologie de la santé." *Anthropologie et sociétés* 24, no. 1: 95–116.

Foucault, Michel. 2008a. *Nascimento da biopolítica: Curso no Collège de France (1978–1979)*. São Paulo: Martins Fontes.

Foucault, Michel. 2008b. *Segurança, território, população: Curso no Collège de France (1977–1978)*. São Paulo: Martins Fontes.

Freire, Jussara, and Cesar Pinheiro Teixeira. 2016. "Humanidade disputada: Sobre as (des)qualificações dos seres no contexto de 'violência urbana' do Rio de Janeiro." *Terceiro milênio: Revista crítica de sociologia e política* 6, no. 1: 58–85.

Grillo, Carolina. 2013. "Coisas da vida no crime: Tráfico e roubo em favelas cariocas." PhD diss., Graduate Program in Anthropology, Social Sciences and Philosophy Institute, Federal University of Rio de Janeiro.

Herzfeld, Michael. 1997. *Cultural Intimacy: Social Poetics in the Nation-State*. New York: Routledge.

Leite, Márcia. 2000. "Entre o individualismo e a solidariedade: Dilemas da cidadania e da política no Brasil." *Revista brasileira de ciências sociais* 15, no. 44: 73–90.

Machado, Carly. 2014. "Pentecostalismo e o sofrimento do (ex-)bandido: Testemunhos, mediações, modos de subjetivação e projetos de cidadania nas periferias." *Horizontes antropológicos* 20, no. 42: 153–80.

Machado da Silva, Luiz Antonio. 2008. *Vida sob cerco: Violência e rotina nas favelas cariocas.* Rio de Janeiro: Nova Fronteira.

Mariz, Cecília Loreto. 1999. "A teologia da batalha espiritual: Uma revisão bibliográfica." *Revista brasileira de informação bibliográfica em ciências sociais—BIB* 1, no. 41: 33–48.

Mbembe, Achille. (2003) 2018. *Necropolítica.* São Paulo: N-1 Edições.

Misse, Michel. 2022. *Malandros, marginais e vagabundos: A acumulação social da violência no Rio de Janeiro.* Rio de Janeiro: Editora Lamparina.

Misse, Michel, Carolina Grillo, Natasha Neri, and Cesar Pinheiro Teixeira. 2013. *Quando a polícia mata: Homicídios por "auto de resistência" no Rio de Janeiro (2001-2011).* Rio de Janeiro: Booklink.

Novaes, Regina. 2003. "Errantes do novo milênio: Salmos e versículos bíblicos no espaço público." In *Religião e espaço público,* edited by Patrícia Birman and Márcia Leite. São Paulo: Attar.

Rocha, Carolina. 2021. "A culpa é do Diabo: As políticas de existência na encruzilhada entre neopentecostalismo, varejo de drogas ilícitas e terreiros em favelas do Rio de Janeiro." PhD diss., IESP/UERJ (State University of Rio de Janeiro).

Rocha, Lia. 2012. "Representações e autorrepresentações: Notas sobre a juventude carioca moradora de favelas e os projetos sociais de audiovisual." In *Rio de Janeiro: Um território em mutação,* edited by Angela Moulin Santos, Glaucio José Marafon, and Maria Josefina Sant'anna. Rio de Janeiro: Gramma/FAPERJ.

Rocha, Luciane. 2016. "De-matar: Maternidade Negra como ação política na pátria mãe (gentil?)." In *Antinegritude: O impossível sujeito Negro na formação social brasileira,* edited by Osmundo Pinho and João Vargas Cruz das Almas. Belo Horizonte: Fino Traço Editora.

Schutz, Alfred. (1970) 2012. *Sobre fenomenologia e relações sociais.* Rio de Janeiro: Vozes.

Teixeira, Cesar Pinheiro. 2008. "O Pentecostalismo em contextos de violência: Uma etnografia das relações entre evangélicos pentecostais e traficantes de drogas em Magé." *Ciências sociais e religião / Ciencias sociales y religión* 10, no. 10: 181–205.

Teixeira, Cesar Pinheiro. 2011. *A construção social do ex-bandido: Um estudo sobre sujeição criminal e pentecostalismo.* Rio de Janeiro: 7Letras.

Teixeira, Cesar Pinheiro. 2012. "'Frios,' 'pobres' e 'indecentes': Esboço de interpretação de alguns discursos sobre o crimonoso." In *Conflitos de (grande) interesse: Estudos sobre crimes, violências e outras disputas conflituosas,* edited by Michel Misse and Alexandre Werneck. Rio de Janeiro: Garamond.

Teixeira, Cesar Pinheiro. 2015. "O policial social: Algumas observações sobre o engajamento de policiais militares em projetos sociais no contexto de favelas ocupadas por UPPs." *Dilemas: Revista de estudos de conflito e controle social* 8, no. 1: 77–96.

Teixeira, Cesar Pinheiro. 2016. "O testemunho e a produção de valor moral: Observações etnográficas sobre um centro de recuperação evangélico." *Religião and sociedade* 36, no. 2: 107–34.

Teixeira, Cesar Pinheiro. 2023. *Matar, converter, incluir: A trama da violência urbana no Rio de Janeiro*. Rio de Janeiro: Editora Lamparina.

Teixeira, Cesar Pinheiro, and Beatriz Brandão. 2019. "Sobre as formas sociais da mudança individual: O testemunho em centros de recuperação pentecostais." *Anthropológicas* 30, no. 1: 136–57.

Tilly, Charles. 1978. *From Mobilization to Revolution*. Boston: Wesley.

Vital, Christina. 2015. *Oração de traficante: Uma etnografia*. Rio de Janeiro: Garamond.

Zaluar, Alba. 1985. *A máquina e a revolta: As organizações populares e os significados da pobreza*. São Paulo: Brasiliense.

18

Genderphobic Binarism / Binarismo Gênerofóbico

The War against Gender as a Political Weapon

VITÓRIA MOREIRA

In recent decades, feminist and LGBTQ+ movements have managed to obtain greater prominence in political debates at all levels, from local to global. Nevertheless, the popularization of these struggles has been accompanied by a growing resistance to the incorporation of the concept of gender. For those who oppose what they call gender ideology, the concept of gender is an ideological farce that denies the natural or divine division between the sexes. For these movements, what is at stake is the traditional family and the relationship between the human and divine. Often associated with right-wing and authoritarian populist rhetoric, movements combating gender ideology mobilize diverse and sometimes unlikely alliances against what they consider, ultimately, to be a civilizational threat. The context of Rio de Janeiro is exemplary in revealing how this discourse has been used to mobilize emotions, build collective identities, and even try to rewrite the history of queer and feminist struggles. In this chapter, I argue that the political experience in Rio de Janeiro exposes the strategic plasticity of the idea of gender ideology. It thus contributes to understanding the transnational mobilizations that oppose the gender perspective and the uncomfortable reflections it raises.

These feminist and LGBTQ+ movements have become increasingly prominent around the world and have achieved several advances in the recognition of minorities' rights. Since the 1990s, a growing number of international organizations have recognized sexuality and gender within a human rights framework that could provide regional and national legislative changes. In Latin America, this international context coincided with several processes of redemocratization in the 1990s, giving feminist and LGBTQ+ movements a window of opportunity to incorporate their demands into the political agendas of different countries. Those demands achieved new success amid successful elections of center-leftist governments in the early 2000s (Biroli and Caminotti 2020). Despite the ambivalent relations between these governments and those demanding gender equality, laws strengthening affirmative action quotas and gender parity were strengthened or regulated in this period, and legislative and judicial changes began to favor gender equality on the subcontinent (Biroli and Caminotti 2020).

In Brazil, feminist movements have historically developed within a context of campaigns for redemocratization, especially since the 1970s. In the 1990s, there was an increase in the number of NGOs with feminist and LGBTQ+ movements focused on the executive branch (Costa 2005), a trend that continued during the first decade of the twenty-first century. Nevertheless, the progress of sexual and gender rights guidelines has also encountered increasing resistance from more conservative sectors of society, which have been mobilizing transnationally against feminist and LGBTQ+ demands. Such forces began condemning the very concept of gender as an ideological trap that would aim to destroy the pillars of the traditional family and the Christian religion. I call this phenomenon *genderphobic binarism* because this right-wing discourse rejects the socially constructed character of gender roles and states that binary sexual distinctions naturally and irrevocably determine human social behavior.

For conservative groups, antigender mobilization creates a common language for political mobilizations not necessarily connected to sexuality. Therefore, the reactive nature of these movements does not prevent them from mobilizing their own agendas—as in the case of Rio de Janeiro, where mobilization around the fight against gender ideology campaigns constituted an opportunity for the rise of conservative political leaders. One of the characteristics of what is commonly called gender backlash in Latin America is that it promotes alternative frameworks for gender rights and relations. These groups seek to delegitimize one of the basic foundations of national and international policies since the 1990s: that gender is a social construction that creates power inequalities and hierarchies.

In this chapter, I introduce the concept of genderphobic binarism and analyze its expression in the context of Rio de Janeiro. First, I introduce gender and the diffuse notion of gender ideology, arguing that genderphobic binarism centers on the rejection of gender and the glorification of innate sexual characteristics. I then present how this discourse is expressed in the context of Rio de Janeiro, where gender ideology offers the possibility of a broad platform for political mobilization. Finally, I conclude with considerations about the complexity of the genderphobic discourse and the need to understand it beyond the idea of backlash.

Gender and the Gender Ideology Fallacy

Currently, gender is often used to refer to issues related to women (descriptive use), deal with relationships between men and women (relational use), or designate the culturally constructed interpretations of bodies into a male-female framework (binarism). Initially, *gender* served to indicate a rejection of the biological determinism implicit in the use of *sex* or *sexual difference* and emphasized the relational aspect of normative definitions of femininity (Scott 1986, 1054). The work of philosopher Judith Butler (1999)—the preferred target of attacks by "genderphobic" activists—challenges the neutrality of biology as a science by stating that gender is, in fact, sex. For her, sex, being a human notion, is as culturally constructed as gender, although it is camouflaged as prediscursive, or prior to culture. Anything, according to this argument, prior to culture and the body itself is a construction, having no significant existence before the mark of its gender (Butler 1999, 13). Butler does not deny the existence of bodies and genitalia. Rather, she states that the interpretation built around these bodies and genitalia is not presocial—elaborated by people who, inevitably, are in social and historical contexts. For Butler, gender is made; it is not a noun, nor a set of fluctuating attributes, but an achievement. It is compulsory heterosexuality that operates to standardize gender and sexuality.

Even among feminists, gender (as an analytical and political term) is not adopted unanimously. For its critics, it removes the focus on women, obscuring what would be the main object of feminist studies—the existence of a universal system of oppression of women by men. The use of gender has become popular in recent decades, partly because of its power to highlight the characteristics of social arrangements based on sexual differences. Therefore, one of its main contributions is demystifying the idea that social roles traditionally assigned based on sex are inevitable or even desirable.

In contrast to feminist debates, there is a growing conservative discourse that rejects the use of gender and defines it as a tool not for analysis, but for domination and destruction of traditional forms of social relations. According to this view, gender is an ideology that threatens not only traditional structural arrangements but, ultimately, human life as such. *Ideology* is used here to designate "situations in which people are persuaded by shady means to adopt convictions without being given any possibility of criticizing the position adopted in an imposing way" (Zapater 2015). The characterization of a discourse as ideological, therefore, is usually a way of delegitimizing it, designating it as pure opinion or guesswork. The essence of the antigender narrative is based on the idea that gender and sex are being used interchangeably but that the science that determines sex also determines, naturally and irrevocably, social behavior. According to this logic, the social construction of gender roles cannot, or should not, be independent of binary biological sex. The relevance of the concept of gender as an analytical and political mobilization tool is denied, arguing that biological differences between two sexes determine human behavior in a natural and immutable way.

I propose here to call this discourse—central to Brazilian conservative activism—genderphobic binarism. It is, in the first place, a reclamation of the supposed binary and complementary character of sexual distinctions that not only hinders the recognition of intersex people but also carries a deterministic interpretation. The normative discourse depends on the mobilization of fear. It presupposes, therefore, a true phobia of gender, which is understood as a trap that aims to destroy traditional social structures and values, especially the heteronormative family. Two factors inspire that fear on the part of conservative institutions. First, because it is a broad and flexible term, the word *gender* can be used in different feminist mobilization strategies, including those related to reproductive rights and LGBTQ+ groups (Buss and Herman 2003). Second, the idea of gender as a social construction challenges the supposed complementarity between women and men and, therefore, undermines the idea of a natural family (O'Leary 1997; Buss and Herman 2003, 113). In this sense, the framing of gender issues as a threat to the innocence of children, an idea that has great power for popular mobilization and serves to condemn gender as a weapon of manipulation of children and youth and of insurrection against parental authority, is particularly relevant.

Genderphobic binarism rejects the politicization of public-private distinctions evoked by feminist thinking and promotes family rights over individual rights (Biroli and Caminotti 2020). It reinforces heteronormative and cisnormative discourses. Antigender movements argue that feminists, human rights groups, and LGBTQ+ activists are united in a global project against the heteronormative family and therefore constitute a threat to the natural and divine order. However, while evoking religious premises, genderphobic binarism also uses the defense of science and empiricism to challenge the usefulness of the concept of gender and to condemn it as an ideology. Cardinal Dom Orani Tempesta (2020), archbishop of the Archdiocese of São Sebastião in Rio de Janeiro, exemplifies this thought by arguing that "those who insist on the ideological indoctrination of children and adolescents do not disseminate scientific knowledge, as they propagate, but work tirelessly, as one can see, for an ideology against God." Gender would be, according to this logic, an unnatural invention and, therefore, a radical rebellion against the will of God, who would be responsible for defining the existence and behavior of men and women.

In Latin America, genderphobic binarism focuses its efforts on fighting gender ideology, a shapeless aggregate of assumptions that serve as a strawman of feminist and LGBTQ+ movements. The organized narrative against gender ideology was originally a Catholic project developed in the context of mobilizations by the Holy See at different United Nations conferences in the 1990s (Patternote and Kuhar 2018). Specifically, 1995 is often pointed out as the turning point for the popularization of the concept. In the discussions leading up to the 1995 Fourth World Conference on Women in Beijing, the use of the term *gender* raised strong opposition from conservative religious countries—both Christian and Islamic—who shared the Vatican's fear that the word "could become, among the institutionalization of sexual and reproductive rights, a vehicle for the international recognition of abortion, additional attacks on traditional motherhood and a legitimation of homosexuality" (Patternote and Kuhar 2018, 11).

During the early 2000s, the backlash against gender turned to laws, judicial decisions, and public policies that dealt with topics such as same-sex marriage, adoption by same-sex couples, and sex education (Biroli and Caminotti 2020, 1). Through deploying and producing fear around gender ideology, the Catholic Church made it possible to create spaces where intellectuals and activists could meet and exchange views and strategies—the creation of a "powerful network of mobilization and diffusion" (Patternote and Kuhar 2018, 11). Because of its extremely elastic and flexible character, the notion allowed historically disparate social and religious groups to come together in opposition to it. In Latin

America, transnational networks propagated the idea that the traditional family would be at risk if gender ideology is not defeated, which makes it possible to unite secular and religious, Catholic, and evangelical actors (Biroli and Caminotti 2020, 3). It is precisely its abstract and indefinite character that makes it possible to adapt this set of ideas to different local contexts and political strategies. And it constituted an umbrella term that managed to become an especially effective electoral weapon.

Rio's War on Gender

In Brazil, the fight against gender is concentrated around education, arguing to protect children against what would be seen as a harmful instrument of mass manipulation and destruction of the family. Though never explicitly mentioned, gender was a priority in the National Education Plan approved in 2014 and education plans enacted in 2015 in state legislative assemblies and city councils, which regulate teaching for ten years (Miguel 2016). At the national level, the Escola sem Partido movement (roughly, School without Political Parties) is a significant example of the power to mobilize genderphobic binarism. Created in 2004 to fight against an alleged Marxist indoctrination in schools—and linked to the ultraliberal think tank Instituto Millennium—the movement focused in its initial period on the defense of liberal economic banners (Miguel 2016, 600). Because of its intersections with Christian religious discourse, genderphobic binarism in Rio de Janeiro is closely connected with the rise and expansion of Pentecostal and Neo-Pentecostal churches in recent decades, as well as the resurgence of more conservative currents of Catholicism. However, it also transcends religious discourse by advocating the natural or biological character of binarism and opens doors for different social groups to adhere to this discourse.

In the municipal legislative sphere, the most recent fight against gender ideology was led by the former councilor of Niterói and current federal deputy Carlos Jordy. In 2016, during hearings on the municipal education plan in Niterói, Jordy advocated to include the fight against gender ideology within the document, which was blocked by the efforts of City Hall and the Department of Education. Despite this, antigender mobilization succeeded in popularizing the idea and bringing it into debates about public education in Rio and other parts of the country.

In a panel discussion on the topic at the City Hall of Londrina, in 2017, Jordy characterized gender ideology as an atrocity and a macabre plan (Parlatório

Livre 2017). According to him, it is a distortion of feminism, which in its first and second generations would, even if problematic, have focused on defending civil and political rights. The gender ideologues, in turn, would be astute manipulators who use feminists—who think they are fighting for equality between men and women—to attack heterosexuality and masculinity, and not machismo. According to Jordy (2017), "the gender agenda is the negation of human nature, of biology itself, and feminist movements are used as a maneuver by people who are very aware of what is happening behind the scenes so that this agenda can be disseminated . . . always with the defense of fighting against intolerance." Therefore, paradoxically, genderphobic binarism can transcend the binary view of "us against them" by recognizing diversity among feminist and LGBTQ+ fields. In this case, however, this recognition works to strengthen the conservative perspective on gender relations.

In addition to coordination efforts in legislative policy, Rio's antigender movements are also strongly present in public universities, where groups of conservative religious students compete for power through the promotion of Christian studies meetings. In April 2018, one of these events made headlines when a group of students from the Fluminense Federal University (UFF) prevented an event of the Christian University Movement on the university premises, which resulted in a conflict between the two groups and accusations of violence on both sides. A year earlier, in June 2017, the same university had been the target of a notice sent by then councilman Carlos Jordy, who, based on complaints, suggested investigating the use of university bathrooms by transgender students. Mobilizing the rhetoric of fear, Jordy claimed that although there was no law that would support the ban on the use of bathrooms by transgender people, "I would not like a daughter or relative to have to go through this" (Mendes 2017). From an antigender perspective, transgender people are sick, victims of gender dysphoria, and are being used by gender ideologues as an instrument to advance their goal of eliminating any sexual distinction.

Outside the university environment, the antigender movement spreads through events organized by conservative groups, often held in Catholic and evangelical churches (both traditional and new). In these events, the genderphobic narrative mixes with the fight against cultural Marxism with a supposed dominance of the left in education and with the propagation of historical revisionist theories. In 2016—a time for discussing education plans—councilor Carlos Bolsonaro announced, on his website, that he was committed to combating "gender ideology," which he characterized as an attempt to "teach homosexuality and sex" to children as young as five years old in schools (Bolsonaro Family 2016). In the same year, during the period of municipal elections, "gender ideology" accusations were used against the candidate for mayor Marcelo Freixo, of the Socialism and Freedom Party (PSOL) when he was accused of having projects to "define sexuality in schools" (*O Globo* 2016).

The strategic utility of gender ideology produces significant electoral results, not only because of the power to mobilize its assumptions but also because of the loopholes it creates. By evoking the idea of gender ideology, genderphobic binarism makes room for disinformation campaigns that, even if not explicitly announced as part of the multiple definitions of the term, are easily linked to and guarantee it even more popularity.

Conclusion

Although rooted in Christian religious thought and promoted by Catholic and evangelical groups, genderphobic binarism transcends the borders of religion and is incorporated into secular debates of great prominence. The plasticity of gender ideology works strategically to enable alliances between different conservative groups and to offer a gateway of support from feminist activists. Through referencing biological sciences and the distinction between gender ideologues and authentic feminists, the antigender movement seeks to build a broad alliance against challenges to gender-based hierarchies. Rio de Janeiro is an example of how gender ideology is formed through a shapeless aggregate of ideas. The focus on education allows groups to mobilize fears through a call to protect children and, with that, allows for campaigns for disinformation and defamation.

In the foreground, genderphobic binarism is concerned with the threat that feminists and gender scholars bring to heterosexuality and traditional family organizations—both seen as biological facts. It is in direct opposition to progressive policies that propose the normalization of alternative family arrangements and the recognition of LGBTQ+ people. The elasticity of the genderphobic discourse and the plurality of its actors call into question its perception as a reaction movement or backlash since it is also capable of bending the binarism embedded in the idea of "us against them" (Patternote 2020). If, on the one hand, genderphobic binarism has the characteristics of a counteroffensive, or backlash, to the expansion of minority rights, then it appears, on the other hand, as a complex mobilization platform built from the feeling of fear of a malleable enemy. Understanding this characteristic is necessary in order to recognize that the challenges brought by this discourse are diverse and indeterminate and that its flexibility allows adaptations and reinventions that must be carefully mapped by social movements and progressive forces.

REFERENCES

Biroli, Flávia, and Mariana Caminotti. 2020. "The Conservative Backlash against Gender in Latin America." *Politics and Gender* 16: 1–3.

Bolsonaro Family. 2016. "Em que pé anda a ideologia de gênero e sexualidade para as crianças nas escolas do Rio." *Blog Família Bolsonaro*, October 26. http://familiabolsonaro.blogspot.com/2016/08/bolsonaro-ideologia-de-genero-e.html.

Buss, Doris, and Didi Herman. 2003. *Globalizing Family Values: The Christian Right in International Politics.* Minneapolis: University of Minnesota Press.

Butler, Judith. 1999. *Gender Trouble: Feminism and the Subversion of Identity.* New York: Routledge.

Costa, Ana Alice Alcântara. 2005. "O movimento feminista no Brasil: Dinâmicas de uma intervenção política." *Revista Gênero* 6, no. 2: 1–20.

Jordy, Carlos. 2017. "Conheça mais sobre o que está por trás da ideologia de gênero." YouTube video, June 21. https://www.youtube.com/watch?v=3d8uV_4-_YI.

Mendes, Wilson. 2017. "Vereador denuncia uso de banheiros da UFF por 'homens que se intitulam qualquer coisa diversa.'" *O Globo: Extra*, June 13. https://extra.globo.com/noticias/rio/vereador-denuncia-uso-de-banheiros-da-uff-por-homens-que-se-intitulam-qualquer-coisa-diversa-21472112.html.

Miguel, Luis Felipe. 2016. "Da 'doutrinação marxista' à 'ideologia de gênero'—Escola Sem Partido e as leis da mordaça no parlamento brasileiro." *Direito e Práxis* 7, no. 15: 590–621.

O Globo. 2016. "Candidatos à prefeitura do Rio participam de debate na TV Globo." September 30. https://g1.globo.com/rio-de-janeiro/eleicoes/2016/noticia/2016/09/candidatos-prefeitura-do-rio-participam-de-debate-na-tv-globo.html.

O'Leary, Dale. 1997. *The Gender Agenda: Redefining Equality.* New York: Vital Issues.

Parlatório Livre. 2017. "Parlatório Livre—Ideologia de Gênero—Carlos Jordy." YouTube video, September 11. https://www.youtube.com/watch?v=Ip5Xk5ZXlIo.

Patternote, David. 2020. "Backlash: A Misleading Narrative." Sexuality Policy Watch, June 16. https://sxpolitics.org/backlash-a-misleading-narrative/20996.

Patternote, David, and Roman Kuhar. 2018. "Disentangling and Locating the 'Global Right': Anti-gender Campaigns in Europe." *Politics and Governance* 6, no. 3: 6–19.

Scott, Joan. 1986. "Gender: A Useful Category of Historical Analysis." *American Historical Review* 91, no. 5: 1053–75.

Tempesta, D. Orani João. 2020. "Ainda a questão da ideologia de gênero." Arquidiocese de São Sebastião, June 14. https://pt.aleteia.org/2020/06/10/ainda-a-questao-da-ideologia-de-genero/.

Zapater, M. 2015. "Afinal, existe a tal 'ideologia de gênero'?" *Carta Capital, Justificando,* November 20.

19

Legal Limbo of Urban Indigeneity /
Limbo Jurídico da Indigeneidade Urbana

Indigenous Mobilizations and the Traps of State Visibility

MARCOS ALEXANDRE DOS SANTOS ALBUQUERQUE

This chapter explores the case study of urban Indigenous activists in Rio de Janeiro, tracing the growth of the Indigenous urban population and what that has
meant for the legal rights and visibility of such groups. I use the concept of legal
limbo to capture the particular recolonial predicament the state deploys for urban
Indigenous citizens. If the state still recognizes Indigenous peoples only through
their villages, lands, and tribes, then can an urban Indigenous individual or
people—who migrated away or have been forcibly displaced from their ancestral villages—still make legal claims as Indigenous? And to which state authority
would they make these claims? This chapter focuses on the occupation of the
Museu do Índio, near the Maracanã Stadium complex, and the government's
response to such actions. Thanks to movements such as this, the municipal
and state government can no longer ignore the legal rights of Rio's Indigenous

peoples. This chapter explores both the victories and limitations of movement organizations that have emerged in recent years.

The Urban Indigenous of Brazil

The Brazilian census of 1991 indicated a total of 294,000 Indigenous people in the country, with 223,000 living in rural regions (76.1 percent of the total) and 71,000 residing in urban areas (23.9 percent). In the 2000 census, new data revealed that the Indigenous population had doubled, at 734,000, most of whom lived in cities (383,298), while the remaining 350,000 were recorded in rural areas. In the 2010 census, the Indigenous population increased annually by 1.1 percent (817,963). Urban areas, on the other hand, witnessed a decrease of 68,000 (315,180), with the biggest population decline in the southeast region. According to speculation, "these people who have ceased to classify themselves as indigenous in the urban areas may have no affinity with their people of origin and the inclusion of questions related to ethnic belonging and the language spoken at home may have been a factor of influence in regard to the declaration of being or not indigenous" (Santos and Teixeira 2011, quoted in IBGE 2012, 12). Identification with a certain lineage was considered a possible reason for changing figures across the decades, rather than an objective migration, emigration, or immigration.

A new reality is beginning to emerge with regard to the distribution of the country's Indigenous population. Of the twenty municipalities with the largest number of Indigenous inhabitants, ten are capital cities. A larger trend suggests an explanation of why this redistribution has occurred. Brazil became the country with the most unequally concentrated pattern of rural landownership in the world. The Brazilian Institute of Geography and Statistics' Agricultural Census of 2006 shows that the concentration of large landowners' share of the land in Brazil continues to increase, which has reduced the number of establishments with less than 10 hectares. Small landowners are mostly poor rural Brazilians, about 2.5 million people, who occupy 2.7 percent of the national territory (IBGE 2012). Recent numbers indicate that "it is the agribusiness farmers, who represent less than 1% of the establishments, but control 46% of all land" (IBGE 2012, 2). There are 16 million people in the country who remain landless and 23 million rural workers who survive in poverty. In the northeast region, the territory occupied by small properties (under 10 hectares) has decreased dramatically. In comparison to 1980, there was a decrease of 707,000 hectares, and compared to 1996, 325,000 hectares (8 percent less). The "map of conflicts involving environmental injustice and health in Brazil" elaborated by Fundação Oswaldo

Cruz Health Foundation (FIOCRUZ) and Federação de Órgãos para Assistência Social e Educacional (FASE), released in May 2010 (Fiocruz 2010), shows that the most affected populations are primarily Indigenous (33.67 percent), followed by family farmers (31.99 percent) and quilombolas (21.55 percent). The Indigenous population ends up following the same path as the poor in the countryside, heading for the large cities for economic opportunity.

Simultaneous with the growing movement of landless peoples to big urban spaces is the increasingly broad network of support for Indigenous social and political representation. To be sure, migration to cities has been happening since at least the 1950s, during a period of intense urbanization in the country. But an increase in Indigenous associations—with the promulgation of Article 231 of the 1988 Constitution, which legally codified Indigenous rights—and subsequent mobilization and social visibility of Indigenous peoples within cities may be a further incentive for migration. Democratic opening and the consolidation of rights minimized prejudices and the social invisibility of Indigenous people, thereby making formal identification less socially and politically costly. Put simply, "the indigenous identity in urban centers is clearly configured as a contextual social identity. The same person can consider himself to be indigenous in some contexts and not in others" (Baines 2001, 15–16).

In order to achieve recognition and consolidation of differentiated rights, Indigenous people in cities have led their own autonomous organizations. The issue officially gained attention in 2006, during the First National Conference on Indigenous Peoples. During the World Urban Forum in 2010, the former president of Brazil's National Indian Foundation (FUNAI), Márcio Meira, said that "most of the indigenous population still lives—and I hope they will keep on living—in their traditional territories. But Brazilian cities are increasingly receiving indigenous peoples" (Abdala 2010). FUNAI expects Indigenous peoples never to leave their lands. This logic is present in the agency's management model, which is why it was never prepared to meet demands by Indigenous peoples in cities. The agency believes its role "should not be to implement the programs itself, but to develop the lines of policies that should be implemented by the federal government within the scope of the direct action of the ministries" (de Carvalho 2007).

In the midst of this legal limbo, some states and municipalities—mostly through human rights secretariats—have been creating public policies for the Indigenous population. In general, what such articulations between the federal, state, and municipal governments have accomplished is a division of work assisting the Indigenous population, allocating duties to different ministries and secretariats. As a result, it ends up not establishing a clear direction at the federal level for policies to assist Indigenous peoples, producing few actions. For more than fifteen years, the bill for the new Statute of Indigenous Peoples has been in the National Congress, testing the possibility that specific rules may be established in the new text that explicitly guarantee the rights of Indigenous peoples in urban contexts. Valuing the autonomy of community associations and recognizing them as a legitimate instrument of representation and dialogue—defined by the Brazilian constitution and the 169th International Labor Organization (ILO) Convention ratified by Brazil in 2004—is only one step in the direction of meeting the needs of urban Indigenous peoples.

The Case of Rio

The relationship between cities and Indigenous lands is revealing. Of the total of 15,894 Indigenous people in the state, 450 live on Indigenous lands and 15,444 in cities. The decrease in the Indigenous population in the state was 7.8 percent in total; 7.9 percent in urban areas and 6.8 percent in rural areas. The absolute decrease in the capital between 2000 and 2010 was 8,858 and in the group of other municipalities 11,182. The average annual decrease between 2000 and 2010 was 8.0 percent in the capital and 7.7 percent in other cities. One report concludes that "the indigenous population decrease was significant in the urban areas of 20 Federation Units, especially in the States of São Paulo, Rio de Janeiro, and Minas Gerais. In these states, the 2000 Demographic Census revealed the largest population increases in relation to that carried out in 1991" (IBGE 2012, 14). These numbers reveal at least two things: the decrease in the Indigenous population in rural areas as part of the migration process to cities, as well as the urbanization of these areas; and, on the other hand, the decrease in numbers in cities due to the census's new procedures described in the previous section.

As stated above, in 2010 there were 15,894 Indigenous people in the state of Rio de Janeiro, and in the largest cities in Greater Rio, the Indigenous population was recorded at 11,961 people, or 75.25 percent of the total Indigenous population in the state (the capital holds 44.6 percent of the total state). Therefore, most of the urban Indigenous population is concentrated in the Greater Rio region, where the largest cities in the state are located. Legislative change toward the representation of these groups has lagged despite the data available about their growing relevance.

In 2004 and 2005, a small group of Indigenous people started to meet in spaces provided by unions. These small meetings were intended to organize Indigenous people in the city in order to build a social movement to support enacting public policies for Indigenous people. In October 2006, this group organized the occupation of the former Indigenous Museum (Museu do Índio) that was abandoned in 1977. As the building is located in the external area of the Maracanã Stadium complex, the group called the occupation Aldeia Maracanã. As a result, Indigenous organizers began to revitalize the space, build small mud houses around the building, plant vegetable gardens and fruit trees, organize events to promote Indigenous culture, and sell handicrafts. In the process, they demanded that public authorities restore the building for the promotion of Indigenous culture and rights. At the beginning of the occupation, there were seventeen ethnic groups with about forty-seven Indigenous people. Throughout this occupation, this number varied slightly, but Indigenous residents continued to rotate leadership roles. In addition to the Guaraní of the state of Rio de Janeiro, the main ethnicities present were migrants from the north and northeast of the country.

The Indigenous plea for the restoration of the building seemed legitimate because all public demonstrations made by technicians and commissions that surveyed the site declared that the building was not at risk of collapse and that it could be fully restored. The Indigenous Museum is a national historical and architectural landmark. In the second half of the nineteenth century, it was intended for use by the Duke of Saxe, son-in-law of Emperor Dom Pedro II. It was the first headquarters of Brazil's Indian Protection Service (SPI), the predecessor of FUNAI in 1910, where Marshal Candido Mariano Rondon operated, and of the Indigenous Museum founded by Darcy Ribeiro in 1953. The building hosted the SPI Studies and Research Section, where important Brazilian anthropologists like Eduardo Galvão and Roberto Cardoso de Oliveira worked. These facts rendered the museum's rescue an important historical event for the Indigenous population and movement. Aldeia Maracanã came to occupy the building and promote the history and the forms of Indigenous social and cultural organization. The Aldeia Maracanã functioned as a node for congregation, an instrument of organization, and a field of visibility for the Indigenous presence in the city.

Although the group had strongly insisted on promoting a dialogue with the public authorities, demanding the participation of the state in the reform and promotion of space for the Indigenous cause, the government of the state of Rio de Janeiro was silent on the case until the end of 2012. It was then that the government began harassing the group through legal orders to vacate the space. In December 2013, the military police's Shock Squad began intimidating organizers, sometimes without court orders. The expulsion of the Indigenous group from the area was part of the reform policy that the government was carrying out due to the 2014 World Cup soccer tournament. Meanwhile, the state government did not manage to create an effective dialogue aimed at solving the problem.

The entire Maracanã complex underwent a process of forced removal of poor communities and the world that they had built.

In March 2013, the Indigenous group was finally expelled by a strong police apparatus with the excessive use of force by the Shock Squad (the militarized SWAT team equivalent in Brazil). The event made headlines for a week, showing images that shocked national and international audiences. Most of the group was housed in public improvised spaces until 2016, when they were transferred to a building with twenty apartments in a block of a housing project of the federal government—a project known as Minha Casa, Minha Vida (My house, my life), in the center of the city of Rio de Janeiro (with the transfer of properties free of charge to the Indigenous group). In March 2014, this group founded the Indigenous Association Aldeia Maracanã (AIAM) and then, together with the State Secretariat for Human Rights, organized the State Council for Indigenous Rights (CEDIND), instituted by state decree in January 2018. CEDIND is a permanent collegial body—but of an advisory nature—and is linked to the State Secretariat for Human Rights and Policies for Women and the Elderly (SEDHMI).

Conclusion

The means of survival for many Indigenous peoples, prior to urban migration, was wage labor on farms and in civil construction in neighboring cities and capitals of the country. The Indigenous diaspora for the cities and economic capitals of the country created the consequent invisibility of this population in the urban environment. As a paradigmatic example, Rio de Janeiro's Indigenous peoples find great difficulty in getting their rights enforced. The main instrument for contesting the authenticity of Indigenous peoples, whether by the government—which keeps them administratively in a legal limbo—or by society itself, is the assumption that their urbanity would disqualify them as Indigenous. Therefore, the logic goes, they should not have access to specific rights, such as health and education.

The anti-Indigenous discourse in the cities introduces a new kind of repressive language, as can be seen in the term *villageless*, which carries the assumption that the Indigenous gave up their protection and assistance from public agencies (FUNAI and others). This is a form of political and administrative prejudice. Political-administrative prejudice maintains the SPI policy, while FUNAI's contributions diminish, constituting a legitimate omission. One must consider the context of mobility: "an understanding of indigenous societies and cultures cannot go without critical reflection and recovery of their historical dimension" (de Oliveira 1999, 8).

REFERENCES

Abdala, Victor. 2010. "Cresce número de indígenas que vive em cidades brasileiras." Notícias FUNAI (Government of Brazil). https://www.gov.br/funai/pt-br/assuntos/noticias/2010/numero-de-indigenas-vivendo-em-cidades-e-cada-vez-maior-no-brasil.

Baines, Stephen G. 2001. "As chamadas 'aldeias urbanas' ou índios na cidade." *Revista Brasil indígena* 2, no. 7: 15–17.

de Carvalho, Priscila D. 2007. "Índios na Cidade." WRBI. https://webradiobrasilindigena.wordpress.com/indios-na-cidade/.

de Oliveira, João Pacheco. 1999. *Ensaios em antropologia histórica*. Rio de Janeiro: Editora UFRJ.

Fiocruz. 2010. "Mapa de conflitos injustiça ambiental e saúde no Brazil." https://mapadeconflitos.ensp.fiocruz.br/.

IBGE. 2012. "Os indígenas no Censo Demográfico 2010: Primeiras considerações com base no quesito cor ou raça." Rio de Janeiro: Instituto Brasileiro de Geografia e Estatística.

Santos, Ricardo, and Pery Teixeira. 2011. "O 'indígena' que emerge do Censo Demográfico de 2010." *Cadernos de Saúde Pública* 27, no. 6 (June): 1048–49. http://www.scielo.br/pdf/csp/v27n6/01.pdf.

20

Terreiro Politics and Afro-religious Mobilizations /
Política do Terreiro e Mobilizações Afro-religiosas

Practices of Black Resistance against Christian Supremacism and Religious Racism

ROSIANE RODRIGUES DE ALMEIDA AND LEONARDO VIEIRA SILVA

The political performance of Afro-religious people has given rise to a contemporary model of activism based on the sociocultural diversity of African-descendant religious practices. In August 2018, for example, scant media attention was given to the dozens of Afro-religious community members, representing a variety of Afro-Brazilian religious traditions, who occupied the municipal legislative chamber in Rio de Janeiro. They did so to defend animal sacrifice, which is sanctioned in their religions and represents a key spiritual and collective ritual. The Supreme Court, the highest court in Brazil, was at the time considering the constitutionality of such practices, which were common among Afro-Brazilian diasporic religions, including those of the Yoruba people, many of whose descendants in Brazil are identified as Nagô and maintain aspects of that West African language and identity. The Nagô are also known as the Ketu Nation of Candomblé practitioners. The community we identify here as Afro-religious also importantly integrates influences and traditions from the non-Yoruba, commonly referred to as Bantu, peoples who originated in the area currently known as Angola and the Congo (which historically was the Kingdom of the Kongo). This diverse legacy integrates the descendants and cultural contributions of the Fon of the Benin and Dahomey regions, who practice Jeje, which is a branch of Candomblé (often called the Vodum of Brazil). The varied religious communities that emerged from this set of diverse legacies also included the terreiro communities or nations of Omolokô and Umbanda. The word *terreiro* signifies the shrine, sacred house, or religious community center where Afro-Brazilian rituals, ceremonies, and gatherings take place.

During the event in which the Afro-religious community leaders and members entered and occupied Rio de Janeiro's legislative chamber, all participants wore white or colored robes—women wore skirts, camisus, gowns, ojás, and coastal cloths, and men wore eketés and/or abadás. Their protest chants were accompanied by the sound of atabaques, agogôs, and songs in Yoruba (Nagô and Ketu) languages, Mbundu, Kikongo (Bantu) languages, Fon and Fon-gbé (Jeje) languages, and Portuguese. "This type of protest—The Staircase washing of the Rio Legislative Chamber—did not dispense with liberal-modern models of rights claims but does transcend this frame, drawing upon the richness of Afro-religious methods and epistemologies. Nevertheless, this protest event was entirely distinct from more festive gatherings by Afro-religious communities that occupy public spaces, like the festival Presente a Iemanjá, which takes place annually on the city's beaches and celebrates Iemanjá, the Mother of All Waters and Mother of All Orixás (according to all the related African religious traditions listed above)" (R. R. Almeida 2019).

The staircase washing of the legislative chamber takes up public space, centers diasporic discourse and slogans, and reimagines the body politic. It questions public norms so that it can demand civil rights, centering the focus on terreiros rather than other religious representations (Catholics, Evangelicals, Buddhists, Jews, Muslims). These actors introduce a new epistemology when they sing to Xangô (a Yoruba god), as they cry out for justice, or when they praise Pambu Njila (in the Congo-Angola Candomblé tradition). In this action, practitioners of the Jeje branch of Candomblé evoked Bessém, the spirit of continuity and good fortune. With this reverence, the demonstrators invoke transformation and favorable resolution. Such epistemic challenges and collective remembering have enabled a reconfiguration of the fight against racism (R. R. Almeida 2014,

2019). It is distinct from the tactics and discourses of other secular Brazilian Black social movements, though it remains in dialogue with them as well as with Black, religiously informed politics in North America and Africa.

This chapter highlights the complexity and diversity of Black practices among Afro-religious peoples in Brazil, in traditional terreiro communities. Afro-religious movements emerged in the 1990s and came to represent a diverse range of individuals and organizations. Based on the ethnographies carried out in Rio involving religions of African descent, we developed the terms *terreiro politics* and the Afro-religious as concepts. Both concepts help make sense of attacks throughout the 1980s by members of the Neo-Pentecostal churches, who were opposed to the terreiros. We examine such conflicts and the inadequacy of the term *holy war* to account for these events. We explore the possibility of explicating allegations of discrimination as religious racism, as opposed to religious intolerance. The political performance of Afro-religious people has given rise to a contemporary model of activism based on the sociocultural diversity of religious practices. Such a scenario has enabled a reconfiguration of the global fight against racism, not aligning entirely with other Black Brazilian movements but remaining in dialogue, more generally, with Black movements in North America.

For the reader in North America or Europe, the prefix *Afro-* might seem outdated. But in Brazil, *Afro-* is not a stigmatized expression and is still widely used by antiracist and Black social and political movements to highlight the African-diasporic or African-descendant aspects of a particular political, cultural, or social formation. In that context, our concept of the Afro-religious emerged from our research and experiences in Rio de Janeiro. It was there that we encountered a diversity of institutions, organizations, and religious people of African origin, who were fighting for the rights of the terreiros. A body of literature captures ethnographies pertaining to the ethnic, racial, and religious nature of these conflicts (Miranda 2010, 2018; R. R. Almeida 2014, 2019; Miranda and Boniolo 2017; Miranda, Correa, and Almeida 2019; L. Lima, Berbet, and Vieira Silva 2019; Vieira Silva 2020).

Afro-religious people are agents (Ortner 2007) of what we call terreiro politics, understood as the unique concepts and practices cultivated by leaders and followers of Black and Afro-religious communities, and used to fight Christian supremacism in public policies.[1] Terreiros are the African-descendant communities' equivalent to churches or mosques. They also function as religious community centers for the collective practice of Afro-Brazilian religious traditions. Terreiros are spaces that house shrines, sacred rituals, and social and solidarity functions. These practices are particularly important for racialized communities and the very high percentage of LGBTQ-identified Black women participants in these communities. Terreiros are often located in working-class areas occupied by militarized police, vigilante militias, or narco-faction organizations. Since the 1980s, these communities have been targeted intensively by Pentecostal missionaries, who seek to convert and violently attack Black and African religious practices. Dogmatic Christians believe such traditions to be practices of the devil or heresies. In Brazil, public space has always been religious, often dominated by the Christian tradition (Miranda 2019).[2] The concepts of terreiro politics and Afro-religious mobilization help make sense of the new forms of resistance that have emerged from communities responding to the surge of attacks by members of the Neo-Pentecostal churches (particularly from the Universal Church of the Kingdom of God) against leaders and followers of the terreiros. Here, we utilize new methods and concepts in order to provide an alternative to the racist religious conflict discourse—animated by the press, media, and Pentecostal institutions. The term *religious conflict* positions Christian supremacism on the side of civilization and Afro-religious terreiro communities on the side of barbarism—justifying religious racism, attacks on terreiros, and even lynching or cultural genocide. Religious intolerance erases anti-Blackness, racism, and the specific anti-African dimension of these attacks.

In terms of urban-geographic distribution of the terreiros and their relationships to community needs and rivals, the great majority of terreiros are located in the dense urban territory of the city, including its more centrally located favelas as well as urban peripheries. There tend to be fewer terreiros in rural areas, where they often articulate with quilombos. There is a certain competition between terreiros and Neo-Pentecostals, with the latter making new alliances with narcotic organizations or/and militia units to intensify their fight against the terreiros' way of life.

We reject the notion that "saintly people do not do politics" (Segato 1991; Prandi 1991), since this inaccurately suggests that Afro-Brazilian Orixás are Catholic saints absorbed through syncretism and that their followers are apolitical. The idea that the terreiros[3] do not make politics ignores the countless activities (organizational, social, public, etc.) organized around religious groups. Afro-religious people have developed methods for securing their rights without dissociating their politics from religion.

Understanding the political experiences of Black Brazilians as it relates to the terreiro is not a novel idea (Vogel, Mello, and Barros 1992). Previous accounts point to three distinct ways in which Black people mobilize: (1) in quilombos, (2) in the face of slavery's pain and suffering, and (3) in the terreiros (Vogel, Mello, and Barros 1992). We consider the terreiro as territory constituted from the familias-de-santo (V. Lima 2003)—established in the diaspora and which may or may not occur through consanguineous ties. These spaces involve solidarities and intragroup disputes related to rituals and liturgies, perpetuated and classified as traditional (Candau 2019; Asad 2017). The reproduction of these memorial practices provides the distinctions between the nations, families, and lineages that constitute the terreiros and guide Afro-religious ways of life.[4]

Terreiro politics confront the idea that African-based religions exclusively follow a Yoruba/Nagô model, founded in the mid-nineteenth century in Salvador (Bahia). Homogeneity and ritual purity, crystallized in ethnographic research since Nina Rodrigues, reified Bahian terreiros and Candomblé as a model for African peoples (and their descendants). For Afro-religious people, it is strategic to combat the assumption that there is a unique form of doing, located in only one region, established by exclusive and pure relations. The purpose of this strategy is to highlight the complexity and diversity of Black practices. Observers must value the multiplicity of liturgical, ritualistic, scientific, memorial, botanical, medicinal, and culinary frameworks maintained in the terreiros.

Forms of Afro-religious activism grow out of alliances between the familias-de-santo. For example, take the case of young Kaylane, who—on June 14, 2015—was stoned in the street for wearing clothing characteristic of her religion. The attackers raised the Bible and called everyone a devil, claiming that the girl and everyone who was with her would go to hell. This aggression unleashed an alliance between those belonging to different saint-families, which were linked to the Yoruba, Jeje, and Congo-Angola. The events resulted in a mobilization in the northern part of Rio. To offer another example, during resistance to the aggression against Yalorixa Carmem de Oxum in the Baixada Fluminense, evangelical traffickers (narco-factions who are also Pentecostal missionary militias) set out to destroy the shrines, icons, and community spaces of the terreiros. Traffickers even filmed their own actions as they destroyed the sacred spaces and then distributed the video on social media. Attackers uttered phrases that reverberated: "Look here, my friends. The chief devil is right there. Break everything and blow out the candle. The blood of Jesus has the power. All evil has to be undone in Jesus' name. You are the head devil, who serves dogs" (Bom Dia Rio 2017). The video gained national visibility and was aired by TV stations in prime time. These attacks take place daily in the lives of Afro-religious people.

In response to these actions—and in order to pressure the state to respond—Babalorixa Adailton Moreira (Ilé Asé Omin Oju Aro), a respected female terreiro leader, together with Yalorixa Meninazinha (Ilé Omolu Oxun), another prominent woman leader, organized Luto Na Luta (Struggle while mourning). This movement's first activity, at the Omiojuaro headquarters, included more than one hundred people as well as government representatives who identify with religious groups (e.g., deputies, federal and state prosecutors, delegates, councilors) and members of Black and women's social movements (Miranda and Vieira Silva 2018). In this way, it is no longer the religious who go to the representative bodies to demand rights. It is the terreiro that summons the authorities through mobilization, set in motion by its own terms and needs. At that time, differences in linguistic, liturgical, and memorial practices (i.e., those fluid boundaries that differentiate saint families) momentarily became less salient and gave way to collective identity resisting racism. Shared meanings of pain and suffering help foster this unity, but strategies to understand the violence suffered are distinct to each tradition. During this moment, Babalorixa Adailton said, "We are here today because our people are being persecuted. Therefore, we are here to think of ways to change all this. More than that, [we are here] to receive Yalorixa Carmem de Oxum, who was a victim of these racist monsters, who preached violence, transphobia, homophobia, and sexism. . . . Her pain is our pain. Part of us was also destroyed" (Miranda and Vieira Silva 2018, i–ii). These alliances are distinct from the operational logics of dominant Brazilian political parties and social movements. The intention here is to encompass the performance of those Afro-religious political struggles and, simultaneously, their ethnic-racial-religious diversity (Das and Poole 2008).

But the concept of Afro-religious does not belong to any one specific Afro-religion. Rather, it represents actors that emerge in the public sphere who are affected by, among other factors, religious practices and traditions. This activism politicizes the terreiros through education, public security, health, culture, art, and law. This concept considers the sociohistorical formation of Afro-Brazilian religions equally important. To understand Afro-religious agency, one may revisit identities built into Candomblé terreiros. Traditions that emerge in such spaces do, of course, intersect with other Black and LGBTQI+ movements. Mobilization sustains itself through intimate alliances established between the terreiros, built between the familias-de-santo, from a complex network of affinities, solidarities, and disputes guided by their distinct logic (V. Lima 2003).

Fabricated Holy War: Thirty Years of Struggle for the Recognition of Rights

During the 1980s in Rio, the diverse tendencies within the Afro-religious community began to join forces against the first surge of Pentecostal-supremacist missionary activities and rapid expansion (R. R. Almeida 2019). Terreiros came together to demand recognition of guaranteed civil and social rights for the terreiros populations. Afro-religious people moved into the public eye in order to resist the ideological basis of Pentecostalism, which in its spiritual battles "tries not to see Afro-Brazilian religions as folklore, popular belief, ignorance or imagination, but recognizing that their deities 'exist,' even though they are 'actually' demonic spirits that deceive and threaten the Brazilian people" (Silva 2007, 210).[5]

In 1989, Candomblé priests and priestesses delivered a document titled "The Fabricated Holy War" to the Federal Public Ministry.[6] Mãe Beata de Iemanjá, Mother Meninazinha de Oxum, and Father Adailton Moreira brought attention to the occupations and depredations of the terreiros and the growing physical violence.[7] Since then, a series of denunciations and reports have been produced by nonreligious activists. These texts contained news of rights violations (threats, intimidation, physical assaults, murders, fires, and bomb attacks) in the terreiros and were presented to Brazilian authorities at municipal, state, and federal levels. At that time, according to these reports, there was already an understanding, on the part of Afro-religious people, that the persecution of the terreiros was a political act with a religious veneer.

Rio de Janeiro, in the late 1970s, hosted the rise of Christian supremacist movements. This political tradition was most notably developed and crystallized by the Igreja Universal do Reino de Deus, which uses the theology of spiritual battle as a justification for pursuing and demonizing ethnic-racial differences. It erects racism and related forms of discrimination as a liturgical model. The suggestion that the holy war mentioned above was fabricated reveals a different understanding of the events within the terreiros in relation to the persecution suffered by its populations. But the Universal Church of the Kingdom of God and, later, several other Evangelical-Pentecostal denominations were able to manage the discourse (Maggie 1992). This persecution, in addition to proselytism, was based on territorial disputes for control of the favelas and Rio's peripheries (though the battle later expanded to prisons).

Meanwhile, in the last ten years, Evangelical-Pentecostal movements have attempted to mobilize to seize political, economic, and social power. They did so by gravitating toward North American evangelical fundamentalism (R. R. Almeida 2017), expressed not only by the number of grandiose newly built churches but also due to the increase in evangelical blocs in legislatures in Brazil and the presence of faith-based businesses in the financial and communication markets. Activists of the terreiros have insisted that the rise to power by the Evangelicals—led by the Universal Church of the Kingdom of God and adhered to by most Christian segments—was not due to religious disputes of a strictly proselytizing character. Rather, it was based on material, economic, and political domination. Evangelical seizures of power, denounced since 1989, were consolidated during the 2018 elections.

About the Guarantee of Rights

In 2010, the Fluminense Nucleus of Studies and Research (NUFEP) produced a report compiled from lawsuits filed by victims of Afro-religious discrimination in Rio de Janeiro (Miranda, Mota, and Pinto 2010).[8] In all, the researchers found thirty-four lawsuits that were pending at the Special Criminal Courts (JECRIMs) in the metropolitan region of Rio de Janeiro, of which only one had a known outcome.[9] The lack of accountability in the cases continues despite Law 7716/89, which criminalizes racism and religious discrimination. According to activists, "anti-black racism and the persecution of the terreiros is an ingrained and naturalized aspect in Brazilian society" (R. R. Almeida 2015). For the Afro-religious, the structural and institutionalized racism that orders relations in Brazil means the lawsuits that intend to guarantee the victims' rights are not accepted among legal experts and practitioners.

Although some Afro-religious people urge the judiciary to rule on such issues, a lack of confidence that the state apparatus will manage these conflicts is not uncommon (Miranda 2011, 2018, 2019; Miranda, Correa, and Pinto 2011; Pinto 2011; R. R. Almeida 2017; L. Lima, Berbet, and Vieira Silva 2019). Afro-religious people claim that in many cases, the judge's understanding changes the criminal classification to crimes with less offensive potential than those of Law 7716/89. In the majority of such cases—of ethnic, racial, and religious discrimination—legal practitioners tend to disregard the motives of the perpetrators (de Oliveira 2008).

Ethnographies also point out that, in the absence of state enforcement of civil rights, Afro-religious people calculate risks before pursuing legal action. Class biases also tend to affect the likelihood of success in legal accountability. Afro-religious activists advise, guide, and monitor such legal claims. If a case will not be legally durable, conflicts are managed informally (e.g., in schools, hospitals, or public institutions) through dialogue with the perpetrators and victims.[10]

Religious Intolerance, Religious Racism

If, until recently, mobilization of activists was shaped by the fight against religious intolerance, disputes between Pentecostals and Afro-religious movements produced the phrase *religious racism* among the latter and within Black social movements (R. R. Almeida 2015).[11] This change is not only semantic (Miranda 2018), since religious racism intends to show that violence against terreiros and their adherents conforms to a model different from other forms of racism (Nogueira [1954] 2006). But religious intolerance is insufficient due to ethnic and racial factors that remain irreducible and undeniable (Flor do Nascimento 2017). Alternatively, religious racism would help explain the exceptional dynamics of racism projected onto African and Indigenous peoples within the terreiros.

It is in this context that activists refuse to identify cases of ethnic-racial-religious discrimination beyond skin color. Religious racism occurs amid Pentecostals' proximity to Black movements, but it simultaneously dismisses the demands for guaranteed rights of Afro-religious people. Such groups argue that the terreiros have been "whitened" (R. R. Almeida 2015). But out of these disputes, one must not ignore the history of Blackness of the terreiros and their ways of life (Munanga 2004). Displacement has brought the struggles of the Afro-religious closer to African American frameworks, which explicitly fight anti-Blackness. As disputes between Pentecostals and Afro-religious movements continue, race relations simultaneously transform within the terreiros—calling for a dynamic approach to monitoring discrimination and racism in conflict.

NOTES

1 On agents: "Individuals/people/subjects are always inserted in webs of relationships, affection or solidarity, power or rivalry, or, often, in some mixture of the two. Whatever 'agency' they seem to 'have' as individuals, it is actually something that is always interactively negotiated. In this sense, they are never free agents, not only in the sense that they are not free to formulate and achieve their own goals in a social vacuum, but also in the sense that they are not able to completely control these relationships for their own ends. As social beings—a true and inescapable fact—they can only act within the many webs of relationships that make up their social worlds" (Ortner 2007, 74).

2 Terreiro politics, as a concept, has been built in dialogue with the research carried out by Ana Paula Mendes de Miranda in Rio de Janeiro, Sergipe, and Alagoas.

3 Terreiro is a generic designation for all places where the rituals of Afro-Brazilian religions take place (Sodré 2002). This is also a social space and dates back to a community that is linked to those on the African continent.

4 There is a complex network of relationships between the terreiros, based on ethnic differences (which can be roughly classified as Jeje, Nagô/Yoruba, and Congo-Angola), founding myths (which gave rise to families), and the internal divisions of these families into lineages.

5 Pentecostalism refers to evangelical churches that practice "prosperity theology" and "spiritual battle" (Campos 2005). Ricardo Mariano (2004) uses the term *neo-Pentecostalism* for the phenomenon.

6 Elaborated by the Ipelcy Institute, which gathered reports on cases of violation of property rights and religious conscience of the supporters (R. R. Almeida 2019).

7 Mãe Beata de Iemanjá was a women's rights, LGBTQI+, and Afro-religious activist who became a protagonist in the fight against racism. She passed away at the age of

eighty-seven in 2018. Mother Meninazinha de Oxum is coordinator of the National Network of Terreiros and Health (Renafro) and leader of Ilé Omolu Oxum in São João de Meriti (RJ). Father Adailton Moreira is the current leader of Ilé Axé Omiojuaro, in Nova Iguaçu, Rio de Janeiro.

8 NUFEP is part of the Federal Fluminense University.

9 That case began in 2009, when Cirene Dark (umbandista) was tied up, tortured, and set on fire in her home by a domestic worker, Nádia Pereira, who was an evangelical pastor. The lawsuit condemned the perpetrator of the crime for religious intolerance after the victim had died (GospelMais 2009).

10 The informal approach remains a tradition of Afro-religious people systematically ignored by the state. There are of course limitations to this approach. The Afro-religious community cannot resolve conflicts informally when aggression is committed by members of armed groups (drug traffickers and militia members), who may expel grieving parties from the terreiros or intimidate residents (R. R. Almeida 2019). It is worth remembering, here, the aforementioned case that involved evangelical traffickers ordering the destruction of the terreiro (Torres 2017).

11 "It points to experiences of victimization due to prejudice and discrimination due to its religious and ethnic affiliations, especially in view of the growth in the number of followers of neo-Pentecostal religions in the country" (Miranda 2011, 1).

REFERENCES

Almeida, Ronaldo. 2006. "A circulação pentecostal: Circulação e flexibilidade." In *As religiões no Brasil: Continuidades e rupturas*, edited by Faustino Teixeira and Renata Menezes, 111–22. Petrópolis: Vozes.

Almeida, Ronaldo. 2008. "Os Pentecostais serão Maioria no Brasil?" *Revista de estudos da religião* 8: 48–58.

Almeida, Ronaldo. 2017. "A onda quebrada—evangélicos econservadorismo." *Cadernos pagu* 50: 1–27.

Almeida, Rosiane Rodrigues de. 2014. "Quem foi que falou em igualdade?" Master's thesis, Universidade Federal Fluminense.

Almeida, Rosiane Rodrigues de. 2015. *Quem foi que falou em igualdade?* Rio de Janeiro: Autografia.

Almeida, Rosiane Rodrigues de. 2019. "A luta por um modo de vida: As narrativas e estratégias dos membros do Fórum Nacional de Segurança Alimentar e Nutricional dos Povos Tradicionais de Matriz Africana (FONSANPOTMA)." PhD diss., Universidade Federal Fluminense.

Asad, Talal. 2017. "Pensando sobre tradição, religião e política no Egito contemporâneo." *Política e Sociedade* 16, no. 36: 263–84.

Bom Dia Rio. 2017. "Vídeo registra traficante obrigando mãe de santo a quebrar imagens em um terreiro da Baixada Fluminense." *O Globo*, September 15. https://g1.globo.com /rio-de-janeiro/noticia/video-registra-traficante-obrigando-mae-de-santo-a-quebrar -imagens-em-um-terreiro-da-baixada-fluminense.ghtml.

Campos, Leonildo S. 2005. "As origens norte-americanas do pentecostalismo brasileiro: observações sobre uma relação ainda pouco avaliada." *Revista USP* 67 (November): 100–115.

Candau, Joel. 2019. *Memória e identidade*. São Paulo: Contexto.

Das, Veena, and Deborah Poole. 2008. "El estado y susmárgenes: Etnografías comparadas." *Cuadernos de Antropología Social*, no. 27: 19–52.

de Oliveira, Luís Roberto Cardoso. 2008. "Exist eviolência sem agressão moral?" *Revista brasileira de ciências sociais* 23, no. 67: 135–46.

Flor do Nascimento, Wanderson. 2017. "O fenômeno do racismo religioso: Desafios para os povos tradicionais de matrizes africanas." *Revista Eixo* 6, no. 2: 51–56.

GospelMais Noticias. 2009. "Pastora e Missionária da Assembléia de Deus é presa após agredir umbandista." May 9. https://noticias.gospelmais.com.br/pastora-e-missionaria -da-assembleia-de-deus-e-presa-apos-agredir-umbandista.html.

Lima, Lana Laga da Gama, Bernardo Molina Berbet, and Leonardo Vieira Silva. 2019. "Administração institucional de conflitos envolvendo discriminação étnica, racial e religiosa em Campos dos Goytacazes." In *As crençasna igualdade*, edited by Ana Paula Mendes de Miranda, Fabio Reis Mota, and Lenin Pires. Rio de Janeiro: Autografia.

Lima, Vivaldo da Costa. 2003. *A família de santo nos candomblés jejes-nagôs da Bahia: Um estudo de relações intragrupais*. São Paulo: Corrupio.

Maggie, Yvone. 1992. *Medo de feitiço: Relações entre magia e poder no Brasil*. Rio de Janeiro: Arquivo Nacional.

Mariano, Ricardo. 2004. "Expansão pentecostal no Brasil: O caso da Igreja Universal." *Estudos avançado* 18, no. 52: 121–38.

Miranda, Ana Paula Mendes de. 2010. "Entre o público e o privado: Considerações sobre a (in) criminação da intolerância religiosa no Rio de Janeiro." *Anuário antropológico* 35, no. 2: 125–52.

Miranda, Ana Paula Mendes de. 2011. "Combate à intolerância ou defesa da liberdade religiosa: Paradigmas em conflito na construção de uma política pública de enfrentamento ao crime de discriminação étnico-racial-religiosa." Paper presented at 33° Encontro Anual da ANPOCS, Caxambu, Minas Gerais, October 24–28. Accessed March 27, 2021. https://www.anpocs.com/index.php/papers-33-encontro/gt-28/gt05-26 /1805-anamiranda-combate/file.

Miranda, Ana Paula Mendes de. 2018. "Intolerância religiosa e discriminação racial: Duas faces de um mesmo problema público?" In *A antropologia e a esfera pública no Brasil: Perspectivas e prospectivas sobre a Associação Brasileira de Antropologia*, edited by Antonio Carlos de Souza Lima et al. Rio de Janeiro: E-papers.

Miranda, Ana Paula Mendes de. 2019. "A 'política dos terreiros' contra o racismo religioso e as políticas 'cristofascistas.'" *Vibrant* 17: 17–54.

Miranda, Ana Paula Mendes de, and Roberta Machado Boniolo. 2017. "Empúblico, é preciso se unir: Conflitos, demandas e estratégias políticas entre religiosos de matriz afro-brasileira nacidade do Rio de Janeiro." *Religião e sociedade* 37, no. 2: 86–118.

Miranda, Ana Paula M. de, Roberta M. Correa, and Vinicius Cruz Pinto. 2011. "Conciliação no papel: O tratamento dado aos casos de intolerância religiosa em Juizados Especiais Criminais no Rio de Janeiro." *Confluências* 18, no. 2: 21–43.

Miranda, Ana Paula M. de, Roberta de Mello Correa, and Rosiane Rodrigues de Almeida. 2019. "O 'renascimento' da intolerância religiosa e as formas de administração institucional de conflitos no Brasil." In *Liberdade religiosa e direitos humanos*, edited by Ricardo Perlingeiro, 111–46. Niterói: Nupej/TRF2.

Miranda, Ana Paula Mendes de, Fabio Reis Mota, and Paulo Gabriel Hilu Pinto. 2010. *Relatório sobre a Comissão de Combate à Intolerância Religiosa: Balanço de dois anos de atividade*. Niterói: NUFEP.

Miranda, Ana Paula Mendes de, and Leonardo Vieira Silva. 2018. "O atabaque está chamando! Uma análise das estratégias de mobilização dos adeptos das religiões afrobrasileiras no enfrentamento da intolerância religiosa no município de Duque de Caxias." *PIBIC/UFF Research Report*: 1–11.

Munanga, Kabenguele. 2004. "Uma abordagem conceitual das noções de raça, racismo, identidade e etnia." In *Programa de educação sobre o negro na sociedade Brasileira*. Niterói: EDUFF.

Nogueira, Oracy. (1954) 2006. "Preconceito racial de marca e preconceito racial de origem: Sugestão de um quadro de referência para a interpretação do material sobre relações raciais no Brasil." *Tempo social* 19, no. 1: 287–308.

Ortner, Sherry B. 2007. "Poder e projetos: Reflexões sobre a agência." In *Conferências e diálogos: Saberes e práticas antropológicas, 25ª Reunião Brasileira de Antropologia*, edited by Miriam Pillar Grossi, Cornelia Eckert, and Peter Henry Fry, 17–80. Blumenau: Nova Letra.

Pinto, Vinícius Cruz. 2011. *Picuinha de vizinho u problema cultural? Uma análise dos sentidos de justiça referente aos casos de "intolerância religiosa."* Monografia em ciências sociais. Rio de Janeiro: Universidade Federal Fluminense.

Prandi, Reginaldo. 1991. "A religião e a multiplicação do eu: Transe, papéis e poder no candomblé." *Revista USP* 1, no. 9: 133–44.

Rufino, Luiz, and Marina Santos de Miranda. 2019. "Racismo religioso: Política, terrorismo e trauma colonial: Outras leituras sobre o problema." *Problemata* 10, no. 2: 229–42.

Sá, Leonardo. 2015. "As questões do poder na perspectiva da antropologia política." *Áltera revista de antropologia* 1, no. 1: 82–111.

Segato, Rita Laura. 1991. "Uma vocação de minoria: A expansão dos cultos afro brasileiros na Argentina como processo de re-etnicização." *Dados* 34: 240–78.

Silva, Vagner Gonçalves da. 2007. "Neopentecostalismo e religiões afro-brasileiras: Significados do ataque aos símbolos da herança religiosa africana no Brasil contemporâneo." *Mana* 13, no. 1: 207–36.

Sodré, Muniz. 2002. *O terreiro e a cidade: A forma social negro-brasileira*. Rio de Janeiro: Imago Ed.; Salvador, BA: Fundação Cultural do Estado da Bahia.

Torres, Ana Carolina. 2017. "Polícia do Rio investiga vídeo em que tráfico ordena depredação de centro espírita com porrete: 'Diálogo.'" *Globo*, September 13. https://extra .globo.com/casos-de-policia/policia-do-rio-investiga-video-em-que-trafico-ordena -depredacao-de-centro-espirita-com-porrete-dialogo-21815587.html.

Vieira Silva, Leonardo. 2020. "Nem impuro, nem misturado: A construção do Nagô afrosergipano da Sociedade de Culto Afro Brasileiro Filhos de Obá (SCAFO) e suas estratégias político-religiosas." Master's thesis, Universidade Federal Fluminense.

Vogel, Arno, Marco Antônio da Silva Mello, and José Flávio da Silva de Barros. 1992. "Enigma e escândalo: A sociedade hierárquica e o sincretismo na romaria afrobasileira." *Série ciências sociais* 4: 190–213.

21

Kaleidoscopic Arabness / Arabitude Caleidoscópica

Performative Identities and Diasporic Arenas of
Syrian-Lebanese Communities

PAULO G. PINTO

The analysis of Arab identities in Rio de Janeiro shows how Arab/Syrian-Lebanese ethnicities have been negotiated, transmitted, and reinvented in Brazilian society. Discrete ethnic and national codifications of linguistic and cultural heritage of Arabic-speaking immigrants emerged between 1890 and 1930. Meanwhile, between 1915 and 1960, various ethnic and religious urban social institutions were created to transmit these codifications to Brazilian-born generations. Despite the creation of a community with numerous ethnic and national identities—of Arabic-speaking immigrants and their descendants—there was no consensus about their identity. This created what I call kaleidoscopic identities, which present ever-moving patterns of identity that remain highly contextual. The data analyzed here was collected during ethnographic fieldwork with the Arab/Syrian-Lebanese community and supplemented with archival research conducted within institutions in Rio de Janeiro and São Paulo.

Brazil was one of the main destinations for Arabic-speaking immigrants who left the Middle East for the Americas in the late nineteenth and early twentieth centuries. Between 1871 and 2001, the country received a total of 162,355 immigrants from the Middle East, with the bulk of immigration falling between 1884 and 1939, when 107,135 entered the country (Pinto 2010, 134; Lesser 2001, 97). While most immigrants went to São Paulo, Rio de Janeiro received the second largest contingent. The implementation of a quota system in 1934 effectively ended mass immigration and started a long process of cultural assimilation, as well as the creation and negotiation of ethnic identities within the Brazilian framework.[1]

The low numbers of recent immigrants from the Middle East—despite a global increase during the 2010s[2]—meant that the mechanisms for negotiating identities were central to building a diasporic community. The actual population of Middle Eastern immigrants and their descendants in Brazil is subject to speculation (est. 1–12 million). While the lower figures are obviously closer to the demographic reality, these estimates are sometimes reflective of strategies for visibility in Brazilian society (Karam 2007, 10–13).[3]

The idea that Arabic-speaking immigrants and their descendants form well-integrated communities with boundaries defined by shared identities is constantly challenged.[4] Two major identification systems—Arab and Syrian-Lebanese—while partially overlapping, point to different definitions of Arabness. Both spheres are defined by the fact that their cultural references are expressed in Arabic. But Arab identity supposes a necessary connection between language and culture, proposing an ethnic sphere of belonging. Syrian-Lebanese identity, on the other hand, stresses diasporic attachment to a political and territorial entity where Arabic is simply the dominant linguistic context for cultural traditions that are distinct from those of other Arabic-speaking territories.

Within these broader spheres of belonging, there are smaller ones that are defined by national identities—notably, Lebanese, Syrian, or Palestinian. While they may intersect both major spheres, they do not fully overlap with them. Palestinians often do not fit into the Syrian-Lebanese identity. At the extreme end of the spectrum of possibilities, the proponents of Lebanese national distinctiveness reject Arab and, sometimes, Syrian-Lebanese identities, usually mobilizing mythical references to the Phoenicians. These national identities are themselves crossed by religious affiliations, social class, and generational differences. Instead of a shared overarching identity or a combination of related identities, we have a dynamic mosaic of ever-changing combinations that are not always seen as compatible. In order to make sense of this, I deploy the notion of kaleidoscopic Arabness, which constitutes a field of discursive and performative identity-forming practices based on the combination, articulation, contrast, or opposition of discrete diasporic imaginaries.[5]

This configuration of Arabness is stronger in the large urban centers of Brazil, where ethnic identities were shaped throughout the twentieth century by both local and transnational debates on nationalism in the Middle East (Karam 2007; Lesser 2001; Pinto 2010). In places where there is a strong presence of recent immigrants who arrived after the 1970s (e.g., Foz do Iguaçu), there are other configurations (Macagno, Montenegro, and Béliveau 2011). Rio de Janeiro, the focus of this analysis, presents stronger kaleidoscopic dynamics of Arab identities. This is due to the fact that the city received the second largest influx of Arabic-speaking immigrants in the country during the first half of the twentieth century, becoming one of the intellectual, demographic, and institutional centers for the production and negotiation of ethnic identities and imaginaries in Brazil. This diaspora has not experienced a significant influx of immigrants from the Middle East since the 1970s.[6] Also, the Arabic-speaking community in Rio de Janeiro was established when Rio was Brazil's national capital and diplomatic and cultural metropole until 1960. Thus, the Arabic-speaking community engaged multiple rich, contradictory flows of transnational political projects coming from the Middle East. These flows intersected the global city of Rio and generated more multiangled, fragmented, and context-specific performances of its various identities than in many other communities across Brazil. This is clear in the creation of institutions that embodied such transnationally articulated richness and multiangled contradictions as the Lebanese League (Liga Libanesa), one of the direct responses to the 1958 civil war in Lebanon and its corresponding political tensions.

While the multiangled perspective inscribed in the notion of kaleidoscopic Arabness was built upon the analysis of ethnographic data from Rio de Janeiro, it also can be used to understand ethnic dynamics in other diasporic Arabic-speaking communities in Brazil and other countries, with the ethnographic analysis showing how and in which degree it applies. The idea of kaleidoscopic identities can also be used to understand the cultural dynamics of identity formation in other diasporic communities.

Community Fragments, Institutions, and the Construction of Diasporic Identities

When Arabic-speaking immigrants from the Middle East started to arrive in significant numbers in Brazil in the last decade of the nineteenth century and the first decades of the twentieth century, they met a society that already had images of them. Some of these representations derived from European orientalism, while others were developed thereafter by Brazilian intellectuals in response to the growing presence of Middle Eastern immigrants. Still, representations were fostered by the immigrants themselves in order to create a shared history distinct from the Ottoman past, or to negotiate their cultural differences within the country (Pinto 2016).

The iconic symbol of Brazilian orientalism, the Turk (turco), was used to designate Middle Eastern immigrants irrespective of their ethnic, religious, or national origins. While it was originally an administrative category used to classify immigrants arriving with Ottoman passports (Knowlton 1960, 37), the turco quickly became an ethnic stereotype invested with negative moral and cultural meanings. Ethnic and religious institutions emerged and countered these stereotypical representations. Between the 1890s and the 1950s, the list of ethnic and religious institutions created by Arabic-speaking immigrants in Rio became quite long, with the earliest ones promoting a shared Syrian identity. The Syrian Union Society (Sociedade União Síria) and the Syrian Society (Sociedade Síria) were created in 1897; the Society of Young Syrians (Sociedade dos Jovens Sírios) in 1902; the Syrian Youth Society (Sociedade da Mocidade Síria) and the Syrian Masonic Lodge (Loja Maçônica Síria) in 1904; the Syrian Brazilian Club (Clube Sírio Brasileiro) in 1916; and the Syrian Athletic Club (Clube Atlético Sírio) in 1921 (Safady 1972, 122–26).

These early attempts at a shared territorial and historical identity were crossed by other diasporic identities affected by nationalist projects in the Middle East. In 1912, the Arab Charitable Society (Sociedade Beneficente Árabe) was founded in order to link Arab nationalism to a Syrian identity. However, Lebanese particularism was fostered by institutions such as the Cedar of Lebanon Society (Sociedade Cedro do Líbano), created in 1912, and the Phoenician Club (Clube Fenício) of 1915 (Safady 1966, 196). Syrian nationalism was also represented by a branch of the Syrian Independence Party (Hizb al-Istiqlal al-Surya), created in Rio in 1921, and the Syrian Federation (Federação Síria) of 1923 (Safady 1972, 125). In 1935, the Lebanese Brazilian Club (Clube Líbano-Brasileiro) was founded, and one year later the Syrian-Lebanese Club (Clube Sírio-Libanês) emerged. Defenders of Lebanese nationalism founded the Mount Lebanon Club (Clube Monte Líbano) to counter this in 1946.

Events in the Middle East also led to the creation of diasporic institutions connected to nationalist projects. Thus, the Nakba led to the creation of the Palestinian Charitable Society (Sociedade Beneficente Palestina) in 1949 (Pinto 2010, 102).[7] The Lebanese League (Liga Libanesa) was created in May 1958, aiming to affirm Lebanese national identity against the rise of Nasserism and pressure for Lebanon to join the United Arab Republic.[8] Religious institutions also had an important role in the circulation and codification of ethnic and national identities, with Arab nationalism being stronger among Muslims and Orthodox Christians and Lebanese nationalism having greater support among Maronite Christians. In 1897, members from the Antiochene Orthodox Church founded the Saint Nicholas Orthodox Society (Sociedade Ortodoxa São Nicolau), which was officially registered in a notary in 1900 and built the Saint Nicholas Orthodox Church in 1918. The Maronite Brotherhood (Irmandade Maronita) was created in 1900 (Barreto [1904] 1951, 75), followed by the Maronite Mission (Missão Maronita) in Rio in 1931 and the Church of Our Lady of Lebanon in 1960. The Greek-Catholic Melchite Council (Conselho Grego Católico Melquita) was founded in 1928, and the Saint Basile Church was consecrated in 1941. The city also saw the emergence of two Muslim institutions—the 'Alawi Charitable Society (Sociedade Beneficente Alauíta) in 1931, and the (Sunni) Muslim Charitable Society of Rio de Janeiro (Sociedade Beneficente Muçulmana do Rio de Janeiro) in 1951 (Pinto 2010, 106–21).

The Arabic press was established as each nationalist project published its own newspaper, promoting an intense political debate that shaped the construction of diasporic identities in Rio de Janeiro. In total, fifty-five Arabic newspapers and magazines were published in Rio de Janeiro between 1896 and 1950. The first newspaper, Al-Raqib (The observer), circulated between 1896 and 1898 and faced Ottoman censorship for its liberal orientation. The influence of competing empires and nationalist imaginaries continued to circulate. Thus, Al-Hamra' (The red one, 1913) supported a French protectorate, while Syrian nationalism was expressed in Suria al-Jadida (New Syria, 1918). Arab nationalism was fostered by Al-Tasahul (Tolerance, 1919). Lebanese nationalism was promoted by Al-Arzat (The cedars), which was published by the Cedar of Lebanon Society and renamed Arzat Lubnan (Cedars of Lebanon) in 1922 (Safady 1972, 282–91).

The plurality of identities represented by these institutions and publications fostered contestation, with constant shifts in the meaning or connections between ethnic and national boundaries. In this context, the construction of "common denominators" (Eriksen 1998) that could create a shared sense of community beyond national or religious differences was marked by tensions and contradictions. While some institutions and publications stressed particularisms and differences, others tried to foster shared identities through compromise. The Syrian-Lebanese identity, for example, was adopted during the 1910s in order to accommodate the rejection of Arab identity by certain Maronite Lebanese nationalists. These efforts remained partial, since every compromise alienated part of the community, as was seen in the Palestinians' reservations toward Syrian-Lebanese identity.

After four decades of constructing and maintaining diasporic identities, these institutions gradually lost importance, and the transmission of identities was pushed into the private sphere. The interdiction of foreign-language publications in Brazil between 1941 and 1945 led to the irreversible decline of the Arabic press, while the increasing intolerance toward public expressions of ethnicity and simultaneous cultural and linguistic assimilation of new generations led to sharp declines in ethnic institutions, most of which disappeared after the 1950s.[9]

Ethnic Performances, Cultural Intimacy, and the
Communication of Arabness

With the decline of a formal, organizationally driven ethnic public sphere in Rio de Janeiro, the main arena for the transmission of Arab identities became the family. Declining public expressions of ethnicity were accompanied by cultural traditions embedded in the affective familial relationships and practices of domestic conviviality (Pinto 2018). Often certain family members (parents, grandparents, uncles, and aunts) were described as iconic figures who embodied Arabness, which was expressed in stories about the homeland or the process of immigration. A forty-nine-year-old university professor of Lebanese descent summarized this experience: "My aunts were very dear to me, as was my grandmother. . . . They were my idols. . . . My grandmother was a woman of wise words, very affectionate, very intelligent, a woman of action. To understand that all this was connected to the Arab community, and of course it was, was something very interesting and seductive. My connection to this identity is an affective one" (interview by author, Rio de Janeiro, 2009).

A key element in this process was Middle Eastern culinary traditions, kept by the families and carried on by descendants, which was more common than the inheritance of the Arabic language itself. As discrimination against Arabic-speaking immigrants was very much centered on the language, many families consciously avoided teaching it to new generations (Pinto 2010, 85). A forty-nine-year-old writer of Lebanese and Palestinian descent described how food was a concrete symbol through which ideas of Arabness were passed on during his childhood: "My mother, who is an excellent cook, learned it from my grandmother. . . . Culinary lineages . . . that's how we got the identity" (Pinto 2018, 72).

Even rituals and objects connected to Middle Eastern religious traditions were usually lived through family conviviality, becoming lieux de mémoire (spaces of memory).[10] The above-mentioned university professor remembered the celebration of Orthodox Easter in her family as an arena of expression and experience of Arabness: "We had a separate Easter [from Catholic Easter] with a long Mass [in the Orthodox church] which lasted all night long. Then . . . we had a huge breakfast. There were colored eggs, and the kids would play, competing to see which egg would break all the others."

The transformations of family dynamics invited changes and adaptations in the way these traditions were lived. After some decades, Easter breakfast transformed into an Easter lunch in order to accommodate the younger generations, who preferred to go to the beach during the holiday.

The experience of this cultural intimacy contributed to ways of being in the world or, in other words, configurations of the self (Csordas 1990).[11] These configurations were expressed through affective idioms, codified into objects that worked as concrete symbols or mnemonic devices that evoked affective experiences. Thus, a thirty-seven-year-old physician kept the copper pans that his great-grandmother had brought from Syria as decorative pieces in his home; a fifty-year-old university professor kept photographs of her grandmother; and another university professor kept the narghile (water pipe) of her grandfather.

Texts written in Arabic have an important role in this process. Nevertheless, their meaning often is not in the linguistic message they convey, as most descendants cannot read Arabic, but rather in their visual connection to a cultural and linguistic universe that gives authenticity and concreteness to their owner's particular construction of Arabness. Thus, a forty-eight-year-old lawyer of Lebanese descent kept his Muslim grandfather's Quran as part of his "family patrimony." Similarly, some families kept Bibles in Arabic, Turkish, or Armenian as part of their heritage, although they had no religious use anymore. A university professor kept the correspondence that her grandparents exchanged during the period when one was in Lebanon and the other in Brazil. And a writer remembered the library of his grandfather as something important in his literary trajectory, although he could not read Arabic at that time. Many families kept all kinds of documents, such as property titles, wills, or certificates, as concrete symbols of their connection to the Middle East through their ancestors, despite ignoring the documents' actual content.

Some texts, mainly books, were also constantly reassigned meaning in order to connect the biography of the individual with the cultural tradition transmitted in the family. Sometimes the larger context of the tradition was lost, and orientalist imaginaries were mobilized in order to give meaning to concrete symbols that had become opaque to those who kept them as identity references. One clear example of this was an eighty-year-old fortune teller in a suburb of Rio, whose father probably had been a Druze shaykh from Lebanon. She had a

Druze religious book, which she described as a text full of "secret knowledge" from the "Orient." During consultations, she used the book as an oracle, which she opened to "read" the future in a trance-like murmur and afterward "translated" it to her clients.[12]

These configurations of the self that are expressed through concrete symbols of Arabness serve as a basis for cognitive, affective, and practical dispositions or habitus (Bourdieu [1972] 2000, 256–85) that index ethnic differences when mobilized in the larger society. Traditionally, this habitus was expressed through participation in community life organized by ethnic and religious institutions or by maintenance of Middle Eastern cultural traditions. However, the decline of these institutions allowed for new forms of expression to emerge amid a more open society, during the redemocratization of Brazil in the 1980s.

New ethnic idioms appeared as many people started to reinvent cultural content for their identities and/or diasporic ties to imagined homelands in the Middle East. This process enhanced the kaleidoscopic character of Arabness and Middle Easternness in Rio de Janeiro, for while the ethnic and religious institutions still shaped its public expressions, they had lost part of their disciplinary and normative power. This allowed for more complex and fluid ethnic idioms to appear. While the main lieu de mémoire of the Arab/Syrian-Lebanese community—the Saara, a commercial district in downtown Rio where Arabic-speaking immigrants established themselves in the early twentieth century (Pinto 2010, 147–51)—still projects an idealized diasporic identity emphasizing a tolerant and hard-working community in contrast to a conflict-ridden Middle East, other diasporic forms of Arabness have emerged.

While these new diasporic mobilizations provide arenas for the expression of ethnic selves, they have also enhanced the debates about the meaning and extent of Arabness and Middle Easternness. So when there was a march in protest of the Israeli bombardment of Lebanon during the war of 2006, there was a fierce debate within the Lebanese League because many of its members refused to be associated with any kind of support to Hezbollah's vision of Lebanese national identity. Similarly, during the 2011 Syrian Civil War, there was an intense mobilization of members of the Orthodox and 'Alawi communities—of both Syrian and Lebanese descent—in support of the Syrian regime, which they considered to be a defender of secular Arab nationalism against imperialist aggressors. Sunni Muslim communities, on the other hand, tended to mobilize in favor of the victims of the conflict or, sometimes, the Syrian opposition, presenting a different diasporic connection to the Arab world.

Thus, the kaleidoscopic character of Arabness allows it to provide a performative framework that articulates public imaginaries fostered by ethnic and religious institutions and subjectivities shaped within the familial context. The experiential and embodied codifications of Arabness that ground ethnic subjectivities can be articulated with diverse ethnic or national imaginaries and performances of identity. This kaleidoscopic dynamic, in which fragments are rearranged, hidden, connected, or contrasted in order to create a different pattern in each context, allows the constitution of a community that is never fully integrated or stable but does not break apart either. This ever-changing configuration of Arabness allows it to be constantly reinvented as a source of meaning, creativity, and cultural distinction by the descendants of Arabic-speaking immigrants in the cultural landscape of Rio de Janeiro.

NOTES

1 The quota system was removed from the Brazilian constitution in 1946, but it continued to inform legislation until the 1960s (Seyferth 2014, 123–28).

2 The policy of facilitating visas for Syrian refugees between 2013 and 2017 did not create a significant influx of people from the Middle East. In 2018, there were only 3,326 Syrian refugees officially registered in Brazil (UNHCR 2018).

3 The latest of these studies was a publication in July 2020 of research commisioned by the Arab-Brazilian Chamber of Commerce (Câmara de Comércio Árabe Brasileira). The organization estimated the number of Brazilians of Arab descent at 11.6 million, or 6 percent of the country's population (Sousa 2020).

4 The imaginaries that shape identity are central to the constitution of bonds, affections, and forms of belonging that produce and maintain political, ethnic, or cultural communities (Anderson 1991).

5 I use the notion of performative identity as a way to understand complex identities and shifting collectivities that are formed and acquire concrete reality through practices such as secular and/or religious rituals, political mobilizations, and cultural expressions, rather than through the adherence of a stable collectivity to a shared symbolic system or social imagination.

6 The data analyzed here are the result of bibliographic, archival, and ethnographic research, as well as interviews with members of the community in various periods from 2006 to 2019.

7 Nakba (catastrophe) is the Palestinians' term for the destruction of large parts of Palestinian society, through war and ethnic cleansing, during the partition of Palestine and the creation of Israel in 1948–49 (Pappe 2006).

8 The United Arab Republic was created by a union between Egypt and Syria in 1958. In the minutes of the first assembly of the Lebanese League, it decided to support "the firm, steadfast and highly patriotic attitude of the Lebanese government in face of the revolution unleashed by the partisans of Gamal Abdel-Nasser in the Lebanese Republic" (Archive of the Lebanese League, https://www.instagram.com/ligalibanesa1958/).

9   The pressure toward cultural assimilation appears as recurrent tropes of "becoming more Brazilian than the Brazilian" in the literature produced by Arabic-speaking immigrants, sometimes through mythical references to their integration in Brazil's rural hinterlands (Jorge 1935, 30; Ferreira 2014).

10   The notion of lieux de mémoire or spaces of memory refers to arenas of remembrance in which identities are inscribed in specific temporalities (Nora 1984). Tobias Boos (2016) pointed to the maintenance of Lebanese institutions in Argentina as spaces of memory even after their associative and political functions sharply declined. A similar dynamic can be seen in Rio.

11   Cultural intimacy refers to spheres of cultural engagement where identities are constructed and lived through ideals of authenticity and familiarity—in short, the feeling of being "among us" (Herzfeld 2005, 1-6).

12   She did not know how to read Arabic.

REFERENCES

Anderson, Benedict. 1991. *Imagined Communities: Reflection on the Origin and Spread of Nationalism*. London: Verso.

Barreto, Paulo. (1904) 1951. *As religiões no Rio*. Rio de Janeiro: Ed. da Organização Simões.

Boos, Tobias. 2016. "Las asociaciones libanesas en Argentina: Lugares de memoria, espacio de representación cultural." *Thule: Rivista Italiana di Studi Americanistici* 3841: 977-1006.

Bourdieu, Pierre. (1972) 2000. *Esquisse d'une théorie de la pratique: Précédé de trois études d'ethnologie Kabyle*. Paris: Seuil.

Csordas, Thomas. 1990. "Embodiment as Paradigm for Anthropology." *Ethos* 1, no. 18: 5-47.

Eriksen, Thomas. 1998. *Common Denominators: Ethnicity, Nation-Building and Compromise in Mauritius*. London: Berg.

Ferreira, Silvia C. 2014. "*Turco* Peddlers, Brazilian Plantationists, and Transnational Arabs: The Genre Triangle of Levantine-Brazilian Literature." In *The Middle East and Brazil: Perspectives on the New Global South*, edited by Paul Amar, 279-95. Bloomington: Indiana University Press.

Herzfeld, Michael. 2005. *Cultural Intimacy: Social Poetics and the Real Life of States, Societies, and Institutions*. New York: Routledge.

Jorge, Salomão. 1935. "Carta Aberta ao Dr. José Maria Whitaker." In *As vantagens da imigração Syria no Brasil: Em torno de uma polêmica entre os Snrs. Herbert V. Levy e Salomão Jorge no "Diário de São Paulo,"* edited by Amarílio Junior. Rio de Janeiro: Off. Gr. Da S.A. A Noite.

Karam, John. 2007. *Another Arabesque: Syrian-Lebanese Ethnicity in Neoliberal Brazil*. Philadelphia: Temple University Press.

Knowlton, Clark. 1960. *Sírios e Libaneses em São Paulo*. São Paulo: Editora Hucitec.

Lesser, Jeffrey. 2001. *Negociando a identidade nacional: Imigrantes, minorias e a luta pela etnicidade no Brasil*. São Paulo: UNESP.

Macagno, Lorenzo, Silvia Montenegro, and Verónica Béliveau. 2011. *A tríplice fronteira: Espaços nacionais e dinâmicas locais*. Curitiba: UFPR.

Nora, Pierre. 1984. *Les lieux de mémoire*. Vol. 1. Paris: Gallimard.

Pappe, Ilam. 2006. *The Ethnic Cleansing of Palestine*. London: Oneworld.

Pinto, Paulo G. 2010. *Árabes no Rio de Janeiro: Uma identidade plural*. Rio de Janeiro: Cidade Viva.

Pinto, Paulo G. 2016. "Labirinto de espelhos: Orientalismos, imigração e discursos sobre a nação no Brasil." *Revista de estudios internacionales mediterráneos* 21, no. 1: 47–57.

Pinto, Paulo G. 2018. "Primos e patrícios: Intimidade cultural e representações na construção da etnicidade Árabe/Sírio-Libanesa no Rio de Janeiro." *Confluenze: Rivista di studi Iberoamericani* 10, no. 1: 60–83.

Safady, Jorge. 1972. "A imigração Árabe no Brasil (1880–1970)." PhD diss., University of São Paulo.

Safady, Wadih. 1966. *Cenas e cenários dos Caminhos da Minha Vida*. Belo Horizonte: Santa Maria.

Seyferth, Giralda. 2014. "O Estado Brasileiro e a imigração." In *Caminhos da imigração: Memória, integração e conflitos*, edited by Miriam Santos, Regina Petrus, Hélion Póvoa Neto, and Charles Gomes, 109–34. Rio de Janeiro: Léo Christiano Editorial.

Sousa, Thais. 2020. "Comunidade árabe é 6% da população brasileira, diz pesquisa." ANBA, July 22. https://anba.com.br/comunidade-arabe-e-6-da-populacao-brasileira -diz-pesquisa/.

UNHCR. 2018. *Global Trends: Forced Displacement in 2018*. UN High Commissioner for Refugees. https://reliefweb.int/attachments/5ee61624-975c-3354-9b7e-f2c1e9c8185a /5d08d7ee7.pdf.

22

Decarceral Archetypes / Arquétipos Decarcerais

Rio de Janeiro as a Model Laboratory for the Abolition of Prison-Based Torture

TAMIRES MARIA ALVES

Organizations that monitor, prevent, and combat torture are emerging in the South, but anti-incarceration is still considered a predominantly northern effort. This chapter highlights the relationship between prisons and the antitorture and prison abolition organizations and movements that have emerged around them. Such organizations have been established in response to a global effort toward more equitable treatment of incarcerated individuals, or to advocate for decarceral models. The State Mechanism for Preventing and Combating Torture in Rio de Janeiro (MEPCT/RJ) represents one body within the international commitment to inspect and defend human rights. Created in 2010 and linked to the Legislative Assembly of the State of Rio de Janeiro (ALERJ), the organization is a pioneer and technical laboratory for the promotion of public security policies at a global level. Following the same line of reasoning and looking at methodologies in the South, an alternative allows southern populations to struggle to predict and prevent abuses. It is necessary to face decarceral archetypes not as an object of research but as a method toward freedom.

The main way to challenge neoliberal practices is no longer done institutionally, through parties or policy, but through what has been called epistemological political transformation (Santos 2019). The spirit of resistance demands that we no longer accept that the only valid knowledge comes from the North. It is necessary to reinterpret the world before transforming it. In facing the conservative and dominant epistemologies of the North, alternative approaches to rights and campaigns against repression are needed. I argue that through the epistemological shift toward the South, we could reinterpret social struggles against domination. Such an argument, to be sure, has been previously made: "The epistemologies of the South refer to the production and validation of knowledge anchored in the experiences of resistance of all social groups that have been systematically victims of the injustice, oppression and destruction caused by capitalism, colonialism and patriarchy. I call the vast and very diverse scope of these experiences Anti-Imperial South. It is an epistemological South . . . that has in common the fact that this knowledge is born in struggles against capitalism, colonialism and patriarchy" (Santos 2019, 17). Decolonizing abolitionist knowledge requires incorporating distinct justice paradigms and critiques from marginalized communities to avoid replicating colonial structures (Alves 2021). The ethical dilemma of extracting knowledge from incarcerated people necessitates a shift from exploitation to collaborative engagement, giving them agency and voice. Civil society actors protect grassroots movements from co-optation by maintaining financial independence and community-led decision-making (Souza 2014). To create more inclusive and equitable MEPCT/RJ frameworks, it's essential to engage in ongoing self-critique, community consultations, and dialogue with affected communities to address colonialism and extractivism while advancing justice (Alves, Lopes, and Borges 2023).[1] In the same effort, I present a decolonizing methodology that is not extractivist and can produce and invent transnational pedagogies for the management of the prison crisis. The idea is that after understanding the above, there can be bridges and articulations of effective scientific knowledge that can be implemented in other spaces. These alternative arenas seek to combat and prevent the violation of human rights, as is done locally with MEPCT/RJ.[2]

My main argument is that these new epistemological views are necessary to comprehend the efforts of activists, intellectuals, and certain political leaders to emphasize the need to abolish prisons and imprisonment procedures. Prisons have grown and increased their presence in Brazil during the past decade, despite the fact that traditional legitimizing discourses (primarily those of re-socialization) are no longer valid justification for their continuation. The lack of a credible rationale for the continued operation of prisons has not stymied their continuation. The objective has shifted to neutralizing the enemy rather than resocializing.

Following the same line of reasoning and looking at methodologies in the South, an alternative now allows southern populations to be able to predict their signifiers, procedures, and techniques without having the West as a mirror to be mimicked. This can only be accomplished if the methodology is decolonized, allowing scientific knowledge and memory from the South to be prioritized. To achieve the goal, it is necessary to face decarceral archetypes not as an object of research but as a methodological effort, so that new fertile epiphanies on these themes of repeated violation of human rights are faced not only from the point of view of those who defend people in prison, but above all those who resist punitive practices. Prisoners must be approached not only as objects of research but also as articulators of their own struggle. In this process, it will be crucial to look at the "productive power on the frontier—the strategic role it plays in the making of the world" (Mezzadra and Neilson 2013, vii).

The Deprivation of Liberty

A colonial perspective of knowledge naturalized an unequal relationship between the North and the South, fostering "a new way to legitimize the old ideas and practices of superior/inferior relations between dominant and dominated. . . . The conquered and dominated peoples were placed in a natural situation of inferiority, and consequently also their phenotypic traits, as well as their mental and cultural discoveries. In this way, race became the first fundamental criterion for the distribution of the world population in the levels, places and roles in the power structure of the new society" (Quijano 2005, 118). Like many other cities in the Global South, Rio de Janeiro occupies a territory with high levels of social inequality measured by the Gini index and with a significant part of its population being Black and brown people.[3] It shares a racialized colonial history that continues to marginalize and punish the populations that have built it.

According to data from Infopen 2019, approximately 51,029 people were arrested within the state of Rio de Janeiro, although there was prison capacity only for 31,485. The Black and brown population—although it does not reach even half the number of people in the Rio state and is only 55 percent of the population of Rio city—represents more than 75 percent of the prisoners today.[4] These percentages indicate a disproportionate targeting familiar to Black and brown people in other contexts. This should not suggest that these populations commit a greater number of crimes but that they face exceptional forms of persecution by the state and the institutions of coercion that constitute it (de Almeida 2019; Alves 2021). In light of this differential treatment, this chapter uses MEPCT/RJ as a method that seeks to reduce suffering and liberation through the technical production of knowledge. The humane treatment of the prison population simultaneously addresses racism and human rights abuses in the South.

Rio's State Mechanism and Committee for Preventing and Combating Torture

The MEPCT/RJ was created through a 2010 law (No. 5,778) and is linked to ALERJ. The intention of creating an organization that should concentrate on creating a system for preventing torture was formalized from 1993 onward at the UN World Human Rights Conference. The initiative understood that the best way to avoid torture was through prevention rather than reaction (OHCHR 2022). The MEPCT/RJ and corresponding law, more specifically, emerged from the ratification of the following protocols: the 2007 United Nations Optional Protocol to the Convention against Torture and Other Cruel, Inhuman, or Degrading Treatment or Punishment; the 2006 Integrated Action Plan for the Prevention and Combat of Torture in Brazil; and the 2009 National Human Rights Plan III. After creation, enforcement began in 2011. The committee (CEPCT/RJ; the Rio State Committee for the Combat and Prevention of Torture) is composed of sixteen institutions that address both government and civil society. Its main objective is to formulate public policies based on the recommendations postulated by the MEPCT/RJ.

The MEPCT/RJ operates in close proximity to the National Truth Commission and is linked to the UN through its Subcommittee on Preventing and Combating Torture.[5] The MEPCT/RJ is made up of six members, elected by the committee, based on the UN Optional Protocol. Its function is to monitor the risk of torture and ill treatment. Through planning and conducting regular visits (without prior notice), members create reports to describe the living conditions inside prison units. Throughout the process, officials establish relationships with management authorities, the technical staff, and the prisoners. They also provide recommendations for institutional measures so that individuals deprived of their liberty are treated appropriately and according to international and national human rights standards. It also promotes seminars and presents bills—together with CEPCT/RJ—that aim to combat mass incarceration and torture. It communicates to the Public Ministry and public defender when it finds instances of torture, since these bodies have the legal prerogative to act. Therefore, the purpose of the MEPCT/RJ is not to defend the vilified or to accuse the individual who orchestrated the act. Rather, it intends only to prevent torture, making its work innovative and essential for the South (Alves 2021).

Visits follow a script, and reports are primarily descriptive. The inspection aims to verify conditions regarding health, education, housing, work, hygiene, legal counseling, religious practice, infrastructural conditions, and other incidents. Investigations also function as an audit, monitoring the various institutional agents. Along with the on-site monitoring, analysis considers official state and national data, articles by experts on the subject, information on what has been debated about people deprived of their liberties at national and international levels, and recommendations made by competent authorities. The recommendations are the way that the MEPCT/RJ (2012) primarily promotes the prevention of torture.

Although in many countries there are agencies that make visits to spaces where possible abuses of human rights occur, the creation of organized bodies allows sustained monitoring. Being linked to the legislative administrative sphere, rather than the executive, offers the MEPCT/RJ relative autonomy.[6] The local character of MEPCT/RJ is relevant because countries with continental dimensions face different challenges in prisons located in more or less affluent regions, close to or far from large centers, in border locations, with the imprisonment of Native and Indigenous peoples, among others. In Brazil, primary spaces of rights abuses may include immigration centers, transit zones of international airports, police stations, educational systems (for children under eighteen), prisons, psychiatric institutions, and places of administrative imprisonment, among others.

Subaltern Resistance to Incarceration

Thus, decarceral archetypes serve as devices of resistance to the punishing practices fostered by the prison system. While I emphasize the central role of the MEPCT/RJ in the extrication agenda in this work, it is necessary to recognize that the MEPCT/RJ's action is strengthened and deepened by other abolitionist and decarceral institutions that the state has expanded. During the COVID-19 epidemic, the MEPCT/RJ and the State and National Fronts for Extrication collaborated to establish the Plataforma Desencarcera, RJ!, a website for anonymous reporting of human rights abuses and torture in prison settings. It is directed at prisoners and their families who have complained about maltreatment during the epidemic, during which both family and MEPCT/RJ visits were suspended. The argument presented here is not about refining measures that ostensibly reduce prisoner misery but about creating strategies and processes for the abolition of prison facilities. In the Brazilian context and in an unprecedented manner, institutions in Rio de Janeiro are attempting to abolish prisons through initiatives that include the use of state resources.

The MEPCT/RJ and affiliated bodies represent but one decarceral archetype in a larger global effort to improve the tools that defend human rights and prevent torture. Several organizations have disbanded in recent years, while others have arisen as abolitionist organizations. We highlight here the Frentes pelo Desencarceramento no Brasil, which is active in the majority of the federation's states. Also, the Laboratory of Critics and Alternatives to Prison (LabCap) consists of academics and antiprison activists. Additionally, there are organizations of family members and persecuted individuals, including Redes de Mães contra a Violência do Estado; Rede Nacional de Feministas Antiproibicionistas (RENFA); Liberta Elas; Elas Existem; Escrevivendo a Liberdade; Voz do cárcere; Cooperativa Libertas; and Amparar, Associação de amigos(as) e familiares de presos. There are other groups of individuals who have had firsthand experience with the prison environment—systems-impacted peoples or their families—such as Todas Unida and ONG Eu sou Eu. There are also religious associations that assist imprisoned individuals or survivors of the prison system, such as Luz para a Liberdade and Pastoral Carcerária. Although they do not proclaim themselves to be abolitionists, they attempt to alleviate prisoners' suffering. Countless innovative groups are arising and must be mapped for future research.

These groups operate within a sphere of oppression and anti-Blackness that is by no means new.[7] But to face mass incarceration at a global level, one might begin with monitoring the mechanisms and victims of oppression. There is a transnational pattern across several continents that those who are overrepresented in the imprisoned population are young, Black people, immigrants, poor people. These patterns must be named and addressed—including by agencies such as MEPCT/RJ and CEPCT/RJ. It would be possible to build through observation of their best practices and extend beyond them. If experiences within Rio's asylum spaces are similar to other prisons of the world, it seems to be that some form of inspection that is sustainable and enforceable must emerge. The MEPCT/RJ is a type of inspection laboratory that can be seen as part of civil society, in a space familiar with punitive policing and authoritarian governments. These tools are dependent upon efforts made by civil society that seek not only to combat torture and ill-treatment but also to prevent these same subjects from being victimized by the state and others.

The tools employed involve not only the inclusion of traditional political agents—such as the Public Ministry, the Public Defender's Office, and Governor's cabinet agencies—but also a constellation of actors in nongovernmental groups. Through CEPCT/RJ and MEPCT/RJ, civil society actors such as family members of individuals affected by abuses, rights and justice reform organizations, and the press, torture and abuse of prisoners may be more effectively monitored and prevented. These dynamics occur in Rio and Brazil, but also in southern neighbors such as Argentina (e.g., Madres e Abuelas de Plaza de Mayo) and Uruguay. The mothers of tortured, murdered, and neglected prisoners play a prominent role in these issues. But one must also consider the cooperation of prison unit directors, police officers, and prisoners themselves when attempting to articulate demands for reform. Epistemologies of the South that focus on decarceration make it possible to reimagine actors and agencies that traditionally do not dispute the agenda. Decentering practices against incarceration in the North may more readily allow for more robust and dynamic epistemologies (Santos 2019, 194).

It is possible to take the MEPCT/RJ as an example of what a laboratory might look like for the abolition of torture of prisoners who end up there predominantly because of historically unequal marginalization and punishment. The institution seems to be close to a space and network that could "develop conditions that foster and feed the anti-authoritarian elements of . . . human relations" (Mathiesen 1989, 117).

This chapter has sought to demonstrate that the methodologies used in the South to promote more humane treatment of prisoners can come from the epistemologies of the South. Rio's experience is but one example of a larger global civil society strategizing to resist mass incarceration and the systematic abuse of prisoners. New spaces and new laboratories must emerge to inspect, monitor, and gradually abolish threats to freedom. Here an effort was made to critically map policies that focus on preventing and combating torture. Despite the failure to comply with the agreements signed, institutions have mobilized, and have been mobilized by, civil society in defense of such protection. These organizations are little explored by researchers and observers. The MEPCT/RJ together with CEPCT/RJ act as pioneering technical laboratories for the prevention of torture and the promotion of public security policies at a global level. Decarceral archetypes demonstrate not only structural and institutional changes but also the ability to act as nontraditional actors within a very familiar system.

NOTES

1 Extractivist methodologies are oriented toward the extraction of knowledge in the form of raw material, human or nonhuman. The extraction is unilateral: those who extract are never extracted, so to speak (Santos 2019).

2 It is worth mentioning that there is little documentation of the MEPCT/RJ in Brazilian databases. This reinforces how it is necessary to investigate and detail work better. For this research, it was necessary, above all, to look at the laws that led to its promulgation, as well as the reports produced by the organization and ALERJ.

3 Gini Index, 2019 (social inequality index): 0.543 (IBGE 2019, 5).

4 The Brazilian census data last consulted in 2020 (PNAD—Pesquisa Nacional por Amostra de Domicílios) refers to Indigenous and unreported populations only in an aggregated metric, totaling 0.6 percent.

5 The National Truth Commission was installed in Brazil in 2012 by Law 12528/2011 to investigate serious violations of human rights that occurred between 1946 and 1988.

6 In the Brazilian case, it is important that state mechanisms exist because the prison administrations are state responsibility. But if Brazil is tried internationally for torture and ill-treatment, it will hardly be enforceable (Freixo 2016).

7 Cesar Kiraly argues that a part of society has accepted the inevitable use of cruelty in politics, since this would be "an unavoidable component in the composition of institutions" (2007, 5).

REFERENCES

Alves, Tamires Maria. 2021. *Enjaulados: Escolha punitiva brasileira e perspectivas desencarceradoras*. Mercês Curitiba: Editora Appris.

Alves, Tamires Maria, and Thaís Gonçalves Cruz. 2021. "Seletividade, punitividade e o novo arranjo criminal: O padrão de comportamento das instituições penais como elemento propulsor do PCC." *Simbiótica: Revista eletrônica* 8, no. 1: 21–52.

Alves, Tamires Maria, Twig Santos Lopes, and Afonso Borges. 2023. "O enfrentamento à violência de gênero no estado do Rio de Janeiro: Dinâmicas, fluxos e desafios." Rio de Janeiro: Editora FGV, August 18. https://bibliotecadigital.fgv.br/dspace/handle/10438/34112.

de Almeida, Silvio Luiz. 2019. *Racismo estrutural*. São Paulo: Pólen.

Freixo, Marcelo. 2016. "Desintegração do sistema prisional, segurança pública e exclusão social." *Ciência e saúde coletiva* 21, no. 7: 2171–78.

IBGE. 2019. "Gini Index." Accessed April 1, 2024. https://agenciadenoticias.ibge.gov.br /en/agencia-news/2184-news-agency/news/27603-northeast-is-the-only-region-with -increase-in-income-concentration-in-2019.

INFOPEN. 2019. "Levantamento Nacional de Informações Penitenciárias." Ministério da Justiça e Segurança Pública. Brasília, DF: Departamento Penitenciário Nacional. https://dados.mj.gov.br/dataset/infopen-levantamento-nacional-de-informacoes -penitenciarias/resource/225de757-416a-46ab-addf-2d6beff4479b.

Kiraly, Cesar Louis Cunha. 2007. "Crueldade e justiça no contexto da teoria política moderna." Paper presented at 31° Encontro ANPOCS Anais, October 22–26, Caxambu, 1–30.

Mathiesen, Thomas. 1989. "La politica del abolicionismo." In *Abolicionismo penal, traduzido por Mariano Ciafardini e Mirta Bondanza*, 109–25. Buenos Aires: Editora Ediar.

MEPCT. 2012. "Relatório anual do Mecanismo de Prevenção e Combate à Tortura 2012." Mecanismo Estadual de Prevenção e Combate à Tortura do Rio de Janeiro, May 6, 2015. https://www.cnj.jus.br/wp-content/uploads/conteudo/arquivo/2016/06/cf63b40b 37ea1dbc619b2a03e2e76121.pdf.

Mezzadra, Sandro, and Brett Neilson. 2013. *Border as Method, or, The Multiplication of Labor*. Durham, NC: Duke University Press.

OHCHR. 2022. "Committee against Torture Meets with Subcommittee on Prevention of Torture." Office of the United Nations High Commissioner for Human Rights, April 25. https://www.ohchr.org/en/press-releases/2022/04/committee-against-torture -meets-subcommittee-prevention-torture.

PNAD (Brazilian National Census). 2020. "PNAD 2019—Dados sociais e raciais." Instituto Brasileiro de Geografia e Estatística, January. https://www.ibge.gov.br/estatisticas /sociais/educacao.html.

Quijano, Aníbal. 2005. *A colonialidade do saber: Eurocentrismo e ciências sociais*. Perspectivas latino-americanas. Buenos Aires: CLACSO.

Santos, Boaventura de Sousa. 2019. *O fim do império cognitivo*. Belo Horizonte: Autêntica.

Souza, Luisa. 2014. "Implementation of State Mechanisms for Torture Prevention in Brazil: Constructing an Institutional Design in Light of Regional Challenges." Paper prepared for Projeto Justiça Criminal do Instituto Terra, Trabalho e Cidadania, funded by Instituto Lafer, São Paulo.

23

The Social Life of Corpses / Vida Social dos Mortos

Transcending Institutional Framings of Death in Rio de Janeiro

FLÁVIA MEDEIROS

This chapter traces the process through which death and life are registered and inscribed on papers and bodies. Ethnographic data reveal the mechanisms of power that work on organizing, classifying, and controlling dead bodies, while the quantification of death is used by the state to build public policies. This work is the result of research on police control regimes, state violence, and what I conceptualize as the institutional building of dead people. Public institutions are central to this process, especially in offices of the civil police of Rio de Janeiro and in courts. Here I present situations at the Medical-Legal Institute during the forensic exam of two bodies that were shot during a military police incursion. Through this case, I discuss how bodies and papers constitute ways to produce and reproduce death, as well as how bodies became social others throughout the process of "killing the dead." The ultimate goal here is to reflect on how violence, politics, race, and deaths are related in an institution responsible for defining the paths of the social life of those who do not return.

Just One Shot

Two rabecões parked at the entrance of the Instituto Médico Legal (IML, Medical-Legal Institute) carried six corpses.[1] Only one of them was identified by his own name from the identification document that was found in his pocket. A line with the six bodies lying on trays and wrapped in black bags formed in the hall. To carry out the autopsy, the medical examiners chose to use only one of the three rooms available. There were two necroscopic tables, and examinations were carried out at each one by the same medical examiner responsible for the autopsies performed (almost simultaneously). While two police officers—specifically, autopsy technicians—were dedicated to cutting, manipulating, and suturing the bodies, the medical expert (who is also a police officer at the Civil Police of Rio de Janeiro State) observed them and asked questions, occasionally looking for his clipboard to take notes and observations on a document called Injury Schemes. "Any tattoos?" the expert asked, referring to marks produced on the skin by gunpowder residue deposited in the abrasion ring and the bullet wound. The technician replied, "a blood tattoo," noting that the volume of blood that covered those bodies due to hemorrhages—produced by the bullet wounds—made it difficult to identify such evidence.

One of the unidentified corpses had been hit in the head by a rifle bullet. He was a thin, brown man with black curly hair, who was about thirty years old. The autopsy technician sawed open the skull and separated the posterior piece. He removed the brain from the corpse to carry out an examination (evaluating weight, texture, and color) and to collect the projectile that remained. The other corpse was a Black man of strong complexion, approximately thirty-five years old. The man was shot in the left side of his chest, with a puncture through the skin, reaching ribs, muscles, and heart. On his right forearm was a tattoo with the inscription, "Claudia, eternal love." The coroner commented, "He left Claudia a widow," while documenting the message on the body. The technician looked for other bullet wounds. "There is nothing else there—easy autopsy to finish," he said. The technician confirmed, "Yes. Just one shot! Police killed him."[2]

Institutional Building of the Dead

The institutionalization of death constitutes a series of scientific and bureaucratic practices that define whether a body is dead, which personal identity corresponds to that corpse, how that death occurred, and who was responsible. The IML (the equivalent of the coroner's office and morgue in Rio de Janeiro, the site of forensic postmortem medicine) is one of the institutions that is responsible for such practices and is therefore partially responsible for establishing truth (Foucault 1996). It does this through registers of an inquisitorial nature, characteristic of police bureaucracy in Rio de Janeiro (Lima 1995).

This chapter presents an ethnography conducted at the IML in Rio de Janeiro (Medeiros 2016) to identify mechanisms, practices, discourse, and categories that constitute public institutions. The IML is part of a heterogeneous group of interests that reproduces and negotiates morality, classification, and truth. The daily lives and deaths of individuals and institutions are described and analyzed here to understand the existence of the dead and the ways in which these deaths are managed to configure a process called the "institutional building of the dead" as a main part of the social life of corpses (Medeiros 2018). The chapter then describes the role of the state in these classification systems, and how the daily life of police institutions exercises power over corpses (their bodies and roles). The dead are given a certain life outside of the one lived by the individual now gone. The routine and daily manipulation carried out on the physical body of the deceased and in bureaucratic-institutional elaborations creates a new kind of truth about the one who is dead.

How Police Kill

More than expressing personal opinion or deduction about the dynamics that led to death, the technician's statement above, about the death by "just one shot," demonstrates how much police violence is a part of everyday life. It is naturalized within the IML's institutional routines. Professionals at the IML regularly deal with this "opaque zone" of police violence, in which they manage and gestate those killed by their police powers (Tiscornia 2005, 4). Although they valued their position as policemen, the agents marked the differences between the police they were (i.e., Technical-Scientific Police) and the police they were not (i.e., military police). In this demarcation, IML police officers disidentified with certain police practices, demonstrating dexterity in identifying the cause of death. More than knowing that the police kill, the technician's statement about the body of that individual also revealed another aspect—that the police at IML know how the police kill: with "just one shot."[3]

Medical examiner experts, in a sense, read and listen to bodies, and maintain authority over this process while building a narrative about lifeless individuals. The IML professionals, for example, considered the way the body explained its life through marks, tattoos, scars, the appearance of their clothes and teeth, the condition of organs, and the coffin that the family chose for the funeral. In this sense, the dead body was the main tool among a series of others necessary for the medico-legal objectification of death in the production of records.[4] A medico-legal definition establishes what in Latin is called the causa mortis. But I identify this as a process of "killing the dead" (Medeiros 2016). In addition to being a procedure for the construction of truth, the reports were considered containers for scientific legitimacy, due to their methods and presentation style, which necessarily depended on extremely effective bureaucratic work. In the process, experts come to see the body as an object (Good 2003; Foucault 2007). Anatomy laboratories, considered sacred among those initiated in the field of medicine, are only possible because of the existence of corpses. Thus, these bodies represent a central element in the construction of medical knowledge and in the establishment of medicine as a legitimate and disciplined knowledge (Martins 1983).

In necroscopic exams, the medical examiner apprehended the corpses by their fragments: organs, members, fabrics, and parts that informed the body's aesthetics. When looking at body parts, the body speaks because the experts are trained to understand it as a language from anatomical-clinical perspectives. But they also make it final, they kill the dead, by rendering the body an object of medico-legal knowledge.

Registering the Dead

I went to another table, where the corpse was waiting for the necroscopic examination to begin. His foot was lacerated but, according to the coroner, only the rifle shot would have killed him. After being photographed, the Black man's body was stripped naked. "What was he doing in a Speedo on a Tuesday?" the expert asked. It was possible to observe five holes embroidered with blood and charred flesh, each indicating a bullet wound entrance on the back of the body. After the dead man's back was viewed, he was turned in the supine position, which allowed the coroner to observe six bullet exit wounds on the front of his body. This indicated that he had been shot in the back, probably after trying to run from the shots fired at him.

The necropsy technician who performed the examination with the expert searched for the projectiles' trajectories inside the body with the help of a metal rod. The expert and technician decided that it was time to open up the body. After cutting, the expert observed internal organs of the body and identified lesions in the chest and abdomen. Both lungs and the liver were hit, and the path of one of the shots was mapped out. One of the projectiles had fragmented when hitting the sternum, located in the center of the chest, explaining how there were more exit holes than entrance wounds. One expert concluded, "They shot him in the foot to stop him from running."

Corpses' hands are observed as part of the protocol for examining cadavers that appear to be shot by a firearm. In this process, the expert identified traces between the thumb and index finger and said that the man's hands were "dirty with powder," an indication that the dead man had used a firearm. In the face of this evidence, the expert did not hesitate to raise suspicion about the dead man. Faced with the expressions of the medical examiner and the autopsy technician, the body of the deceased was once again objectified, to some degree because of the suspicion that, in a way, made the dead man responsible for his own death. The expert's suspicions, however, would not be included in his official records (the Medical-Legal Report and the death certificate).[5]

When he left the room of technicians and corpses, the medical examiner crossed the corridor of the necropsy service and went to the typing room at Laudos, where the necropsy technician was waiting for him to type the Medical-Legal Report. She sat down in the available chair next to the computer and asked the policeman to start typing the report: "So, dear, can we?" The swivel chair allowed the expert to position himself diagonally and keep his back to the computer screen, with notes and papers on the table. Sometimes he looked at the wall, sometimes at the floor, while dictating the description of the corpse that was typed by the technician: "Characteristics of the corpse: Man, about thirty years old, curly hair. . . . No, he was curly. Black curly hair. Average physical build. One meter and seventy-three. Eighty kilos. Corpse wore . . . I feel ridiculous saying that! What was the dress again?" The expert looked at the notes and went to another medical examiner who was also on duty. "He wore a white and yellow T-shirt, blue Tactel shorts, and black beach trunks with a white side band," he said. "Yes! Thanks," he said, looking like he had forgotten the "Speedo on a Tuesday" comment mentioned during the examination a few minutes ago. The expert and typist then moved on to the examination: "external lesions: abrasion collar with tattooing, smoke and slight presence of burn edges." Some wounds also demonstrated an "edge of excoriation and ecchymotic wiping," and "internal inspection indicated laceration of the lungs and liver," this being defined as the cause of death due to "firearm projectiles."

In the construction of the medical report, the expert moved between two distinct and complementary physical spaces that characterize the scope of the control of forensic medicine. In this movement, the expert exercises his power and control, leaving the medical-scientific laboratory and registering his truth in the bureaucratic-administrative registry. In the shift from oral to written documentation (Eilbaum 2012), the police officer responsible for typing reports had an intermediate function. Through fact production and truth claims, the reports helped reify the truth of the state, backed by public faith in official records. The categories used were technical terms describing shots but suggesting innocence or guilt in death.

After preparing the report, the expert filled out, stamped, and signed the Death Declaration Draft, an intermediate document delivered to the autopsy technician of the Death Identification and Release Service (SILO), who in turn is the one who filled out the death certificate. The death certificate draft is made official through signature and stamp. In addition to the insignia, the expert wrote down the cause of death, explaining the contents that should appear in the official death records of the corpse and the categories to be used in the death registry in the Ministry of Health's Mortality Information System. Although filling out the death certificate is a "medical act," the document was filled out by an IML police officer who works as a necropsy technician, and not the medical examiner, who, as noted before, is also a police officer. After the technician filled out this declaration, the coroner signed, conferring authority, and making those papers a public document. As the "authorized voice" (Bourdieu 2008) to establish what the body says and what can be said about that lifeless body— as well as the expert's suspicion about the dead person's guilt—policemen are dedicated to reproducing systems of classification and control over the dead.

Continuity of the Dead

The routine of the policemen who worked at IML relied on continuous classification and identification of the dead and producing truths to kill the dead. Some classifications were considered legitimate and institutional, giving movement to the bureaucracy that carried out this institutional construction. In contrast to the scope of the bureaucracy, other representations emerged through comments and jokes, opinions and practices, and feelings and perceived senses. These supplementary elements were part of the institutional routines but were not fixed in the public records. Each category—corpses, bones, hams, shots, dead, rotten, and so on—referred to a moral statement on the body that, when expressed, informed the different ways of existing and being classified as dead.

Corpses had only one way to enter the IML: by hearse. But there were at least four categories for their exit: identified-claimed, unidentified-claimed, unclaimed-unidentified, and unclaimed-identified. These forms referred to the individual's death status, so that they could be inserted in social relationships, as when the family presented themselves as the dead person's relatives. The unidentified were also subjected to the IML's procedures when seeking notary confirmation, but the absence of documentation or social ties was noted (Ferreira 2009; Medeiros 2014a). Unidentified corpses were, in general, also classified as unclaimed, since the deceased had no documentation, and it was not possible to confirm a bureaucratically defined existence. Unclaimed bodies were recorded only after a period of seventy-two hours after entering the IML. The dead were the responsibility of an exclusive sector that organized the records and funeral procedures, in specific cemeteries and burials made possible by a charity foundation.[6]

The Dead as Social Others

"Bring this body over here," said a civil policeman to the fireman responsible for the hearse, on arrival at IML. "Put this body over there," said a medical examiner to a police officer (a necropsy technician), at the end of the examination procedure that had defined the cause of death. "The bodies have arrived," the policeman informed the social worker, who was at the reception desk tending to the relatives of the young people killed in a massacre. "Madam, the body is being examined," said the social worker to the mother of a dead young man, who was waiting to continue the bureaucratic and funeral procedures concerning the death of her son. As an expert medical examiner said in an interview at IML, the "person ends with the end of life." According to this interlocutor, people have a name, family, action, social relationships, and, above all, an embodied life. The end of biological life would remove from the body the attributes of a person and transform them into "social others" (Gell 1998), into dead people. The social others function as a tool for establishing a truth about death. Their bodies support the biographies of those who once lived. These inert bodies provoked reactions, created relationships, and caused a diversity of actions—"not moving is an action in that sense" (Gell 1998, 125). The agency of corpses moves beyond the assertion that they "apparently do nothing. They generally just stay there, remaining immobile" (128). Medical examiners, experts, autopsy technicians, homicide police, and the related all contribute to managing the corpses' death and life.

Even though the body has no life, these agents designed actions for it that refer to the construction of truth about both death and evidence. The dead represent a corporeal status of what was already marked by life, while there was no death there. Despite being institutionally dead, some victims considered outside the pale of morality were deemed unworthy of classification and became tools for managing state-sponsored death and violence. This ethnographic analysis of the management of deaths, the institutional "killing" of the corpse, and the social life of the dead demonstrates how the dead are produced by violence as well as by the technical-bureaucratic and moral practices that express the centrality of death in the daily lives of the living.

NOTES

1   The rabecão is a hearse-like vehicle used by the military fire department, exclusively responsible for the removal and transportation of corpses to the IML in the state of Rio de Janeiro.

2   All data were built through participant observation at the IML authorized by the director of the institute, performed for nine months in 2011, and registered in my research journal after. The interlocutors and corpses are anonymized in order to preserve their identities (Medeiros 2014b, 2016).

3   The IML is part of the Technical-Scientific Police of Rio de Janeiro and State Civil Police.

4   In addition to the bodies, records in the form of papers, photographs, radiographs, and a series of official documents for the declaration of death.

5   The Medical-Legal Report uses language that is registered and characterized as the truth of the facts, constructed in a monological and technical way by the medical examiner, who also exercises police authority. In it, the expert reports what "the body spoke" through the knowledge constructed by medicine and presents the narrative as the official version of what happened to a body due to death. The death certificate is a national document with universalizing intentions, which establishes the legal distinction between the dead and the living. It is the state's instrument to contribute to the official quantification of the population, since all individuals killed in Brazil must be tied to a death certificate. Upon the presentation of the death certificate to a civil registry office, an official document is provided certifying the death of an individual. This document authorizes the burial of the deceased, through the Burial Guide, in addition to giving rights to possible heirs. The continuity of the corpse and the possibility of exercising rights and fulfilling duties after death is, therefore, intrinsically linked to the death certificate.

6   An employee, a necropsy assistant, called among colleagues in his sector a phantom, worked at dawn and was responsible for transporting the bodies from the cold room to the cemetery. The nickname given by his colleagues reveals how frightening the work undertaken by this police officer can be considered, reinforcing

the invisibility of the unclaimed dead. If the family does not present itself or does not wish to take responsibility for the body by presenting itself as a declarant, it is considered to be an identified but unclaimed or abandoned body. The most frequent cases of abandoned bodies I found at IML were newborn babies. In many situations the family goes to the IML, presents itself as a declarant, and collects the death certificate, but never contacts a funeral home. The police link this abandonment to the family's lack of finances to cover the expenses of a funeral. Also, "there is a lack of knowledge, even the ignorance of people, because nowadays he can bury people for free [by dropping the body at the police station]. Sometimes, people even know about it, but it is later and then they are afraid to return. They have forgotten. They have moved on with life and do not want to experience suffering again," explained an employee from the Unclaimed Sector. In these cases, the body remains in the refrigerator at the IML. The police from the Unclaimed Sector activate the competent judicial bodies so that, under judicial authorization, the abandoned body can be destroyed (Medeiros 2014a).

REFERENCES

Bourdieu, Pierre. 2008. *A economia de trocas linguísticas: O que falar quer dizer*. São Paulo: Editora da Universidade de São Paulo.

Eilbaum, Lucía. 2012. *O bairro fala: Conflitos, moralidades e justiça no conurbano bonaerense*. São Paulo: Hucitec Editora; ANPOCS.

Ferreira, Letícia Carvalho de Mesquita. 2009. *Dos autos da cova rasa: A identificação de corpos não-identificados no IML-RJ, 1942–1960*. Rio de Janeiro: FINEP/E-Papers.

Foucault, Michel. 1996. *A ordem do discurso: Aula inaugural no Collége de France, pronunciada em 2 de Dezembro de 1970*. São Paulo: Edições Loyola.

Foucault, Michel. 2007. *Vigiar e punir: História da violência nas prisões*. Petrópolis: Vozes.

Gell, Alfred. 1998. *Art and Agency*. Oxford: Oxford University Press.

Good, Byron J. 2003. *Medicina, racionalidad y experiência: Uma perspectiva antropológica*. Barcelona: Edicions Bellaterra.

Lima, Roberto Kant de. 1995. *A polícia da cidade do Rio de Janeiro: Seus dilemas e paradoxos*. 2nd ed. Rio de Janeiro: Ed. Forense.

Martins, Jose de Souza, ed. 1983. *A morte e os mortos na sociedade brasileira*. São Paulo: Hucitec.

Medeiros, Flavia. 2014a. "O 'monstro' e o 'homem': Aspectos da construção institucional de mortos no Instituto Médico Legal do Rio de Janeiro." *Dilemas: Revista de estudos de conflito e controle social* 7, no. 2: 347–65.

Medeiros, Flavia. 2014b. "Visão e cheiro dos mortos: Uma experiência etnográfica no Instituto Médico-Legal." *Cadernos de Campo* 23: 77–89.

Medeiros, Flavia. 2016. *"Matar o morto": Uma etnografia do Instituto Médico-Legal do Rio de Janeiro*. Niterói: Eduff.

Medeiros, Flavia. 2018. *"Linhas de investigação": Uma etnografia das técnicas e moralidades numa Divisão de Homicídios da Polícia Civil do Rio de Janeiro*. Rio de Janeiro: Autografia.

Tiscornia, Sofía. 2005. *Activismo de los derechos humanos y burocracias estatales: El caso Walter Bulacio*. Buenos Aires: Editores del Puerto.

Part IV
Futurity

24

Travestirevolutionary Occupy Movements /
Ocupações Possessórias Travestirevolucionarias

*Solidarity Economies, Anticapitalist Housing Politics,
and Nonbinary World Making*

INDIANARE SIQUEIRA

In this chapter, I detail my work as a revolutionary trans activist who founded CasaNem (n.d.; Evoé Cultural, n.d.), an LGBTQIAPN+ (lesbian, gay, bisexual, trans and travesti, queer, intersex, asexual, pansexual, nonbinary and allies) urban squatter movement that occupies unused buildings to repurpose them as trans housing collectives and centers for community education, health, and human rights promotion. CasaNem was officially affiliated with the Internationalist Front of the Houseless (Frente Internacionalista dos Sem Têto or FIST) yet left the network after an incident of transphobia. We spearheaded the founding of the Brazilian Network of Shelters for LGBTQIAPN+ (Rede Brasileira de Casas de Acolhimento, or REBRACA), which includes more than twenty houses throughout Brazil. As described by journalist Brunella Nunes (2016), "a symbol of struggle, resistance and power, CasaNem, in Rio de Janeiro, is what we can call home. This is where transsexuals, transvestites, and transgender people find shelter, support, and even a new family to call their own. Through workshops, debates, parties, and concerts, the space empowers the LGBTQIAPN+ public in situations of social vulnerability and serves as an inspiration to the world." CasaNem simultaneously offers economic, social, and political alternatives. Our movement subverts normative economic transactions so often unchallenged in increasingly gentrified cities (Cortêz 2023). We fundraise for the LGBTQIAPN+ community through our studio projects (such as the CosturaNem–SewNem) and our vegan KuzinhaNem restaurant at the Palco Lapa Cultural Institute. All of the profits from the restaurant are divided between the Palco Lapa, CasaNem, and the LGBTQIAPN+ people who participate in our projects.

A travesti whore (the word *puta* in original Brazilian Portuguese text), I am also a founder of Transrevolução, a nongovernmental organization (TransRevolução 2013; Transrevolução, n.d.). Travesti is a gender identity in Brazil that refers to someone who identifies with the female gender but does not identify as a woman nor seek to change their genitalia. The term, highly stigmatized in the past, has been resignified by our trans movement. Because of this, the term *travesti* also has a strong political connotation. The translators of this chapter have left this term in Portuguese as its history and significance are utterly different than the English translation *transvestite*. The struggles and politics, as well as concepts and practices described in this chapter, cross several fields, deconstructing theory into practice. Our radical concept of transvestigênere moves beyond travesti and transsexual—terms originally created by a cisgender society to refer to transgender bodies. With the word *transvestigênere*, the idea is to go beyond the body, appearances, sexual orientation, genitalia (important in the idea of transsexuality), or gender (central to transgender expressions). Here, I blend our radical social movement's manifesto with a utopian vision statement.

Occupations and Squatting

I am a vegan transvestigênere and whore, a supplementary city councilmember for Rio de Janeiro, and a member of the Brazilian Network of Prostitutes and Puta Davida Collective. Like many prostitute activists in Brazil, I reclaim and reframe the word *puta/whore* as a way to fight the stigma surrounding prostitution. While generally used in a derogatory sense in Brazilian society, it can also be used to describe something cool, somewhat like the words *bitchin'* or *fucking awesome* in English. Through these ways of being, I deconstruct theory into practice, addressing struggles and politics across many fields—education, sex work, gender violence, and power struggles within LGBTQIAPN+ activisms.

Let me begin with CasaNem. *Nem* is a slang term in Rio de Janeiro used to indicate affection toward another person and does not have a specific gendered connotation. To prepare transvestigêneres for the Brazilian college entrance exam in 2015, we decided to call the prep course PreparaNem. *CasaNem* was adapted from this original term and signifies a space of neutrality—neither yours nor theirs (but ours), neither man nor woman, and neither private nor public. Since 2016, it has served as a shelter and cultural center with courses and trainings for LGBTQIAPN+, sex workers, activists, and displaced trans youth. During the pandemic, we have also received and distributed hundreds of food baskets and necessary supplies to the homeless and other vulnerable groups—including LGBTQIAPN+ and sex workers—throughout metropolitan Rio.

CasaNem was involved in six different occupations before coming to Copacabana in 2019. In July 2020, we successfully postponed a pending eviction from Copacabana. At the time, I was quarantined at my house in Santíssimo, a neighborhood in the western region of Rio de Janeiro. I had stepped away from the occupation and Transrevolução due to my precandidacy for Congress, as a member of the Workers' Party (PT). On August 24, 2020, the building was repossessed under a court order. CasaNem was relocated to the Pedro Alves Cabral School in Copacabana for a short time, before the Rio de Janeiro state government granted CasaNem a floor of a building in the Flamengo neighborhood, right next to the Castelinho (Little castle). Ironically, prior to being granted to us, the building had housed the Assembly of God Evangelical Church. Evangelical churches have been claiming places of social movements, porn theaters, and clubs for some time. CasaNem takes these puta territories back.

We aren't from Mars or Venus; we're from Pluto. A manifesto of CasaNem would describe a different, parallel world—one where problems are discussed and not hidden hypocritically. CasaNem represents revolutionary change, a place where people are respected, where bodies can exist, and where there aren't imposed standards, correct formulas, or traditional rules to be followed. With this opportunity, people can create moments and relationships, and learn and teach one another. CasaNem is the world in motion, as it should be—only we strive for more freedom. The CasaNem manifesto declares the freedom to be yourself.

This is the world that we carry inside ourselves. As children, we expect the world to be completely free. Preexisting political, economic, and sociocultural structures show us that we are not. There are rules to be followed. Suppression of freedoms creates frustrations, depressions, and other impositions. You must have a diploma; you have to answer to society and begrudgingly contribute what you would have freely given. It is a capitalist formula for existence.

Urban occupation and squatting are naturally an anticapitalist struggle. CasaNem—alongside FIST, the Movimento dos Trabalhadores sem Teto (MTST), and other Rio-based organizations—conducts political trainings to unlearn fixed ways of seeing the world. The point is not to pay rent. There is an estimated shortage of 7 million homes, with people facing inadequate housing or houseless situations in Brazil (Fierro 2020; Frente Internacionalista dos Sem Teto—Fist, n.d.; Habitat for Humanity, n.d.). If you occupy all those properties, you end the problem of homelessness. But there isn't public interest in this due to real estate speculation. Why destroy more space to build new buildings if we already have so much unused property? We occupy space in favor of the right to housing, but it goes beyond that: we fight for the right to the city. Through squatting, groups and movements transform space. Even if we are evicted, owners and governments should pay us for our labor in reforming these spaces. It's a favor.

Occupations should help train people. We, as a movement, see squatting as an autonomous practice and prefer not to interfere but rather help with logistics, legal matters, and meetings. We are occasionally invited to help create cooperatives with other organizations, all for the sake of building a solidarity-based economy. Education, for example, can thrive through a communal approach, with global evidence of the success of such solidarity-based models.

In reality, CasaNem is different. We influence our surroundings when we occupy buildings, due to the physical presence of our bodies. Often the space where we establish ourselves isn't used to seeing transvestigênere people. Casa-Nem's travestirevolutionary squatting movements are, thus, about changing our external environment, rather than the converse.

Wherever it arrives, CasaNem expects attacks. It thus has a policy of being more closed to its neighbors, of being less involved with the neighborhood unless the neighborhood is welcoming. If that doesn't happen, then the house closes its doors and becomes a sanctuary. Copacabana is something of a halfway case. Part of the neighborhood welcomes us and understands, and another part does not. We only open up within those neighborhoods that embrace us. (This was the case with Lapa.) There are neighborhoods where we change people's minds. People start to see things differently. We don't look like bandits or victims, and the neighbors begin to see what we produce—art, politics, and knowledge. They see that we are a group of people that have been pushed out of our homes.

The Power of the Puta/Whore and the Brothel

People say there's prostitution because whorehouses exist, with arguments that prostitution is violence against women. But people with experience in prostitution know that this is not the case, that societal violence is directed toward women and the LGBTQIAPN+ community, among others. Violence in brothels represents a reproduction of the violence in society. Fear of discussing labor is most visible when one works at a whorehouse and is afraid to talk to the owner to demand one's labor rights.

The difference is that whorehouses empower. There will never be whores without houses. In Niterói, in 2014, police expelled everyone from the Caixa Building. Aninha—who worked in the building and led protests against police violence prior to the eviction—stressed the inevitable resistance of whores in their struggle to find spaces to exist. She has this wonderful phrase: "Look, the whorehouse might lack putas, but there's no lack of whorehouses for whores." This is the power we have: to know that we are necessary. We're going to use this to improve our conditions. It's this power—of knowing there is never enough labor in the world—that will lead to honest discussions about prostitution. We Brazilian sex worker activists insist on reclaiming the terms *prostitute* and *prostitution*, which we usually prefer to the term *sex work*, which is now more common in English-speaking contexts. Similar to the positive reappropriation of the word *puta* by feminist and trans activists in Brazil, many militants use the terms *prostitute* and *prostitution* as a way to reject respectability politics and destigmatize terms long attributed to laborers who sell sex.

Socialism is not prepared for prostitution, not at all. There are things that are natural but that human beings can do without. You can die from a lack of food or water, but you won't die from a lack of sex. But there are people who will exchange sex for other things. If the socialist revolution happens, let's say, and one still does not have what one needs—and people who have food and water want to have sex—one would have sex with them. Prostitution won't end with the arrival of a socialist revolution. Sexuality and the exchange of sex for things will continue. The name may change, but prostitution will exist.

The problem with some social movements is that they frame their notions of progress only in relation to the formal, normative labor market. They repeat the refrain, "The only option for travestis and transsexuals can't be prostitution." But we putas believe that more can be made of prostitution, which is more profitable, less formal, and more flexible than many forms of work.

Prostitution has more to do with anarchism, embracing vital ways to achieve freedom. Nobody rules anyone, and nobody is a boss. The raw material needed can be found within the body, emotions, and ability to provoke others' emotions. Socialism came from anarchism, with many women leading it. Women who believed in sexual freedom. Women who didn't want to get married. These women got involved with other issues. It was these free women who were at the head of the revolution. They were called whores who didn't want a home, but who practiced their sexuality freely or exchanged sex to survive. The revolution has always been led by whores.

I started by saying that prostitution goes beyond sex for money. Prostitution produces knowledge—it produces a solidarity economy, bartering, and art. Prostitution, of course, can be turned into capital, and it contributes directly to capital. Prostitution is the anarchic inside-out version of normative princess schools, whereby conventional patriarchal society teaches girls to be mothers. It romanticizes this role without mentioning the economic challenges of pregnancy and how to raise a child without dependency on a male breadwinner. Consequently, one loses one's freedom and is told to submit to a husband—a pattern that has led to girls being targeted for violence and escalating rates of femicide.

Even prostitutes take time to break free. When that happens, it is transformative. You understand the world and its gears. You begin to walk lighter. They will accuse you of being insensitive, romantic, and crazy. They just won't call you a whore because that's what you're going to say about yourself, thereby taking power away from them. One subverts the order. Prostitution is the most organized form of anarchy.

Transvestigêneres and the Trans Revolution

In 2009, at the National Meeting of Travestis and Transsexuals, a workshop took place to decide the definitions of each of these two terms. This was a continuation of a previous debate about the transgender category, which occurred at the fifth National Meeting of Travestis and Transsexuals in 1997 (organized by the Philadelphia Group, of which I was president and founder, and the Brenda Lee Support House). It was at this earlier meeting that transgênero was proposed as a translation. There was zero acceptance of the term, with responses like, "We're going to be colonized again?!" and "No, we won't accept a foreign term! Our language is Brazilian, Portuguese."

Previously, in 1995, the travesti/transsexual movement wanted to organize an exclusively transsexual network, with transsexual defined as only those who wanted sexual reassignment surgery. By the time two workshops were organized in 2009 about related terms, participants were asking: What does it mean to be a travesti or a transsexual in Brazil? Transsexual means identifying with the opposite gender from that on your birth certificate. This includes making bodily modifications to achieve one's desired body standard: cosmetic surgery, prosthesis implantation, injecting liquid silicone (which is a crime against public health), taking hormones, and so on. But travestis have no problem with their genitals. They can be active or passive in sex, and they usually survive through prostitution. I replied that people didn't need to take hormones or undergo surgical interventions. I was against injecting silicone, so I didn't fit into the definitions of travesti or transsexual. The only term I was left with was *transgender*, which was an umbrella for all of this. And that is a word that was not created by the movement. Once again, there were the accusations of colonizing ideas. Instead of fighting old battles, I said, "Let's stop fighting and create a new word mixing all three terms": transvestigêneres.

If travesti is defined by appearance, transvestigêneres goes further. Transsexuals experience the issue of identifying with the opposite gender, as do travestis. But in addition to the question of changing one's genitalia, there are also the questions of identity and sexual orientation. Transvestigêneres is beyond all of that. We are transvestigênere, with an *e* at the end to neutralize the word's gender in Portuguese. We do not define who is a woman and who is a man, what clothes they can wear, and so on.

Transvestigênere is moving beyond and living freely—traveling with constant movement and moving beyond. It is a constant journey. You can go and even come back. I believe that revolutions need to be made in order to give comfort to people, to return to nature. But technology constantly advances, and we can't turn back the clock. Technology is going to have to be used to liberate and comfort people. People need to work less.

Politics, Theory, and Practice

My election to public office would challenge a great deal. I'd radically blow everything up and suffer the risk of being challenged after the elections for not backing down. Many people also consider me to be a countercandidate and antipolitical. But I have never desired, myself, to go into politics. But people want me to be a politician. In the October 2022 elections, I ran for the Workers Party (PT) as candidate as a representative from Rio de Janeiro state for the national congress; but I was not successful. Perhaps that was my last campaign. I really want to withdraw from public life and live without all the obligations that are imposed on me today. I always have to have an opinion on everything and can't live as freely as I would like to. I constantly analyze things, and this is tiring; it has really begun to hurt me. I want people to practice what they preach and what they theorize.

If politics is transformation, then difference and equity must be embraced. Individuality and collective equality should be applicable to all. It is in this sense that everybody is political because any action you take leads to reflection. So, the question "Is my body political?" is really quite complex. Whores and LGBTQIAPN + people live through practice. We know the hypocrisy of the system because we challenge it with our bodies, incessantly. This isn't theory. In my revolution, theories are about something that has already happened.

I once posted on Facebook that I wanted Judith Butler to feel "the power of the streets and corners because what she deconstructs in theory, we deconstruct with our bodies in everyday practice." I didn't know that she (Judith Butler) was going to be at the "Undoing Gender" conference in Salvador, Brazil, in 2019. I went to the debate and said we had to set fire to the universities or make them into whorehouses, because whores are the ones who know things, and whorehouses are the best places to learn. This Facebook post and my encounter with Judith Butler came up the other day in the WhatsApp group of the Brazilian Prostitute Network. One of the sex workers in the group said, "Ah, Judith Butler. I've heard of her, but we don't know her. Most of us—80 percent of prostitutes—don't know her." I don't see myself as a philosopher but as a practitioner. I have written more than two hundred texts that are being edited into a book. I see how much I have changed in my thinking because we are all constantly changing. We analyze life in our current situation, and we can change at that moment.

At times, the anarchist, anticapitalist, trans, and prostitute movements share struggles and complement each other. At other moments, they diverge from one another. They bring together several issues that people don't want to discuss. The struggles are divided because people don't want to reflect beyond a certain point, regardless of what they say. These questions are very difficult to discuss, even for progressive people. With regard to, say, feminism, we may say that women have reframed the word in their fight against machismo.

The struggle against patriarchy runs through me because I reframe *feminism* just as we reframed the word *slut*. I don't want to fight just for women's rights anymore. I want to fight for everyone's rights. This makes me occupy unused spaces of habitual accumulation. This makes me antiracist, anti-LGBTQIAPN+-phobic. To be against all of that, you need to engage in a total struggle against machismo, against patriarchy, overthrowing and destroying the social structure imposed upon us. This is my struggle: the total destruction of society.

REFERENCES

CasaNem. n.d. Instagram. Accessed February 1, 2024. https://www.instagram.com /casanem_/?hl=en.

Cortês, Pedro. 2023. "Gentrificação suburbana, *displacement* e identidade territorial: O caso de almada." *Forum Sociologico* 2, no. 42: 37–48. https://journals.openedition.org /sociologico/11178.

Evoé Cultural. n.d. "CasaNem." Accessed February 1, 2024. https://evoe.cc/casanem.

Fierro, Alberto. 2020. "The MTST Politics of Social Rights: Counter-conducts, Acts of Citizenship and a Radical Struggle beyond Housing." *International Journal of Politics, Culture, and Society* 33: 513–27.

Frente Internacionalista dos Sem Teto—Fist. n.d. Facebook. Accessed February 1, 2024. https://www.facebook.com/frenteinternacionalista.fist/.

Habitat for Humanity. n.d. "The Housing Need in Brazil." Accessed September 23, 2023. https://www.habitat.org/where-we-build/brazil.

Nunes, Brunella. 2016. "Conheça a Casa Nem, um exemplo de amor, acolhimento e apoio a transexuais, travestis e transgêneros no RJ." Hypeness, August 12. https://www .hypeness.com.br/2016/08/casa-nem-e-um-exemplo-de-amor-acolhimento-e-apoio-a -transexuais-travestis-e-transgeneros-no-rj/.

TransRevolução. 2013. "Seja Bem Vindos(as)!!!" Blogger, February 29. http:// transrevolucao.blogspot.com/2013/02/29-de-janeiro-dia-nacional-da.html.

Transrevolução. n.d. Facebook. Accessed March 30, 2020. https://www.facebook.com /transrevolucao/.

25

Reexistence and "Villaging Up" /
Re-existência e Aldeiamento

Indigenous and Anthropological Activist Praxis at Rio's National Museum after the Catastrophic Fire and through the Bolsonaro Era

ANTONIO CARLOS DE SOUZA LIMA,
CRISTIANE GOMES JULIÃO,
AND LUIZ HENRIQUE ELOY AMADO

On September 2, 2018, the São Cristóvão Palace was destroyed in a catastrophic fire. This palace was a sprawling, mighty architectural monument built in 1803 that served as home to the Portuguese imperial family when Rio de Janeiro was the seat of the global Portuguese empire and then as home of the Brazilian imperial family after independence from Portugal in 1822. In 1891, the republican constitution of Brazil was drafted in the halls of this palace when the monarchy was overthrown. In 1892, the palace was transformed into the National Museum (Museu Nacional, MN). This edifice was unique as a museum, for it has also served as the nation's hub for anthropology scholarship and for collecting the written, cultural, and treaty records of the Indigenous peoples and nations of Brazil. The museum long served as home for the country's highly prestigious Graduate Program in Social Anthropology (PPGAS), and the building hosted many of the most important ethnographic collections of the Indigenous peoples of Brazil. Coming from an anthropological perspective, this chapter focuses on historical texts from the National Museum of the Federal University of Rio de Janeiro (PPGAS/MN-UFRJ). It's worth remembering that the fire happened just before the election of Jair Messias Bolsonaro, and that as soon as he was asked what he would do to rebuild the museum if elected, he replied incisively, "So what? It happened. It caught fire. What am I supposed to do about it? My middle name is Messiah, but I don't work miracles" (Redazione 2018). A very similar stance was taken when he, already president, denied the seriousness of the COVID-19 pandemic, especially in relation to Indigenous peoples. When the São Cristóvão Palace was destroyed in the fire, in it were the main facilities of the National Museum, including the PPGAS, as well as the ethnology and ethnography sectors, which held the most important ethnographic collections of the Indigenous peoples of Brazil.[1] The catastrophic fire also affected the Center for Documentation of Indigenous Languages (CELIN) and the museum's Memory and Archive Sector (SEMEAR). Due to the SEMEAR's character of being the first scientific institution created—and the only one, for a long time—in Brazil in 1818 while under Portuguese colonization, it contained fundamental and unique collections for the study of sciences and the relationship between Indigenous peoples.

As described below, Indigenous organizations' notions of resistance and struggle are, implicitly or explicitly, central to the modes of action (of research and intervention) of Indigenous organizing and trajectories, and these ideas and epistemologies have fundamentally shaped the restructuring of the PPGAS and the National Museum after the fire. The PPGAS/MN became a place of refuge and of dense and rigorous reflection (and not of political indoctrination) on the concrete processes at stake in Brazilian social life, beyond the great left and right narratives. But as we have noted, the majority of literature on interculturality and alternative epistemologies (Souza Lima and Carvalho 2018) does not pay attention to the political, often situational, use of unique notions by Indigenous movements.

In this context it is important to note how anthropology and postgraduate programs have become important spaces of refuge for reflecting and searching for new instruments of action and are directly associated with these notions of resistance and struggle.[2] Coming from an anthropological perspective, this chapter focuses on historical texts from the PPGAS/MN-UFRJ. Ideas of resistance and struggle draw upon the sharp poetic-political vision of Brazil's Indigenous movements, particularly around the concepts of "reexistence" and "villaging up." "Reexistence" means more than resistance, signifying a kind of ontological, transformative re-creation. "Villaging up" means creating new communities of knowledge, action, and refuge after catastrophe as well as bringing the urgencies and histories of the rural Indigenous village to the city. These terms became central to structuring modes of action and processes of reconstructing the National Museum and the PPGAS anthropology program. Similarly, the same Indigenous concepts led us to a deeper and stronger mutual identification after the fire and shaped action in other arenas during the Bolsonaro years against neo-extractivist interests, openly racist attacks, and genocidal policies.

This chapter uses forty years of one researcher's institutional experiences and two types of materials—our testimonials about why we searched for and how we got to the National Museum (Julião and Eloy Amado), and the testimonial videos of some of PPGAS faculty at the seminar "50 Years of Coup: PPGAS and Anthropological Research during the Civil-Military Dictatorship" (PPGAS/MN 2016). In the next section, an autobiographical excerpt captures an Indigenous student's experience amid the devastating impact of the fire. Next, an Indigenous lawyer documents his experience, from defending Indigenous rights through law to becoming an anthropologist with the same mission. Finally, the authors provide a historical overview of the PPGAS/MN and a path of healing and moving forward.

Indigenous Peoples Search for a Postgraduate Program
(Section by Cristiane Gomes Julião)

They killed the National Museum. And that is not a surprise, because the Brazilian state has been systematically dismantling history for some time now, especially as it relates to Indigenous peoples. My story as an Indigenous woman and my relationship to the museum starts a long time ago with Luzia. Luzia is the common name for the human fossil considered the oldest found in the Americas, dating from 12,500 to 13,000 years ago, which was located at the National Museum and, despite the horrible fire, was recovered. My name is now irrelevant; suffice it to say that I am Indigenous. In the MN, there was my story, blood, sweat, services, traces, corners, bones, films, languages, images, wax dolls, relatives, and memories. We, my people, have been alive for about 518 years.

The National Museum was a dream for me, but I never thought that it would ever be possible to engage with it. In 2013, I applied for a master's degree at the PPGAS but did not attend. In 2015, I met Antonio Carlos de Souza Lima at the Acampamento Terra Livre (ATL; Camp Free Land, in English) in Brasília.[3] He encouraged me to try again. It was my second chance. The first time I walked through Quinta da Boa Vista toward the MN, I almost couldn't make it. When I arrived, I felt the spirituality of my ancestors, Indigenous peoples, the Pankararu. At the beginning of that first semester of 2016 in Rio de Janeiro, people welcomed me. In 2018, I defended my master's thesis (Julião 2018). On the day of my defense, I was dressed in white, arrived a little early, sat on a stool in the garden, looking at the fountain, and went to smoke. I understood that I would have to go on and do a doctorate. My dissertation explores the relationship between the Brazilian state and Indigenous peoples in the struggle for land and the environment. It examines how Indigenous people were perceived in law and legal history. As we Indigenous people do all the time—and even more so in the years of Bolsonaro and the pandemic—we have decided to resist and reexist, together with our anthropological colleagues and professors. This is not just a question of fighting but of existing, again and again, in a variety of ways. When they say, "Urban Indians are no longer Indians and have no rights to their territories," we will show that we are the same and different at the same time, and that the flow of history has allowed us to reinvent ourselves without forgetting our traditions. To this end, in these years after the fire, we have been working side by side with the anthropology program to rebuild this museum, which, having come from the colonizers, was already ours many years ago.

There was not a single time that I smoked my campiô pipe, both in the MN and Quinta, that did not inspire me with the historical importance of my endeavor. Even here in my land, I hear these spirits. I dream of them. They warned me to prepare because difficult times were coming. It was their warnings that made me stay here in my land. They are the cries that I heard after they killed the National Museum, and I cry too. I now understand the spiritual burden that I carried. I realized that my relationship with the National Museum is spiritual. Three days after the fire, I looked for remedies to cure burns of an immeasurable degree, to soothe this pain and relieve the bodies and minds of those who felt the agonies of the National Museum. Life goes on, and I needed to connect once with my dreams and my mission. Cristiane Julião is my name. I am Pankararu, and this is my story of the National Museum.

The Museum, Anthropology, and the Indigenous Peoples
(Section by Luiz Henrique Eloy Amado)

Studying in Rio de Janeiro has always been a distant issue for me. I remember the advice of my grandmother, Julieta Antonio Pio, always telling me about the need to study, to go to the big city in search of quality of life. At the law school, at Universidade Católica Dom Bosco (UCDB) in Campo Grande (in the Brazilian state of Mato Grosso do Sul), I discovered a research group coordinated by Professor Marta Brostolin (the Rede de Saberes project).[4] It was my first time hearing about the National Museum of UFRJ. Professor Vera Vargas had returned from earning her doctorate in Rio and reported immense satisfaction in taking classes with Professor João Pacheco de Oliveira. She spoke about the reality of taking classes with someone we only knew from texts. It was on this day, at the end of the study meeting, that Prof. Vera Vargas said: "You need to go to the museum, Eloy." At that moment, my focus was singular: finish the course and pass the OAB test.[5] But even so, I took some time off and researched the National Museum from a distance. This was perhaps the first time that I encountered Professor Antonio Carlos de Souza Lima, who periodically held meetings at UCDB.

I finished my course and started working as a lawyer for Indigenous communities. I only received news from the museum on the day that my sister informed me that she had been accepted into a master's degree program. In the following year, with increasing tensions due to territorial conflicts between farmers and Indigenous communities in Mato Grosso do Sul, persecution increased greatly. It went from simple threats to effective persecution. It was in this context that Professor Antonio Carlos de Souza Lima, watching the news on social media, invited me to leave the state, to spend time in Rio with a research grant and get away from the center of conflicts. I accepted, and, in early 2014, I went to Rio.

The museum was an academic refuge. Conducting research and recording video lessons on Indigenous law for Indigenous leaders, I had the opportunity to live there and take exceptional classes. I had no doubt, as soon as the selection process for doctoral programs opened, that I would apply. I moved to Rio de Janeiro during what became one of the best years of my life. I was able to dedicate myself entirely to my research. The PPGAS had profoundly changed my tools for perceiving the world. I was becoming an Indigenous anthropologist. Undoubtedly, being a PhD at the National Museum is an individual achievement, but with great collective significance. I felt the weight, for the first time, when I returned to my village after the defense of my thesis. In a chiefs meeting, I was no longer just a lawyer. Thinking about my social role among the Terena and the Puxarará, I was able to synthesize my legal and social scientific backgrounds, which shaped my career as a lawyer at the largest Indigenous organization in the country: the Articulation of Indigenous Peoples of Brazil (APIB).[6]

What remains for us is hope that the museum returns, and that it will be an inexhaustible source of knowledge and shelter for all those who will one day need refuge. May we be able to give more to science and to the public university, and to create universal access to knowledge that, at other times, was on the margins. As of September 2023, I was the secretary general of the Ministry of Indigenous Peoples. I say we will continue to do as we have done in every federal government: we will hammer out policy. We will also reconstruct the museum. In fact, we are already doing this. We are establishing the Indigenous presence in geographical, institutional, and symbolic territories all across Brazilian life. We are making our ways of being felt and, in this task, the practices of the majority of Brazilian anthropologists have been our great partner. The museum, which we conceptualize as the village of so many persecuted people, will continue to be our village too.

Beyond Great Narratives

The statements above point to dimensions that lead some Indigenous students to seek the PPGAS/MN, located in Rio de Janeiro. It is attractive to many Indigenous students for its history and tradition of excellence, as well as for its affirmative action system. The PPGAS/MN appears as a space for official collections of Indigenous materials of different natures (ethnographic, paper documents, audiovisual media, etc.), an autochthonic symbol of Indigenous citizenship that has to be recognized and indelibly inserted into the nation's history.

The PPGAS/MN was created in 1968, a few months before the crackdown by the civil-military dictatorial regime established via a military coup in 1964 (Dreifuss 1981). It was the first postgraduate program in anthropology based on modern Brazilian postgraduate models, simultaneously prioritizing research and training (Leite Lopes 1992; Corrêa 1995; Almeida 2013; Souza Lima and Gonçalves Dias 2020). In videos of a seminar on anthropological research in the framework of the dictatorship, participants highlight how it was possible to forge this space and investigative practices associated with it in a historical framework—where democratic freedoms were suppressed through growing escalation of state terrorism.

Out of what Otávio Velho (PPGAS/MN 2016) described as a relative "schizophrenia"—between the suppression of academic freedom and places in terms of undergraduate courses, on the one hand, and the emphasis of the dictatorial regime on producing highly qualified technical staff for the developmental project (especially engineers), on the other—came a postgraduate education in the contemporary social sciences. Giralda Seyferth—at the time also a professor in undergraduate studies at the State University of Guanabara (now Rio de Janeiro State University)—reminded us that teaching undergraduate classes, about the most elementary things, was in itself dangerous. The National Museum itself, at the time, had members linked to the dictatorship. Maria Stella

Amorim detailed the daily and pervasive presence of repressive police action in the lives of teachers and students, and how national security bureaucrats limited the production of knowledge. Velho and Seyferth led us to question the permanence of an authoritarian legacy in the years of redemocratization. Their seminar, held on May 29, 2014—after the 2013 movements but well before the tense electoral campaign in which Dilma Rousseff would be elected—outlined the upsurge of authoritarianism in Brazilian public life.

The Museu Nacional was an institution that promoted better understanding of various forms of domination. Tenured professor at the MN João Pacheco de Oliveira introduced students to classic authors like Bronisław Malinowski, showing how they could potentially be useful for understanding the social struggles of sugarcane workers. The testimonies show a way of doing anthropology. Ethnographic practice remains the fundamental key to the discipline, and the tradition is, today, expanded and redefined by the very presence of Indigenous people, Afro-descendants, and students from the popular classes. Researchers narrate how ethnography was directly linked to the concrete life of interlocutors (peasants, urban workers, Indigenous peoples, etc.). But it was carried out under strict ethical principles, where the political costs of research were permanently and carefully measured, since everyone knew they were tracked by public agencies responsible for national security. Revealing the files from the Department of Public and Social Order (DOPS)—mentioned by more than one of the seminar members, but addressed by José Sergio Leite Lopes—allows us to perceive the permanent tension that researchers were subject to. But a true research agenda is relentless, being pursued incessantly.

The PPGAS/MN would become, as mentioned by Velho and Leite Lopes, a center where many young researchers coming out of the dictatorship's prisons came together in search of training and a space for reflection. As in the contemporary context, for other sectors—especially Indigenous and Afro-descendants—studying was a value in itself and a political act. Studying was resisting and fighting, just as it is today for the Indigenous people who are directly involved in movements in defense of their rights to life and the recognition of autochthony. To study was to resist, but also to reexist, especially for those who came out of the prisons and torture facilities of the military regime to conquer a new existence, new ways of being in the social world and in scientific production. To fight was also to settle, to build new spaces—to village up, to build new villages of knowledge and action. This wasn't simply to spout rhetoric but to work with scientific rigor and political coherence. The centrality of Rio de Janeiro and its symbolic position in Brazil's mental cartography was also a major factor here.

The fire and the current political moment present us with the challenge of building a new institution from the ashes of the materiality of the past but fertilized by the links to the future. The future will be built upon the knowledge generated by generations of trained researchers who constituted a museum that is still very much alive. It will remain a space for refuge and reflection, for the formulation of ideas and struggles intimate to the personal and political lives of every researcher.

We seek to show, throughout the text, how the search for PPGAS/MN is also the search for Indigenous peoples' rights (especially those intensely intertwined with the social struggles of their peoples). We aim to do anthropology that surpasses formulations of great theoretical narratives alien to Indigenous ways of thinking and acting, a method that would allow us to find elements to intervene in reality by formulating new knowledge, essentially through ethnographic practice. We have experienced the search for the construction of an effective symmetry that is not based on the exoticization of traditional Indigenous customs. The Indigenous ways of fighting in the Brazilian public sphere mobilize knowledge. But not everything can be said. There are sacred secrets of many orders that must be respected. Here, too, there are many practices of resistance and struggle that can lead to an effective change of posture, where dialogue is based on true dialogical respect and the ethical-political alliance. Here, too, are many practices of resistance, or rather of reexistence; of struggle and villaging up. Anthropology is once more learning with Indigenous people's ways of thinking and acting that can lead to effective change, where dialogue is based on true dialogical respect and ethical-political alliance.

NOTES

1 According to the Brazilian Institute of Geography and Statistics, the Indigenous population in Brazil (IBGE 2010) was 896,917—around 0.47 percent of the total Brazilian population. Of this total, 324,834 (36.2 percent) lived in cities and 572,083 (63.8 percent) in rural areas. This demographic minority, on the other hand, has a unique wealth on the planet: there are around 305 peoples speaking 274 languages, not counting the people who lost their original languages during the colonial process (IBGE 2010). The 305 peoples are distributed throughout 724 Indigenous lands constitutionally recognized in almost all states of the Brazilian federation. The total Indigenous lands is about 117,377,021 hectares (1,173,770 square kilometers), making up 13.8 percent of the Brazilian territory (which totals 851,196,500 hectares, that is, 8,511,965 square kilometers). The Amazon hosts 424 areas, totaling 115,344,445 hectares, or 23 percent of this wide region, totaling 98.25 percent of the entire area of Indigenous lands in Brazil.

2   We start here from our experience as leaders involved with organized Indigenous movements in Brazil who sought postgraduate education in anthropology at the PPGAS/MN-UFRJ (Julião and Eloy Amado), and also based on our institutional belonging, research, teaching, advising, and promoting affirmative action for Indigenous peoples in higher education programs (Souza Lima).

3   The ATL emerged in 2004 as a way of uniting Indigenous peoples in Brazil in the struggle for rights, consisting of extensive mobilizations in Brasília.

4   The Rede de Saberes program of affirmative action for Indigenous peoples in Mato Grosso do Sul (Vianna 2014; Souza Lima 2018).

5   Every bachelor of law in Brazil, to pursue the profession of lawyer, must take and pass the OAB exam.

6   *Puxarará* is a traditional Terena term to designate white people (Eloy Amado 2019).

REFERENCES

Almeida, Alfredo Wagner Berno de. 2013. "Apresentação: 'A turma do Brasil Central' e a 'antropologia da Amazônia.'" In *Frentes de expansão e estrutura agrária: Estudo do processo de penetração numa área da Transamazônica*, edited by Otávio Guilherme. Manaus: UEA Edições.

Corrêa, Mariza. 1995. "A antropologia no Brasil (1960–1980)." In *História das ciências sociais no Brasil*, edited by Sergio Miceli. São Paulo: Vértice / Ed. Revista dos Tribunais / Idesp.

Dreifuss, René Armand. 1981. *1964: A conquista do estado*. Petrópolis: Vozes.

Eloy Amado, Luiz Henrique. 2019. "Vukápanavo. O despertar do povo Terena para os seus direitos: Movimento indígena e confronto político." PhD diss., Programa de Pós-Graduação em Antropologia Social, Museu Nacional/UFRJ, Rio de Janeiro.

IBGE. 2010. "Atlas do censo demográfico 2010." Brazilian Institute of Geography and Statistics. Accessed February 11, 2021. https://biblioteca.ibge.gov.br/index.php/biblioteca-catalogo?view=detalhes&id=264529.

Julião, Cristiane Gomes. 2018. "Os povos indígenas e o estado brasileiro: A luta pelo território e o meio ambiente ecologicamente equilibrado a partir das leis." Master's thesis, Graduate Program in Anthropology, National Museum, Rio de Janeiro.

Leite Lopes, José Sergio. 1992. "20 anos do Programa de Pós-Graduação em Antropologia Social do Museu Nacional/UFRJ." *Comunicações do PPGAS* 2: 1–8.

PPGAS/MN. 2016. "Abertura—50 anos do Golpe: O PPGAS e a pesquisa antropológica durante a ditadura civil militar." YouTube video, posted by Revista Mana, May 19. https://www.youtube.com/watch?v=l-xd_tM8Cpk.

Redazione. 2018. "National Museum in Rio, When Jair Bolsonaro Was Saying: By Now It Has Caught Fire, What Am I Supposed to Do with It?" *Finestre sull'Arte*, August 10. https://www.finestresullarte.info/en/policy/national-museum-in-rio-when-jair-bolsonaro-was-saying-by-now-it-has-caught-fire-what-am-i-supposed-to-do-with-it.

Souza Lima, Antonio Carlos de. 2018. "Ações afirmativas no ensino superior e povos indígenas no Brasil: Uma trajetória de trabalho." *Horizontes Antropológicos* (online) 24: 377–448.

Souza Lima, Antonio Carlos de, and Luis Felipe dos Santos Carvalho. 2018. "Intercul turalidade(s): Das retóricas às práticas. Uma apresentação." In *Interculturalidade(s): Entre ideias, retóricas e práticas em cinco países da América Latina*, edited by Antonio Carlos de Souza Lima, Luis Felipe dos Santos Carvalho, and Gustavo Lins Ribeiro, 7–42. Rio de Janeiro: Contra Capa; Associação Brasileira de Antropologia.

Souza Lima, Antonio Carlos de, and C. Gonçalves Dias. 2020. "Anthropology and the State in Brazil: Questions Concerning a Complex Relationship." *Vibrant* 17: 1–21.

Vianna, Fernando de Luiz Brito. 2014. *Indígenas no ensino superior: As experiências do pro grama Rede de Saberes, em Mato Grosso do Sul*. Rio de Janeiro: E-Papers.

26

De-hygienization Clusivities /
Clusividades de De-higienização

Urban Renewal and Parastatal Power in Vila Mimosa

THADDEUS GREGORY BLANCHETTE, SORAYA SIMÕES,
LAURA REBECCA MURRAY, THAYANE BRÊTAS, AND ANA PAULA DA SILVA

Rio is a city of mixed cities
Rio is a city of camouflaged cities
With mixed, camouflaged, parallel governments
Hidden, hiding commandos
—FERNANDA ABREU, "Rio 40 Graus"

This chapter is written by people with different subjectivities, living and working in Rio, who are linked through a messy, wide-scale Weltanschauung. Our ontology is rooted in the interface between Carioca urban theory, ethnographic practice, and political organization around sex/work, gender, and racism. As Rio has passed through one of its periodic cycles of urban renovation, demolition/

construction, and decay, we, the authors of this chapter, were brought together during an enduring commensality over the past two decades. Perhaps it is better described as a commensal positionality: a knowing of oneself that is also open to others and rejects the other, not as a being, but as an unknowable and radically different nonself. It is this commensality that has been the fundamental condition for our work (some of which is presented elsewhere in this volume). Rio de Janeiro is a propitious space for such commensalities to develop alongside the city's well-known exclusions and marginalizations. This is why we speak of *clusivity* in our title and relate it to the notion of *(re)creation*. We define them thus:

1   Clusivity—the difference between *we* that includes and *we* that excludes the addressee.
2   (Re)creation: the (often regenerative and entertaining) cycle of building anew things that supposedly existed elsewhere and which suffer change in the process.

Our ontology cohered as clusivity through a commensal positionality constructed in sex/work-dominated spaces—a knowing of oneself open to learning from others and rejecting the concept of the other. Rio is a propitious space for such commensalities to develop alongside its well-known exclusions. This is why we speak of clusivity. This linguistic concept, applied to sociology, embraces both inclusion and exclusion, presuming interaction between the (re)created groups that Fernanda Abreu (2016) refers to in our epigraph. The frontiers of these groups are porous, no matter how tightly patrolled; for the city to survive, these borders must be negotiable.

Rio de Janeiro, the Marvelous City, has been a contact zone for more than four centuries (Pratt 1992). We've learned to pay attention to the (un)certainties created by Carioca commensalities in this ambiguous space—which creates hidden hierarchies of social power.

Even early Portuguese colonial administrators complained about the parallel powers that made managing Rio difficult (Fragoso 2000). If one can point to a longue-dureé phenomenon typifying the city, this is it, and it's something often missed in the spectacles of Rio's beaches, favelas, music, and murder rates.

This chapter tracks and reconceptualizes a series of attempts to remake Rio according to the model of the cities of the Global North, highlighting local elites' plans to whiten, Europeanize, and (later) Americanize a city that has remained obdurately nonwhite. Adopting the perspectives of major Carioca urbanists, we unpack the imported concept of gentrification in Carioca contexts, suggesting that the emic category of hygienization might better conceptualize the desire of the city's elites to create a Paris (New York, London, Barcelona) in the tropics. We take the red-light district of the Mangue/Vila Mimosa as our empirical object of analysis, tracing how it was originally founded as a way of segregating sex work from the healthy, family-oriented city in the 1920s, and how it has been remade since then.

Gentrification and Higienização: Sweeping Back
the Ocean with a Broom

Gentrification was the word on our lips in describing sex/work and processes of change in the city in the early 2000s. This was a theoretical import that rode into Rio on waves of foreign capital, as petroleum prices rose and the municipal economy exploded with the prospect of hosting mega sporting events. It quickly became clear to us, however, that Rio wasn't London or Paris, and certainly not New York.

Our first indication of gentrification's theoretical and practical insufficiency came when Governor Sérgio Cabral hired ex–New York mayor Rudy Giuliani as a consultant in 2009. Giuliani had popularized "quality of life policing," whereby eliminating traces of "urban disorder" (broken windows, graffiti, poorly lit streets, prostitution) reduced middle-class insecurity and transformed inner cities (Harcourt and Ludwig 2006; Chronopoulos 2017).

A few months after Giuliani's visit to Rio, we noticed changes on R. Imperatriz Leopoldina, Rio's oldest prostitution zones (Graham 1991). The graffiti had been cleaned off the walls, cobblestones reset, and tables moved off the street. Sodium lamps had replaced burned-out streetlights. Underneath them, sex workers stood, pleased with how the bright light increased their security while making them visible to clients. We doubted Rudy Giuliani had counted on this effect.

Years passed, more changes occurred, and we began to feel a sense of déjà vu. The city, decrepit and characterized as primitive, receives an influx of capital. Elites decree a makeover according to imported models. These plans are already outdated and unworkable when they are dropped into the Brazilian context, but money pours in anyway. Decayed areas are identified. Populations are marked for removal. Contracts materialize. Bank accounts fill and drain. Projects are mired in literal and metaphoric mud as conditions aren't what gringo blueprints presumed. Accusations of corruption multiply. The population takes to the streets. Finally, the commodity-driven boom fueling everything busts. Work grinds to a halt, the refitted alongside the decrepit. Before long, the jewels of the late(st) urban renewal project are being sold at auction, squatted in, or abandoned to the elements. Rio has seen this before, in cycles that have repeated since the late nineteenth century. Entire books have been written about this phenomenon (M. Abreu 1987). Taking our cue from them, we began to employ the term *higienização* (or hygienization) instead of *gentrification* to describe what was happening.

Higienização is an established category in the Brazilian human sciences. It has been explained for Anglophone audiences as distinct from gentrification, according to five characteristics:

> (1) It is a process whereby low-income people are forced from specific urban areas, not necessarily for ground rent maximisation or investment opportunities, but primarily to impose/restore hygienic urban landscapes; (2) the state, and more specifically state violence, play central roles; (3) low-income residents facing displacement are frequently depicted as tres-passers, perceived as out of place, and therefore pathologized and consid-ered delinquent; (4) it tends to repress and induce urban informality, by smothering it [in] one space, and then—rather than address the drivers of social inequality—ensuring it reemerges elsewhere; and (5) it is often justified according to modernist discourses that emphasise the greater urban good. (Garmany and Richmond 2019, 139)

While we agree that these characteristics are constitutive of higienização, they aren't what distinguishes it from gentrification. We also disagree with Jeff Garmany and Matthew Richmond's claim that higienização has not been theorized. It has been discussed by Lilia Schwartz (1999), Sérgio Carrara (1996), and Henrique Cukierman (2007), among many others. Its lack of comparison with gentrification is because higienização began to be problematized about the same time as gentrification—long before the latter concept arrived in Brazil (M. Abreu 1987; Leeds and Leeds 1978; Velho 1973; Maggie 1975; Valladares 1978). Higienização has two particular features not touched upon by Garmany and Richmond (2019), which distinguishes the term from gentrification: its con-stant incompleteness and its reliance on parastatal formations (a concept we discuss further below). While it tries to smother urban informality, higieni-zação doesn't reproduce inequality as a side effect; it overlays, coexists, and even depends upon informality in an urban palimpsest whose function it is to reproduce inequality.

Like many cities in the South, Rio lacks the capital to be like the cities of the Global North. Yet, as Brazil's postcard to the world, Rio must present itself as modern and Western. Capital for urban development is only occasionally avail-able. Wealth disparities are enormous. The means to remake decrepit neighbor-hoods are lacking and tend to be plowed into the city's core (the Center and

South Zone) because returns are more assured there.[1] This results in a city that inverts the classic Chicago School theories of urban ecology:

> The Rio metropolitan area suffers from a basic paradox: because it has to be the same as the foreign metropolises on which it depends, Rio has the exact opposite configuration to those cities. In U.S. American metropolitan areas, for example, the strata which enjoy higher purchasing power seek out the urban peripheries and low density land occupation solutions so that they can enjoy the amenities of modern urbanization. For the same reason, the upper classes in Rio are concentrated in the city's nucleus, in high density solutions. . . . The solution has been to pile up the rich around what urban assets exist so that they could enjoy them to the fullest, while preventing the poor from entering the city's core . . . or driving them out. (M. Abreu 1987, 17)

Readers might note that today, downtown areas are valued as residential space in the United States, precisely because of gentrification. The march toward suburbia described by the Chicago School (Park, Burgess, and McKenzie 1925) has not ended, however (Garreau 1992). In fact, the urban centralization Mauricio Abreu describes has been shaping Rio since the late nineteenth century.

The cities of the "developed world" are today adopting patterns long established in the Global South (Davis 2006). What has typified gentrification in the Global North—redevelopment of urban cores—was prefigured in Rio's urban evolution. Another factor must be considered: geography. Carioca urbanization initially occurred in valleys and along the coasts, avoiding the surrounding mountains. These hilltops—which became the infamous favelas—were later colonized by refugees from the city's first urban renewal projects. Populations were removed during the urban demolition campaigns implemented by the "Haussman of Rio," urban reformer Pereira Passos (mayor of the city, 1902–6), who was obsessed with destroying cortiços (workers' tenement buildings) in the city center (Garmany and Richmond 2019, 128). The resident populations of these cortiços were then often relocated uphill nearby. This was the case with the Pig's Head, Rio's most notorious cortiço. Demolished in 1893 by the city's original hygienizing mayor, Barata Ribeiro, its residents were relocated to constitute the first favela up on the hill called the Morro da Providência (Vaz 2002; Santucci 2008). In this case, population removal meant a shift of a mere 50 meters north and 100 meters up the hill.

In what would become a characteristic of higienização, Barata Ribeiro's and Pereira Passos's urban renewals never ended. More than a century after the destruction of the Pig's Head, another wave of urban demolitions ran through the area, in order to clear space for the hosting of the World Cup and Olympics staging areas, also in the vicinity of Morro da Providência. These removals targeted some of the fifty remaining nineteenth-century cortiços along the district's avenues, tenements that were still inhabited by some of Rio's poorest citizens (Briso 2016).

Higienização is what makes Rio the "city of camouflaged cities," sardonically celebrated in our epigraph (M. Abreu 1987). Elites attempt to sweep out poor, symbolically unclean populations from the city core to (re)create a modern Western (white) city. This is a Sisyphean task for those caught up in the sweeping. Borders between different clusivities in Rio are (re)created in this process but are fractal, porous, shifting, patrolled, and (re)negotiated. As a result, the reputations (and real estate values) of core neighborhoods can fluctuate wildly. Copacabana, in particular, has rocked back and forth between decadence and elegance for over half a century (Velho 1973).

This constant pulsing incompleteness is higienização's primary characteristic. It's like sweeping back the sea with a broom: a temporary clearance maintained through exhausting labor. The moment work stops, informality flows back in. In fact, it often never disappears. Formal structures promoted by higienização grow over and around informality, incorporating it. This leads us to higienização's second characteristic: its reliance on parastatal formations.

"Quem é Dono Desse Pedaço?": Haunted by the Parastatal

Parastatal formation is a concept pioneered by Paul Amar that contemplates "forms of public-private partnership, NGO mobilization, and development of expertise" in diverse areas of public policy, including the management of human rights and welfare (Amar 2013, 7).[2] In thinking about Rio, we stipulate that the parastatal must necessarily contemplate the informal and illegal partnerships state actors create with nonstate actors, which are often glossed as corruption.

Higienização depends on the fact that the res publica is often intentionally left in the hands of nonstate actors. As Denise Ferreira da Silva (2007) points out, swaths of Rio de Janeiro belong to the "space of necessitas," understood as devoid of human agency, managed by outside forces through state representatives operating at the intersection of the (in)formal. This is the sphere of parallel powers sardonically celebrated by Fernanda Abreu (2016), where informality isn't produced by higienização but is always already part of it.

The state relies upon parastatal formations precisely because it doesn't serve the majority. The parastatal is the quintessential expression of "counterpoised antagonisms" (Araújo 1994) that are key to understanding Brazil, which anthropologist Antonio Carlos de Souza Lima sees as characteristic of Lusophone coloniality (Freyre [1933] 1980; Souza Lima 2008). This is generated when a society based on masters and slaves becomes a nation-state with pretensions to liberal democracy. This is the milieu of Sérgio Buarque de Holanda's ([1936] 1995) "cordial man" and Roberto da Matta's (1984) "home and street" where some are owed every consideration and the rest nothing more than the law demands. Garmany and Richmond (2019) miss the fact that not only does higienização not address the "drivers of social inequality," but it also actively counts upon, cultivates, and incorporates them to manage the city. In other words, parastatal formations can't be seen as a bug in Rio's urban evolution: they are a primary feature.

The parastatal haunts urban (re)organization in Rio in the sense described by Avery Gordon, in "which abusive systems of power make themselves known and their impacts felt in everyday life, especially when they are over and done with" (2008, xvi). There's another dimension to this haunting, however. As Gilberto Velho (1994) remarked, Cariocas are inclined to believe that one may interact with occult entities. We'd say that Cariocas pay attention to the hidden forces operating behind the curtains, without which reality is inexplicable. The parastatal is also what makes higienização always already incomplete (in a way that gentrification is not). The parastatal allows the city to function by permitting constant (re)negotiation of clusivities, allowing us to include an other or exclude one of us without making this into a more general rule. If the divisors between social worlds in Rio are porous, it is the parastatal that makes them so.

Higienização of Sex Work

We now must return to our roots as a collective focused on sex work by describing higienização in Rio's largest red-light district. As the direct descendent of the Mangue (chapter 7, this volume), Vila Mimosa (VM) can trace its history to early twentieth-century attempts to hygienize prostitution. Today's district was born in an earlier incarnation through an association between prostitutes and brothel owners located in the remnants of the Mangue (Moraes 1996). This association resettled VM on the far side of Praça da Bandeira after higienzação sweeps in the 1980s and '90s. The (re)creation of the new Vila was accompanied by accusations that the indemnity the city paid to sex workers to vacate the old Mangue had been stolen by the then-president of the Prostitutes' Association (accusations vehemently denied and never proven). As a result, today's VM was almost completely built by the old brothel owners. These people and their descendants hold power today (Simões 2002, 2010a, 2010b).

Currently, VM contains some sixty establishments offering commercial sex. The main warehouse of the Vila is owned by a small group that has registered it as a generic commercial enterprise. Individual bars are owned via contracts made with the warehouse owners—contracts that don't exist on paper outside of VM. Bar owners don't directly profit from sex work. That would be illegal. Instead, they rent private rooms in their establishments. The property owners of the Vila have an NGO (AMOCAVIM) that supports professional training, humanitarian aid, and health care for sex workers but doesn't press for the decriminalization or regulation of sex work. It deals with police, the Human Rights and Women's Secretariats, researchers, the Health Department, and any legal issues. It finances and manages humanitarian projects in and around the Vila. Made up mostly of women, AMOCAVIM is aided by a male-dominated, informal private security force.

The problems VM hands off to the police are those that cause scandals: principally, drug dealing and exploitation of minors. Here's a composite ideal, typical example of how the parastatal organization of Vila Mimosa functions, drawn from our field notes:

A representative of the Human Rights Secretariat comes into the Vila as part of citywide preparations for a municipal mega event. They meet with AMOCAVIM, promising improvements to Vila Mimosa. They note that some women in the bars look young. Two days later, AMOCAVIM reminds bar owners that prostitution of minors is illegal and the city is on alert against it. One bar owner ignores the warning. A week later, police invade his bar, arresting him, his manager, and two seventeen-year-old girls. The busts get media attention locally but aren't noticed by the (inter)national press. VM is cleaned. The warehouse gets a new facade from the Women's Secretariat. AMOCAVIM hosts the state anti-human trafficking outreach project during the mega event. The closed bar is shuttered, its owner stripped of his contract by AMOCAVIM. Because exploitation of minors can't be proven, he's released after the event with charges partially dismissed. He is a persona non grata in Vila Mimosa, however.

This story shows how prostitution is effectively regulated; how an embarrassing situation is dealt with by giving credit to the police; and how VM can negotiate improvements to its facilities, providing better working conditions and increased profitability—all without direct state management of prostitution. It also shows how clusivities are operationalized. The bar owner is included in a formally illegal market (running a house of prostitution) as long as he doesn't violate other laws seen as much more serious within the current political environment (sexual exploitation of minors). When he persists, someone in his community reports him to the police and makes a public example of him. He is then excluded from the formally illegal market by its parastatal brokers, even though he has not been convicted of any crimes. The market for commercial sex thus continues merrily along in VM while Rio can say—to its international partners producing the mega event—that it is repressing sexual exploitation.

Again, informality is not specific to prostitution in Rio de Janeiro. The city relies on it to function. Higienização is thus a strategic weapon. In the case of prostitution, it is mobilized by moralities and real estate markets, coated in stigmatizing language, and operationalized by parastatal formations—but all ultimately to very little effect, if the desired effect is, indeed, the abolition of prostitution.

The broom of higienização thus periodically sweeps through Rio's oldest red-light district with the aid of allied state and nonstate actors. It carries some of the neighborhood's denizens with it, but most hunker down until it passes. We catch snapshots of this process because we pay attention to the semioccult—to the clusivities implied by people's speech, whom they talked to, whom they drank with, and what happened next. This is often more important than reading what Brazilian laws say about prostitution. Certain clusivities are made and unmade in higienização's sweeps. We can understand this by looking at commensality, or "sharing time" (Fabian 1983), with a series of state and nonstate actors in and around Vila Mimosa and through participating in several state commissions and groups on trafficking and mega events.

NOTES

1 The core includes Barra da Tijuca. While the symbolic cleansing of urban land-scapes is a principal driver of higienização, it also concentrates on profitable territorialization, or what Garmany and Richmond call "ground rent maximization" and "investment opportunities" (quoted in M. Abreu 1987, 18, 74–75).

2 "Quem é dono desse pedaço?" means "Who owns this piece [of territory]?" (M. Abreu 1987).

REFERENCES

Abreu, Fernanda. 2016. "Rio 40 Graus." YouTube, July 29. https://www.youtube.com /watch?v=AhuJ3dUVQvc.

Abreu, Mauricio de. 1987. *Evolução urbana do Rio de Janeiro*. Rio de Janeiro: Zahar.

Amar, Paul. 2013. *The Security Archipelago: Human-Security States, Sexuality Politics, and the End of Neoliberalism*. Durham, NC: Duke University Press.

Araújo, Ricardo Benzaquen. 1994. *Guerra e paz: Casa-grande e senzala e a obra de Gilberto Freyre nos anos 30*. São Paulo: Editora 34.

Briso, Caio Barreto. 2016. "Cortiços do Rio Antigo resistem na Zona Portuária." *O Globo*, June 11. https://oglobo.globo.com/rio/corticos-do-rio-antigo-resistem-na-zona-portuaria-20419840.

Carrara, Sérgio. 1996. *Tributo a Vênus: A luta contra a sífilis no Brasil, da passagem do século aos anos 40*. Rio de Janeiro: FIOCRUZ.

Chronopoulos, Themis. 2017. "Broken Windows Policing and the Orderly City: New York since the Late Twentieth Century." *The Gotham Center for New York City History* (blog), October 19. https://www.gothamcenter.org/blog/broken-windows-policing-and-the-orderly-city-new-york-since-the-late-twentieth-century.

Cukierman, Henrique. 2007. *Yes, nós temos Pasteur: Manguinhos, Oswaldo Cruz e a história da ciência no Brasil*. Rio de Janeiro: Ediouro.

da Matta, Roberto. 1984. *A casa e a rua: Espaço, cidadania, mulher e morte no Brasil*. Rio de Janeiro: Rocco.

da Silva, Denise Ferreira. 2007. *Toward a Global Theory of Race*. Minneapolis: University of Minnesota Press.

Davis, Mike. 2006. *Planet of Slums: Urban Involution and the Informal Working Class*. New York: Verso.

de Holanda, Sérgio Buarque. (1936) 1995. "O homem cordial." In *Raízes do Brasil*. São Paulo: Companhia das Letras.

Fabian, Johannes. 1983. *Time and the Other: How Anthropology Makes Its Object*. New York: Columbia University Press.

Fragoso, João. 2000. "A nobreza da República: Notas sobre a formação da primeira elite senhorial do Rio de Janeiro (séculos XVI e XVII)." *Topoi (Rio de Janeiro)* 1: 45–122.

Freyre, Gilberto. (1933) 1980. *Casa grande e senzala*. Rio de Janeiro: José Olympio.

Garmany, Jeff, and Matthew Richmond. 2019. "Hygienisation, Gentrification, and Urban Displacement in Brazil." *Antipode* 52, no. 1: 124–44.

Garreau, Joel. 1992. *Edge City: Life on the New Frontier*. New York: Anchor.

Gordon, Avery. 2008. *Ghostly Matters: Haunting and the Sociological Imagination*. Minneapolis: University of Minnesota Press.

Graham, Sandra Lauderdale. 1991. "Slavery's Impasse: Slave Prostitutes, Small-Time Mistresses, and the Brazilian Law of 1871." *Comparative Studies in Society and History* 33, no. 4: 669–94.

Harcourt, B. E., and J. Ludwig. 2006. "Broken Windows: New Evidence from New York City and a Five-City Social Experiment." *University of Chicago Law Review* 73, no. 1: 271–320.

Leeds, A., and E. Leeds. 1978. *A sociologia do Brasil urbano*. Rio de Janeiro: FIOCRUZ.

Maggie, Yvonne. 1975. *Guerra de Orixá: Um estudo de ritual e conflito*. Rio de Janeiro: Zahar.

Moraes, Aparecida F. 1996. *Mulheres da vila: Prostituição, identidade social e movimento associativo*. Rio de Janeiro: Vozes.

Park, R. E., E. Burgess, and R. McKenzie. 1925. *The City*. Chicago: University of Chicago Press.

Pratt, Mary Louise. 1992. *Imperial Eyes: Travel Writing and Transculturation*. New York: Routledge.

Santucci, Jane. 2008. *Cidade rebelde: As revoltas populares no Rio de Janeiro no início do século XX*. Rio de Janeiro: Casa da Palavra.

Schwartz, Lília Moritz. 1999. *The Spectacle of the Races: Scientists, Institutions, and the Race Question in Brazil, 1870–1930*. New York: Hill and Wang.

Simões, Soraya. 2002. "Vila Mimosa II: Um novo conceito de zona." Master's thesis, PPGA/ICHF-UFF.

Simões, Soraya. 2010a. "Identidade e política: A prostituição e o reconhecimento de um métier no Brasil." *Revista de antropologia social dos alunos do PPGAS-UFSCar* 2, no. 1: 24–46.

Simões, Soraya. 2010b. *Vila Mimosa: Etnografia da cidade cenográfica da prostituição carioca*. Niterói: EdUFF.

Souza Lima, Antonio Carlos de. 2008. "Traditions of Knowledge in Colonial Management of Inequality: Reflections on an Indigenist Administration Perspective in Brazil." *World Anthropologies Network*, no. 3 (April): 7–32.

Valladares, Licia do Prado. 1978. *Passa-se uma casa: Análise do programa de remoção de favelas do Rio de Janeiro*. Rio de Janeiro: Zahar.

Vaz, Lilian Fessler. 2002. *Modernidade e moradia: Habitações coletivas no Rio de Janeiro nos séculos XIX e XX*. Rio de Janeiro: 7 Letras.

Velho, Gilberto Cardoso Alves. 1973. *A utopia urbana: Um estudo de antropologia social*. Rio de Janeiro: Zahar.

Velho, Gilberto Cardoso Alves. 1994. "Unidade e fragmentação e sociedades complexas." In *Projeto e Metamorfose: Antropologia das sociedades complexas*. Rio de Janeiro: Zahar.

27

Puta Politics / Putapolítica

The Innovative Political Theories and Protest Praxis of Putas

LAURA REBECCA MURRAY

Sex worker activists in Brazil have redefined theories of politics and activism through their innovative and revolutionary practices for over three decades. In this chapter, I draw on my activist engagement and ethnographic research with the Brazilian prostitute movement to discuss puta politics, a concept inspired by the movement.[1] I use this term as an attempt to capture and translate the endless rhythms of Brazilian puta ativistas. The term *puta* could be directly translated into English as *whore*, but that would erase the other significations of it as a becoming (de Olivar 2013) and its positive connotation as an adjective. For example, a party could be called a "puta festa!" (bitchin' party). Inspired by this exclamatory energy of puta activism as a political force field, I focus my attention on how puta politics has operated in several protests in Rio de Janeiro, starting with a 1991 protest heavily critiqued by Gabriela Leite, the cofounder of the prostitute movement in Brazil, up to the International Women's Day March in 2020. I pay particular attention to how putas have mobilized their subjectivities, bodies, allies, and political know-how to draw attention to state abuses, societal stigmas, and injustices. My core argument is that puta politics has mobilized distinctive forms of subversive protest while also advancing political, feminist decolonial, and social movement theory in exciting ways, and thereby also deserves its own category in political thought.

"All rhythms, especially the innumerable." Gabriela Leite (1994) quoted this line from Manuel Bandeira's poem "Poética" in one of her first writings about politics published in *Beijo da rua* (Kiss from the street), the Brazilian Prostitute Network's newspaper founded in 1988. In her piece, she chronicles a protest organized by an NGO in response to US Navy officers being prohibited from visiting prostitutes at the Praça Mauá, a public square and adjacent neighborhoods near the port that served as a traditional area for prostitution in Rio de Janeiro. Few sex workers at the Praça Mauá joined the protest, telling *Beijo da rua* reporters that it did not matter if the Americans stopped at the Praça Mauá or not; they would simply go to Copacabana (a more upscale neighborhood with a small red-light district) and wait for them there.

In her column, Gabriela argued that the protest's format was inappropriate for the context. The protest was conceived and executed by the NGO rather than prostitutes who worked in the area. Gabriela implicated herself in the critique, saying that like many from her generation, she grew up thinking that exercising one's citizenship meant protesting in the streets. Yet, as she says, "these are not the only ways people have to confront adversity" (Leite 1994). Going after the clients in other parts of Rio is also a form of protest—a creative and pragmatic way to subvert a ridiculous regulation (and earn cash while doing so). Gabriela recognized this creativity and flexibility and ended the column with a call for the movement to harness more fluid and diverse forms of activism and to bet "on the diversity and cultural complexity of Brazil, or as Manuel Bandeira says, 'All rhythms, especially the innumerable.'"

Gabriela's column was titled "Putas Políticas" (Political whores), and her political philosophy combined with that of Lourdes Barreto, who cofounded the Brazilian Prostitute Network with Gabriela in 1987, to form the base of the puta politics concept presented in this chapter. Gabriela and Lourdes dedicated their lives (and in the case of Lourdes, continues to dedicate) to developing a unique kind of politics around prostitution. My own close interactions with Gabriela and Lourdes as a researcher, activist, filmmaker, and friend since 2005 have meant that I have had the privilege of being able to observe and learn from their political brilliance as I've watched them taking on and taking down diverse institutional structures and hierarchies time and time again.

Being and Doing Politics

Sex workers in Brazil say that they are in politics and are also doing politics. As Maria de Jesus Almeida da Costa, founder and leader of the Association of Sex Workers from São Luis de Maranhão (APROSMA), told me at the thirty-year anniversary meeting of the prostitute movement in 2017, "I am politics. Because I think that everyone is political, we go to the streets, we show our faces, we are mothers, we are women, girlfriends, everything . . . so we are politics." As Maria de Jesus emphasizes, politics forms a constitutive part of puta subjectivity, as does moving and negotiating a variety of subjectivities to form alliances with diverse institutional structures, allies, and conquest spaces.

Prostitution as a profession is one that relies on sex workers' abilities to negotiate with a variety of types of clients, with diverse political persuasions, temperaments, physical and mental needs, desires, and fantasies. As puta ativista Patricia Rosa reminded viewers in an online event in 2020, "doing politics is exactly that. It is talking, and putas do this. They talk to everyone, they open up to everyone, they get close to everyone, they kiss, have sex . . . and we know how to do that very well and together, we do it better" (Núcleo de Solidariedade 2020). This combination of professional and political know-how that comes from being a sex worker, and moving between political boundaries of their own and others, requires being especially attuned to contradiction and hypocrisy.

In fact, exposing contradiction is central to puta politics. Fast-forward twenty-nine years from the protest that opens this chapter to March 9, 2020, at the corner of the Avenida Rio Branco and Presidente Vargas in Rio de Janeiro, just a few blocks from the failed protest Gabriela described at the Praça Mauá. The International Women's Day March, that year, was held on Monday (rather than Sunday) to gain more visibility. I arrived at the march with my fourteen-month-old son and nineteen-year-old stepdaughter, and while the energy was upbeat and powerful, there was an underlying tension due to the constant attacks of bolsominions (supporters of Bolsonaro) on women's rights in general and women's rights activists in particular. The three of us were weaving through the crowd when all of a sudden Indianare Siqueira appeared—in a bright rainbow shirt covered in protest stickers and a gas mask. Indianare (see chapter 24, this volume) is a travesti puta ativista, founder of the revolutionary project and occupation CasaNem, and member of the organizing committee of the annual march.[2] She had fought hard to have prostitutes' rights recognized as a part of the platform of the Women's Day March, confronting many feminists who are vehemently against prostitution.

Indianare immediately took my hand and said, "You need to go to the children's wing." With her arm raised high in the air, she led us through the crowd in the contrafluxo (against traffic, against the grain). People opened up in front of us, eager to make room for Indianare and the mother she was pulling along. We made it to the wing that was protected by trans members of the CasaNem holding hands to form a circular barrier around us. We marched together, and a chorus of mothers, children, putas, and travestis shouted, "As gays, as trans, as bis e as sapatão, estão todas reunidas para fazer a revolução, com as putas!"[3]

CasaNem's role at the march was brilliant. As a human chain protecting families, they destroyed the far right's frequent discriminatory slander that often presents travestis as threats to, rather than protectors of, children. The symbolism was even more powerful due to a controversy just several days earlier involving a well-known doctor in Brazil and his embracing of a travesti in jail.[4]

It also reminded me of a time, four years earlier, when Indianare spoke at an event I organized at the Institute for Social Medicine at the State University of Rio de Janeiro (IMS/UERJ). A colleague's baby started to fuss in the middle of Indianare's talk, and as they got up to leave, Indianare stopped in midsentence and brilliantly defended why babies need to be accepted in academic and work spaces. She noted that the exclusion of babies means the exclusion and isolation of mothers and their ability to participate, which, as she emphasized, falls much more heavily on poor women of color. My colleague sat back down, and her son, as if he understood and appreciated Indianare's recognition, sat quietly for the rest of her talk.

Jacques Rancière (1999) has described such disruptions that break with "the established order" as one of the defining characteristics of politics. Puta politics is exactly this: CasaNem's presence at the Women's March and Indianare's defense of the baby at the academic talk disrupted established orders of activism and the academy. Indianare frequently criticizes the family as an oppressive structure in Brazil, yet she also sees the connections between her fight and that of mothers and children. She also frequently criticizes the transphobic and prostitute-shaming tendencies of some strands of feminism, yet considers herself a puta feminista.[5] This deeper understanding of connections—between sometimes feuding or sharply contrasting ideologies and subjectivities— fosters a sense of solidarity with others that in turn mobilizes body politics as a transversal component of all feminist fights. This is something many feminists frequently say, but that no group has so brilliantly harnessed and expressed, through their actions and politics, as putas.

Puta: Word, Becoming, and Politics

For Gabriela Leite, the word *puta* was an attitude toward life and politics. Her preference for the word is related to her disdain for political correctness and stems from her noticing a fundamental contradiction in its use as the common derogatory expression *filho da puta* (son of a whore). As she told me in a recorded interview (Um Beijo para Gabriela 2013), she thought it was completely unfair that the children of her colleagues—whom she considered to be amazing and dedicated mothers—represented one of the worst things you can be called in Portuguese. Gabriela believed that by reclaiming the word and building on the positive connotation it also carries as an adjective in Portuguese, the stigma around the word would start to disappear. Speaking out and gaining visibility is central to puta politics because, as Gabriela, Lourdes, and Brazilian sex worker authors (Prada 2018; Moira 2017) have strongly emphasized, putas' central and marginalized place in Brazilian gender and sex hierarchies depends on upholding their invisibility and silence.

Gabriela's embrace of the word *puta* also reflected her exhaustion with the sanitized world where contradictions lay hidden, relegated to the shadows with other inconvenient truths and populations. Through puta politics, the movement frequently exposed connections between seemingly contradictory parts rather than ignoring their differences while synthesizing them into one. Movement activists play on socially constructed contradictions that putas, through their experiences and subjectivities, understand to be profoundly connected and not contradictory at all. In fact, it is precisely the stigma surrounding prostitution that makes them appear as contradictions. Puta ativistas have tirelessly argued that using the word *puta* disrupts stigmatizing processes and forces people to see putas as mothers, protectors, feminists, and workers while also defending prostitution within a framework of sexual rights. In this way, puta politics is multiple and simultaneously disobedient, conforming, challenging, and destabilizing.

Putas wield a kind of "fugitive power" that is seen "not as an eternal essential characteristic, but as a field of power" (de Olivar 2013, 313). Like Félix Guattari's idea of "becoming-woman" (Deleuze and Guattari 1987, 242), de Olivar's "devir-puta" (becoming-whore) describes a force that rejects categorization and subverts labor, gender, and sexuality norms. The puta is in this sense also a great strategist, since "there is an important power in the clear capacity to alternate between a deep silence and constraining noise" (313); becoming-whore is essentially a grammar that makes political, affective, and sexual alliances possible. This fluid and transgressive nature creates a force field that goes beyond the sexual and is inherently political.

Indeed, the prostitute movement in Brazil harnessed power into a way of doing politics that intentionally and proudly breaks with normative paradigms of sexuality and activism. In this way, puta politics must also be placed in the genealogy of Latin American decolonial feminist thought and praxis. In particular, I see important connections with work that questions the politics of purity and separation and that explores the unclassifiable and unmanageable nature of mestizaje/mestiçagem (mixed race) as a fundamental source of resistance (Lugones 1994, 460). To resist logics of control, Maria Lugones recommends "festive resistance" through blurring, mixing, renaming, and "caricaturing the selves we are in the worlds of our oppressor, infusing them with ambiguity" (1994, 478).

Ambiguity is of particular importance to the concept of puta politics, as it is central to sex workers' ability to move between diverse subjectivities in their interactions with state and parastate actors and to respond to the country's ability to "assert sexual rights while reigning in police militarism under the framework of a mix of humanitarian legalism and worker empowerment" (Amar 2013, 199). As described by my coauthors and me in this volume (see chapter 26), the design of Brazil's administrative and legal systems allows it to operate simultaneously along informal and formal channels. This requires people to adopt flexibility and agility to move between conflicting and often even contradictory regulations and laws. These fractured bureaucratic fields are best described as fertile ground for what Sherry Ortner (1996) refers to as "serious games." The theoretical category was developed to move beyond binaries and more effectively incorporate an analysis of power, struggle, and gender into understandings of social life. As Ortner states, social life consists of "webs of relationships and interaction between multiple, shifting interrelated subject positions, none of which can be extracted as autonomous 'agents'; and yet at the same time there is 'agency'— that is, actors play with skill, intention, wit, knowledge, intelligence" (1996, 12).

Throughout my ethnographic and activist work, I constantly observed how prostitute activists acted with a profound understanding of how to play these serious games. Lourdes succinctly and brilliantly summarized their political strategy for me at a 2017 HIV/AIDS-related workshop in João Pessoa, Paraíba. At the time, Lourdes was worried that a harsh letter sent by the Brazilian Prostitute Network to the Ministry of Health might jeopardize future funding. Shaking her arm that had been recently tattooed—with the words *Eu sou Puta*

(I'm a whore)—toward me, Lourdes said, "You need to learn that doing politics is about knowing how to hit without hurting."[6]

Lourdes's brilliance at negotiating with and mobilizing a variety of actors to support prostitute rights is notorious in Brazil. Her work dates back to the 1970s, when she fought against extreme police violence in Belém's red-light district during the country's dictatorship. The prostitute movement's founding coincided with the redemocratization process in the 1980s. From the beginning, prostitutes—led by Gabriela and Lourdes—held a protagonist's role in the development of the National HIV/AIDS Program. While the movement's activism was first in response to egregious police violence (still ongoing), the HIV epidemic and sex workers' strong reaction against being cast as vectors and victims inspired them to keep pleasure and sex at the center (Murray, Kerrigan, and Paiva 2018).

This was not always easy, as prostitutes always fought for, and were not given, this kind of approach. In, for example, a 1989 *Beijo da rua* article about an event called AIDS and Prostitution organized by the Institute for Studies on Religion, *Beijo da rua* editor Flavio Lenz quotes Gabriela talking about how she rebelled against an agenda that had been organized to feature doctors and specialists: "I felt that people were distant from everything and that the doctors were, of course, involved in a debate with themselves. So, the next morning, I came back in a low cut black dress, high heels, exaggerated make-up, and I talked about my life" (Lenz 1990, 4). Gabriela's intervention illustrates the movement's approach to refusing victimization and bringing sexuality back to the center of the conversation. Rather than adjusting her appearance to be more appropriate and consistent with the doctors' perspectives, Gabriela broke protocol and demanded to be heard. Indeed, she hit without hurting, and it worked.

Daspu, Catwalk Protests

Daspu is perhaps the best example of this provocative and powerful form of politics. Founded in 2005, Daspu (Of the whores) is a clothing line conceived of at a bar table in a "climate of happiness and celebration" (Lenz 2008, 58). The initiative would later grow into a national and international media phenomenon. Passarellas-passeatas (Daspu director Elaine Bortolanza's term meaning *catwalk protests*) have occurred in a variety of spaces ranging from red-light districts to conference stages, museums, occupations, nightclubs, and samba schools (Bortolanza 2011). Collections were first designed by professionals in partnership with sex workers and played on cultural symbols of sex and prostitution. T-shirts with phrases such as "We're bad but we could be worse" and "The profession is the world's oldest prostitution" sell quickly and are always in high demand. As Davida's organizational structure changed over the years, Daspu came to incorporate more aspects of performance focused on models and messages rather than a more traditional idea of a clothing collection or a catwalk.[7] By mixing prostitutes and nonprostitutes together, the catwalk creates a space of safety, ambiguity, and obfuscation that also led many sex workers—who might have not been ready otherwise—to openly come forward and participate.

One particularly memorable November 2015 fashion show took place at the Institute of Philosophy and Social Sciences (IFCS in Portuguese) at the Federal University of Rio de Janeiro (UFRJ, just a few blocks from both protests mentioned thus far). The fashion show was the closing event to a week-long course organized by Prostitution Policy Watch on the history of the sex worker movement. And although we barely even had enough money to print the course's program, the head of extension projects at the UFRJ was so enthusiastic about the course and the fashion show that she worked hard to ensure the necessary infrastructure was available for the event. The night before the performance, a professional sound system and stage were installed, and bright purple and red lighting transformed the front of the IFCS into a puteiro, of which Lourdes Barreto played the madame. A performance ensued with cis and trans sex workers, UFRJ students, activists, and academics. At the end, when the Daspu official music would typically come on and all of the models would come back to the stage to dance, the professional DJ system went out. The music would not play. Only the microphones worked. Indianare and Betania Santos, a Black puta ativista from Campinas, immediately grabbed the microphones and closed the fashion show with powerful words about prostitute rights and the importance of putas in resisting the increasingly strong, reactionary, and violent political right.

In writing about it here, I am reminded of a recent post by Indianare in which she states that "brothels are schools of insubordination for those who are willing to learn an orgasmic and ecstatic freedom." Through its bright lights and performance, the fashion show transformed the IFCS into an example of insubordination and resistance. Indianare also points to an important issue: to learn from putas, one must be disposte.[8]

I want to end with an email that I received from Gabriela in 2012 that lays out many of the primary pillars of puta politics and touches on something that is frequently misunderstood about prostitute activism:

> I always thought about innovating the way to do politics. I always thought about a light militancy, with irony. Denouncing, but with happiness. The

results of these thoughts were the more informal national encounters, meetings in bars, serenades. . . . It was also always very difficult to take these cheerful ideas forward because the majority of people, brought up politically within a rhetoric and way of doing politics with protests, meetings with points of order, discourses in defense of democracy but with attitudes that weren't always democratic etc., etc., always seemed strange to others and they didn't understand that what we were doing was politics. (Gabriela Leite, email to author, October 2012)

Indeed, as Gabriela notes, unfortunately not everyone is disposte to understand. Puta politics disrupts the hierarchies and divisions between institutional structures and the street through its use of irony and informality. It engages culture as a site of contention and advocates for sex worker rights from a place of pleasure, rather than as victims or vectors of disease. The playful and provocative nature of the movement's politics does not mean it is not serious or extremely aware of what is at stake. As both Lugones and Ortner also emphasize, these qualities are actually part of the game and necessary to changing racist and sexist societies with deep roots of inequality embedded in colonial structures.

Political activity "makes visible what had no business being seen, and makes heard a discourse where once there was only place for noise" (Rancière 1999, 30). Encounters with the state require decades of hitting without hurting—as was accomplished by Gabriela in 1989, Indianare at the 2020 Women's March, and Lourdes when getting her tattoo at the AIDS conference. These strategies expose hypocrisies and discriminatory subtexts in spaces that are supposed to be in partnership with sex workers but that often replicate hierarchies and prejudices. In these spaces, puta politics makes speech heard—like Gabriela did when dressing up in a low-cut dress and lipstick. And just like the Daspu fashion show described above, when the music ends, the discourses for radical changes come through loud and clear.

NOTES

The research presented in this chapter is drawn from my PhD project in medical anthropology at Columbia University (fieldwork conducted 2011–24), postdoctoral project at the Institute of Social Medicine/State University of Rio de Janeiro (IMS/UERJ, 2016–18), and activism in Brazil (2005–present) as part of the NGO Davida (which became the Coletivo Puta Davida in 2020), Brazilian Prostitute Network (Rede Brasileira de Prostitutas), and Prostitute Policy Watch (Observatório da Prostituição) at the Federal University of Rio de Janeiro.

1 I use the words *prostitute, prostitution, sex workers,* and *sex work* throughout the text. All these terms are used in Brazil, yet the activists who inspire the concept discussed in this chapter overwhelmingly prefer *prostitute,* or *puta* in Portuguese. As further discussed here, they have reclaimed the terms as part of their political strategies to fight the stigma surrounding prostitution.

2 Travesti is a gender identity in Brazil that refers to someone who identifies with the female gender but does not identify as a woman nor seek to change their genitalia. The term, previously highly stigmatized, has been resignified by the trans movement and because of this also has a strong political connotation.

3 "The gays, the trans, the bis, and the dykes are all united to start a revolution, with putas!"

4 The controversy occurred when Dr. Drauzio Varella appeared on the *Globo* program *Fantástico* in a segment about prisons and stated that, as a doctor, he cared for everyone equally, regardless of their crime. The day after the program aired, Bolsonaro's supporters discovered that the travesti featured was in jail for murdering a child and spread this widely on social media in messages laced with homophobia and transphobia common in the extensive and inflammatory moral panics spread by bolsominions.

5 There is much more to say about prostitution and feminism more broadly than is possible in this short text. I refer readers to a series of important works written by sex workers, such as Juno Mac and Molly Smith's (2018) *Revolting Prostitutes* and, in Brazil, *Putafeminismo* (Puta feminism) by Monique Prada (2018), that highlight how issues central to sex worker rights activism are at the core of feminist debates.

6 Lourdes tattooed her arm when she was seventy-one years old at a Brazilian AIDS conference in a powerful act of resistance, blurring and countering a series of prejudices about age, sexuality, and prostitution.

7 Davida, like many NGOs focused on sexuality and HIV/AIDS in Brazil, saw its funding and support for its activities drastically reduced from 2008 forward. We have been without an office space and have had intermittent, small project-based funding since 2010. These setbacks and structural changes in state support for sex worker rights were a large part of my dissertation research.

8 Gender-neutral word for *willing.*

REFERENCES

Amar, Paul. 2013. *The Security Archipelago: Human-Security States, Sexuality Politics and the End of Neoliberalism.* Durham, NC: Duke University Press.

Bortolanza, Elaine. 2011. "Daspu: Zonas de passagem." In *Moda em ziguezague: Interfaces e expansoes,* edited by Cristiana Mesquita and Rosane Preciosa. Sao Paulo: Estacao das Letras e Cores.

Deleuze, Gilles, and Félix Guattari. 1987. *A Thousand Plateaus: Capitalism and Schizophrenia.* Minneapolis: University of Minnesota Press.

de Olivar, Jose Miguel. 2013. *Devir puta: Políticas de prostituição de rua na experiência de quatro mulheres militantes.* Rio de Janeiro: Ed. UERJ.

Leite, Gabriela. 1994. "Coluna da Gabi: Putas políticas." *Beijo da rua*, no. 4 (May): 2.

Lenz, Flavio. 1990. "As Rosas já Falam: Prostitutas e travestis decidem como trabalhar com Aids e prostituição." *Beijo da rua*, no. 4: 4.

Lenz, Flavio. 2008. *Daspu: Moda sem vergonha*. Rio de Janeiro: Objetivo.

Lugones, Maria. 1994. "Purity, Impurity and Separation." *Signs* 19, no. 2: 458–79.

Mac, Juno, and Molly Smith. 2018. *Revolting Prostitutes*. London: Verso.

Moira, Amara. 2017. *E se eu fosse puta*. São Paulo: Hoo.

Murray, Laura Rebecca, Deanna Kerrigan, and Vera Paiva. 2018. "Rites of Resistance: Sex Workers' Fight to Maintain Rights and Pleasure in the Centre of the Response to HIV in Brazil." *Global Public Health* 14, no. 6–7: 939–53.

Núcleo de Solidariedade Técnica/UFRJ. 2020. "Putas, Profissionais do Sexo, Trabalhadoras Sexuais: O que revindicam? Por que lutam? Com Soraya Silveira Simões, Lourdes Barreto and Patricia Rosa." Online conference, August 13. Accessed April 4, 2024. https://www.facebook.com/soltec.ufrj/videos/2739856589626828/.

Ortner, Sherry B. 1996. *Making Gender: The Politics and Erotics of Culture*. Boston: Beacon.

Prada, Monique. 2018. *Putafeminismo*. São Paulo: Veneta.

Rancière, Jacques. 1999. *Disagreement: Politics and Philosophy*. Minneapolis: University of Minnesota Press.

Um Beijo para Gabriela. 2013. "Porque Gabriela gosta da palavra puta / Why Gabriela Prefers the Word Puta (Whore)." YouTube video, June 12. https://www.youtube.com/watch?v=CvKkGPiXvoo.

28

Heartbreaking Lyrical Ontology /
Ontologia Lírica Comovente

*Aldir Blanc and Popular Music as Guides to
Carioca Modes of Being in the World*

BRYAN MCCANN, VICTORIA BROADUS, AND
JOÃO GABRIEL RABELLO SODRÉ

Aldir Blanc died of COVID-19 on May 4, 2020, at the age of seventy-three during the pandemic that ravaged Brazil and the world (Sukman 2020). Blanc left
behind a singular body of work, one that deeply shaped Brazilian popular music
and also serves as a guide to Carioca modes of being in the world. Blanc was
one of Brazil's greatest lyricists and cowriter of hundreds of popular songs as
well as short stories. Most of this work is about Rio de Janeiro, and even when
it is not, it tends to embody a Carioca spirit—florid, earthy, subversive, and
suffused with love for the gritty, obstreperous, and heartbreaking moments of
everyday city life. The Aldir Blanc style, or Blanquian approach, was well bal-
anced, disdainful of categorical imperatives, and off-kilter. The Blanquian approach draws our attention to startling juxtapositions. This chapter synthesizes
key themes in Blanc's work and interprets them as a method for engaging with

life in the contemporary global city—themes like resistance against abuses of power, rejections of overweening authority, refraining from snitching, being a flaneur, knowing yourself, cultivating a fine appreciation of the vulgar without eschewing the refined, and celebrating the sensual and absurd. The principles of the Blanquian method are flexible but coherent.

Aldir Blanc leaves an extraordinary legacy as one of Brazil's greatest popular musical lyricists and a prolific author of semifictional crônicas, or chronicles of everyday life in his native Rio. Blanc's influence in his lifetime was profound: together with his first major collaborator, João Bosco, he made a decisive contribution to the soundtrack for redemocratization. Their songs helped inspire popular mobilization against the military dictatorship of the 1970s and shaped aspirations for the pluralistic democracy that ensued. They called attention to abuses of power and evoked visions of a better Brazil, one that dreams of social justice and celebrates the sensual, raffish, and unpretentious.

But while Blanc's work is often overtly political, he avoids sloganeering and shuns dogma. In the samba "Plataforma," he warns,

Don't bring slogans or pennants
we don't need anyone
to organize our Carnival.
I'm not a candidate for anything,
my business is the middle of the night.[1]

Instead, he advocates a samba "que balance e abagunce"—that shakes things up and makes a mess. Lyrics to many Blanc songs include compendiums of disparate elements thrown together, apparently willy-nilly. "Linha de Passe" (Passing route), for example, begins, "armadillo's burrow, sausage and salami and a zebu bull / oxtail soup with manioc meal, skirt-chaser."[2] These agglomerations may be aleatory but not accidental. Blanc is telling us something. In fact, he is telling us three things. First, that Brazil is chaotic, but the chaos has meaning, a cultural DNA with identifiable sequences. Afro-Brazilians inherit the local color of Carioca folkways, spliced and recombined in endless variations with cosmopolitan points of reference. Second, the music of the language is part of its message: *toca de tatu* (armadillo's burrow) may have various referential valences, such as the famed Buraco de Tatu, or Armadillo's Hole, which is a quilombo, or settlement of runaway slaves in colonial Brazil. Third, the play between meaning and music is part of what Blanc identifies as the "toma-lá-dá-cá do samba," or give-and-take of samba—its collective, improvisatory nature.

In doing so, he points us toward a heartbreaking lyrical ontology: a way of engaging Brazil, and more specifically Rio de Janeiro, the city he captured with unsurpassed insight and grace. Blanc's work rejects exploitation and abuse of power while tolerating contradiction and disorder. He celebrated the earthy and the marginal without rejecting the erudite and the elegant. Know your own weaknesses without expecting to outgrow them. Value solidarity without expecting deference and find both humor and tragedy in the humble dramas of life in the city. Following Aldir Blanc through the streets of the city can tell us how to live in Rio and about how Rio lives in the bodies and dreams of its inhabitants. The city speaks through Blanc's work. In transcribing it, he teaches us how to follow.

Knowledge from the Botequim

Aldir Blanc Mendes was born on September 2, 1946, in the neighborhood of Estácio, in Rio's Central Zone, an area vital to the emergence of samba. Blanc's upbringing was marked by a mother with postpartum depression and a father who, his civil service job notwithstanding, was fond of horse racing and billiards. These emotional and financial constraints led Blanc to be effectively raised by his maternal grandparents in Vila Isabel, a neighborhood in Rio's North Zone. Vila Isabel was well known in Brazil's popular musical circles as the home of the late Noel Rosa (1910–37), one of the first white samba composers to collaborate with favela musicians, several of whom hailed from nearby favelas (Macacos and Salgueiro). Blanc inherited Rosa's mantle as an acerbic observer of the Carioca lower-middle and working class. His lyrics and short stories reflect his experiences in a side of the city perceived as garish and provincial, and in contrast to the cosmopolitan image of the oceanfront South Zone neighborhoods of Copacabana and Ipanema. Blanc's work reveals a suburbano perspective permeated by contrasts, bohemian life, flaneurs, humor, eroticism, and resistance (de Souza 2003, 33–38; McCann 2004, 47–48; 2014, 96; Vianna 2013, 15–26; Caldeira 2007).

In his twenties, Blanc attended medical school while also participating in the Movimento Artístico Universitário, a group of young artists that regularly met in the North Zone's Maracanã neighborhood (Vianna 2013, 28–43). In 1970, Blanc coauthored his first nationwide hit, "Amigo é pra essas coisas," with composer Sílvio da Silva. The lyrics present both sides of a conversation between two friends—one who laments the misfortune of his recent breakup, the other who seeks to console him with a series of platitudes. The characters sit in a botequim, a traditional Carioca neighborhood bar, where they call for rounds of draft beer and reminisce. Aldir said when he first heard the melody, he imagined a dialogue. The lyrics serve as an early example of "Blanc's ability to create a story suggested by the melody" (Vianna 2013, 40).

So sentar um pouco?
Faça o favor
A vida é um dilemma
Nem sempre vale a pena
Pô, o que é que há?
Rosa acabou comigo
Meu Deus, por quê?
Nem Deus sabe o motive
Deus é bom
Mas não foi bom pra mim
Todo amor um dia chega ao fim
Triste
É sempre assim
Eu desejava um trago
Garçom, mais dois
Não sei quando eu lhe pago
Se vê depois.[3]

The unpretentious setting, the keen observations of local color and dialogue, and the empathy with humble figures would all become signatures of his work.

It should come as no surprise that Blanc's medical specialization was psychiatry. He graduated in 1971 and began a medical residency in a psychiatric hospital in Engenho de Dentro, another working-class neighborhood in Rio's North Zone. Several observers have drawn the connection between Blanc's training in psychiatry and his incisive lyrics. For his part, the poet inverted the analysis: "It wasn't psychiatry that opened the mind of the lyricist. Maybe I was a good psychiatrist at the time because I was already a musician, a percussionist, and a lyricist" (Carvalho, Sampaio, and de Morais 2004). In any event, Blanc also met João Bosco in the early 1970s. Bosco, a talented guitarist and composer from Minas Gerais, had an innovative approach to samba rhythm on guitar and proved a perfect match for the lyricist. As his musical career began to take off and his frustrations with the restrictions of the psychiatric profession grew, Blanc abandoned the latter to concentrate on the former.

Resistance and Solidarity

In an interview with the cartoonist Lan (quoted in Moura 2001), Aldir said his work was 90 percent chronicles of daily life and love, and the remaining 10 percent were protest songs (músicas engajadas). This is not strictly true, as subtle forms of everyday resistance are woven throughout his repertoire. (Or as he put it, "everything I do is against any type of totalitarianism.")[4] But the most penetrating political songs—the 10 percent he referred to—date from the long military dictatorship and from his partnership with João Bosco. Blanc observed, "I am enormously proud of those songs . . . for what they represented in the era. And I am proud of having participated in the process. The popular composer is a kind of spokesperson. It is a cliché, but he is the voice for the voiceless" (Moura 2001, 9).

Blanc wrote Brazil's voiceless into his songs and, in turn, into Brazil's popular memory.

> Glory
> to all the inglorious struggles
> that over the course of our history
> we'll never forget

goes the famous chorus of "O mestre-sala dos mares." The song is a tribute to João Cândido, leader of the 1910 Revolta da Chibata. The Revolt of the Lash was a rebellion by enlisted sailors against the practice of corporal punishment in Brazil's navy, when white officers commonly whipped Black sailors in a practice inherited directly from the brutal tradition of slavery. Having only been abolished in 1888, this draconian anti-Blackness was well within the memory of João Cândido and his coconspirators. The revolt continues to serve as a stark example of Brazil's deep racial inequalities and leaders' attempts to deny them.

Blanc and Bosco struggled to get the song approved by the censors (Carvalho, Sampaio, and de Morais 2004). The military regime promoted the illusion of a racially harmonious nation, and any suggestion to the contrary was simply banned. Blanc revised a few phrases and changed the name of the song from "Almirante negro" (Black admiral) to "O mestre-sala dos mares" (Standard bearer of the seas).[5] The new title refers to the dignified mestre-sala who, along with the female porta-bandeira, leads a samba school's Carnival parade—an image that unites samba, dignity, and Black resistance. With those changes, censors cleared the song, and it became an anthem of popular mobilization against authoritarianism. Its claims for racial justice are equally relevant today, decades after the end of the dictatorship.[6]

Four years later, "O bêbado e a equilibrista" (1979) became even more influential in the push toward redemocratization. The samba had begun as a fairly straightforward homage to Charlie Chaplin, who died in late 1977. Bosco wrote the music over the melody for "Smile," Chaplin's instrumental theme from *Modern Times* (1936). He showed the song to Blanc, who had heard from his friends, Henfil and Chico Mário, about their mano in exile.[7] Blanc suggested to Bosco that they make the song about a Chaplin-like character, longing for those who had been forced into exile by the military regime. It was a brilliant combination. The opening line immediately set the scene in Rio's North Zone, in the context of the depredations of the military regime: "Afternoon was falling like a viaduct."[8]

In November 1974, an elevated highway, under construction since 1969, collapsed on the corner near where Aldir had lived as a teenager, killing twenty-nine people. The tragedy exemplified the regime's disregard for human lives, especially those of poor Brazilians. The regime cut corners, accepted kickbacks, and neglected the safety of infrastructural projects. The lyrics describe a drunk who reminds the narrator of Chaplin, dressed in black and mourning for those in exile. But this lament is leavened by dreams of "the return of Henfil's brother / along with so many people who took off like a rocket's tail."[9] As in Chaplin's movies, the spirit of popular resistance prevails: "hope dances on the tightrope with a parasol."[10] The song, in Elis Regina's transcendent rendition, provided release for an emotionally exhausted nation after fifteen years of authoritarian rule.

"O mestre-sala dos mares" and "O bêbado e a equilibrista" put Blanc and Bosco in the vanguard of redemocratization. More subtly, they expressed a tolerant humanism, sensitive to the hard-earned pleasures of everyday life. Though a crucial step toward addressing these concerns, redemocratization could not in itself resolve any of them. Blanc continued to denounce abuse of power and authority well after this moment:

> The law is a cudgel against those who have nothing,
> but for those who have all the money,
> law is a permissive stepmother,
> giving out banana with marmalade.[11]

He wrote those words in "Muambeiro," a collaboration with the composer Guinga. Blanc rejected overweening authority, a sensibility he said was distinctly Carioca. When Lan asked him if he considered Rio the cultural center of the country, he responded yes, largely due to the Carioca's aversion to gurus: "[Guru] is a word I hate, and there is no excrement from the end of the millennium worse than the guru" (Moura 2001, 8). Blanc advocated a streetwise Carioca sensibility skeptical of all claims to authority based on credentials, lineage, wealth, or bluster.

Solidarity and the Botequim

While Blanc lampooned vain authorities, he celebrated the embodied, relational knowledge of the streets and the botequims. His collaboration with composer Maurício Tapajós offers one of the clearest examples. Blanc joined Tapajós in a struggle to enforce copyright laws and demand transparency in royalty payments for composers and musicians. When Tapajós died of a heart attack in 1995, Blanc was bereft. Reflecting on their shared political commitment several years later, he remarked, "Maurício was the one who was my closest companion in the sense of having a politics of doing anything to avoid reneging on a commitment. . . . I will never belong to anything that could have offended Maurício" (Carvalho, Sampaio, and de Morais 2004). The comments suggest that, for Blanc, the foundations of unswerving commitment were not necessarily shared political goals, which were transitory, but something deeper—trust, admiration, friendship, and, in a word, solidarity.

For Blanc, the botequims of Rio's North Zone were the natural locus for that kind of solidarity. "My heart holds filthy botequims" is the opening line of "Bandalhismo," another Blanc and Bosco composition.[12] They continue to revere the botequim in "Mãos de Aventureiro," where the narrator feels that "the call of the samba and the botequim" becomes more powerful than any aspiration to domestic tranquility.[13] Affection for the botequim runs through Blanc's work, from his earliest hit, "Amigo é pra essas coisas," to one of his later works, "Saíndo a francesa." The latter is a collaboration with Moacyr Luz, written in memory of Maurício Tapajós. In its verses, Blanc refuses to believe the news of Tapajós's death, and insists,

> Me encontra com o riso de sempre no bar
> A gente vai ter muito o que conversar
> . . .
> E discutir a importância da velha amizade
> Redimensionar a palavra "saudade":
> é nela que tudo que amei sobrevive!

This translates as "You'll find me in the bar, with the same laugh as always. We'll have lots to talk about . . . discussing the importance of enduring friendship, adding new dimensions to the word *saudade*, for it is in this that everything I have loved survives." It is only fitting that this late work brings Blanc full circle and makes explicit his long-running exploration of the connections between solidarity, saudade, and the botequim. The song's title refers to a "French exit," or leaving without saying goodbye. In mourning Tapajós's sudden death, it foreshadows Blanc's own sudden fade two weeks after falling ill with COVID-19.

From Lyrics to Crônicas

Such concerns run through Blanc's crônicas, as well as his lyrics. Indeed, Blanc noted that the crônicas and lyrics were so intertwined that they were "mixed together inseparably" (Hoepers 2017). But in the crônicas, Blanc had more space to explore the city as a microcosm of Brazilian society. In the short story "Uma entrevista bomba," the narrator pretends to be a building manager in the neighborhood of Grajaú (Rio's North Side; Blanc 1996, 97–99). In the Carioca imaginary, the area is known as a housing spot for military officers. Instigated by controversies surrounding repression in the 1964–85 military dictatorship, the undercover character interviews retired colonel Uraí Ariranha, who had just published his "neo-memoir," *Não matei mas chutei o saco*. The tragicomic dialogue with the colonel reveals the persistence of an alternative history of the post-1985 regime:

NARRATOR: I would like to . . .
COLONEL: I am the one who speaks here. I hate authoritarianism. I don't admit being treated like a common criminal. It was a war. We applied the death penalty and shot the enemy. . . .
NARRATOR: Any regrets, colonel?
COLONEL: I can't regret what has not happened.
NARRATOR: A sex symbol?
COLONEL: Pinochet. (Blanc 1996, 99)

Blanc's choice of an Indigenous name for Colonel Uraí Ariranha seems to represent a twofold critique: first, of the persistent official ideology of colorblindness. Second, the words speak to the authoritarian regime's aggressive and superficial nativism, as seen in the Indigenous names of military airplanes produced by the then-state-owned Embraer in the 1970s. As for its context, the short story reflects the public debate of the 1990s. While a new democratic regime was consolidating, a portion of the population's antidemocratic desires persisted. The piece exemplifies Blanc's style of social commentary.

In another short story, the Indigenous sign appears in another position. In "Porque me abandonaste," the narrator-author encounters his father, Araripe, who has been fatally shot, and whose deceased body lies stretched out on a brass table (Blanc 1996, 226). This macabre treatment is intercalated with a biting reference to a Neo-Pentecostal church (deliberately restricted to lower-case treatment), which condemns art as worse than crime: "Staring at him, on the dirty brass table, I heard bells, music, many. . . . I thought flowers would come out of the ears of a corpse, laughter from the mouth. And more music from the hole in the head. From early life, only blood could testify, running down from his eyes. I would like to be a musician, but the universal church pastor yelled that more dangerous than an armed criminal, is only an idiot with a guitar in his hands." The story presents a snapshot of Rio's racial and social inequalities in the 1990s (which still endure). Blanc's piece was set in the context of a growing Americanization of Brazil and adherence to neoliberal reforms by Fernando Henrique Cardoso. It is a story about cyclical aspects of violence and abandonment.[14]

Simple and Absurd

Aldir spent the last few decades of his life in his apartment in the Muda neighborhood. But he said that as far as he was concerned, he still lived in Vila Isabel: "The street I live on now, in Muda, is a piece of Vila Isabel. I believe that. I believe it because it's absurd" (Blanc 1996, 24). Faith in the absurd permeates Aldir's lyrics. Doubt, disorder, ambiguity, and contradiction are accepted as the driving forces of daily life. The title of the album *Simples e absurdo* (Simple and absurd), a collaboration between Blanc and the composer and performer Guinga, neatly expresses Blanc's predilection for combining the everyday with the arcane in unexpected ways. Blanc's exploration of dichotomies reaches its height with "Catavento e Girassol" (Pinwheel and sunflower). This tempestuous, opposites-attract story is also a metaphorical exploration of a divided city. The narrator is a gato do subúrbio, or cat from the suburbs (Engenho de Dentro), while his love interest is a litorânea who "lives in the breeze of Arpoador" (a subsection of posh Ipanema). The narrator goes to humble, suburban Cacique de Ramos for Carnaval, while his lover goes to the expensive beach resort in the restored colonial village of Paraty (Vianna 2013, 76). These Carioca opposites anchor the song as it whirls through universal contradictions: one is a pensive worrier, the other spontaneous; one laid-back and withdrawn, the other flashy and expansive. Yet in a destruction of dichotomies typical of Aldir's work, the suburbano singer sees himself, in his inverse, in the litorânea. "I am you, who vanishes down the mirror's drain, suggests the narrator."[15] Like the North and South Zones of the city they represent, the unnamed characters cannot get along or leave each other behind. They create each other through their interdependence, establishing self-definitions through opposition.

Blanc leaves us a method for understanding Rio, and in so doing an understanding of Rio as method. Carioca humanism of the Blanquian school requires tolerance, acceptance of disorder and contradiction, empathy, solidarity, and the troublesome condolence of nostalgia. As a poet haunted by the city, Blanc was aware that epidemics are cyclical in Rio. The 1918–19 Spanish flu hit Rio hard. Yellow fever and cholera ravaged the city repeatedly in the nineteenth and early twentieth centuries, dengue and Zika in the twentieth and twenty-first. Chikungunya, Chagas, variola—the names would fit perfectly in a Blanc compendium. "Ah, to begin again, to begin again like songs and epidemics," Blanc put it in "Caça a raposa."[16] Blanc knew that Rio was capable of rebirth but would never be free of its freighted and unequal past.

Brazil was devastated by COVID-19 in 2020–21, and Rio in particular. It hit favelas and dense North Zone communities particularly hard, with the same kinds of racial and class disparities seen elsewhere. It ravaged the city Blanc loved and illuminated for us. The vaccine arrived too late for Blanc. Unceremonious to the end, he had already made his French exit, and left without saying goodbye. But, as always, he has left us directions. In "Pra quem quiser me visitar," a collaboration with Guinga, he tells us where to find him: "To my friends who stayed behind, a messenger will bring a pair of wings and a parachute to whomever wants to visit me."[17]

NOTES

1   Não traz lema nem divisa / que a gente não precisa / que organizem nosso carnaval / não sou candidato a nada / meu negócio é madrugada.
2   Toca de tatu, linguiça e paio e boi zebu / Rabada com angu, rabo-de-saia.
3   May I sit for a little bit? / Please do / Life is a dilemma / It is not always worth it / Oh, what is happening? / Rosa broke up with me. / God, why? / Not even God knows why / God is good / But he was not good to me. / Every love comes to an end / Sad / It is always like that / I wanted to smoke / Waiter, two more / I don't know when I will pay you / We'll see about it later.
4   Tudo o que faço está engajado contra qualquer tipo de totalitarismo.
5   In fact, two previous versions had been rejected by the censors, the first titled "Almirante negro" and the second "O dragão do mar."
6   The equally critical "O rancho da Goiabada" (1976) similarly paired uplifting music with biting lyrics, becoming part of the mobilization for redemocratization. Another Blanc-Bosco anthem of resistance from the same year, "Ronco da Cuíca," was rejected by censors. It was also banned from radio, TV, and live shows.
7   Henfil was the political cartoonist Henrique de Souza Filho. Aldir said at the time he didn't realize the mano was the leading sociologist Herbert "Betinho" de Souza.
8   Caía a tarde feito um viaduto.
9   A volta do irmão do Henfil / com tanta gente que partiu / ao rabo de foguete.

10 A esperança dança na corda bamba de sombrinha.

11 A lei é pau em quem não tem nada / mas pra quem solta a grana / a Lei é a mãe-joana / dando banana com marmelada.

12 Meu coração tem botequins imundos.

13 O chamado do samba e do botequim.

14 Blanc's crônica supports Amar's (2013, 139–71) analysis of the "infra-nationalism" of 1990s Brazil, characterized by elitist and occasionally militaristic interventions in working-class and Afro-Brazilian neighborhoods, superficially softened by humanistic and technocratic discourse to win the support (or at least acceptance) of some sectors of the left.

15 "Eu sou você que se vai no sumidouro de espelho" would literally translate to "I am you who goes down the mirror's drain."

16 Ah, recomeçar, recomeçar, como canções e epidemias.

17 Aos meus amigos que ficaram / um portador há de levar / um par de asas, e um paraquedas / pra quem quiser me visitor.

REFERENCES

Amar, Paul. 2013. *The Security Archipelago: Human-Security States, Sexuality Politics, and the End of Neoliberalism*. Durham, NC: Duke University Press.

Blanc, Aldir. 1996. *Um cara bacana na 19a: Contos, crônicas e poemas*. Rio de Janeiro: Editora Record.

Caldeira, Jorge. 2007. *A construção do samba*. São Paulo: Mameluco.

Carvalho, Alexandre Ribeiro, Andre Sampaio, and José de Morais, dirs. 2004. "Aldir Blanc—Dois prá lá, dois pra cá." Inventarte, TVE (Rede Brasil), TV Cultura de São Paulo. YouTube video, posted by Mídia NINJA, 2020. https://www.youtube.com /watch?v=BoCGEpcsNQg.

de Souza, Tárik. 2003. *Tem mais samba: Das raízes à eletrônica*. Coleção todos os cantos. São Paulo: Editora 34.

Hoepers, Kathleen. 2017. "Aldir Blanc: 'Resistimos porque do contrário morreríamos.'" Catraca Livre, August 8. https://catracalivre.com.br/samba-em-rede/aldir-blanc -resistimos-porque-do-contrario-morreriamos/.

McCann, Bryan. 2004. *Hello, Hello Brazil: Popular Music in the Making of Modern Brazil*. Durham, NC: Duke University Press.

McCann, Bryan. 2014. *Hard Times in the Marvelous City: From Dictatorship to Democracy in the Favelas of Rio de Janeiro*. Durham, NC: Duke University Press.

Moura, Roberto. 2001. "Aldir Blanc: Dados biográficos sem nenhum compromisso com a isenção." In *A poesia de Aldir Blanc: Melodias e letras cifradas para guitarra, violão e teclado*, edited by Roberto M. Moura and Luciano Alves, 6–15. São Paulo: Irmãos Vitale Press.

Sukman, Hugo. 2020. "Aldir Blanc tornou-se como poeta a voz dos que não têm voz." *O Globo*, May 4. https://oglobo.globo.com/cultura/aldir-blanc-tornou-se-como-poeta -voz-dos-que-nao-tem-voz-24409939.

Vianna, Luiz Fernando. 2013. *Aldir Blanc: Resposta ao tempo—vida e letras*. Rio de Janeiro: Casa da Palavra.

29

Bandungian Futurities / Futuridades Bandungianas

A Future-Oriented Practice for South-to-South Solidarities

BEATRIZ BISSIO

This chapter argues for the continued relevance of the Bandung Conference and its legacy, which defined racism as one of the most perverse legacies of colonialism, and centers on how some experiences, in Rio de Janeiro, can be interpreted as a way to revive, extend, and animate the relevance of the Bandung project through Global South solidarity mobilization. The future needs to be Bandungian, as there is no way to build a free, just, and solidarity-based society without eliminating the scourge of racism. Humanity is facing a practical and theoretical challenge. Practical because it is necessary to win the hearts and minds of the world's people, and to believe again in concepts that have been emptied to the point of losing all meaning—the most important of which is democracy. And we have to forge new theoretical tools to remove the ideological veil that justifies neocolonial aggressions and imperialistic interventions disguised as humanitarian initiatives. It is necessary to use these tools to the maximum extent possible and expand our understanding of social phenomena with other theoretical references that are capable of giving more appropriate answers to the threats of today.

Global Catastrophes and Collective Responses

The challenges that we have faced in previous years reveal the fragility of formally established certainties that have made up our politics, culture, and environment until now. Therefore, this moment invites us to put aside our traditional views on society, domestic and international politics, and concepts consolidated as modernity, and to use our own lenses to unravel the knot. The failure of most of the West in responding to the 2020 COVID-19 pandemic revealed the perversities of the political-social system prevalent in our societies and has exposed the limitations of Eurocentric ways of interpreting reality. These logics remain present in most traditions within the contemporary social sciences. We are facing a practical and theoretical challenge. It is practical because it is necessary to win the hearts and minds of our people and believe again in concepts that have been emptied (such as democracy), and theoretical because we have to forge new tools to remove the ideological veil that seeks to disguise neocolonial aggressions and imperialistic interventions as humanitarian initiatives.

In a pioneering form in the 1940s, Uruguayan artist Joaquín Torres García painted South America in an "inverted" form and proclaimed, "the South must be our compass" (Ramirez 1992, 53). This aesthetic provocation had parallels in the social sciences. Intellectuals, thinkers, and activists from the Global South, but also from the North, sought to pave the way toward a new understanding of history and international relations.

In the 1950s and 1960s, in a Cold War scenario between the two superpowers, African and Asian countries were fighting to restructure themselves as autonomous. The Bandung Conference (Indonesia, April 18–24, 1955) brought together leaders from some thirty Asian and African nations, responsible for the destiny of 1.5 billion human beings. Focused on the idea of creating their own space in a bipolar world—would it be appropriate to call it an imagined community?— people were fighting in favor of peaceful coexistence and nonintervention in the internal affairs of other countries. They enshrined the principles of sovereignty and territorial integrity of all nations and to the defense of human rights as a fundamental value (Guitard 1962).

Indonesian president and independence leader Sukarno offered a speech during the opening session, as the conference host. He emphasized that all the chiefs of state and government present were united by more important things than those which superficially divided them. He insisted, "We are united, for instance, by a common detestation of colonialism in whatever form it appears. We are united by a common detestation of racialism. And we are united by a common determination to preserve and stabilize peace in the world" (Sukarno 1955, 4). The recognition of equality of all races and all nations, large and small, was one of the Ten Principles of Bandung. Sukarno's proposal, directly or indirectly, inspired theoretical analyses. Bandungian futurities, as a concept, aim to adapt the intention of the Bandung Conference to twenty-first-century realities. It is a synthesis of that historical experience and present innovative practices.

Critical, subaltern, and decolonial theories renewed the interpretations that had prevailed. In these early decades of the twenty-first century, in order to understand the changes that humanity is going through, we need theoretical references that do not discard the contributions made to history and the advancement of humanity by the cultures of Africa, the Arab world, Asia, and the ancient civilizations of the Americas.

Issues that human beings have argued about since the beginning of history are discussed again today. Debates and human experiments continue to oscillate between individualism and collectivism, equality, and freedom. Such debates on the topic ignited political discussions for decades in the twentieth century, within the framework of the ideological struggle between capitalism and socialism/communism. The argument in favor of freedom, as it was understood in that context, was basically the defense of the capitalist system (free enterprise and markets). The central argument of this current revolved around criticism of the state in the Soviet model, in which individual rights were subjected to collective logic. In contrast, those who understood that equality is the most important element for life in society pointed to the fallacy of freedom in the capitalist system. By leaving the driving force of the economy in the invisible hands of the market, capitalism only offers an illusory freedom for most.

The 2020 pandemic is revealing that obscene levels of global social inequality are threatening the very survival of a huge part of human existence. Without an organized society, we humans cannot survive. In a crisis, collective action is necessary. In view of the dystopian social, economic, and environmental reality present in our societies—and in view of the incapacity or lack of political will of elites to assume responsibility—the most vulnerable segments of our societies are bearing the burden and suffering the most. Popular organizations did not wait for the state to act and emerged, seeking their own answers. An interesting phenomenon appeared: what in English we would call de-linking, or separation from the state, in favor of autonomous decision-making.

Rio de Janeiro, mainly in the favelas, was a rich field of experimentation for these initiatives during the ongoing pandemic. In schools, among street vendors, at hairdressers' salons, and in small neighborhood businesses, mutual aid thrived—with residents supplying food and hand sanitizer to the excluded and offering water through taps installed provisionally on street corners and by neighbors at bus stops. The initiatives, which are already inspiring others, aimed to support the thousands left without work due to the indifference of the wealthy and of the incumbent government and emerged through spontaneous action. The usually female leadership of these initiatives represents a long tradition of women leading collective movements. It is clear that behind these spontaneous actions there was an organizational experience of movements—grassroots, favela-based, or comprising associations of small farmers. These movements have shown that it is possible to organize through decentralized decision-making, valuing already-existing skills from community members. In fact, the work that is being done by grassroots organizations emerged long before the pandemic. The struggle for social and economic transition away from extractivist models and for the abandonment of monoculture and market-based forms of food and goods distribution have long been the struggle of food sovereignty activists.

The Global Antiracist Fight: Remembering the Bandung Conference

This is, of course, not exceptional to Brazil, Rio, or the Americas; the same is happening in Africa and Asia. A transcontinental dialogue between these movements is growing, predominantly led by Black and Indigenous people. Given this reality, it is important to remember a phrase written by the sociologist and US historian W. E. B. Du Bois. In his seminal work, *The Souls of Black Folk* (1903), he traces the poverty and exploitation of African Americans in the years of Reconstruction. He concludes in a now-famous statement that "the problem of the 20th century is the problem of the color line" (10). Perhaps if he were alive, Du Bois's feelings and his assessment of the current situation would be the same. Structural racism is still everywhere, and a global response is necessary. From the Black Lives Matter movement to the global response to the killings of George Floyd and, earlier, Marielle Franco, the Black and Indigenous movements and all those committed to the antiracist struggle are pressing against one of our most pervasive forms of violence and exploitation.

Therefore, after all these years, the conference held in Bandung, Indonesia, in 1955 continues to be relevant. The radical fight against racism would become one of the main banner flags of the conference's struggle. One of the ideologues of Negritude (Blackness), Senegalese poet and political leader Léopold Senghor, perceived the 1955 Bandung Conference as the global expression of consciousness and a path to dignity. It was, in his eyes, the death of the inferiority complex (Swan 2018). At a time when racism is again debated worldwide, it is important to pay tribute to the Bandung Conference. It demonstrated that combating racism must be the central strategy for overcoming colonial and neocolonial legacies and for the struggle to eliminate the secular exploitation of most of humanity.

In June 1992, Rio de Janeiro hosted the United Nations Conference on the Environment and Development (UNCED), also known as the Earth Summit, and the city became indelibly associated with the struggle to preserve our natural habitat. Rio has all the conditions to be a laboratory of innovative practices that can claim the heritage of Bandung and the Earth Summit and, in a certain way, transcend them.

Bandung was the representation of the majority's wishes, thought of in statist terms. Rio de Janeiro, together with other Global South capitals, can go further. It can represent the intersection of population initiatives and practices, supported by public policies (understanding, without doubt, that a democratic state is needed in this process). This junction may be the foundation of a future Bandungian intention.

Using Bandungian logic to imagine futures is not some kind of postpandemic enlightenment, since the metaphor would represent a rescue of Eurocentrisms and the divorce of rationality from spirituality, as well as a pseudo-science of white supremacy. The era that is being born must in fact be novel. In Rio de Janeiro, there are signs of change coming from those whom Frantz Fanon ([1963] 2005) deemed "the wretched of the Earth." They are bringing along with them the consciousness of their collective strength, inspired by their ancestors. But as we are immersed in a process of change, signs of the new are imprecise and the old resists being replaced. In the words of Antonio Gramsci, "the crisis consists precisely in the fact that the 'old' is dying and the 'new' cannot be born; in this interregnum, the monsters appear" (2005, 556).

The resurgence of solidarities across Africa, Asia, and Latin America continues today. These alliances have cultivated community values instead of privileging individualism and consumerism promoted by capitalism. The Indigenous peoples of Ecuador, Peru, and Bolivia define their worldview as the philosophy of living well (buen vivir) in which there is harmony between human beings and Pachamama, Mother Earth. Similar to South Africa's ubuntu philosophy, it encompasses the idea of unity and respect among humans, other living beings, the environment, and the cosmos. The Indigenous peoples of Argentina define the current stage of society as terricide, a stage in which humans are leading the environment to destruction. Latin American Indigenous communities defend a new legal definition for the natural habitat, equating it with the human being—nature as worthy of rights. It is no coincidence that the new paradigms are being proposed mainly by Black and Indigenous populations, decimated by the genocide caused by colonialism, neocolonialism, and environmental exploitation.

The future is being sown by communities that cultivate a deep relationship of respect and love for nature and have a strong sense of responsibility toward future generations. At a moment when science warns of the proximity of a point of no return, only cultures with a deep sense of communalism and with relationships to the natural world can imagine new proposals for social organization. The model of the world as a machine, which prevailed mainly in the eighteenth and nineteenth centuries, led human beings to control nature. If, on the contrary, we think of our planet as a web of relationships between our natural habitat and life in all of its manifestations, we will feel the responsibility to take care of it. This is a true paradigm shift.

In the absence of guidance and leadership from above, global catastrophe will be resolved by those already living in precarity. If we think of this learning as an embryo of something new, the possibilities for changes in future behavior are encouraging. Our societies have the potential for a practical response to the mistakes (crimes) of elites. They have the potential to offer an alternative model of knowledge production that weaves contemporary and ancestral thought. All this energy, solidarity, and accumulation of experiences of self-organization cannot be dissolved even during a global crisis. To be sure, the next era will not be easy. We will have lost a lot, in human and material terms. The balance of these years will be dramatic. For this reason, we must formulate new models and praxis, capable of ensuring a different future for our societies.

Brazil has experienced the erosion of its institutions, economy, environment, public health, and democracy. In the struggle to forge a new future, after pandemic and authoritarianism, Rio de Janeiro could function as a laboratory. We can draw inspiration from the Earth Summit in 1992. Simultaneous with UNCED, a large gathering of nongovernmental organizations (NGOs) was held in Aterro de Flamengo Park, a beautiful area located by Guanabara Bay, forty kilometers from the RioCentro conference site. Its title was the World Forum. That extremely rich forum was a mixture of NGO networking, political demonstrations, and cultural events, and it involved more than 20,000 foreign participants in addition to more than 200,000 local residents who participated or at least visited the site during the conference.

Inspiring Vital Energy

Rio de Janeiro has a unique energy, inspiring remarkable events like the 2005 World Social Forum. That energy comes from its people, who have developed over centuries the art of overcoming difficulties and systematic exclusion in order to persevere. And the cities' communities realized these advances through art— music, dance, carnival, capoeira, funk, poetry, and theater. But above all, this energy has manifested in the exercise of solidarity and in the exaltation of freedom. This city's communities have reidentified themselves as the original children of the Americas, children of Africa, children of immigration. They became aware of resulting from a crucible of races and cultures that enabled them to extend a hand to other formerly colonized peoples from the most distant continents. The feeling of belonging shared and transmitted between peoples and nations fuels the will to build alternatives. This is a legacy of the South-South solidarity honoring the spirit of Bandung, but it could go much further.

Rio de Janeiro is a powerful reference for the creative capacity of the Global South and its willpower to advance toward a different future. The end of the Third World inferiority complex that, according to Léopold Senghor, represented Bandung has been renewed in the creative vitality represented by Rio de Janeiro, and in this vast city of contradictions and creativities, Bandungian echoes inspire the construction of futures.

REFERENCES

Du Bois, W. E. B. 1903. *The Souls of Black Folk.* New York: New American Library Press.

Fanon, Frantz. (1963) 2005. *Wretched of the Earth.* New York: Grove Press.

Gramsci, Antonio. 2005. *Selections from the Prison Notebooks.* Edited by Quintin Hoare and Geoffrey Nowell-Smith. London: Lawrence and Wishart.

Guitard, Odette. 1962. *Bandung y el despertar de los pueblos coloniales.* Buenos Aires: EUDEBA.

Ramirez, Mari Carmen. 1992. *El Taller Torres-García: The School of the South and Its Legacy.* Austin: University of Texas Press.

Sukarno. 1955. "Opening Address Given by Sukarno (Bandung, 18 April 1955)." In *Asia-Africa Speaks from Bandung,* 19–29. Djakarta: Ministry of Foreign Affairs, Republic of Indonesia. https://www.cvce.eu/en/obj/opening_address_given_by_sukarno_bandung _18_april_1955-en-88d3f71c-c9f9-415a-b397-b27b8581a4f5.html.

Swan, Quito. 2018. "Blinded by Bandung? Illuminating West Papua, Senegal, and the Black Pacific." *Radical History Review* 131: 58–81.

30

De-kill / De-matando

Black Mothers' Epistemology of Violence and Mourning in Rio de Janeiro

LUCIANE ROCHA

Here is a horrifying, outrageous, and unacceptable event: as usual in Duque de Caxias, a city in the metropolitan region of Rio de Janeiro, its residents sit on the sidewalks during summer evenings to talk and for some fresh air while the children play. On December 4, 2020, two girls who are cousins, and very close to each other, took their showers and went to the street to join their mothers and wait for their grandmother to arrive from work. When the grandma got off the bus, she saw the police shooting from a vehicle toward the street where her house was located. Arriving at home, she found Emily Victoria killed in front of the property's gate, shot in the head. Rebecca Beatriz was a little further away, with a gunshot wound to the chest. Taken to the hospital, both were pronounced dead. The same rifle bullet killed the two cousins, ages four and seven years old, respectively. They were Black. They were two beautiful Black little girls (Record TV Rio 2020).

In June 2021, six months after this killing, the case investigation was still inconclusive. The police and several witnesses testified that there was no crossfire between the police and the criminals. However, neighbors and family members affirm that the police fired moments before the bullet hit the girls. The five officers involved deny the story. Ana Lucia Moreira, the mother of Emily Victoria, explained: "They [the police] just do this, shoot. Look and shoot. When I realized [that the bullet hit Emily], I just took the document [to court]. Because I already knew, my daughter was already stretched out dead. My daughter was shot in the head with a rifle. My daughter was already dead. My niece had time to run but died beside her mother's water tank" (Coelho 2020).

Before writing about this killing, I announced the horror of this event to the reader. My intention was not to create a trigger warning on the upcoming disturbing content but to evoke a particular reading of this repugnant incident to those who normalize Black death.[1] Unfortunately, murders such as those of Emily and Rebecca are not unusual. According to the *Fogo Cruzado* (2021) database, from 2016 to 2021, there were thirty-nine cases of children shot during police operations—of these, twelve died. For Black people, the repetition of this violence produces a trail of blood, trauma, and sorrow on a neighborhood level. The killings of Emily and Rebecca demonstrate a pattern in the security policies of Rio that makes Black people the target of systematic and sordid violence (Rocha 2017). However, our deaths are normalized and made trivial by the state. Some societal sectors justify them by suggesting that all persons killed were involved with crimes or were victims of the unfortunately violent consequences ostensibly part of such territories (Rocha 2015). Ana Lucia Souza, a cousin of the girls, inquires:

> We leave to work to contribute to this murderous government, and that's what they give us in return, they kill our children, our future. This has to end. This has to stop. How long will they kill innocent people? Emily was shot in the head with a rifle. Do you understand what this is? What did she do to deserve a gunshot in the head? What has a four-year-old done to deserve this? What were they holding in their hands? What will they say? Will they say they were on drugs, with guns and that they exchanged shots? This causes us a lot of anger. We know that nothing will happen. When this happened to the girls, all of us in the family were coming back from our jobs. Our salaries pay for public security, but what protection do we have? None! (Coelho 2020)

Ana Lucia's words of mourning show the suffering that will never cease for this family. Her grief exposes the violence inherent in Black lives and contains a deep analysis of the relationship between the state and the Black and poor population. She talks about the anger and explains how the state and members of civil society justify the deaths. Each of these deaths produces a family in mourning, and in many cases, an activist mother emerges.

The activism of Black mothers, whose offspring—children, adolescents, and adults—were killed in Rio de Janeiro, has been the subject of my primary intellectual and political engagement since 2008. Their struggles not only encompass their own fights against poverty, racism, and gender discrimination but are also the consequences of violent acts perpetrated or facilitated by the state against their family members. Just like those of the women in Emily and Rebecca's families, the narratives of other mothers with whom I collaborated throughout these years show vertexes that, put together, allow us to delineate the Black mothers' epistemology of the state, emerging from their outraged luta. In this luta, mourning is used as a catalyst fuel for seeking justice.

The long-term engagement with activist mothers allowed me to hear many stories of state violence and surveillance upon Black communities: testimonies of mothers who fought to avoid or stop their teenagers' involvement with criminality, mothers of innocent young Black men whose criminal activity was invented by the police to justify the killing, women whose sons were killed while incarcerated, mothers of children deceased because of stray bullets, and many other cases. Through participant observation in protests, judicial hearings, and trials, as well as in-depth interviews, I learned their epistemology of state violence and their strategies for their "motherwork" (Collins 2000; Nascimento [1949] 2003), uninterrupted in this part of the African diaspora.[2] But above all, my interaction with them allowed me to witness their strength and courage while mourning. Following their logic, my work as an activist scholar is to testify (Rocha 2018). In this chapter, I review interviews and observations to demonstrate one of the main methods of resistance against state violence, those acts of de-killing. I argue that in trying to de-normalize the killings of their children, Black mothers position themselves as the main antagonists of the state.

I USE THE term *de-kill* (*de-matar*) as a way to analyze the acts of courage performed by Black women, particularly mothers, to seek justice for the death of their children or to keep alive young Black men or women who are physically and symbolically condemned to death by society members and justice systems. These mothers have their mourning diminished through the pejorative category *mãe de bandido* (bandit mothers), which is used to blame them for the death of their offspring by accusing them of failing to raise and educate their children properly. The concept of de-killing helps us to see that, while Black mothers fight against the status of mãe de bandidos, their acts make their antagonist position with the state evident. In this chapter, I recall the activism of three mothers whose stories I heard in three different phases of my research: Deize Carvalho, Nilza Maria da Silva, and Ana Paula Oliveira. I portray these three mothers in this chapter not only because of the strength and relevance of their activism, but also because the cases show different aspects of anti-Black violence in Rio de Janeiro. Respectively, but not limited to each case, the stories demonstrate: (1) the demonization and brutality against the male Black body in the justice system; (2) the spectacle of Black suffering in recent public security campaigns carried out by the government; and (3) how the mothers worked to change the narrative about their sons and use the state apparatus in their favor (namely, through public defense).

One of the first stories I heard during fieldwork was about the activism of Deize Carvalho. Her oldest son, Andreu Carvalho, became involved in petty robberies and was caught and held in the DEGASE unit (Ilha do Governador).[3] On January 2, 2009, just a day after his detention, Deize received the news that her son had died after falling on the floor while trying to escape. The cause of death was recorded as due to concussion injuries, meningeal bleeding, and head trauma. After the burial, she pursued a search for truth and justice, noticing the discrepancy between the official story and the bruises on her son's body. Newspaper articles about the murder portrayed Andreu as being "1.9 m tall (roughly 6.2ft)" and "aggressive" (Carvalho 2014, 73) and that he had laughed and mocked the police at the time of the arrest. These accounts dehumanized Andreu and reinforced the violent Black man stereotype, justifying his death as inevitable and welcome. According to the agents' testimony, Andrew attacked one of them as they retaliated. However, young inmates reported the police officers verbally provoking Andreu and kicking him. These claims stated that the officers whipped Andreu with cables five times and beat him with a makeshift weapon (a coconut inside a plastic bag). The assaults might have continued even after Andreu was on the ground.

With the support of organizations working against police brutality, Deize battled for and acquired permission to exhume her son's body for a second autopsy. Through that procedure, she discovered that Andreu was not killed but overkilled.[4] The seventeen-year-old had a broken skull, dislocated jaw, and severely lacerated torso—"the dead had a voice" (Carvalho 2014, 74). Her de-killing work resulted in the incrimination of the agents, but the judicial process was still ongoing thirteen years after the killing. She gave performances and public speeches—one of her methods of de-killing—before the judicial hearings, which, according to her, "energized and gave strength to face the murderers in the courtroom."

In February 2012, I saw Deize Carvalho in action for the first time. In a protest in front of the court building, she drew public attention to the abuses committed by state agents, demanded justice, and received support from other mothers and activists. Deize's discourse and performance were very emotional and brought out various resistance elements. The first element was the way she marked her positionality. She stated, "Today, 1,498 days after the death of my son, I'm here as a citizen from the favela who has come down the hill to the asphalt to cry for justice." This positionality as a citizen of the favela is crucial because it contradicts a notion that symbolically (but not only) categorizes favela residents as favelados and in opposition to the citizens of the asphalt. It also shows that favela residents have not achieved full citizenship yet, since they have to come to spaces other than the favela for their voices to be heard. She also delineates Andreu's positionality as someone who committed mistakes but was still a citizen and had the right to be alive, like any other human being. In her own words, she told us, "My son, who was human, was a citizen like anyone else. Made mistakes, yes, made mistakes, but nobody has the right to slaughter another human being in a room."

Deize's speech presents a second element, which is naming the oppressor. Deize named not only people, such as the violent agents of discipline, the governor, and the public security secretary, but also the institutions that help oppress poor and Black people. At the end of her talk, Deize concluded, "The process of fighting for justice for my son is as painful as the pain of childbirth, except that today, the contractions will reduce only when this trial is over, and I successfully say everything I know. I have no fear of retaliation or death for my fight. My greatest good, my son, they already took." Through my interaction with Deize for nine years, I have grasped that her courage in denouncing brutality relies upon hopes of avoiding other deaths. Her strength is fed by the memories of Andreu's life and death, which indicates that the fuel will never end.

On November 27, 2011, the police invaded the community of Complexo de Alemão in order to install a Police Pacification Unit (UPP). The community response to this event introduced Brazil to its citizen Dona Nilza Santos. Her mothering strategy became known because of her successful attempt to de-kill Diego dos Santos, best known by his drug-dealer name, Mister M. According to the police investigation, Diego/Mister M was the leading security guard of the leader of the gang organization that controlled Complexo do Alemão. He had been accused of associating with drug trafficking (RJ no Ar 2010).[5] On that day as military police and army troopers were preparing to invade Alemão, with the operation being broadcast live on popular TV channels, Dona Nilza saw the heavy weapons carried by the officers, heard the call from the general commander of police asking the drug dealers to surrender, and realized that this was her last chance to de-kill her son. She managed to convince Diego/Mister M to surrender peacefully. While waiting in the police station, Dona Nilza spoke in a TV interview: "I have never accepted having a child involved with this. Then I took that opportunity, I talked to him, and he accepted." The next day, TV presenter Ana Maria Braga (Mais Você, 2010) made a spectacle out of Diego's arrest and reminded her audience that "everybody has a mother—the singer, the officer, and also drug dealers." I understood that Braga gave this context because Dona Nilza's act created a contradiction in Rio's social imagination about the mãe de bandido. Braga asked her how she was feeling that day with a smile on her face, to which she replied, "I am sad. I am sad, but Diego is alive. Diego is arrested but alive. I believe that he will be free one day. He is already in a new life."

In both appearances in the media, Nilza emphasized that she is the mother of Diego, not Mister M. She repeated his real name in almost every sentence, making him a subject, which I interpreted as an act of de-killing. Naming is one of the first acts of motherwork. In African traditions, naming has power. It can shape someone's character, mold their social identity, and even influence their destiny (Olatunji et al. 2015). "His name is Diego," she said. In my interpretation of her act, Mister M symbolized the past, violence, unhuman, and the dead, whereas Diego is reborn, bright and alive. She brought her son back to her. The second way that Dona Nilza de-kills Diego is by quoting him in her narrative. When talking about how her attempt to take Diego to the police station was successful, she said, "I called him, and he asked me, 'To go where?' I said I was going home, and he said, 'Home, no, because the police will kill me. I'll keep running—it will be the same thing. They're gonna kill me anyway'" (RJ no Ar. 2010). Diego was socially dead (Patterson 1982). By narrating the story with quotes, Dona Nilza gives him a voice, thus de-killing him. Her strategy to ensure that Diego would be kept alive also involved understanding the police structure to circumvent their practice. She narrates that she saw a police car and an officer that she knew from a social project in the community. She did not tell him about her plan to search the favela looking for Diego. Instead, after she crossed the favela with him, she approached the police officer with a witness and told him, "'Look, lock up my son because I want him alive. I want you to give him an opportunity.' Diego gave him his arms, the police officer handcuffed him, and we went to the police station" (RJ no Ar. 2010). Dona Nilza knew that, through this strategy, no police would say that he was trying to escape and kill him. Her act of being a witness while giving him to the officer was her third de-killing act. The reporter asked if she was afraid that Diego would go back to a life of crime. Very secure and calm, she replied, "No, he will not go. I am sure that he will not go. This is a new life" (RJ no Ar. 2010). She believed him, her fourth de-killing act. Diego graduated and became a filmmaker for an NGO, played soccer in the Botafogo FA club, and the most recent information in the news said he became a photographic model (Fontes 2013). Diego is alive.

This is how Ana Paula Oliveira, mother of Johnatha Oliveira, explains how she started her search for justice:

> When my son died, I didn't believe it. I went into a kind of coma. I didn't eat; I didn't get out of bed. One day, I managed to get up and went to watch TV. When the news started, they talked about my son's case and said he "supposedly had involvement with drug trafficking." They spoke at the end, right after showing the population's protest. At the very end, like someone who says he was just another unimportant and justifies his death. That made me outraged. The other day I gathered my things and went to seek justice for my son. (Interview with author, August 7, 2017, Rio de Janeiro)

Like many mothers who turn their grief into a political struggle, Ana Paula turned her outrage at the naturalization of her son's death into fuel to get out of her social coma, push the direction of the justice system, and become an activist against state violence. The strategy of disseminating news that associates Black people who were murdered with criminality is not new. The media has the practice of using phrases such as "has been arrested before" or "possible dealer," which justify deaths. This is because they dehumanize the person and consequently naturalize the deaths in these territories.

Therefore, Ana Paula's political struggle fundamentally involves denaturalizing these narratives. She told me in an interview that she will not "allow herself to be called mãe de bandido"—a category that also criminalizes the mothers as they continue to exercise their motherhood within institutions of justice—and that "the real criminals will be held responsible." Johnatha Oliveira was murdered by the military police in May 2014, shot in the back as he was returning from his girlfriend's house in the favela of Manguinhos. He was rescued by residents but arrived dead at the local emergency care unit (UPA). When analyzing the progress of the case in the NUDEDH, I verified that the police investigation shows that the police officer said that "they were moving through the favela in search of a drug-selling point when they heard shots and shot back."[6] They also claimed that they "recognize[d] Johnatha for his involvement in local crime."

Ana Paula's work encompasses presenting moral evidence about Johnatha that disqualifies the narrative that says he was a criminal. To this end, she was enlisted in the judicial process as a witness, with the strategy of talking about his life and contrasting with the image created by the police. Fundamental to Ana Paula's action is the political acts she organizes before each hearing and preserving her son's memory through photos posted on her social networks. She says they need to show the state and society that their children are loved and they are good mothers. This narrative of affection and longing is attested in the justice system by revealing the cruel nature of death and translating their suffering to the judge, a judicialization of Black suffering (Rocha 2020). The validation of this mother's struggle is also documented through the recurring submission of newspaper reports about her activism to the public defender's office, which proves her outrage and shows that she has not given up fighting for her son. Her suffering is visible and moves the justice system.

The public defender working with her on the case considers that all this mobilization since the beginning of the police investigation has resulted in abundant evidence for the case to have been referred to the popular jury. Although the process is still ongoing, Ana Paula already sees positive signs in her acts. According to her, "justice has been done every day that I open my mouth and manage to add one more mother here in the favela to the luta (struggle). They look up to me to not let their children's cases go unpunished. The struggle has results" (interview with author, August 7, 2017, Rio de Janeiro).

IN THIS CHAPTER, I demonstrated key methods of resistance against state violence used by mothers who had their lineage threatened or interrupted by the police in Rio de Janeiro. Ana Paula Oliveira, Dona Nilza da Silva, Deize Carvalho, Ana Lucia Souza, and Ana Lucia Moreira are Black women who raised their voices and created strategies to avoid deaths or seek justice, the de-killing acts. Their experiences show that in trying to denormalize the killings of their children, they position themselves as the main antagonists of the state. They use their outrage, anger, and grief as a source of power to seek justice for their cases and address their communities' general concerns. While they transform their mourning into political practice, their fight with the state allows them to understand its function from a privileged position. Their state analysis unveils what can be called the Black mothers' epistemology of the state. I argue that the suffering caused by the terror and how they pursue their lutas reveals their antagonist position to the state, making them a distinct political group. Black mothers' de-killing is in opposition to Black annihilation. It is an alternative in the sense that it utilizes love, care, and protection in the face of terror and gratuitous violence. It uses power to ensure life instead of death and suffering.

NOTES

1 Lei 9.180/21, also known as the Agatha Felix Law, established to honor the seven-year-old Black girl killed by a stray bullet in Complexo do Alemão (Phillips 2019), requires priority in the investigation of a child's death (Castro 2021). However, in the case of Emily and Rebecca, despite the fact that several witnesses testified that the police fired the bullet, the investigation was paralyzed one year after the event. The different treatment of Black death in the Brazilian judicial system is evident if we compare it with cases involving non-Blacks. For example, the inquiry into the murder of eight-year-old Bernardo Boltrini in Rio Grande do Sul concluded in a little over a month, the killing of five-year-old Isabela Nardoni in São Paulo in just one month, and the murder of four-year-old Henry Borel in Rio de Janeiro in just two months (Do R7 2021). Although these three cases did not involve the police, specialists say that the main reason for the quick investigation, trial, and verdict was the general social pressure that motivated the justice system. Why does Black suffering not provoke the same effect?
2 Brazil has the largest Black population outside of the African continent, due to centuries of human trafficking by the Portuguese. According to the Brazilian census of 2010 (IBGE 2010), the Black (pardo and preto) population was roughly 51 percent of the national total. The historical constraints of racism, anti-Blackness, sexism, poverty, and violence have led Black women to continuously develop strategies to secure their children's physical and cultural survival.
3 The Departamento Geral de Ações Socioeducativas (DEGASE) is the institution responsible for the execution of socio-educational measures, recommended by the Statute of Children and Adolescents (ECA), applied by the judiciary to young people in conflict with the law.
4 Military concept that describes the excessive use of force in killing an individual or organism.
5 I use the term *drug retail* to call attention to the apparatus necessary to successfully complete international drug trafficking. This apparatus is not owned by the young Black men killed daily in the favelas.
6 From 2015 to 2018, I conducted research at the Human Rights Defense Center of Rio de Janeiro Public Defender's Office (NUDEDH), studying cases in which mothers had a relevant role in the actions of the criminal justice system.

REFERENCES

Carvalho, Deize. 2014. *Vencendo as adversidades: Autobiografia de Deize Carvalho*. Rio de Janeiro: Nós por Nós Editora.
Castro, Claudio. 2021. "Lei no. 9.180 de 12 de janeiro de 2021." JusBrasil. https://gov-rj .jusbrasil.com.br/legislacao/1157629043/lei-9180-21-rio-de-janeiro-rj.

Coelho, André. 2020. "Moradores de Duque de Caxias protestam contra morte de primas Emilly e Rebeca." *GloboNews*, June 12. https://g1.globo.com/rj/rio-de-janeiro /noticia/2020/12/06/moradores-de-duque-de-caxias-protestam-contra-morte-de-irmas -emilly-e-rebeca.ghtml.

Collins, Patricia Hill. 2000. "Rethinking Black Women's Activism." In *Black Feminist Thought: Knowledge, Consciousness, and the Politics of Empowerment*, 201–24. New York: Routledge.

Do R7. 2021. "Mortes e agressões: Relembre casos de crianças vítimas de familiares." *Portal R7*, April 8. https://noticias.r7.com/cidades/fotos/mortes-e-agressoes-relembre -casos-de-criancas-vitimas-de-familiares-08042021#/foto/6.

Fogo Cruzado. 2021. "Em quase 5 anos, 100 crianças foram baleadas no Grande Rio." April 18. https://fogocruzado.org.br/100-criancas-baleadas-grande-rio/.

Fontes, Carol. 2013. "Ex-traficante Mister M se reinventa no Botafogo FA e vira modelo fotográfico." *Globo*, September 24. http://ge.globo.com/outros-esportes/noticia/2013 /07/ex-traficante-mister-m-se-reinventa-no-botafogo-fa-e-vira-modelo-fotografico.html.

IBGE. 2010. *Atlas do Censo Demográfico 2010*. Instituto Brasileiro de Geografia e Estatística. https://censo2010.ibge.gov.br/apps/atlas/.

Mais Você. 2010. "Ana Maria recebe convidados para falar sobre a situação do Rio de Janeiro." *Last O Globo*, November 29. Accessed February 1, 2020. http://gshow.globo.com /programas/mais-voce/v2011/MaisVoce/0,,MUL1632942-10345,00-ANA+MARIA+RE CEBE+CONVIDADOS+PARA+FALAR+SOBRE+A+SITUACAO+DO+RIO+DE+JA NEIRO.html.

Nascimento, Maria. (1949) 2003. "Infância agonizante." In *Quilombo—vida, problemas e as-pirações do negro*, edited by Abdias do Nascimento. Rio de Janeiro: Editora 34 Ltda.

Olatunji, Abdulganiy, Moshood Issah, Yusuf Noah, A. Y. Muhammed, and Abdul-Rasheed Sulaiman. 2015. "Personal Name as a Reality of Everyday Life: Naming Dynamics in Select African Societies." *Journal of Pan African Studies* 8, no. 3: 72–90.

Patterson, Orlando. 1982. *Slavery and Social Death: A Comparative Study*. Cambridge, MA: Harvard University Press.

Phillips, Dom. 2019. "Brazilians Blame Rio Governor's Shoot-to-Kill Policy for Death of Girl." *Guardian*, September 22. https://www.theguardian.com/world/2019/sep/22 /brazilians-blame-rio-governors-shoot-to-kill-policy-for-death-of-agatha-felix-girl-8.

Record TV Rio. 2020. "Emily, de 4 anos, e Rebeca, de 7, são mortas em tiroteio no Rio." *Portal R7*, December 5. https://noticias.r7.com/rio-de-janeiro/emily-de-4-anos-e-rebeca -de-7-sao-mortas-em-tiroteio-no-rio-05122020.

RJ no Ar. 2010. "Traficante do Complexo do Alemão se entrega convencido pela mãe." Video. *Portal R7*, November 29. https://noticias.r7.com/rio-de-janeiro/rj-no-ar/videos /traficante-do-complexo-do-alemao-se-entrega-convencido-pela-mae-21102015.

Rocha, Luciane O. 2015. "De-matar: Maternidade negra como ação política na 'Pátria Mãe Gentil.'" In *Antinegritude o impossível sujeito negro na formação social brasileira*, 197–202. Rio de Janeiro: Cachoeira Editora UFRB.

Rocha, Luciane O. 2017. "Morte íntima: A gramática do genocídio antinegro na Baixada Fluminense." In *Motím: Horizontes do genocídio antinegro na diáspora*, edited by João Costa Vargas and Ana Flauzina, 37–66. Brasília: Brado Negro.

Rocha, Luciane O. 2018. "Maternidad indignada: Reflexiones sobre el activismo de las madres negras y el uso de las emociones en investigación activista." *Anthropologica* 36, no. 41: 35–46.

Rocha, Luciane O. 2020. "Judicialização do sofrimento negro: Maternidade negra e fluxo do sistema de justiça criminal no Rio de Janeiro." *Sexualidad, Salud y Sociedad—Revista Latinoamericana*, no. 36: 181–205.

Contributors

ROSIANE RODRIGUES DE ALMEIDA holds a PhD and a master's degree in anthropology from the Fluminense Federal University (PPGA/UFF). Her doctoral (ethnographic) work received the Lélia Gonzalez Prize for Best Thesis, given by the Black Anthropology Collective of the Brazilian Association of Anthropology (ABA), in 2020. She is the author of *"We" Do Brasil: Contents for the Application of Laws 10639/03 and 11645/08* (2012), *Quem foi que falou em igualdade?* (Who was it that talked about equality?, 2014) and *Para pensar diferente: Cidadania, igualdade e direitos* (To think differently: Citizenship, equality and rights, 2016).

JOSÉ CLÁUDIO SOUZA ALVES holds a PhD in sociology from the University of São Paulo and is a professor at the Federal Rural University of Rio de Janeiro. He has been active in the area of human rights in the Baixada Fluminense since 1984 and is the author of *Dos barões ao extermínio: Uma história da violência na Baixada Fluminense* (From barons to extermination: A history of violence in Baixada Fluminense, 2003).

TAMIRES MARIA ALVES is professor of public security and criminology at Fundação CECIERJ and coordinator of the postgraduate program in professional and technological education at the Federal Institute of Espírito Santo (IFES). She holds a PhD in political science from the Fluminense Federal University (UFF), is a cofounder of the Laboratório Críticas e Alternativas à Prisão (UFF), and is coordinator of the group Migrar não é Delito (UFRJ). She is also the author of *Enjaulados: Escolha punitiva e estratégias desencarceradoras* (Caged: Punitive choices and decarceral strategies, 2020).

PAUL AMAR (PhD and MA from New York University, BA from Duke University) serves as director of the Orfalea Center for Global and International Studies, and as professor and recently as chair in the Department of Global Studies at the University of California, Santa Barbara. Amar is a political scientist and anthropologist with affiliate appointments in political science, feminist studies, sociology, comparative literature, Middle East studies, and Latin American and Iberian studies. Before beginning his academic career, he worked as a journalist in Cairo, as a police reformer and sexuality rights activist in Rio de Janeiro, and as a conflict-resolution and economic development specialist at the United Nations.

His books include *Cairo Cosmopolitan* (with Diane Singerman, 2006); *New Racial Missions of Policing: International Perspectives on Evolving Law-Enforcement Politics* (2010); *Global South to the Rescue: Humanitarian Superpowers and Global Rescue Industries* (2011); *Dispatches from the Arab Spring: Understanding the New Middle East* (with Vijay Prashad, 2013); *The Middle East and Brazil: Perspectives on the New Global South* (2014); *The Tropical Silk Road: The Future of China in South America* (with Lisa Rofel, María Amelia Viteri, Consuelo Fernández-Salvador, and Fernando Brancoli, 2022); and *Cairo Securitized: Reconceiving Urban Justice and Social Resilience* (2024). His book *The Security Archipelago: Human-Security States, Sexuality Politics, and the End of Neoliberalism* (Duke University Press, 2013) was awarded the Charles Taylor Award for Best Book of the Year by the American Political Science Association. In 2019, Prof. Amar was awarded Mentor of the Year by the Latin American Studies Program at UCSB. He has enjoyed a number of long-term research, teaching, and institution-building residencies in Brazil over the past twenty-five years, including as visiting Fulbright professor in the Departments of Anthropology, Political Science, and International Relations, and is cofounder of the Center for Middle East Studies at the Fluminense Federal University in the state of Rio de Janeiro, as visiting scholar at the Federal University of Rio de Janeiro (IFCS-UFRJ), adjunct professor at the Afro-Brazilian Studies Center (UCAM, Rio de Janeiro), research fellow at the Center for the Study of Security and Citizenship (CESeC-UCAM), and most recently as visiting Fulbright professor of social sciences and cofounder of the new Center for Global Studies at the State University of Rio de Janeiro (UERJ).

MARCELO CAETANO ANDREOLI holds a PhD in urbanism from the Federal University of Rio de Janeiro and is an assistant professor in the Department of Architecture and Urbanism at the Federal University of Paraná. He has experience with popular settlements, urban policy, country-city relations, and projects for popular agroforestry settlements (through the PLANTEAR group). He is currently a member of the group Comuns Urbanos na América Latina (CUAL) and is a research member of the Laboratório de Habitação e Urbanismo (LAHURB/UFPR). He is the author of *Qualidade da habitação de interesse social em três escalas* (Quality of public housing on three scales, 2017).

BEATRIZ BISSIO holds a PhD in history and is currently deputy director of the Institute of Philosophy and Social Sciences at the Federal University of Rio de Janeiro. Uruguayan-naturalized Brazilian, she worked for more than two decades as a journalist in the international arena, interviewing Nelson Mandela, Agostinho Neto, Fidel Castro, Yasser Arafat, Samora Machel, Muammar Gaddafi, Saddam Hussein, Xanana Gusmão, Julius Nyerere, General Omar Torrijos, and General Juan Velasco Alvarado. She is the author of *O mundo falava árabe* (The world spoke Arabic, 2012).

THADDEUS GREGORY BLANCHETTE is currently a professor of anthropology at the Federal University of Rio de Janeiro, PPGAS–Museu Nacional, and NUPEM. He graduated with a PhD in social anthropology from the National Museum (UFRJ, 2006), a master of arts in social anthropology from the National Museum (UFRJ, 2001), and two bachelors of arts in sociology and in Latin American studies (University of Wisconsin–Madison, 1997). Together with his partner, Ana Paula da Silva, he is the author of more than fifty peer-reviewed publications on migration, sex work, human trafficking, and policing in Brazil and the world.

FERNANDO BRANCOLI is an associate professor of international security and geopolitics at the Institute of International Relations and Defense at the Federal University of Rio de Janeiro (IRID/UFRJ). He holds a PhD in international relations from San Tiago Dantas (Unesp, Unicamp, and PUC-SP) and is a fellow at the Center for Advanced Study at Princeton University. Brancoli is also the author of *Bolsonarismo: The Global Origins and Future of Brazil's Far Right* (2023). Further, he is a visiting researcher at the Orfalea Center for Global and International Studies at the University of California, Santa Barbara. He has conducted field research in the Middle East and North Africa, with an emphasis on Syria, Afghanistan, and Libya. Areas of academic interest include critical security studies, human rights, Middle East international policy, and privatization of violence.

THAYANE BRÊTAS is a PhD candidate in global urban studies at Rutgers University–Newark. She graduated from Federal University of Rio de Janeiro (UFRJ) with a degree in law and a master's degree in contemporary juridical theories (society, human rights, and art). She has worked for the Human Rights Lab of UFRJ and for projects of the Prostitution Policy Watch in partnership with the Puta Davida collective and the Brazilian Network of Prostitutes. She currently has publications in *Revista enfoques* and the *Beijo da rua* newspaper.

VICTORIA BROADUS is a visiting assistant professor of history at Oberlin College. She obtained her PhD in 2023 at Georgetown University, where her dissertation focused on Afro-descended work and ritual songs known as vissungos; the social and cultural formation of Brazil; and how those regional cultural forms relate to other Black Atlantic cultural practices. She has taught courses in Latin American history and the history of Rio. She received the Graduate Student Teaching Assistant Award for the Humanities for 2018–19. Before beginning the PhD program, she lived in Brazil for six years, where she became increasingly interested in studying Brazilian music and began playing choro music on trombone.

FATIMA CECCHETTO holds a PhD in public health (2002) from the State University of Rio de Janeiro and is a researcher at the Oswaldo Cruz Institute (IOC). She is also a professor in the graduate program at the National School of Public Health (ENSP) and a collaborator at the Jorge Careli Latin American Center for the Study of Violence and Health (CLAVES). She is the author of *Violência e estilos de masculinidade* (Violence and styles of masculinity, 2004). Her research focuses on anthropology and public health.

LEONARD CORTANA (Guadeloupe/France) earned his PhD in the cinema studies department at NYU Tisch School of the Arts and served as an affiliate researcher at the Berkman Klein Center, Harvard Law School. He is currently a public humanities fellow at the Museum of the City of New York. His doctoral research examines the transnational circulation of narratives about racial justice and activist movements between Brazil, South Africa, France, and overseas departments, and the United States, emphasizing the memorialization of political assassinations and the spread of the legacy of assassinated antiracism activists. He was a 2022 United Nations Fellow for People of African Descent and was a senior fellow and consultant for the 2023 fellowship at the UN Geneva headquarters. He holds undergraduate degrees in comparative politics and Spanish from Sciences Po Aix en Provence (France) and an EU Commission NOHA master's degree in humanitarian assistance from Deusto University (Spain). Cortana also earned a BA in cinema and aesthetics from Sorbonne University Paris I. Prior to his doctoral studies, he became a trainer for the European Commission's Youth Program projects and designed methodologies in theater and storytelling for social inclusion. Cortana is also a filmmaker. His last documentary, *Marielle's Legacy Will Not Die*, follows activist movements spreading the intersectional legacy of Afro-Brazilian activist and politician Marielle Franco in Rio de Janeiro, Brazil.

MARCOS COUTINHO is an urbanist and planner. He earned his BA from PUC-Rio and MA from the Institute of Urban and Regional Research and Planning (IPPUR/UFRJ). His research emphasizes Ibero-American colonial societies, cultures, and histories of race, particularly the interaction between Europeans, Africans, and their descendants in the city of Rio de Janeiro. He writes about religious and social practices in urban environments and the structures and legacies of slavery in the Portuguese Empire (sixteenth to nineteenth centuries), analyzing institutions such as the Catholic Church (and Black brotherhoods within the church) as vectors of urban expansion beyond liturgical scope. He has published articles in the journals *Rocalha* (2021), *Mosaico* (2022), and *Imagem Brasileira* (2022).

MONICA CUNHA is an elected city council member in Rio de Janeiro, specialist in antiracist education, and human rights defender who advocates for the rights of children and young people. In 2003, she founded Movimento Moleque, an organization gathering mothers whose children were threatened, attacked, or killed by the police. Movimento Moleque is part of the Network of Communities against Violence (Rede de Comunidades e Movimentos contra a Violência), an organization supporting people affected by state or police violence and their families.

ANA PAULA DA SILVA has a PhD in cultural anthropology from the postgraduate program in sociology and anthropology at UFRJ (PPGSA/IFCS/UFRJ). She is the author of *Pelé e o complexo de vira-latas: Discursos sobre raça e modernidade no Brasil* (Pelé and the mixed-race complex: Discourses on race and modernity in Brazil, 2014). She has a master's degree in sociology and anthropology from PPGSA/IFCS/UFRJ and holds a postdoctoral degree from the University of São Paulo (USP).

DENISE FERREIRA DA SILVA is the Samuel Rudin Professor in the Humanities in the Department of Spanish and Portuguese Languages and Literatures, New York University. Her artistic and academic work reflect and speculate on questions crucial to contemporary philosophy, political theory, Black thought, feminist thought, and historical materialism. She is the author of *Unpayable Debt* (2022), *Dívida impagável* (2019), and *Toward a Global Idea of Race* (2007). Her articles have been published in journals such as *Social Text*; *Theory, Culture and Society*; *philoSOPHIA*; *Griffith Law Review*; *Theory and Event*; and the *Black Scholar*, among others. Her artworks include the films *Serpent Rain* (2016), *4 Waters: Deep Implicancy* (2018), *Soot Breath/Corpus Infinitum* (2020), *Ancestral Claims/Ancestral Clouds* (2023) with Arjuna Neuman, and *Poethical Readings* (2015) and *Sensing Salon* (2016), with Valentina Desideri. She has taught at UC San Diego, University of British Columbia, and Queen Mary University of London and has visited Birkbeck University of London, University of São Paulo, and Université de Paris VIII and is currently an adjunct professor at Monash University in Art, Design and Architecture and a faculty member at the European Graduate School.

AMANDA DE LISIO is an assistant professor of culture, policy, and sustainable development at the School of Kinesiology and Health Science at York University, where she is also affiliated with the City Institute. Her research is focused on development and displacement in host cities during FIFA and Olympic events. Her dissertation was funded by the Social Sciences and Humanities Research Council (SSHRC) and examined the impact of event urbanism on women's informal, precarious labor. Prior to York University, she taught classes on urban geography, political economy, and the sociology of health and physical culture at the University of Toronto (2015–20) and held postdoctoral fellowships at Bournemouth University (2016–18) and Brock University (2018–20). Her work has been published in academic and popular presses in English and Portuguese.

LUIZ HENRIQUE ELOY AMADO is an Indigenous lawyer and anthropologist who is currently the secretary general of the Ministry of Indigenous Peoples. Previously, he was the Legal Department's coordinator at the Articulation of Indigenous Peoples of Brazil (APIB) and at the Coordination of Indigenous Organizations of the Brazilian Amazon (COIAB). He has advocated for Indigenous rights before the Brazilian Supreme Court (STF) and in international organizations. He was also a member of the Working Group on Indigenous Rights for Access to Justice and Procedural Singularities, of the National Council of Justice (CNJ). He holds a PhD in social anthropology from the National Museum (UFRJ) and a PhD in sociology of law from the Fluminense Federal University, and a postdoctorate in anthropology from the École des Hautes Études en Sciences Sociales (EHESS), Paris. He held a research internship at Brandon University, focusing on Indigenous territorial conflicts, through the Canadian government's Emerging Leaders in the Americas Program (ELAP). He was also a member of the Indigenous Affairs Commission (CAI) at the Brazilian Association of Anthropology (2019–20). He was a member of the Indigenous Peoples and Torture Working Group of the World Organization to Combat Torture and was a member of the Special Commission for the Defense of Indigenous People's Rights of the Federal Council of the Brazilian Bar Association (OAB, 2012–16).

He is also an associate researcher at the Laboratory for Research in Ethnicity, Culture and Development (LACED) (National Museum/UFRJ). He is the founder of the Revista Terena Vukápanavo and received an honorable mention for best doctoral thesis in social sciences (ANPOCS) in 2019. He has published several books in the fields of law and anthropology and their interfaces.

MARIELLE FRANCO was a feminist, sociologist, and city councilor in the Municipal Chamber of Rio de Janeiro. Franco completed her master's thesis in public administration from Fluminense Federal University. Franco's scholarship and work for the city reflected her commitment to working-class neighborhoods and against police killings and rights abuses. Raised in Maré, she worked to protect the rights and visibility of queer, women, and Black residents of Rio. She worked with the Commission for Human Rights in the Legislative Assembly of the state of Rio de Janeiro, alongside Marcelo Freixo. Her work, together with the PSOL, was also fundamental in enabling the party to denounce various corruption schemes in the city linked to the mafia in control of the public transport system as well as the contractual and construction companies involved in constructing stadiums for the World Cup and the Olympic Games. On March 14, 2018, she was assassinated by two gunmen. Franco's work against police violence and surveillance continues to inspire LGBTQI+ and Black organizers and scholars globally.

CRISTIANE GOMES JULIÃO is a member of the Indigenous community of the Pankararu people, located in the Sertão de Itaparica, Pernambuco. Julião has a degree in geography from the Higher Education Center of Vale do São Francisco (2007) in Belém do São Francisco/Pernambuco state and a master's in social anthropology from the National Museum, Federal University of the State of Rio de Janeiro, where she is completing her doctorate. She is a member of the Articulation of Indigenous Peoples of the Northeast, Minas Gerais and Espírito Santo (APOINME) and the National Articulation of Indigenous Women Warriors of Ancestrality (ANMIGA). As a representative of Indigenous movements, she is a member of the National Genetic Heritage Council (CGen) / Ministry of the Environment and Climate Change.

BENJAMIN LESSING is associate professor of political science and director of the Center for Latin American Studies at the University of Chicago. He studies armed conflict and governance by criminal groups that do not seek formal state power, such as drug cartels, prison gangs, and paramilitaries. His first book, *Making Peace in Drug Wars*, shows how state crackdowns triggered armed conflict between drug cartels and the state in Brazil, Colombia, and Mexico, and how smarter policies can quell it. His second book, *Criminal Leviathans: How Gangs Govern from Behind Bars*, under contract, shows how mass incarceration and drug repression in Brazil, El Salvador, Colombia, and even the United States have fostered sophisticated criminal shadow governments in prisons and urban peripheries that simultaneously defy and undergird the modern carceral state.

ROBERTO KANT DE LIMA received his PhD in anthropology from Harvard University and is a professor emeritus in the graduate program in anthropology, Fluminense Federal

University (UFF), and coordinator of the National Institute of Science and Technology, Institute for Studies on Conflict Management (www.ineac.uff.br). He is a full member (since 1978) and was vice president of the Brazilian Association of Anthropology; founding member of the UFF Teachers Association (ADUFF-S-Sind); member, since 1978, of the Brazilian Society for the Progress of Science; and since 2018, full member of Brazilian Academy of Science. He is the author of *A polícia da cidade do Rio de Janeiro: Seus dilemas e paradoxos* (Rio de Janeiro city police: Their dilemmas and paradoxes, 1994) and has been published in several journals and edited volumes.

BRYAN MCCANN is a professor of Latin American history and chair of the history department at Georgetown University. He is the author of several books and numerous articles on Brazilian social and cultural history, including *Hard Times in the Marvelous City: From Dictatorship to Democracy in the Favelas of Rio de Janeiro* (2014) and *Hello, Hello Brazil: Popular Music in the Making of Modern Brazil* (2004). He completed his PhD in history at Yale University in 1999.

FLÁVIA MEDEIROS is an associate professor in the Department of Anthropology at the Federal University of Santa Catarina (UFSC), a professor of anthropology at UFSC (PPGAS/UFSC), and a professor of justice and security at the Federal Fluminense University (PPGJS/UFF). Medeiros holds a PhD in anthropology from UFF. She is the author of *Matar o morto: Uma etnografia do Instituto Médico-Legal* (Killing the dead: An ethnography of the Medico-Legal Institute, 2016) and *Linhas de investigação: Uma etnografia das técnicas e moralidades numa divisão de homicídios da região metropolitana do Rio de Janeiro* (Lines of investigation: An ethnography of techniques and morality in a homicide division in the metropolitan region of Rio de Janeiro, 2018). She is also one of the editors of the collection *Casos de repercussão: Perspectivas antropológicas sobre rotinas burocráticas e moralidades* (Cases of repercussion: Anthropological perspectives on bureaucratic routines and morality, 2018). She is an activist at the National Network of Anti-prohibitionist Feminists (RENFA).

ANA PAULA MENDES DE MIRANDA has a PhD in social anthropology from the University of São Paulo (2002). She is an associate professor in the Department of Anthropology at Fluminense Federal University (UFF). Ana Paula holds a research scholarship at the National Council for Scientific and Technological Development (CNPq) and at the Carlos Chagas Filho Foundation for Research Support of the State of Rio de Janeiro (FAPERJ). She is currently the coordinator of the courses in public policy, criminal justice, and public security, and was an assistant coordinator of professional programs in the areas of anthropology and archaeology (CAPES, 2018–22). She is the founder of Ginga, for research in race, Afro-brazilian religions, public policy, and activism at Fluminense Federal University. She is also a researcher at the National Institute of Science and Technology in the Institute of Comparative Studies in Conflict Management (INCT/InEAC). Together with Ilzver de Matos Oliveira and Lana Lage da Gama Lima, she organized and edited *As tramas da intolerância e do racismo* (The schemes of intolerance and racism, 2023).

SEAN T. MITCHELL is associate professor of anthropology and chair of the Department of Sociology and Anthropology at Rutgers University, Newark. His book *Constellations of Inequality: Space, Race, and Utopia in Brazil* (2017) won the 2018 Sérgio Buarque de Holanda Social Science Book Prize from the Latin American Studies Association Brazil Section. He is also the coeditor of *Anthropology and Global Counterinsurgency* (2010) and *Precarious Democracy: Ethnographies of Hope, Despair, and Resistance in Brazil* (2021). He writes about inequality in Brazil and elsewhere.

RODRIGO MONTEIRO is an adjunct professor in the Department of Social Sciences at the Fluminense Federal University in Campos dos Goytacazes. Monteiro has a PhD in public health from the Institute of Social Medicine of the State University of Rio de Janeiro (2009) and a master's degree in the social sciences from the State University of Rio de Janeiro (2001). His research focuses on violence, poverty, education, youth, and sports.

VITÓRIA MOREIRA is a scholar of gender, politics, and human rights and is a PhD candidate in the Department of Global Studies at the University of California, Santa Barbara. Her research focuses on the global antigender movement and the political ideas and transnational networks connecting right-wing political leaders and civil society groups opposing feminism and LGBTQI+ rights.

JACQUELINE DE OLIVEIRA MUNIZ is an adjunct professor at the Department of Public Security, Institute for Comparative Studies in Conflict Management (INEAC/UFF). She completed a postdoctoral program in strategic studies at PEP-COPPE/UFRJ and has a PhD in political science (political science and sociology) from the Brazilian Society of Instruction, SBI/IUPERJ (1999). She is also a member of the Strategic Studies Group (GEE-COPPE/UFRJ), a founding partner of the Latin American Police and Civil Society Network, and a member of the Brazilian Public Security Forum.

LAURA REBECCA MURRAY is an assistant professor at the Center for Public Policy Studies in Human Rights (Universidade Federal do Rio de Janeiro, NEPP-DH/UFRJ). She has a PhD in socio-medical sciences from Columbia University and completed a postdoctorate program at the Instituto de Medicina Social (Universidade Estadual do Rio de Janeiro, IMS/UERJ). She is a member of the Coletivo Puta Davida and Rede Brasileira de Prostitutas, and is founding member and researcher at the Observatório da Prostituição/UFRJ. She directed *A Kiss for Gabriela* (2013), a film about prostitute-activist Gabriela Leite's historic run for federal office. Murray co-coordinated the participatory photography project *What You Don't See: Prostitution as We See It* about sex work and the 2016 Summer Olympic Games in Rio de Janeiro (www.oquevcnaove.com).

OSMUNDO PINHO is a scholar of the National Council for Scientific and Technological Development (CNPq) and a professor at the Federal University of Recôncavo da Bahia (UFRB) in Cachoeira. He teaches social sciences at UFRB and ethnic and African studies at the Federal University of Bahia (UFBA). He is an associate researcher at the Institute of African Studies at the Federal University of Pernambuco (UFPE) and is a coordinator of the Territoriality, Violence and Heritage Group in the Recôncavo da Bahia (UFRB/CNPq). In 2014 he was a visiting researcher at the Department of African Studies at the University of Texas–Austin. Pinho received his PhD from the University of Campinas (UNICAMP) and was a Richard E. Greenleaf Fellow at the Latin American Library at Tulane University in New Orleans. He is the author of *Cativeiro: Antinegritude and Ancestralidade* (Cativeiro: Anti-Blackness and ancestry, 2021) and a coeditor (with João H. C. Vargas) of *Antinegritude: O impossível sujeito negro na formação social brasileira* (Anti-Blackness: The impossible Black subject in Brazilian social formation, 2016).

PAULO G. PINTO is an associate professor in the Department of Anthropology at the Fluminense Federal University (UFF) and the author of *Árabes no Rio de Janeiro: Uma identidade plural* (Arabs in Rio de Janeiro: A plural identity, 2010). Pinto holds a PhD in anthropology (2002) from Boston University.

MARÍA VICTORIA PITA is a CONICET researcher at the Institute of Anthropological Sciences (UBA) and NCT-InEAC (UFF) and a professor of anthropological sciences (FFyL/UBA) and human rights at the Universidad Nacional de Lanús (UNLa). She has participated as a researcher in projects at the Centro de Estudios Legales y Sociales (CELS). Since 2014, she has been a member of CONICET's Red de Investigaciones en Derechos Humanos. Some of her fieldwork photographs have been recognized by the education and communications officer of the Royal Anthropological Institute and by the Colegio de Graduados en Antropología de la República Argentina. She holds a PhD in anthropology from the Universidad de Buenos Aires.

JOÃO GABRIEL RABELLO SODRÉ is an attorney in Brazil who worked at the public defender's office of Rio de Janeiro between 2015 and 2017. Sodré is also a PhD candidate in the history department at Georgetown University and holds two master's degrees, from the Department of Global Studies at the University of California, Santa Barbara (2019), and the Department of Public Policy (Human Rights) at the Federal University of Rio de Janeiro (2017). Rabello Sodré is broadly interested in topics involving racial justice, slavery and its afterlives, indigeneity, LGBTQIA+ struggles, policing, and the criminal justice system.

LUCIANE ROCHA is an assistant professor of Black studies in the Department of Interdisciplinary Studies at the Kennesaw State University. She holds a PhD in anthropology specializing in African diaspora studies and women's and gender studies from the University of Texas at Austin (2008–14). Her research focuses on Black women's activism against state violence and the anthropology of emotions.

MARCOS ALEXANDRE DOS SANTOS ALBUQUERQUE is a professor of anthropology and art history at the State University of Rio de Janeiro (UERJ). His publications include "Performance como tradução: Política e arte indígena na cidade" (Performance as translation: Indigenous politics and art in the city) in *Revista Concinnitas* (2020) and the book *O regime imagético Pankararu: Performance e arte indígena na cidade de São Paulo* (The regime of Pankararu imagery: Indigenous performance and art in the city of São Paulo, 2017), which received an honorable mention in the Capes de Teses Contest. He holds a PhD in social anthropology from the Federal University of Santa Catarina.

SORAYA SIMÕES is an associate professor at the Institute for Research and Urban and Regional Planning and coordinator of the graduate program. She holds a PhD in anthropology from Fluminense Federal University (2008). Since the early 2000s, Simões has worked with the Brazilian prostitutes movement, especially with the Brazilian Network of Prostitutes. She has been the president of Davida, an NGO founded by Gabriela Leite, and is the author of *Vila Mimosa: Etnografia da cidade cenográfica da prostituição carioca* (Vila Mimosa: Ethnography of the scenic city of prostitution in Rio de Janeiro, 2010). Together with Hélio R. S. Silva and Aparecida Fonseca Moraes, Simões organized and edited *Prostituição e outras formas de amor* (Prostitution and other forms of love, 2014).

INDIANARE SIQUEIRA is a transvestigênere, vegan, atheist, antiracist, anticapitalist, antifascist whore and poet born in Paranaguá, Paraná. She founded and was president of Grupo Filadélfia de Travestis e Liberados, one of the oldest LGBTQIA+ NGOs in Brazil. She is also a founding president of the Transrevolução, the Forúm de TransVestiGeneres de RJ, and the Frente LGBTQIA+. Indianarae is an alternate city council member for Rio de Janeiro and is the creator and director of the PrepareNem college prep course for LGBTQIA+ youth. She founded CasaNem, an LGBTQIA+ urban occupation that is part of the International Federation of Homeless People, and REBRACA, a network of twenty-eight safe houses for LGBTQIA+ people across Brazil. She organizes the Slut Walk and the Trans Visibility Walk in Rio and is a member of the Collective Puta Davida and of the Brazilian Network of Prostitutes.

ANTONIO CARLOS DE SOUZA LIMA is a retired professor of ethnology and anthropology at the Museu Nacional, Federal University of Rio de Janeiro, where he still works as a volunteer, teaching and supervising researchers. He is also a visiting professor of anthropology in the graduate program in anthropology, Fluminense Federal University. He holds a PhD in social anthropology and is a scholar of the National Council for Scientific and Technological Development (CNPq) and of the Carlos Chagas Filho Foundation for Research Support of the State of Rio de Janeiro (FAPERJ). He is the coordinator of several projects aimed at promoting Indigenous presence in higher education through affirmative action. He conducts research in the anthropology of the state, with an emphasis on indigenist policies, public administration, and international cooperation for development, working closely with Indigenous movements in Brazil. He was president of the Brazilian Association of Anthropology (ABA) and was the coordinator of anthropology and archaeology at the Coordination for the Improvement of Higher Education Personnel (CAPES) in 2018–22.

CESAR PINHEIRO TEIXEIRA is a sociologist, serving as professor in the graduate program in political sociology at Vila Velha University. He received his PhD in human sciences (sociology) from the Federal University of Rio de Janeiro. He is the author of *The Social*

Construction of the "Ex-Bandit": A Study on Criminal Subjection and Pentecostalism (2011) and *Kill, Convert, Include: The Plot of Urban Violence in Rio de Janeiro* (2023). He is the coordinator of Encruzilhadas: Center for Studies on Violence, Religion and Territory and a researcher at the Center for Studies on Citizenship, Conflict and Urban Violence at the Federal University of Rio de Janeiro.

LEONARDO VIEIRA SILVA is a PhD student in anthropology (PPGA-UFF) who completed a master's degree in anthropology (PPGA-UFF) and is an active member of the Brazilian Anthropology Association. As a researcher, he is part of the GINGA-UFF research group. He is a member of the Institute for Comparative Studies in Institutional Conflict Management (INCT/InEAC-UFF).

Index

Abreu, Fernanda, 61, 312–13, 315–17, 320nn1–2
academic extractivism, 2, 4–6. *See also*
  decolonization: of knowledge and
  methodologies
accusatory legal model. *See* liberal legal model
activism and resistance: of Afro-religious
  communities, 250–58; of Black mothers,
  354–60; creative forms of, 2, 37, 324–26,
  328–31, 351; education and research as, 303–4,
  306–9; electoral politics and, 141–49; of Indigenous peoples, 243–48, 303–4, 308–9; of
  LGBTQIAPN+ communities, 293–96, 300,
  325–26; in music, 334–43; around prostitution, 297–98, 300, 323–31
affirmative action. *See* diversity and equity
  policies and initiatives
Afro-religious communities: activism and
  resistance of, 250–58; legal protection of,
  257; racism and persecution against, 7–8,
  252–53, 255–58; roots and practices of, 250–51,
  253–54, 255
AIAM (Indigenous Association Aldeia
  Maracanã), 248
Aldeia Maracanã, 246–48
aldeiamento. *See* villaging up of Indigenous
  peoples
Alleluia, Sebastião, 34
Amar, Paul: hypervisibility and, 112, 180; parahumanization and, 101–2, 179; parastatal
  governance and, 98–99, 114, 121, 317, 328;
  research partnerships in Brazil and, 5;
  securitization and, 191

Américas studies, 14
AMOCAVIM (Associação de Moradores do
  Condomínio e Amigos da Vila Mimosa),
  319
anthropology and ethnographic practice,
  302–9
anti-Black racism. *See* racism and racial
  injustice
anti-Black violence: in history, 93; normalization and justification of, 156–61, 353–54, 355,
  358, 359, 360n1; by police and the state, 87,
  91–92, 112, 143, 152, 352–55, 358–59; resistance
  to, 189, 354–60; Revolta da Chibata and, 338
anticorruption investigations, 43–44, 73
antigender movement, 235–36, 238–40
anti-incarceration. *See* prison abolition
antiracist movements. *See* racism and racial
  injustice: resistance to
Arab identities in Rio de Janeiro: cultural
  stereotypes and, 264–65, 269; kaleidoscopic
  formation of, 262–71; role of ethnic and
  religious institutions in, 265–67; role of
  family and cultural traditions in, 267–69
Arabitude caleidoscópica. *See* Arab identities
  in Rio de Janeiro: kaleidoscopic formation of
armed dominions, 57–65, 82, 117–18. *See also*
  governance of territories by armed groups
armed territorial control. *See* governance of
  territories by armed groups
arquétipos decarcerais. *See* decarceral
  archetypes

participation of in research and scholarship, 303–9; population statistics of, 244, 246, 309n1; public policies for, 245–46

infranationalism. *See* Amar, Paul

Inquérito Policial. *See* liberal legal model

inquisitorial legal model and practice: equality before the law and, 45–46, 48–51; hierarchy and, 45–46; policing and, 44–45, 48–51; prisons and, 48, 53–54n13; US judges and, 44

Internationalist Front of the Houseless. *See* Frente Internacionalista dos Sem Têto (FIST)

International Women's Day, 325–26

inventing new words. *See* neologisms

Jardim Catarina favela, 174–79, 181

Jeje culture, 251, 254, 258n4. *See also* Candomblé practice

Jordy, Carlos, 239–40

justice system in Brazil. *See* legal system in Brazil

kaleidoscopic Arabness. *See* Arab identities in Rio de Janeiro: kaleidoscopic formation of

Kalil, Isabela, 74

Ketu Nation of Candomblé practitioners. *See* Candomblé practice

knowledge production: by activist-scholars, 1–3, 12–14; of state bureaucracies, 79–87, 282–89

La Roque, Eduarda, 30

Latin American studies. *See* Américas studies

Lava Jato. *See* anticorruption investigations

Lebanese immigrant communities. *See* Arab identities in Rio de Janeiro

Lefebvre, Henri, 200–205

legal system in Brazil: equality before the law and, 47–48; history of, 46–47; judges in, 44–45, 50, 53n2, 53n30; Portuguese monarchy and, 46–47

Leite, Gabriela, 323–24, 329

Leite, Marcia, 32, 33, 36

LGBTQIAPN+ movements and activism, 234–35, 237, 240, 293–96, 300, 325–26

liberal legal model, 45, 48, 49

Lissovsky, Maurício, 31–32

lugar de fala, 168–69

Lugones, Maria, 328, 331

Luke, Darcy, 4

Lula da Silva, Luiz Inácio, 43–44, 70, 74

lyrical ontologies, 335–36, 342–43

Machado da Silva, L. Antonio, 26, 35, 36, 38

mães de bandidos, 147, 354–55, 358

Maia, César, 131

Malafaia, Silas, 8

Mangue neighborhood, 104–5, 108, 314, 318

Maré favela, 27–28, 36–37

Márquez, Francia, 146

McCann, Bryan, 192

MEPCT/RJ (State Mechanism for Preventing and Combating Torture in Rio de Janeiro), 273–74, 276–79, 280n2

Messenberg, Débora, 74

milicianização. *See* militianization

miliciarquia recolonial. *See* recolonial militiarchy

milícias. *See* militias

military dictatorship in Brazil, 307–8, 335, 338–39, 341

militianization, 124–25, 132–35

militias: death squads and, 91–96; governance of territories by, 57–64, 91–96, 114–16, 117–18; history and growth of, 91–95, 129–33; parliamentary inquiry into, 131–33; police and state participation in, 60–61, 91, 93–96, 111–13, 115–16, 119, 122, 130–34; relationship with factions, 127, 130–35

Minha Casa, Minha Vida, 248

Miranda, Ana Paula Mendes de, 62–63

miscegenation, 152, 154–56

Misse, Michel, 60, 92

Mitchell, Sean T., 72

MN (Museu Nacional), 16–17, 302–9

modernization of Brazil, 176–77, 180, 186–87, 190

Monteiro, Dani, 144

Moreira, Adailton, 254–55, 256, 258n7

Moro, Sergio, 70, 76

Morro da Providência favela, 192, 193, 195, 316–17

Morro do Borel favela, 38

Movimento Moleque, 143, 149n1

Muniz, Jacqueline, 62–63

Museu do Índio, occupation of, 243, 246–48

Museu Nacional (MN), 16–17, 302–9

music. *See* samba music and politics

mutual aid, 5, 118, 164, 169, 348

State Council for Indigenous Rights
(CEDIND), 248
State Mechanism for Preventing and Combating Torture in Rio de Janeiro (MEPCT/RJ), 273–74, 276–79, 280n2
stateness, 79–80, 83, 85–87, 88n7
statistics and data about crime and violence, 79–87, 282–89
stray bullets, 79–80, 82–87
Sukarno, 346–47
syncretism, 120–22
Syrian immigrant communities. See Arab identities in Rio de Janeiro

Tapajós, Maurício, 340
Teixeira, Cesar Pinheiro, 225, 227, 228–29, 230
terreiro politics, 250–58
terreiros. See Afro-religious communities
territorial control by armed groups. See governance of territories by armed groups
transgender people. See transvestigêneres
transgênero. See transvestigêneres
Transrevolução, 294
transsexuals. See transvestigêneres
transvestigêneres: activism of, 293–96, 300, 325–26; meaning of, 19n1, 294, 298–99, 332n2; perspective of the antigender movement on, 240

ultramodernidade. See ultramodernity
ultramodernity: capitalism and, 180–81; gender, sexuality, and race and, 177–79; individualism and, 175–77
Unidade de Polícia Pacificadora (UPP): community resistance to, 36–37; criticisms of, 26–30, 32–38, 75, 118, 191–92, 199–200; disappearances of residents and, 35–36; gentrification and, 33–35; implementation of, 28–29; as military occupation, 26–27, 29, 32, 39; as proximity policing or community

policing, 30–32; Social Forums, 29–30; Social Program, social services, and social policies within, 29–30, 33
United Nations Conference on the Environment and Development. See Earth Summit
United States of America: anti-Black racism and violence in, 153–54, 161, 161n1; inquisitorial legal model and practice in, 44; racism in, 154–55, 161
Universal Church of the Kingdom of God, 8, 253
UPP. See Unidade de Polícia Pacificadora (UPP)
urban centralization in Rio de Janeiro, 170, 316
urban hygienization, 104, 189, 190–92, 313–20
urbanization and expansion of Rio de Janeiro, 103, 167–72, 194, 245
urban reform. See urban hygienization
urban squatting. See squatting

Vargas, João H. C., 175
vereativismo, 142–49
Vigário Geral massacre, 38
Vila Isabel neighborhood, 336, 342
Vila Mimosa neighborhood, 105, 108, 318–20
villaging up of Indigenous peoples, 303–9
violence: moral justification for, 224–30; against women, 297–98. See also anti-Black violence; favelas: violence in; statistics and data about crime and violence
Visão da Favela Brasil Collective, 36
Vodum of Brazil. See Jeje culture

war-ification. See policing: demilitarization of war on drugs, 32
Weber, Max: theory of domination, 61–62
Workers' Party. See PT Party
World Cup. See FIFA World Cup (2014)

Yoruba culture, 250–51, 254, 258n4